T0130674

Get the eBooks FREE!

(PDF, ePub, Kindle, and liveBook all included)

We believe that once you buy a book from us, you should be able to read it in any format we have available. To get electronic versions of this book at no additional cost to you, purchase and then register this book at the Manning website.

Go to https://www.manning.com/freebook and follow the instructions to complete your pBook registration.

That's it!
Thanks from Manning!

Gradle in Action

BENJAMIN MUSCHKO

MANNING

SHELTER ISLAND

Manning Publications Co.
20 Baldwin Road
PO Box 261
Shelter Island, NY 11964

Development editor: Jennifer Stout
Copyeditor: Benjamin Berg
Proofreader: Melody Dolab
Typesetter: Dennis Dalinnik
Cover designer: Marija Tudor

ISBN: 9781617291302
Printed in the United States of America

contents

foreword

When you create a new technology like Gradle, one of the most critical stages of development has nothing to do with writing code. Once the initial versions of your project are used by thousands of developers and a community starts to assemble around it, the challenge becomes communicating with a much larger audience of users who will use the project and pass judgment on its merits, and growing the size of the community ten-fold or a thousand-fold. Gradle has already amassed a large audience, and we've seen tremendous growth over the last two years, but we're getting ready for a still larger influx of end-users.

Therefore, the importance of having a good book cannot be overstated. Developers with a range of skills and abilities need to be able to pick up a book that's easy to understand and which can impart both the syntax and the philosophy behind the tool. Only then will they be able to confidently grow the community that can educate itself using a single, authoritative reference for Gradle. *Gradle in Action* is that book. Additionally, this book gives new Gradle users a very good glimpse into how Gradle fits into a larger view of continuous delivery.

Benjamin is the sort of expert that you hope emerges from an open source community. He has been a long term Gradle contributor and is the author of several popular Gradle plugins. He's both a communicator and a developer. Benjamin has the rare ability to dive into the core details of a particularly challenging development problem and then explain the tool to end-users. We're happy that he has recently joined Gradleware and is now part of the Gradle development team.

I hope you enjoy the book as well as working with Gradle. May your software delivery process become both fun and efficient.

HANS DOCKTER
FOUNDER OF GRADLE
AND GRADLEWARE

preface

When I started my career as a software developer, I was blissfully unaware of the need for project automation. My tool of choice was the IDE, which allowed me to run all tasks required to fully automate my software development cycle. In 2003 Rainer Saw-itzki,[1] an external consultant to the project I was working on, introduced me to Apache Ant. I thought it was the most amazing thing to be able to describe my automation logic with the help of mostly pre-existing functionality and to execute it in a defined order. Despite the fact that the definition language was XML (these were the days when XML was still fashionable), I soon began to become more ambitious by creating artifacts for different target platforms, writing deployment logic for web containers, and setting up a continuous integration server.

Automation requirements have changed significantly since then. My projects have grown in size and complexity. Deployment and delivery models have become far more sophisticated. And while I explored other build tool options to meet these needs over the years, I found that there was always a Catch-22. Many developers accepted the status quo in this space, which left them with painful experiences. Rarely is there a topic that's discussed more religiously[2] than the pros and cons of build tools and why people hate them so much. The purpose of this book isn't necessarily to convince you to switch your current build to Gradle. If you're happy with your setup (whatever you're

---

[1] Thanks again for the object-oriented mindset I picked up by working with you. You've been a great mentor to me.

[2] This topic is on par with Windows versus Linux or the comparison of web application frameworks.

using), by all means, stick to it. I will, however, talk about the massive innovation that Gradle brings to the table and compare it to existing solutions. I invite you to be your own judge.

I started to write this book with a specific goal in mind: teach the core concepts of Gradle, but don't stop there. In a world that embraces software development practices like continuous integration and delivery, you have to take into consideration the tooling ecosystem into which a build system must integrate. Hopefully, I've found the right balance in this book. If you have questions, comments, or ideas, I'd love to hear them. Your feedback might spark the urge to write a second edition or add-on content. Feel free to send me an email or contact me on the book's forum at Manning.

As with all book projects, the page count is limited. To stick to the scope of this book, I had to leave out some of the content I initially planned to write. (This is my first book. With the naïveté of a virgin author, I thought I could fit it all in.) The source code repository of the book, found at https://github.com/bmuschko/gradle-in-action-source, expands on some of this material and lists references to other code examples and resources. I hope you enjoy reading the book as much as I enjoyed writing it.

acknowledgments

When thinking about writing a book, you have no idea how much work it's going to be. It's safe to say that it literally controls your life for an extended period of time. After a while, the writing part becomes easier. The hard part is to start writing every day. This wouldn't have been possible without the support, encouragement, and help of others.

In 2010, I started to evaluate Gradle for the first time as a replacement for a Maven project for a previous employer. I probably wouldn't have done that without the spike initiated by Jonathan Bodner, a long-term acquaintance, whom I deeply admire for his technical insight. He started me on my way to getting excited about Gradle, becoming deeply involved with its community, and writing plugins of my own.

I've been a technical reviewer for books published by Manning for many years before writing my own. It started when I met Dan Allen, the author of *Seam in Action* (Manning, 2008), at one of the No Fluff Just Stuff conferences. After chatting with me for a while, he quickly got me excited about his endeavors and I offered to help him by reviewing his book. My engagement got me a first glimpse of what it means to write a book. I had always wanted to write a book, but never found the appropriate time or topic to jump on it. With Gradle, it just felt right. Thanks, Dan, for your enthusiasm that inspired me to carry on the torch and make it my own.

One of the first things you do before writing a book is put together the outline and table of contents. The first person I showed the draft to was David James, the organizer of the Washington DC–area Groovy user group. Thanks for your outside perspective on the organization of the book, your meticulous attention to detail, and your strong encouragement to make the book a reality.

No commercial book is published without many people in the background. This goes out to everyone involved in the process at Manning Publications. Michael Stephens, who I talked to first, bought into the idea of this book and ultimately trusted me to do a good job. My gratitude also goes to Cynthia Kane, who helped me to find my writing style. I'd also like to thank Jennifer Stout, my development editor, who always tried to get the best out of me, made me think about whole text passages in a different way, and tolerated my impatience. You've been a great help. Thanks also to the whole Manning production and marketing team for guidance along the way and for making the book what it is now. I know you did a tremendous amount of work.

I'd also like to thank the members of the Gradleware team, as well as the Gradle community, for creating Gradle and pushing the boundaries of build automation. Your continued effort and belief in a high-quality product improves the life of many disgruntled build masters around the globe. Special thanks go out to René Gröschke and Luke Daley for their technical insight and their review of the first third of the book. I am also grateful to Hans Dockter, the founder of Gradle, for contributing the foreword and endorsing this book in its early stages, and for the continued promotion through Gradleware.

Thanks to the following reviewers of the manuscript who provided invaluable feedback and gave me a different perspective on the content: Andy Keffalas, BJ Peter DeLaCruz, Chris Grijalva, Chris Nauroth, Dominik Helleberg, Eric Wendelin, Iain Starks, John Moses, Jon Bodner, Marcin Nowina-Krowicki, Mayur S. Patil, Mehrdad Karjoo, Mohd Suhaizal Md Kamari, Nacho Ormeño, Nick Watts, Pawel Dolega, Rob Bugh, Robin Percy, Samuel Brown, Scott Bennett-McLeish, Steve Dickson, Tarin Gamberini, Wellington R. Pinheiro, and Zekai Otles. Thanks also to Barry Kern for his careful technical proofread of the manuscript shortly before it went into production.

Special thanks to Spencer Allain, Jonathan Keam, and Robert Wenner for thoroughly reading every chapter of the book and providing me with line-by-line edits and comments at different stages of development; Michael McGarr and Samuel Brown for bouncing around ideas that involved content on continuous delivery and DevOps; and Baruch Sadogursky from JFrog for the technical review of chapter 14 and for promoting the book even before it was released. I also wish to thank the relentless Author Online forum participants for pushing the content to the next level.

Writing a book requires making sacrifices and puts tremendous strain on personal relationships. I would like to thank my family and friends for being supportive, encouraging, and understanding while I've worked toward completing this ambitious goal. And, yes, there will be time for hanging out without me thinking about the content of the current chapter.

I'm deeply grateful to my wife Sarah for her unending support and optimism. You pushed me to believe in myself, made me take breaks from writing, and tolerated me falling asleep before 9:00 p.m. most days. Without you, the writing process would have been far more grueling than it was.

about this book

Roadmap

This book is divided into three parts. The first part gives an introduction to Gradle's concepts and philosophy, explaining how it compares to other build tools and how to write scripts to automate simple tasks. Part two explores the tool's building blocks and core techniques in greater depth. You should be able to use this knowledge to implement complex, extendable, enterprise builds. The third part describes how Gradle can be used in the context of continuous deliver, focusing on topics like polyglot builds, code quality, artifact assembly, and deployment.

The chapters in part 1, Introducing Gradle, are as follows:

1 *Introduction to project automation*—This chapter gives a gentle introduction into why it's a good idea to automate your projects and how build tools can help get the job done.

2 *Next generation builds with Gradle*—How does Gradle compare to existing JVM-language build tools? This chapter covers Gradle's extensive feature set and how it helps automate your software delivery process in the context of a Continuous Delivery deployment pipeline. As a first taste, you'll write a simple build script and run it on the command line.

3 *Building a Gradle project by example*—This chapter introduces a Java-based web application as a vehicle to demonstrate some of Gradle's core features. We'll explore the use of the Java plugin for standardized and nonconventional use cases and examine productivity tools for fast development turnaround.

Part 2, Mastering the fundamentals, focuses on applying important Gradle concepts to the case study introduced in part 1:

4   *Build script essentials*—What are the main building blocks of a Gradle project? This chapter discusses the use of important domain objects, namely projects and tasks. We'll touch on how these objects map to the corresponding classes in the Gradle API, Gradle's build lifecycle, the incremental build feature, and the mechanics of registering lifecycle hooks.

5   *Dependency management*—No enterprise project can do without reusing functionality from external libraries. This chapter explores Gradle's declarative support for dependency management, version conflict resolution strategies, and the inner workings of its cache.

6   *Multiproject builds*—Does your project consist of multiple, modularized software components? This chapter covers the options for organizing build logic in a multiproject setting, how to declare project dependencies, and the use of partial builds to improve execution time.

7   *Testing with Gradle*—Testing your code is an important activity of the software development lifecycle. By the end of this chapter, you'll write tests with JUnit, TestNG, and Spock and execute them as part of the build lifecycle. You'll also learn how to configure test execution, register listeners to react to test lifecycle events, and organize different types of tests with the help of source sets.

8   *Extending Gradle*—Gradle provides an extensible domain object model. If you want to add completely new functionality to a project or extend the existing domain model, this chapter is for you. You'll learn how to write your own plugin to deploy your sample application to the cloud.

9   *Integration and migration*—In this chapter, we'll look at how Gradle integrates with Ant and Maven. We'll also explore migration strategies in case you decide to go with Gradle long term.

Part 3, From build to deployment, examines how Gradle can be used to bring the example application from the developer's machine into the production environment with the help of a build pipeline:

10   *IDE support and tooling*—IDEs are key enablers for boosting developer productivity. This chapter explains Gradle's capabilities for generating project files for popular IDEs like Eclipse, IntelliJ, and NetBeans. We also discuss how to navigate and manage Gradle-backed projects within these IDEs.

11   *Building polyglot projects*—In this chapter, we'll discuss how Gradle faces the challenge of organizing and building polyglot projects by using your case study application as an example. The languages you'll integrate include JavaScript, Groovy, and Scala.

12   *Code quality management and monitoring*—In this chapter we'll focus on tools that measure code quality and visualize the results to help you pinpoint problem

areas in your code. By the time you finish this chapter, you'll know how to integrate code quality tools with your build.

13 *Continuous integration*—Continuous integration (CI) is a software development practice where source code is integrated frequently, optimally multiple times a day. This chapter discusses the installation and configuration procedures needed to run Gradle on Jenkins, an open-source CI server.

14 *Artifact assembly and publishing*—A build either consumes or produces binary artifacts. This chapter explores the artifact assembly process and the configuration needed to publish artifacts, including their metadata, to a binary repository.

15 *Infrastructure provisioning and deployment*—A configured target environment is a prerequisite for any software deployment. In this chapter, we'll discuss the importance of "infrastructure as code" for setting up and configuring an environment and its services in an automated fashion. Later, you'll implement an exemplary deployment process with Gradle.

Two appendixes cover additional topics:

A *Driving the command line*—This appendix explains how to operate Gradle from the command line. We'll explore tasks available to all Gradle builds, plus command line options and their use cases.

B *Groovy for Gradle users*—If you're new to Groovy, this appendix provides you with a gentle introduction to the most important and widely used language features.

Who should read the book?

This book is primarily for developers and build automation engineers who want to implement a repeatable build that's easy to read and extend. I assume that you have a basic understanding of an object-oriented programming language. You'll get the most out of the content if you have a working knowledge of Java.

In this book, you'll use a lot of Groovy; however, I don't assume you already have experience with the language. For a jump-start on Groovy, look at appendix B, Groovy for Gradle users. The appendix also provides additional references to books that dig deeper into more advanced aspects of the language.

Throughout the chapters, we'll touch on topics you can't circumnavigate when dealing with automated builds. It will be helpful to have some knowledge of tools like Ant, Ivy, and Maven; practices like continuous integration and delivery; and concepts like dependency management. But don't worry if that's not your technical background. Every chapter will explain the "why" in great detail.

Code conventions and downloads

Source code in listings and text is in a `fixed-width font like this` to separate it from ordinary text. Code annotations accompany many of the code listings and highlight important concepts.

The full source code is available from the publisher's website at www.manning.com/GradleInAction and from the GitHub repository at https://github.com/bmuschko/gradle-in-action-source. You'll find additional references to source code repositories that either take some examples from the book to the next level or demonstrate the use of Gradle in contexts not covered in the book.

Author Online

The purchase of *Gradle in Action* includes free access to a private web forum run by Manning Publications where you can make comments about the book, ask technical questions, and receive help from the author and other users. To access the forum and subscribe to it, visit http://www.manning.com/GradleInAction. This page provides information on how to get on the forum once you're registered, what kind of help is available, and the rules of conduct on the forum.

Manning's commitment to readers is to provide a venue for meaningful dialogue between individual readers and between readers and the author. It is not a commitment to any specific amount of participation on the part of the author, whose contribution to the forum remains voluntary (and unpaid). Let your voice be heard, and keep the author on his toes!

The Author Online forum and the archives of previous discussions will be accessible from the publisher's website as long as the book is in print.

About the author

Benjamin Muschko is a software engineer with more than 10 years of experience in developing and delivering business applications. He is a member of the Gradleware engineering team and developer of several popular Gradle plugins.

about the cover illustration

The figure on the cover of *Gradle in Action* is captioned a "Woman from Istria," which is a large peninsula in the Adriatic Sea, off Croatia. This illustration is taken from a recent reprint of Balthasar Hacquet's *Images and Descriptions of Southwestern and Eastern Wenda, Illyrians, and Slavs* published by the Ethnographic Museum in Split, Croatia, in 2008. Hacquet (1739–1815) was an Austrian physician and scientist who spent many years studying the botany, geology, and ethnography of many parts of the Austrian Empire, as well as the Veneto, the Julian Alps, and the western Balkans, inhabited in the past by peoples of the Illyrian tribes. Hand-drawn illustrations accompany the many scientific papers and books that Hacquet published.

The rich diversity of the drawings in Hacquet's publications speaks vividly of the uniqueness and individuality of the eastern Alpine and northwestern Balkan regions just 200 years ago. This was a time when the dress codes of two villages separated by a few miles identified people uniquely as belonging to one or the other, and when members of a social class or trade could be easily distinguished by what they were wearing. Dress codes have changed since then and the diversity by region, so rich at the time, has faded away. It is now often hard to tell the inhabitant of one continent from another and today the inhabitants of the picturesque towns and villages in the Slovenian Alps or Balkan coastal towns are not readily distinguishable from the residents of other parts of Europe.

We at Manning celebrate the inventiveness, the initiative, and the fun of the computer business with book covers based on costumes from two centuries ago brought back to life by illustrations such as this one.

Part 1

Introducing Gradle

Efficient project automation is one of the key enablers for delivering software to the end user. The build tool of choice shouldn't stand in the way of this effort; rather, it should provide you with a flexible and maintainable way to model your automation needs. Gradle's core strength is that it provides you with easy-to-understand but powerful tooling to automate your project end-to-end.

In chapter 1, we'll discuss the benefits of project automation and its impact on the ability to develop and deliver software in a repeatable, reliable, and portable fashion. You'll learn the basic concepts and components of a build tool and how they're implemented with Ant and Maven. By comparing their pros and cons, you'll see the need for a next-generation build tool.

Gradle draws on lessons learned from established build tools and takes their best ideas to the next level. Chapter 2 introduces you to Gradle's compelling feature set. You'll install the Gradle runtime and explore how to write and execute a simple build script from the command line.

Simple build scripts only go so far. Chapter 3 introduces a real-world Java-based web application. You'll learn the configuration needed to compile, unit-test, package, and run the sample. By the end of part 1, you'll have a feel for Gradle's expressiveness and flexibility.

Introduction to project automation

1

This chapter covers

- Understanding the benefits of project automation
- Getting to know different types of project automation
- Surveying the characteristics and architecture of build tools
- Exploring the pros and cons of build tool implementations

Tom and Joe work as software developers for Acme Enterprises, a startup company that offers a free online service for finding the best deals in your area. The company recently received investor funding and is now frantically working toward its first official launch. Tom and Joe are in a time crunch. By the end of next month, they'll need to present a first version of the product to their investors. Both developers are driven individuals, and they pump out features daily. So far, development of the software has stayed within the time and budget constraints, which makes them happy campers. The chief technology officer (CTO) pats them on the back; life is good. However, the manual and error-prone build and delivery process slows them down significantly. As a result, the team has to live with sporadic compilation issues, inconsistently built software artifacts, and failed deployments. This is where build tools come in.

This chapter will give you a gentle introduction into why it's a good idea to automate your project and how build tools can help get the job done. We'll talk about the benefits that come with sufficient project automation, the types and characteristics of project automation, and the tooling that enables you to implement an automated process.

Two traditional build tools dominate Java-based projects: Ant and Maven. We'll go over their main features, look at some build code, and talk about their shortcomings. Lastly, we'll discuss the requirements for a build tool that will fulfill the needs of modern-day project automation.

1.1   *Life without project automation*

Going back to Tom and Joe's predicament, let's go over why project automation is such a no-brainer. Believe it or not, lots of developers face the following situations. The reasons are varied, but probably sound familiar.

- *My IDE does the job.* At Acme, developers do all their coding within the IDE, from navigating through the source code, implementing new features, and compiling and refactoring code, to running unit and integration tests. Whenever new code is developed, they press the Compile button. If the IDE tells them that there's no compilation error and the tests are passing, they check the code into version control so it can be shared with the rest of the team. The IDE is a powerful tool, but every developer will need to install it first with a standardized version to be able to perform all of these tasks, a lesson Joe learns when he uses a new feature only supported by the latest version of the compiler.

- *It works on my box.* Staring down a ticking clock, Joe checks out the code from version control and realizes that it doesn't compile anymore. It seems like one of the classes is missing from the source code. He calls Tom, who's puzzled that the code doesn't compile on Joe's machine. After discussing the issue, Tom realizes that he probably forgot to check in one of his classes, which causes the compilation process to fail. The rest of the team is now blocked and can't continue their work until Tom checks in the missing source file.

- *The code integration is a complete disaster.* Acme has two different development groups, one specializing in building the web-based user interface and the other working on the server-side backend code. Both teams sit together at Tom's computer to run the compilation for the whole application, build a deliverable, and deploy it to a web server in a test environment. The first cheers quickly fade when the team sees that some of the functionality isn't working as expected. Some of the URLs simply don't resolve or result in an error. Even though the team wrote some functional tests, they didn't get exercised regularly in the IDE.

- *The testing process slows to a crawl.* The quality assurance (QA) team is eager to get their hands on a first version of the application. As you can imagine, they aren't too happy about testing low-quality software. With every fix the development team puts into place, they have to run through the same manual process. The team stops to check new changes into version control, a new version is built from an IDE, and the deliverable is copied to the test server. Each and every time, a developer is fully occupied and can't add any other value to the company. After weeks of testing and a successful demo to the investor, the QA team says the application is ready for prime time.

■ *Deployment turns into a marathon.* From experience, the team knows that the outcome of deploying an application is unpredictable due to unforeseen problems. The infrastructure and runtime environment has to be set up, the database has to be prepared with seed data, the actual deployment of the application has to happen, and initial health monitoring needs to be performed. Of course, the team has an action plan in place, but each of the steps has to be executed manually.

The product launch is a raving success. The following week, the CTO swings by the developers' desks; he already has new ideas to improve the user experience. A friend has told him about agile development, a time-boxed iterative approach for implementing and releasing software. He proposes that the team introduces two-week release cycles. Tom and Joe look at each other, both horrified at the manual and repetitive work that lies ahead. Together, they plan to automate each step of the implementation and delivery process to reduce the risk of failed builds, late integration, and painful deployments.

1.2 Benefits of project automation

This story makes clear how vital project automation is for team success. These days, time to market has become more important than ever. Being able to build and deliver software in a repeatable and consistent way is key. Let's look at the benefits of automating your project.

1.2.1 Prevents manual intervention

Having to manually perform steps to produce and deliver software is time-consuming and error-prone. Frankly, as a developer and system administrator, you have better things to do than to handhold a compilation process or to copy a file from directory A to directory B. We're all human. Not only can you make mistakes along the way, manual intervention also takes away from the time you desperately need to get your actual work done. Any step in your software development process that can be automated *should* be automated.

1.2.2 Creates repeatable builds

The actual building of your software usually follows predefined and ordered steps. For example, you compile your source code first, then run your tests, and lastly assemble a deliverable. You'll need to run the same steps over and over again—every day. This should be as easy as pressing a button. The outcome of this process needs to be repeatable for everyone who runs the build.

1.2.3   *Makes builds portable*

You've seen that being able to run a build from an IDE is very limiting. First of all, you'll need to have the particular product installed on your machine. Second, the IDE may only be available for a specific operating system. An automated build shouldn't require a specific runtime environment to work, whether this is an operating system or an IDE. Optimally, the automated tasks should be executable from the command line, which allows you to run the build from any machine you want, whenever you want.

1.3   *Types of project automation*

You saw at the beginning of this chapter that a user can request a build to be run. A user can be any stakeholder who wants to trigger the build, like a developer, a QA team member, or a product owner. Our friend Tom, for example, pressed the Compile button in his IDE whenever he wanted the code to be compiled. On-demand automation is only one type of project automation. You can also schedule your build to be executed at predefined times or when a specific event occurs.

1.3.1   *On-demand builds*

The typical use case for on-demand automation is when a user triggers a build on his or her machine, as shown in figure 1.1. It's common practice that a version control system (VCS) manages the versioning of the build definition and source code files.

In most cases, the user executes a script on the command line that performs tasks in a predefined order—for example, compiling source code, copying a file from directory A to directory B, or assembling a deliverable. Usually, this type of automation is executed multiple times per day.

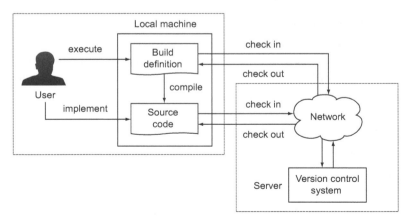

Figure 1.1   On-demand builds execute build definitions backed by a VCS.

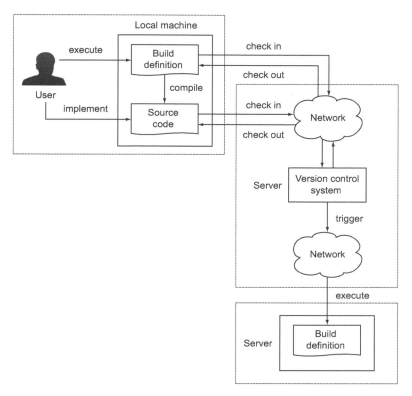

Figure 1.2   Build triggered by a check-in of files into VCS

1.3.2   *Triggered builds*

If you're practicing agile software development, you're interested in receiving fast feedback about the health of your project. You'll want to know if your source code can be compiled without any errors or if there's a potential software defect indicated by a failed unit or integration test. This type of automation is usually triggered if code was checked into version control, as shown in figure 1.2.

1.3.3   *Scheduled builds*

Think of scheduled automation as a time-based job scheduler (in the context of a Unix-based operation system, also known as a cron job). It runs in particular intervals or at concrete times—for example, every morning at 1:00 a.m. or every 15 minutes. As with all cron jobs, scheduled automation generally runs on a dedicated server. Figure 1.3 shows a scheduled build that runs every morning at 5:00 a.m. This kind of automation is particularly useful for generating reports or documentation for your project.

The practice that implements scheduled and triggered builds is commonly referred to as continuous integration (CI). You'll learn more about CI in chapter 13.

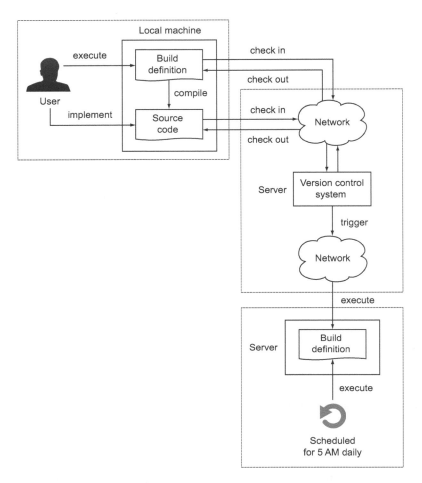

Figure 1.3   Scheduled build initiated at 5:00 a.m. daily

After identifying the benefits and types of project automation, it's time to discuss the tools that allow you to implement this functionality.

1.4   Build tools

Naturally, you may ask yourself why you'd need another tool to implement automation for your project. You could just write the logic as an executable script, such as a shell script. Think back to the goals of project automation we discussed earlier. You want a tool that allows you to create a repeatable, reliable, and portable build without manual intervention. A shell script wouldn't be easily portable from a UNIX-based system to a Windows-based system, so it doesn't meet your criteria.

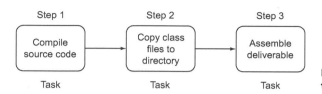

Figure 1.4 **A common scenario of tasks executed in a predefined order**

1.4.1 What's a build tool?

What you need is a programming utility that lets you express your automation needs as executable, ordered tasks. Let's say you want to compile your source code, copy the generated class files into a directory, and assemble a deliverable that contains the class files. A deliverable could be a ZIP file, for example, that can be distributed to a runtime environment. Figure 1.4 shows the tasks and their execution order for the described scenario.

Each of these tasks represents a unit of work—for example, compilation of source code. The order is important. You can't create the ZIP archive if the required class files haven't been compiled. Therefore, the compilation task needs to be executed first.

DIRECTED ACYCLIC GRAPH

Internally, tasks and their interdependencies are modeled as a directed acyclic graph (DAG). A DAG is a data structure from computer science and contains the following two elements:

- *Node*: A unit of work; in the case of a build tool, this is a task (for example, compiling source code).
- *Directed edge*: A directed edge, also called an arrow, representing the relationship between nodes. In our situation, the arrow means *depends on*. If a task defines dependent tasks, they'll need to execute before the task itself can be executed. Often this is the case because the task relies on the output produced by another task. Here's an example: to execute the task "assemble deliverable," you'll need to run its dependent tasks "copy class files to directory" and "compile source code."

Each node knows about its own execution state. A node—and therefore the task—can only be executed once. For example, if two different tasks depend on the task "source code compilation," you only want to execute it once. Figure 1.5 shows this scenario as a DAG.

You may have noticed that the nodes are shown in an inverted order from the tasks in figure 1.4. This is because the order is determined by node dependencies. As a developer, you won't have to deal directly with the DAG representation of your build. This job is done by the build tool. Later in this chapter, you'll see how some Java-based build tools use these concepts in practice.

Directed acyclic graph

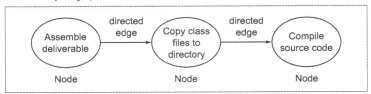

Task dependencies

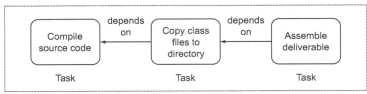

Figure 1.5   DAG representation of tasks

1.4.2   *Anatomy of a build tool*

It's important to understand the interactions among the components of a build tool, the actual definition of the build logic, and the data that goes in and out. Let's discuss each of the elements and their particular responsibilities.

BUILD FILE

The build file contains the configuration needed for the build, defines external dependencies such as third-party libraries, and contains the instructions to achieve a specific goal in the form of tasks and their interdependencies. Figure 1.6 illustrates a build file that describes four tasks and how they depend on each other.

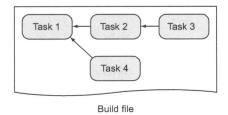

Build file

Figure 1.6   The build file expresses the rules of your build expressed by tasks and their interdependencies.

The tasks we discussed in the scenario earlier—compiling source code, copying files to a directory, and assembling a ZIP file—would be defined in the build file. Oftentimes, a scripting language is used to express the build logic. That's why a build file is also referred to as a *build script*.

BUILD INPUTS AND OUTPUTS

A task takes an input, works on it by executing a series of steps, and produces an output. Some tasks may not need any input to function correctly, nor is creating an output considered mandatory. Complex task dependency graphs may use the output of a dependent task as input. Figure 1.7 demonstrates the consumption of inputs and the creation of outputs in a task graph.

I already mentioned an example that follows this workflow. We took a bunch of source code files as input, compiled them to classes, and assembled a deliverable as output. The compilation and assembly processes each represent one task. The assembly

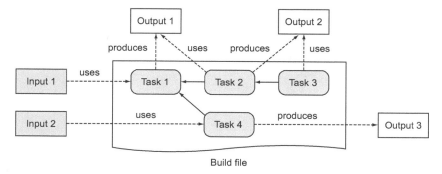

Figure 1.7 Task inputs and outputs

of the deliverable only makes sense if you compiled the source code first. Therefore, both tasks need to retain their order.

BUILD ENGINE

The build file's step-by-step instructions or rule set must be translated into an internal model the build tool can understand. The build engine processes the build file at runtime, resolves dependencies between tasks, and sets up the entire configuration needed to command the execution, as shown in figure 1.8.

Once the internal model is built, the engine will execute the series of tasks in the correct order. Some build tools allow you to access this model via an API to query for this information at runtime.

DEPENDENCY MANAGER

The dependency manager is used to process declarative dependency definitions for your build file, resolve them from an artifact repository (for example, the local file system, an FTP, or an HTTP server), and make them available to your project. A *dependency* is generally an external, reusable library in the form of a JAR file (for example, Log4J for logging support). The *repository* acts as storage for dependencies, and organizes and describes them by identifiers, such as name and version. A typical repository can be an HTTP server or the local file system. Figure 1.9 illustrates how the dependency manager fits into the architecture of a build tool.

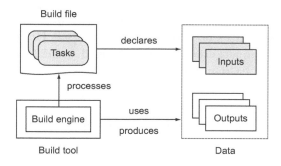

Figure 1.8 The build engine translates the rule set into an internal model representation that is accessed during the runtime of the build.

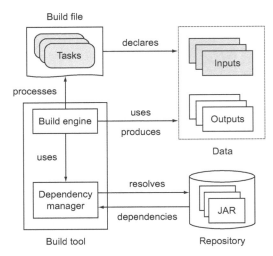

Figure 1.9 The dependency manager retrieves external dependencies and makes them available to your build.

Many libraries depend on other libraries, called *transitive dependencies*. The dependency manager can use metadata stored in the repository to automatically resolve transitive dependencies as well. A build tool is not required to provide a dependency management component.

1.5   Java build tools

In this section, we look at two popular, Java-based build tools: Ant and Maven. We'll discuss their characteristics, see a sample script in action, and outline the shortcomings of each tool. Let's start with the tool that's been around the longest—Ant.

1.5.1   Apache Ant

Apache Ant (Another Neat Tool) is an open source build tool written in Java. Its main purpose is to provide automation for typical tasks needed in Java projects, such as compiling source files to classes, running unit tests, packaging JAR files, and creating Javadoc documentation. Additionally, it provides a wide range of predefined tasks for file system and archiving operations. If any of these tasks don't fulfill your requirements, you can extend the build with new tasks written in Java.

While Ant's core is written in Java, your build file is expressed through XML, which makes it portable across different runtime environments. Ant does not provide a dependency manager, so you'll need to manage external dependencies yourself. However, Ant integrates well with another Apache project called Ivy, a full-fledged, standalone dependency manager. Integrating Ant with Ivy requires additional effort and has to be done manually for each individual project. Let's look at a sample build script.

BUILD SCRIPT TERMINOLOGY

To understand any Ant build script, you need to start with some quick nomenclature. A build script consists of three basic elements: the project, multiple targets, and the used tasks. Figure 1.10 illustrates the relationship between each of the elements.

Build script

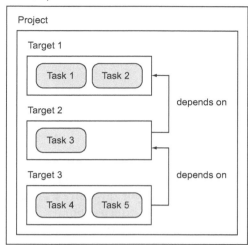

Figure 1.10 Ant's hierarchical build script structure with the elements project, target, and task

In Ant, a *task* is a piece of executable code— for example, for creating a new directory or moving a file. Within your build script, use a task by its predefined XML tag name. The task's behavior can be configured by its exposed attributes. The following code snippet shows the usage of the `javac` Ant task for compiling Java source code within your build script:

```
<javac srcdir="src" destdir="dest"/>
```

Source and destination directories are configured by attributes srcdir and destdir; compile Java source files located in directory src and put class files into directory dest.

While Ant ships with a wide range of predefined tasks, you can extend your build script's capabilities by writing your own task in Java.

A *target* is a set of tasks you want to be executed. Think of it as a logical grouping. When running Ant on the command line, provide the name of the target(s) you want to execute. By declaring dependencies between targets, a whole chain of commands can be created. The following code snippet shows two dependent targets:

```
<target name="init">
    <mkdir dir="build"/>
</target>

<target name="compile" depends="init">
    <javac srcdir="src" destdir="build"/>
</target>
```

Target named init that used task mkdir to create directory build.

Target named compile for compiling Java source code via javac Ant task. This target depends on target init, so if you run it on the command line, init will be executed first.

Mandatory to all Ant projects is the overarching container, the *project*. It's the top-level element in an Ant script and contains one or more targets. You can only define one project per build script. The following code snippet shows the project in relation to the targets:

```
<project name="example-build">
   <target name="init">
      <mkdir dir="build"/>
   </target>

   <target name="compile" depends="init">
      <javac srcdir="src" destdir="build"/>
   </target>
</project>
```

Project encloses one or more targets and defines optional attributes, such as the name, to describe the project

With a basic understanding of Ant's hierarchical structure, let's look at a full-fledged scenario of a sample build script.

SAMPLE BUILD SCRIPT

Say you want to write a script that compiles your Java source code in the directory src using the Java compiler and put it into the output directory build. Your Java source code has a dependency on a class from the external library Apache Commons Lang. You tell the compiler about it by referencing the library's JAR file in the classpath. After compiling the code, you want to assemble a JAR file. Each unit of work, source code compilation, and JAR assembly will be grouped in an individual target. You'll also add two more targets for initializing and cleaning up the required output directories. The structure of the Ant build script you'll create is shown in figure 1.11.

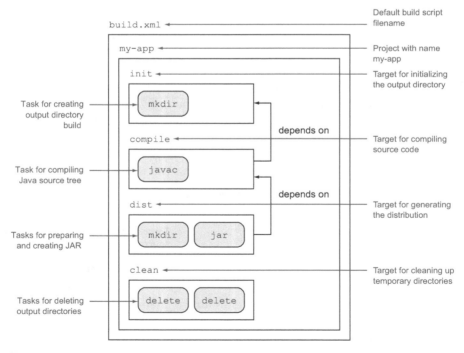

Figure 1.11 Hierarchical project structure of sample Ant build script

Let's get down to business. It's time to implement this example as an Ant build script. The following listing shows the whole project and the targets required to achieve your goal.

Listing 1.1 Ant script with targets for compiling source code and assembling JAR file

```
<project name="my-app" default="dist" basedir=".">
    <property name="src" location="src"/>            Sets global properties for
    <property name="build" location="build"/>         this build, like source,
    <property name="dist" location="dist"/>           output, and distribution
    <property name="version" value="1.0"/>            directories

    <target name="init">                              Creates build directory structure
        <mkdir dir="${build}"/>                       used by compile target
    </target>

    <target name="compile" depends="init" description="compile the source">
        <javac srcdir="${src}" destdir="${build}"     Compiles Java code from
            classpath="lib/commons-lang3-3.1.jar"     directory src into directory build
            includeantruntime="false"/>
    </target>

    <target name="dist" depends="compile"             Creates distribution
        description="generate the distribution">      directory
        <mkdir dir="${dist}"/>
        <jar jarfile="${dist}/my-app-${version}.jar" basedir="${build}"/>
    </target>                                          Assembles everything
                                                       in directory build into
    <target name="clean" description="clean up">       JAR file myapp-l.0
        <delete dir="${build}"/>
        <delete dir="${dist}"/>       Deletes build and
    </target>                          dist directory trees
</project>
```

Ant doesn't impose any restrictions on how to define your build's structure. This makes it easy to adapt to existing project layouts. For example, the source and output directories in the sample script have been chosen arbitrarily. It would be very easy to change them by setting a different value to their corresponding properties. The same is true for target definition; you have full flexibility to choose which logic needs to be executed per target and the order of execution.

SHORTCOMINGS

Despite all this flexibility, you should be aware of some shortcomings:

- Using XML as the definition language for your build logic results in overly large and verbose build scripts compared to build tools with a more succinct definition language.
- Complex build logic leads to long and unmaintainable build scripts. Trying to define conditional logic like if-then/if-then-else statements becomes a burden when using a markup language.
- Ant doesn't give you any guidelines on how to set up your project. In an enterprise setting, this often leads to a build file that looks different every time.

Common functionality is oftentimes copied and pasted. Every new developer on the project needs to understand the individual structure of a build.

- You want to know how many classes have been compiled or how many tasks have been executed in a build. Ant doesn't expose an API that lets you query information about the in-memory model at runtime.

- Using Ant without Ivy makes it hard to manage dependencies. Oftentimes, you'll need to check your JAR files into version control and manage their organization manually.

1.5.2 *Apache Maven*

Using Ant across many projects within an enterprise has a big impact on maintainability. With flexibility comes a lot of duplicated code snippets that are copied from one project to another. The Maven team realized the need for a standardized project layout and unified build lifecycle. Maven picks up on the idea of convention over configuration, meaning that it provides sensible default values for your project configuration and its behavior. The project automatically knows what directories to search for source code and what tasks to perform when running the build. You can set up a full project with a few lines of XML as long as your project adheres to the default values. As an extra, Maven also has the ability to generate HTML project documentation that includes the Javadocs for your application.

Maven's core functionality can be extended by custom logic developed as plugins. The community is very active, and you can find a plugin for almost every aspect of build support, from integration with other development tools to reporting. If a plugin doesn't exist for your specific needs, you can write your own extension.

STANDARD DIRECTORY LAYOUT

By introducing a default project layout, Maven ensures that every developer with the knowledge of one Maven project will immediately know where to expect specific file types. For example, Java application source code sits in the directory `src/main/java`. All default directories are configurable. Figure 1.12 illustrates the default layout for Maven projects.

BUILD LIFECYCLE

Maven is based on the concept of a build lifecycle. Every project knows exactly which steps to perform to build, package, and distribute an application, including the following functionality:

- Compiling source code
- Running unit and integration tests
- Assembling the artifact (for example, a JAR file)
- Deploying the artifact to a local repository
- Releasing the artifact to a remote repository

Every step in this build lifecycle is called a *phase*. Phases are executed sequentially. The phase you want to execute is defined when running the build on the command line. If

Maven default project layout

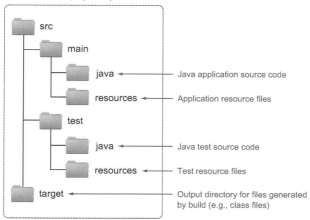

Figure 1.12 Maven's default project layout defines where to find Java source code, resource files, and test code.

you call the phase for packaging the application, Maven will automatically determine that the dependent phases like source code compilation and running tests need to be executed beforehand. Figure 1.13 shows the predefined phases of a Maven build and their order of execution.

DEPENDENCY MANAGEMENT

In Maven projects, dependencies to external libraries are declared within the build script. For example, if your project requires the popular Java library Hibernate, you simply define its unique artifact coordinates, such as organization, name, and version, in the dependencies configuration block. The following code snippet shows how to declare a dependency on version 4.1.7. Final of the Hibernate core library:

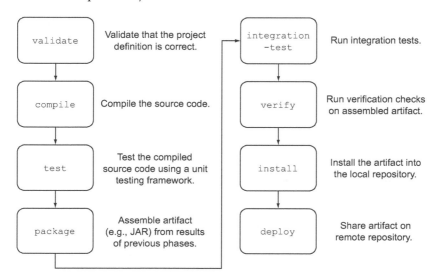

Figure 1.13 Maven's most important build lifecycle phases

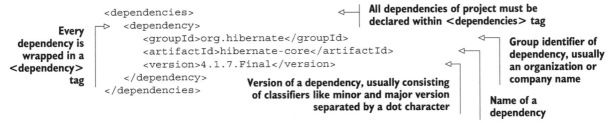

```
<dependencies>
    <dependency>
        <groupId>org.hibernate</groupId>
        <artifactId>hibernate-core</artifactId>
        <version>4.1.7.Final</version>
    </dependency>
</dependencies>
```

All dependencies of project must be declared within <dependencies> tag

Every dependency is wrapped in a <dependency> tag

Group identifier of dependency, usually an organization or company name

Name of a dependency

Version of a dependency, usually consisting of classifiers like minor and major version separated by a dot character

At runtime, the declared libraries and their transitive dependencies are downloaded by Maven's dependency manager, stored in the local cache for later reuse, and made available to your build (for example, for compiling source code). Maven preconfigures the use of the repository, Maven Central, to download dependencies. Subsequent builds will reuse an existing artifact from the local cache and therefore won't contact Maven Central. Maven Central is the most popular binary artifact repository in the Java community. Figure 1.14 demonstrates Maven's artifact retrieval process.

Dependency management in Maven isn't limited to external libraries. You can also declare a dependency on other Maven projects. This need arises if you decompose software into *modules*, which are smaller components based on associated functionality. Figure 1.15 shows an example of a traditional three-layer modularized architecture. In this example, the presentation layer contains code for rendering data in a webpage, the business layer models real-life business objects, and the integration layer retrieves data from a database.

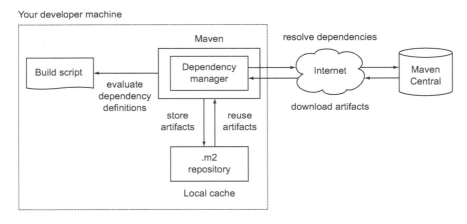

Figure 1.14   Maven's interaction with Maven Central to resolve and download dependencies for your build

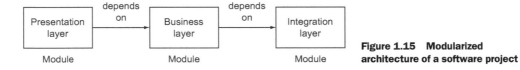

Figure 1.15   Modularized architecture of a software project

SAMPLE BUILD SCRIPT

The following listing shows a sample Maven build script named `pom.xml` that will implement the same functionality as the Ant build. Keep in mind that you stick to the default conventions here, so Maven will look for the source code in the directory `src/main/java` instead of `src`.

Listing 1.2   Maven POM for building standardized Java project

Project definition including referenced XML schema to validate correct structure and content of document. →

```
<project xmlns="http://maven.apache.org/POM/4.0.0"
         xmlns:xsi="http://www.w3.org/2001/XMLSchema-instance"
         xsi:schemaLocation="http://maven.apache.org/POM/4.0.0
                             http://maven.apache.org/xsd/maven-4.0.0.xsd">
    <modelVersion>4.0.0</modelVersion>
    <groupId>com.mycompany.app</groupId>
    <artifactId>my-app</artifactId>
    <packaging>jar</packaging>
    <version>1.0</version>

    <dependencies>
        <dependency>
            <groupId>org.apache.commons</groupId>
            <artifactId>commons-lang3</artifactId>
            <version>3.1</version>
            <scope>compile</scope>
        </dependency>
    </dependencies>
</project>
```

Version of Maven's internal model.

Identifies the organization the project belongs to.

Type of artifact produced by project.

Version of project that factors into produced artifact name.

Name of project that automatically determines name of produced artifact (in this case the JAR file).

Declared dependency on Apache Commons Lang library with version 3.1; scope of a dependency determines lifecycle phase it's applied to. In this case it's needed during compilation phase.

SHORTCOMINGS

As with Ant, be aware of some of Maven's shortcomings:

- Maven proposes a default structure and lifecycle for a project that often is too restrictive and may not fit your project's needs.
- Writing custom extensions for Maven is overly cumbersome. You'll need to learn about Mojos (Maven's internal extension API), how to provide a plugin descriptor (again in XML), and about specific annotations to provide the data needed in your extension implementation.
- Earlier versions of Maven (< 2.0.9) automatically try to update their own core plugins; for example, support for unit tests to the latest version. This may cause brittle and unstable builds.

1.5.3   *Requirements for a next-generation build tool*

In the last section, we examined the features, advantages, and shortcomings of the established build tools Ant and Maven. It became clear that you often have to compromise on the supported functionality by choosing one or the other. Either you choose full flexibility and extensibility but get weak project standardization, tons of boilerplate code, and no support for dependency management by picking Ant; or you go with Maven, which offers a convention over configuration approach and a seamlessly integrated dependency manager, but an overly restrictive mindset and cumbersome plugin system.

Wouldn't it be great if a build tool could cover a middle ground? Here are some features that an evolved build tool should provide:

- Expressive, declarative, and maintainable build language.
- Standardized project layout and lifecycle, but full flexibility and the option to fully configure the defaults.
- Easy-to-use and flexible ways to implement custom logic.
- Support for project structures that consist of more than one project to build deliverable.
- Support for dependency management.
- Good integration and migration of existing build infrastructure, including the ability to import existing Ant build scripts and tools to translate existing Ant/ Maven logic into its own rule set.
- Emphasis on scalable and high-performance builds. This will matter if you have long-running builds (for example, two hours or longer), which is the case for some big enterprise projects.

This book will introduce you to a tool that *does* provide all of these great features: Gradle. Together, we'll cover a lot of ground on how to use it and exploit all the advantages it provides.

1.6 *Summary*

Life for developers and QA personnel without project automation is repetitive, tedious, and error-prone. Every step along the software delivery process—from source code compilation to packaging the software to releasing the deliverable to test and production environments—has to be done manually. Project automation helps remove the burden of manual intervention, makes your team more efficient, and leads the way to a push-button, fail-safe software release process.

In this chapter, we identified the different types of project automation—on-demand, scheduled, and triggered build initiation—and covered their specific use cases. You learned that the different types of project automation are not exclusive. In fact, they complement each other.

A build tool is one of the enablers for project automation. It allows you to declare the ordered set of rules that you want to execute when initiating a build. We discussed the moving parts of a build tool by analyzing its anatomy. The build engine (the build tool executable) processes the rule set defined in the build script and translates it into executable tasks. Each task may require input data to get its job done. As a result, a build output is produced. The dependency manager is an optional component of the build tool architecture that lets you declare references to external libraries that your build process needs to function correctly.

We saw the materialized characteristics of build tools in action by taking a deeper look at two popular Java build tool implementations: Ant and Maven. Ant provides a very flexible and versatile way of defining your build logic, but doesn't provide guidance on a standard project layout or sensible defaults to tasks that repeat over and over in projects. It also doesn't come with an out-of-the-box dependency manager, which requires you to manage external dependencies yourself. Maven, on the other hand, follows the convention over configuration paradigm by supporting sensible default configuration for your project as well as a standardized build lifecycle. Automated dependency management for external libraries and between Maven projects is a built-in feature. Maven falls short on easy extensibility for custom logic and support for nonconventional project layouts and tasks. You learned that an advanced build tool needs to find a middle ground between flexibility and configurable conventions to support the requirements of modern-day software projects.

In the next chapter, we'll identify how Gradle fits into the equation.

Next-generation builds with Gradle

This chapter covers

- Understanding how Gradle compares to other build tools
- Describing Gradle's compelling feature set
- Installing Gradle
- Writing and executing a simple Gradle script
- Running Gradle on the command line

For years, builds had the simple requirements of compiling and packaging software. But the landscape of modern software development has changed, and so have the needs for build automation.

Today, projects involve large and diverse software stacks, incorporate multiple programming languages, and apply a broad spectrum of testing strategies. With the rise of agile practices, builds have to support early integration of code as well as frequent and easy delivery to test and production environments.

Established build tools continuously fall short in meeting these goals in a simple but customizable fashion. How many times have your eyes glazed over while looking at XML to figure out how a build works? And why can't it be easier to add custom logic to your build? All too often, when adding on to a build script, you can't shake the feeling of implementing a workaround or hack. I feel your pain. There has to be a better way of doing these things in an expressive and maintainable way. There is—it's called Gradle.

Gradle is the next evolutionary step in JVM-based build tools. It draws on lessons learned from established tools like Ant and Maven and takes their best ideas to the next level. Following a build-by-convention approach, Gradle allows for declaratively modeling your problem domain using a powerful and expressive domain-specific language (DSL) implemented in Groovy instead of XML. Because Gradle is a JVM native, it allows you to write custom logic in the language you're most comfortable with, be it Java or Groovy.

In the Java world, an unbelievably large number of libraries and frameworks are available. Dependency management is used to automatically download these artifacts from a repository and make them available to your application code. Having learned from the shortcomings of existing dependency management solutions, Gradle provides its own implementation. Not only is it highly configurable, it also strives to be as compatible as possible with existing dependency management infrastructures (like Maven and Ivy). Gradle's ability to manage dependencies isn't limited to external libraries. As your project grows in size and complexity, you'll want to organize the code into modules with clearly defined responsibilities. Gradle provides powerful support for defining and organizing multiproject builds, as well as modeling dependencies between projects.

I know, all of this sounds promising, but you're still stuck with your legacy build. Gradle doesn't leave you in the dust, but makes migration easy. Ant gets shipped with the runtime and therefore doesn't require any additional setup. Gradle provides teams with the ability to apply their accumulated Ant knowledge and investment in build infrastructure. Imagine the possibilities of using existing Ant tasks and scripts directly in your Gradle build scripts. Legacy build logic can be reused or migrated gradually. Gradle does the heavy lifting for you.

To get started with Gradle, all you need to bring to the table is a good understanding of the Java programming language. If you're new to project automation or haven't used a build tool before, chapter 1 is a good place to start. This book will teach you how to effectively use Gradle to build and deliver real-world projects.

In this chapter, we'll compare existing JVM-language build tools with the features Gradle has to offer. Later, you'll learn how Gradle can help you automate your software delivery process in the context of a continuous delivery deployment pipeline. To get a first taste of what it's like to use Gradle, you'll install the runtime, write a simple build script, and run it on the command line. Join me on an exciting journey as we explore the world of Gradle.

2.1 *Why Gradle? Why now?*

If you've ever dealt with build systems, frustration may be one of the feelings that comes up when thinking about the challenges you've faced. Shouldn't the build tool naturally help you accomplish the goal of automating your project? Instead, you had to compromise on maintainability, usability, flexibility, extendibility, or performance.

Let's say you want to copy a file to a specific location under the condition that you're building the release version of your project. To identify the version, you check a string in the metadata describing your project. If it matches a specific numbering scheme (for example, 1.0-RELEASE), you copy the file from point A to point B. From an outside perspective, this may sound like a trivial task. If you have to rely on XML, the build language of many traditional tools, expressing this simple logic becomes a nightmare. The build tool's response is to add scripting functionality through nonstandard extension mechanisms. You end up mixing scripting code with XML or invoking external scripts from your build logic. It's easy to imagine that you'll need to add more and more custom code over time. As a result, you inevitably introduce accidental complexity, and maintainability goes out the window. Wouldn't it make sense to use an expressive language to define your build logic in the first place?

Here's another example. Maven follows the paradigm of convention over configuration by introducing a standardized project layout and build lifecycle for Java projects. That's a great approach if you want to ensure a unified application structure for a greenfield project—a project that lacks any constraints imposed by prior work. However, you may be the lucky one who needs to work on one of the many legacy projects that follow different conventions. One of the conventions Maven is very strict about is that one project needs to produce one artifact, such as a JAR file. But how do you create two different JAR files from one source tree without having to change your project structure? Just for this purpose, you'd have to create two separate projects. Again, even though you can make this happen with a workaround, you can't shake off the feeling that your build process will need to adapt to the tool, not the tool to your build process.

These are only some of the issues you may have encountered with existing solutions. Often you've had to sacrifice nonfunctional requirements to model your enterprise's automation domain. But enough with the negativity—let's see how Gradle fits into the build tool landscape.

2.1.1 Evolution of Java build tools

Let's look at how build tools have evolved over the years. As I discussed in chapter 1, two tools have dominated building Java projects: Ant and Maven. Over the course of years, both tools significantly improved and extended their feature set. But even though both are highly popular and have become industry standards, they have one weak point: build logic has to be described in XML. XML is great for describing hierarchical data, but falls short on expressing program flow and conditional logic. As a build script grows in complexity, maintaining the build code becomes a nightmare.

Ant's first official version was released in 2000. Each element of work (a *target* in Ant's lingo) can be combined and reused. Multiple targets can be chained to combine single units of work into full workflows. For example, you might have one target for compiling Java source code and another one for creating a JAR file that packages the class files. Building a JAR file only makes sense if you first compiled the source code. In Ant, you make the JAR target depend on the compile target. Ant doesn't give any guidance on how to structure your project. Though it allows for maximum flexibility, Ant makes each build script unique and hard to understand. External libraries required by your project were usually checked into version control, because there was no sophisticated mechanism to automatically pull them from a central location. Early versions of Ant required a lot of discipline to avoid repetitive code. Its extension mechanism was simply too weak. As a result, the bad coding practice of copying and pasting code was the only viable option. To unify project layouts, enterprises needed to impose standards.

Maven 1, released in July 2004, tried to ease that process. It provided a standard-ized project and directory structure, as well as dependency management. Unfortu-nately, custom logic is hard to implement. If you want to break out of Maven's conventions, writing a plugin, called a *Mojo*, is usually the only solution. The name Mojo might imply a straightforward, easy, and sexy way to extend Maven; in reality, writing a plugin in Maven is cumbersome and overly complex.

Later, Ant caught up with Maven by introducing dependency management through the Apache library Ivy, which can be fully integrated with Ant to declaratively specify dependencies needed for your project's compilation and packaging process. Maven's dependency manager, as well as Ivy, support resolving transitive dependen-cies. When I speak of transitive dependencies, I mean the graph of libraries required by your specified dependencies. A typical example of a transitive dependency would be the XML parser library Xerces that requires the XML APIs library to function correctly. Maven 2, released in October 2005, took the idea of convention over configuration even further. Projects consisting of multiple modules could define their dependencies on each other.

These days a lot of people are looking for alternatives to established build tools. We see a shift from using XML to a more expressive and readable language to define builds. A build tool that carries on this idea is Gant, a DSL on top of Ant written in Groovy. Using Gant, users can now combine Groovy's language features with their existing knowledge of Ant without having to write XML. Even though it wasn't part of the core Maven project, a similar approach was proposed by the project Maven Poly-glot that allows you to write your build definition logic, which is the project object model (POM) file, in Groovy, Ruby, Scala, or Clojure.

We're on the cusp of a new era of application development: polyglot program-ming. Many applications today incorporate multiple programming languages, each of which is best suited to implement a specific problem domain. It's not uncommon to face projects that use client-side languages like JavaScript that communicate with a mixed, multilingual backend like Java, Groovy, and Scala, which in turn calls off to a C++ legacy application. It's all about the right tool for the job. Despite the benefits

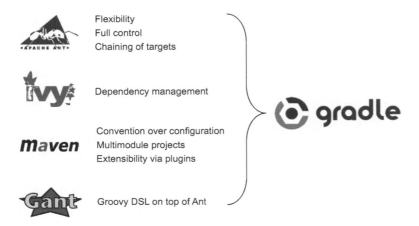

Figure 2.1   Gradle combines the best features from other build tools.

of combining multiple programming languages, your build tool needs to fluently support this infrastructure as well. JavaScript needs to be merged, minified, and zipped, and your server-side and legacy code needs to be compiled, packaged, and deployed.

Gradle fits right into that generation of build tools and satisfies many requirements of modern build tools (figure 2.1). It provides an expressive DSL, a convention over configuration approach, and powerful dependency management. It makes the right move to abandon XML and introduce the dynamic language Groovy to define your build logic. Sounds compelling, doesn't it? Keep reading to learn about Gradle's feature set and how to get your boss on board.

2.1.2   *Why you should choose Gradle*

If you're a developer, automating your project is part of your day-to-day business. Don't you want to treat your build code like any other piece of software that can be extended, tested, and maintained? Let's put software engineering back into the build. Gradle build scripts are declarative, readable, and clearly express their intention. Writing code in Groovy instead of XML, sprinkled with Gradle's build-by-convention philosophy, significantly cuts down the size of a build script and is far more readable (see figure 2.2).

It's impressive to see how much less code you need to write in Gradle to achieve the same goal. With Gradle you don't have to make compromises. Where other build tools like Maven propose project layouts that are "my way or the highway," Gradle's DSL allows for flexibility by adapting to nonconventional project structures.

> **Gradle's motto**
> "Make the impossible possible, make the possible easy, and make the easy elegant" (adapted quote from Moshé Feldenkrais).

Maven

```
<project xmlns="http://maven.apache.org/POM/4.0.0"
         xmlns:xsi="http://www.w3.org/2001/XMLSchema-instance"
         xsi:schemaLocation="http://maven.apache.org/POM/4.0.0
                             http://maven.apache.org/xsd/maven-4.0.0.xsd">
    <modelVersion>4.0.0</modelVersion>
    <groupId>com.mycompany.app</groupId>
    <artifactId>my-app</artifactId>
    <packaging>jar</packaging>
    <version>1.0-SNAPSHOT</version>

    <dependencies>
        <dependency>
            <groupId>junit</groupId>
            <artifactId>junit</artifactId>
            <version>4.11</version>
            <scope>test</scope>
        </dependency>
    </dependencies>
</project>
```

Gradle

```
apply plugin: 'java'
group = 'com.mycompany.app'
archivesBaseName = 'my-app'
version = '1.0-SNAPSHOT'

repositories {
   mavenCentral()
}

dependencies {
   testCompile 'junit:junit:4.11'
}
```

Figure 2.2 Comparing build script size and readability between Maven and Gradle

Never change a running system, you say? Your team already spent a lot of time on establishing your project's build code infrastructure. Gradle doesn't force you to fully migrate all of your existing build logic. Good integration with other tools like Ant and Maven is at the top of Gradle's priority list. We'll take a deeper look at Gradle's integration features and potential migration strategies in chapter 9.

The market seems to be taking notice of Gradle. In spring 2010, Gradle was awarded the Springy award for the most innovative open source project (http://www.springsource.org/node/2871). ThoughtWorks, a highly regarded software development consultancy, periodically publishes a report on emerging technologies, languages, and tools—their so-called technology radar. The goal of the technology radar is to help decision makers in the software industry understand trends and their effect on the market. In their latest edition of the report from May 2013 (http://thoughtworks.fileburst.com/assets/technology-radar-may-2013.pdf), Gradle was rated with the status Adopt, indicating a technology that should be adopted by the industry.

> ### Recognition by ThoughtWorks
>
> "Two things have caused fatigue with XML-based build tools like Ant and Maven: too many angry pointy braces and the coarseness of plug-in architectures. While syntax issues can be dealt with through generation, plug-in architectures severely limit the ability for build tools to grow gracefully as projects become more complex. We have come to feel that plug-ins are the wrong level of abstraction, and prefer language-based tools like Gradle and Rake instead, because they offer finer-grained abstractions and more flexibility long term."

Gradle found adopters early on, even before a 1.0 version was released. Popular open source projects like Groovy and Hibernate completely switched to Gradle as the backbone for their builds. Every Android project ships with Gradle as the default build system. Gradle also had an impact on the commercial market. Companies like Orbitz, EADS, and Software AG embraced Gradle as well, to name just a few. VMware, the company behind Spring and Grails, made significant investments in choosing Gradle. Many of their software products, such as the Spring framework and Grails, are literally built on the trust that Gradle can deliver.

2.2   Gradle's compelling feature set

Let's take a closer look at what sets Gradle apart from its competitors: its compelling feature set (see figure 2.3). To summarize, Gradle is an enterprise-ready build system, powered by a declarative and expressive Groovy DSL. It combines flexibility and effortless extendibility with the idea of convention over configuration and support for traditional dependency management. Backed by a professional services company

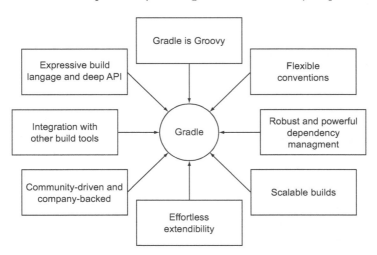

Figure 2.3   Gradle's compelling feature set

(Gradleware) and strong community involvement, Gradle is becoming the number-one choice build solution for many open source projects and enterprises.

2.2.1 *Expressive build language and deep API*

The key to unlocking Gradle's power features within your build script lies in discovering and applying its domain model, as shown in figure 2.4.

As you can see in the figure, a build script directly maps to an instance of type `Project` in Gradle's API. In turn, the dependencies configuration block in the build

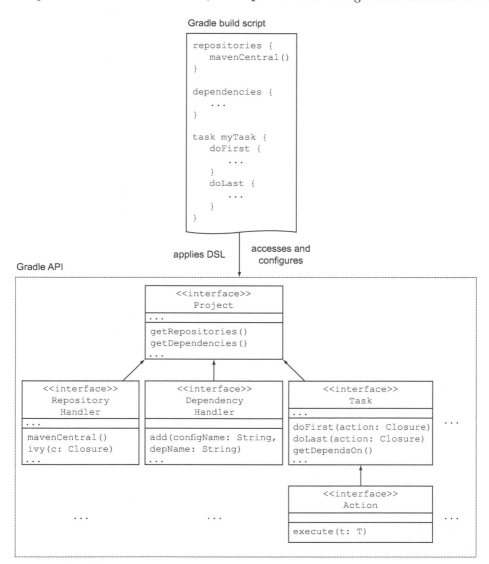

Figure 2.4 Build scripts apply the Gradle DSL and have access to its deep API.

script invokes the method dependencies() of the project instance. Like most APIs in the Java world, it's available as HTML Javadoc documentation on Gradle's website at http://www.gradle.org/docs/current/javadoc/index.html. Who would have known? You're actually dealing with code. Without knowing it, you generate an object representation of your build logic in memory. In chapter 4, we'll explore many of Gradle's API classes and how they're represented in your build script.

Each element in a Gradle script has a one-to-one representation with a Java class; however, some of the elements have been sugarcoated with a sprinkle of Groovy syntax. Having a Groovy-fied version of a class in many cases makes the code more compact than its Java counterpart and allows for using new language features like closures.

Gradle can't know all the requirements specific to your enterprise build. By exposing hooks into lifecycle phases, Gradle allows for monitoring and configuring your build script's execution behavior. Let's assume you have the very unique requirement of sending out an email to the development team whenever a unit test failure occurs. The way you want to send an email (for example, via SMTP or a third-party email service provider) and the list of recipients are very specific to your build. Other builds using Gradle may not be interested in this feature at all. By writing a custom test listener that's notified after the test execution lifecycle event, you can easily incorporate this feature for your build.

Gradle establishes a vocabulary for its model by exposing a DSL implemented in Groovy. When dealing with a complex problem domain, in this case the task of building software, being able to use a common language to express your logic can be a powerful tool. Let's look at some examples. Most common to builds is the notation of a unit of work that you want to get executed. Gradle describes this unit of work as a task. Part of Gradle's standard DSL is the ability to define tasks very specific to compiling and packaging Java source code. It's a language for building Java projects with its own vocabulary that doesn't need to be relevant to other contexts.

Another example is the way you can express dependencies to external libraries, a very common problem solved by build tools. Out-of-the-box Gradle provides you with two configuration blocks for your build script that allow you to define the dependencies and repositories that you want to retrieve them from. If the standard DSL elements don't fit your needs, you can even introduce your own vocabulary through Gradle's extension mechanism.

This may sound a little nebulous at first, but once you're past the initial hurdle of learning the build language, creating maintainable and declarative builds comes easy. A good place to start is the Gradle Build Language Reference Guide at http://www.gradle.org/docs/current/dsl/index.html. Gradle's DSL can be extended. You may want to change the behavior of an existing task or add your own idioms for describing your business domain. Gradle offers you plenty of options to do so.

2.2.2 Gradle is Groovy

Prominent build tools like Ant and Maven define their build logic through XML. As we all know, XML is easy to read and write, but can become a maintenance nightmare if used in large quantities. XML isn't very expressive. It makes it hard to define complex custom logic. Gradle takes a different approach. Under the hood, Gradle's DSL is written with Groovy providing syntactic sugar on top of Java. The result is a readable and expressive build language. All your scripts are written in Groovy as well. Being able to use a programming language to express your build needs is a major plus. You don't have to be a Groovy expert to get started. Because Groovy is written on top of Java, you can migrate gradually by trying out its language features. You could even write your custom logic in plain Java—Gradle couldn't care less. Battle-scarred Groovy veterans will assure you that using Groovy instead of Java will boost your productivity by orders of magnitude. A great reference guide is the book *Groovy in Action, Second Edition* by Dirk Konig et al. (Manning, 2009) For a primer on Groovy, see appendix B.

2.2.3 *Flexible conventions*

One of Gradle's big ideas is to give you guidelines and sensible defaults for your projects. Every Java project in Gradle knows exactly where source and test class file are supposed to live, and how to compile your code, run unit tests, generate Javadoc reports, and create a distribution of your code. All of these tasks are fully integrated into the build lifecycle. If you stick to the convention, there's only minimal configuration effort on your part. In fact, your build script is a one-liner. Seriously! Do you want to learn more about building a Java project with Gradle? Well, you can—we'll cover it in chapter 3. Figure 2.5 illustrates how Gradle introduces conventions and lifecycle tasks for Java projects.

Default tasks are provided that make sense in the context of a Java project. For example, you can compile your Java production source code, run tests, and assemble a JAR file. Every Java project starts with a standard directory layout. It defines where to find production source code, resource files, and test code. Convention properties are used to change the defaults.

The same concept applies to other project archetypes like Scala, Groovy, web projects, and many more. Gradle calls this concept *build by convention*. The build script developer doesn't need to know how this is working under the hood. Instead, you can concentrate on what needs to be configured. Gradle's conventions are similar to the ones provided by Maven, but they don't leave you feeling boxed in. Maven is very opinionated; it proposes that a project only contains one Java source directory and only produces one single JAR file. This is not necessarily reality for many enterprise projects. Gradle allows you to easily break out of the conventions. On the opposite side of the spectrum, Ant never gave you a lot of guidance on how to structure your build script, allowing for a maximum level of flexibility. Gradle takes the middle ground by offering conventions combined with the ability to easily change them. Szczepan Faber, one of Gradle's core engineers, put it this way on his blog: "Gradle is an opinionated framework on top of an unopinionated toolkit." (*Monkey Island*, "opinionated or not," June 2, 2012, http://monkeyisland.pl/2012/06/02/opinionated-or-not/.)

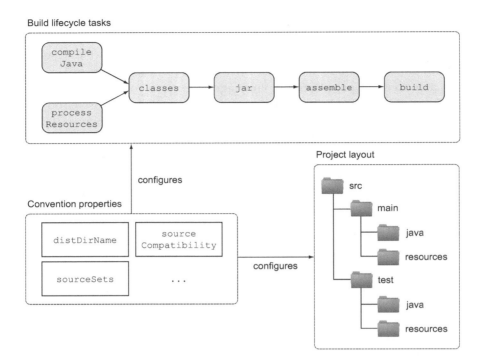

Figure 2.5   In Gradle, Java projects are build by convention with sensible defaults. Changing the defaults is easy and achieved through convention properties.

2.2.4   *Robust and powerful dependency management*

Software projects are usually not self-contained. All too often, your application code uses a third-party library providing existing functionality to solve a specific problem. Why would you want to reinvent the wheel by implementing a persistence framework if Hibernate already exists? Within an organization, you may be the consumer of a component or module implemented by a different team. External dependencies are accessible through repositories, and the type of repository is highly dependent on what your company prefers. Options range from a plain file system to a full-fledged enterprise repository. External dependencies may have a reference to other libraries or resources. We call these *transitive dependencies.*

Gradle provides an infrastructure to manage the complexity of resolving, retrieving, and storing dependencies. Once they're downloaded and put in your local cache, they're made available to your project. A key requirement of enterprise builds is reproducibility. Recall the story of Tom and Joe from chapter 1. Do you remember the last time your coworker said, "But it works on my box"? Builds have to produce the same result on different machines, independent of the contents of your local cache. Dependency managers like Ivy and Maven in their current implementation cannot fully guarantee reproducibility. Why is that? Whenever a dependency is downloaded and stored in the local cache, it doesn't take into account the artifact's origin. In situations where the repository is changed for a project, the cached dependency is considered resolved, even though the artifact's content may be slightly different. At worst, this will cause a failing build that's extremely hard to debug. Another common complaint specific to Ivy is the fact that dependency snapshot versions, artifacts currently under development with the naming convention -SNAPSHOT, aren't updated correctly in the local cache, even though it changed on the repository and is marked as changing. There are many more scenarios where current solutions fall short. Gradle provides its own configurable, reliable, and efficient dependency management solution. We'll have a closer look at its features in chapter 5.

Large enterprise projects usually consist of multiple modules to separate functionality. In the Gradle world, each of the submodules is considered a project that can define dependencies to external libraries or other modules. Additionally, each subproject can be run individually. Gradle figures out for you which of the subproject dependencies need to be rebuilt, without having to store a subproject's artifact in the local cache.

2.2.5 *Scalable builds*

For some companies, a large project with hundreds of modules is reality. Building and testing minor code changes can consume a lot of time. You may know from personal experience that deleting old classes and resources by running a cleanup task is a natural reflex. All too often, you get burned by your build tool not picking up the changes and their dependencies. What you need is a tool that's smart enough to only rebuild the parts of your software that actually changed. Gradle supports incremental builds by specifying task inputs and outputs. It reliably figures out for you which tasks need to be skipped, built, or partially rebuilt. The same concept translates to multimodule projects, called partial builds. Because your build clearly defines the dependencies between submodules, Gradle takes care of rebuilding only the necessary parts. No more running clean by default!

Automated unit, integration, and functional tests are part of the build process. It makes sense to separate short-running types of tests from the ones that require setting up resources or external dependencies to be run. Gradle supports parallel test execution. This feature is fully configurable and ensures that you're actually taking advantage of your processor's cores. The buck doesn't stop here. Gradle is going to support distributing test execution to multiple machines in a future version. I'm sorry to tell you, but the days of reading your Twitter feed between long builds are gone.

Developers run builds many times during development. That means starting a new Gradle process each time, loading all its internal dependencies, and running the build logic. You'll notice that it usually takes a couple of seconds before your script actually starts to execute. To improve the startup performance, Gradle can be run in daemon mode. In practice, the Gradle command forks a daemon process, which not only executes your build, but also keeps running in the background. Subsequent build invocations will piggyback on the existing daemon process to avoid the startup costs. As a result, you'll notice a far snappier initial build execution.

2.2.6 *Effortless extendibility*

Most enterprise builds are not alike, nor do they solve the same problems. Once you're past the initial phase of setting up your basic scripts, you'll want to implement custom logic. Gradle is not opinionated about the way you implement that code. Instead, it gives you various choices to pick from, depending on your specific use case. The easiest way to implement custom logic is by writing a task. Tasks can be defined directly in your build script without special ceremony. If you feel like complexity takes over, you may want to explore the option of a custom task that allows for writing your logic within a class definition, making structuring your code easy and maintainable. If you want to share reusable code among builds and projects, plugins are your best friend. Representing Gradle's most powerful extension mechanism, plugins give you full access to Gradle's API and can be written, tested, and distributed like any other piece of software. Writing a plugin is surprisingly easy and doesn't require a lot of additional descriptors.

2.2.7 *Integration with other build tools*

Wouldn't it be a huge timesaver to be able to integrate with existing build tools? Gradle plays well with its predecessors Ant, Maven, and Ivy, as shown in figure 2.6.

If you're coming from Ant, Gradle doesn't force you to fully migrate your build infrastructure. Instead, it allows you to import existing build logic and reuse standard Ant tasks. Gradle builds are 100% compatible with Maven and Ivy repositories. You can retrieve dependencies and publish your own artifacts. Gradle provides a converter for existing Maven builds that can translate the build logic into a Gradle build script.

Existing Ant scripts can be imported into your Gradle build seamlessly and used as you'd use any other external Gradle script. Ant targets directly map to Gradle tasks at runtime. Gradle ships with the Ant libraries and exposes a helper class to your scripts

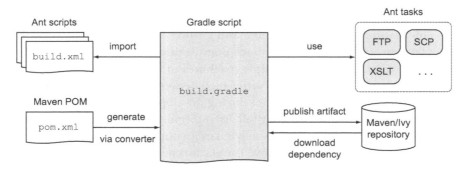

Figure 2.6   Gradle provides deep integration with other build tools and opens the door to gradually migrate your existing Ant or Maven build.

called AntBuilder, which fully blends into Gradle's DSL. It still looks and feels like Ant's XML, but without the pointy brackets. Ant users will feel right at home, because they don't have to transition to Gradle syntax right away. Migrating from Ant to Gradle is also a no-brainer. You can take baby steps by reusing your existing Ant logic while using Gradle's benefits at the same time.

Gradle aims to reach a similar depth of integration with Maven. At the time of writing, this hasn't been realized yet. In the long run, Maven POMs and plugins will be treated as Gradle natives. Maven and Ivy repositories have become an important part of today's build infrastructure. Imagine a world without Maven Central to help access specific versions of your favorite project dependencies. Retrieving dependencies from a repository is only one part of the story; publishing to them is just as important. With a little configuration, Gradle can upload your project's artifact for companywide or public consumption.

2.2.8 *Community-driven and company-backed*

Gradle is free to use and ships with the Apache License 2.0. After its first release in April 2008, a vibrant community quickly started to form around it. Over the past five years, open source developers have made major contributions to Gradle's core code base. Being hosted on GitHub turned out to be very beneficial to Gradle. Code changes can be submitted as pull requests and undergo a close review process by the core committers before making it into the code base. If you're coming from other build tools like Maven, you may be used to a wide range of reusable plugins. Apart from the standard plugins shipped with the runtime, the Gradle community releases new functionality almost daily. Throughout the book, you'll use many of the standard plugins shipped with Gradle. Appendix A gives a broader spectrum on standard as well as third-party plugins. Every community-driven software project needs a forum to get immediate questions answered. Gradle connects with the community through the Gradle forum at http://forums.gradle.org/gradle. You can be sure you'll get helpful responses to your questions on the same day.

Gradleware is the technical service and support company behind Gradle. Not only does it provide professional advice for Gradle itself, it aims for a wide range of enterprise automation consulting. The company is backed by high-caliber engineers very experienced in the domain. Recently, Gradleware started to air free webinars to spark interest for newcomers and deepen knowledge for experienced Gradle users.

2.2.9 *Icing on the cake: additional features*

Don't you hate having to install a new runtime for different projects? Gradle Wrapper to the rescue! It allows for downloading and installing a fresh copy of the Gradle runtime from a specified repository on any machine you run the build on. This process is automatically triggered on the first execution of the build. The Wrapper is especially useful for sharing your builds with a distributed team or running them on a CI platform.

Gradle is also equipped with a rich command-line interface. Using command-line options, you can control everything from specifying the log level, to excluding tests, to displaying help messages. This is nothing special; other tools provide that, too. Some of the features stand out, though. Gradle allows for running commands in an abbreviated, camel-cased form. In practice, a command named `runMyAwesomeTask` would be callable with the abbreviation `rMAT`. Handy, isn't it? Even though this book presents most of its examples by running commands in a shell, bear in mind that Gradle provides an out-of-the-box graphical user interface.

2.3   *The bigger picture: continuous delivery*

Being able to build your source code is only one aspect of the software delivery process. More importantly, you want to release your product to a production environment to deliver business value. Along the way, you want to run tests, build the distribution, analyze the code for quality-control purposes, potentially provision a target environment, and deploy to it.

There are many benefits to automating the whole process. First and foremost, delivering software manually is slow, error-prone, and nerve-wracking. I'm sure every one of us hates the long nights due to a deployment gone wrong. With the rise of agile methodologies, development teams are able to deliver software faster. Release cycles of two or three weeks have become the norm. Some organizations like Etsy and Flickr even ship code to production several times a day! Optimally, you want to be able to release software by selecting the target environment simply by pressing a button. Practices like automated testing, CI, and deployment feed into the general concept of continuous delivery.

In this book, we'll look at how Gradle can help get your project from build to deployment. It'll enable you to automate many of the tasks required to implement continuous delivery, be they compiling your source code, deploying a deliverable, or calling external tools that help you with implementing the process. For a deep dive on continuous delivery and all of its aspects, I recommend *Continuous Delivery: Reliable Software Releases through Build, Test, and Deployment Automation* by Jez Humble and David Farley (Addison Wesley, 2010).

2.3.1   *Automating your project from build to deployment*

Continuous delivery introduces the concept of a deployment pipeline, also referred to as the build pipeline. A deployment pipeline represents the technical implementation of the process for getting software from version control into your production environment. The process consists of multiple stages, as shown in figure 2.7.

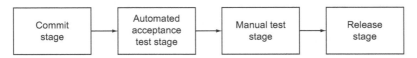

Figure 2.7   Stages of a deployment pipeline

- *Commit stage*: Reports on the technical health level of your project. The main stakeholder of this phase is the development team as it provides feedback about broken code and finds "code smells." The job of this stage is to compile the code, run tests, perform code analysis, and prepare the distribution.
- *Automated acceptance test stage*: Asserts that functional and nonfunctional requirements are met by running automated tests.
- *Manual test stage*: Verifies that the system is actually usable in a test environment. Usually, this stage involves QA personnel to verify requirements on the level of user stories or use cases.
- *Release stage*: Either delivers the software to the end user as a packaged distribution or deploys it to the production environment.

Let's see what stages of the deployment pipeline can benefit from project automation. It's obvious that the manual test stage can be excluded from further discussion, because it only involves manual tasks. This book mainly focuses on using Gradle in the commit and automated acceptance test stages. The concrete tasks we're going to look at are

- Compiling the code
- Running unit and integration tests
- Performing static code analysis and generating test coverage
- Creating the distribution
- Provisioning the target environment
- Deploying the deliverable
- Performing smoke and automated functional tests

Figure 2.8 shows the order of tasks within each of the stages. While there are no hard rules that prevent you from skipping specific tasks, it's recommended that you follow the order. For example, you could decide to compile your code, create the distribution, and deploy it to your target environment without running any tests or static code analysis. However, doing so increases the risk of undetected code defects and poor code quality.

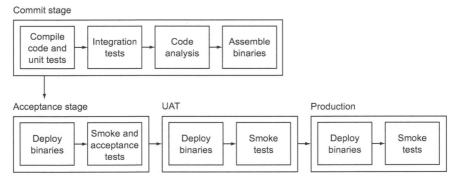

Figure 2.8   Tasks performed in stages of build pipeline

Topics like infrastructure provisioning, automated deployment, and smoke testing can also be applied to the release stage. In practice, applying these techniques to a production environment is more complex than in a controlled test environment. In a production environment, you may have to deal with clustered and distributed server infrastructures, zero-downtime release rollouts, and automated rollbacks to the previous release.

Covering these advanced topics would go beyond the scope of this book. However, there are some great examples of deployment management tools in the wild that you may want to check out, such as Asgard, a web-based cloud management and deployment tool built and used by Netflix (https://github.com/Netflix/asgard). But enough pure theory—let's get your feet wet by installing Gradle on your machine and building your first project. In chapter 3, we'll go even further by exploring how to implement and run a complex Java project using Gradle.

2.4   *Installing Gradle*

As a prerequisite, make sure you've already installed the JDK with a version of 1.5 or higher. Even though some operating systems provide you with an out-of-the-box Java installation, make sure you have a valid version installed on your system. To check the JDK version, run `java -version`.

Getting started with Gradle is easy. You can download the distribution directly from the Gradle homepage at http://gradle.org/downloads. As a beginner to the tool, it makes sense to choose the ZIP file that includes the documentation and a wide range of source code examples to explore. Unzip the downloaded file to a directory of your choice. To reference your Gradle runtime in the shell, you'll need to create the environment variable GRADLE_HOME and add the binaries to your shell's execution path:

- *Mac OS X and *nix*: To make Gradle available in your shell, add the following two lines to your initialization script (for example, `~/.profile`). These instructions assume that you installed Gradle in the directory `/opt/gradle`:

```
export GRADLE_HOME=/opt/gradle
export PATH=$PATH:$GRADLE_HOME/bin
```

- *Windows*: In the Environment Variables dialog, define the variable GRADLE_HOME and update your path settings (figure 2.9).

You'll verify that Gradle has been installed correctly and is ready to go. To check the version of the installed runtime, issue the command `gradle -v` in your shell. You should see meta-information about the installation, your JVM, and the operating system. The following example shows the version output of a successful Gradle 1.7 installation.

Figure 2.9 Updating variable settings on Windows

```
$ gradle -v

------------------------------------------------------------
Gradle 1.7
------------------------------------------------------------

Build time:   2013-08-06 11:19:56 UTC
Build number: none
Revision:     9a7199efaf72c620b33f9767874f0ebced135d83

Groovy:       1.8.6
Ant:          Apache Ant(TM) version 1.8.4 compiled on May 22 2012
Ivy:          2.2.0
JVM:          1.6.0_51 (Apple Inc. 20.51-b01-457)
OS:           Mac OS X 10.8.4 x86_64
```

Setting Gradle's JVM options

Like every other Java application, Gradle shares the same JVM options set by the environment variable JAVA_OPTS. If you want to pass arguments specifically to the Gradle runtime, use the environment variable GRADLE_OPTS. Let's say you want to increase the default maximum heap size to 1 GB. You could set it like this:

```
GRADLE_OPTS="-Xmx1024m"
```

The preferred way to do that is to add the variable to the Gradle startup script under $GRADLE_HOME/bin.

Now that you're all set, you'll implement a simple build script with Gradle. Even though most of the popular IDEs provide a Gradle plugin, all you need now is your favorite editor. Chapter 10 will discuss Gradle plugin support for IDEs like IntelliJ, Eclipse, and NetBeans.

2.5 *Getting started with Gradle*

Every Gradle build starts with a script. The default naming convention for a Gradle build script is `build.gradle`. When executing the command `gradle` in a shell, Gradle looks for a file with that exact name. If it can't be located, the runtime will display a help message.

Let's set the lofty goal of creating the typical "Hello world!" example in Gradle. First you'll create a file called `build.gradle`. Within that script, define a single atomic piece of work. In Gradle's vocabulary, this is called a task. In this example, the task is called `helloWorld`. To print the message "Hello world!" make use of Gradle's lingua franca, Groovy, by adding the `println` command to the task's action `doLast`. The method `println` is Groovy's shorter equivalent to Java's `System.out.println`:

```
task helloWorld {
    doLast {
        println 'Hello world!'
    }
}
```

Give it a spin:

```
$ gradle -q helloWorld
Hello world!
```

As expected, you see the output "Hello world!" when running the script. By defining the optional command-line option `quiet` with `-q`, you tell Gradle to only output the task's output.

Without knowing it, you already used Gradle's DSL. Tasks and actions are important elements of the language. An action named `doLast` is almost self-expressive. It's the last action that's executed for a task. Gradle allows for specifying the same logic in a more concise way. The left shift operator `<<` is a shortcut for the action `doLast`. The following snippet shows a modified version of the first example:

```
task helloWorld << {
    println 'Hello world!'
}
```

Printing "Hello world!" only goes so far. I'll give you a taste of more advanced features in the example build script shown in the following listing. Let's strengthen our belief in Gradle by exercising a little group therapy session. Repeat after me: Gradle rocks!

Listing 2.1 Dynamic task definition and task chaining

```
task startSession << {
    chant()
}
```

```
def chant() {
    ant.echo(message: 'Repeat after me...')       ◁─┐   Implicit Ant
}                                                   ❶  task usage

3.times {
    task "yayGradle$it" << {          ◁─┐   Dynamic task
        println 'Gradle rocks'          ❷  definition
    }
}
```

```
yayGradle0.dependsOn startSession
yayGradle2.dependsOn yayGradle1, yayGradle0        ❸  Task
task groupTherapy(dependsOn: yayGradle2)               dependencies
```

You may not notice it at first, but there's a lot going on in this listing. You introduced the keyword dependsOn to indicate dependencies between tasks ❸. Gradle makes sure that the depended-on task will always be executed before the task that defines the dependency. Under the hood, dependsOn is actually a method of a task. Chapter 4 will cover the internals of tasks, so we won't dive into too much detail here.

A feature we've talked about before is Gradle's tight integration with Ant ❶. Because you have full access to Groovy's language features, you can also print your message in a method named chant(). This method can easily be called from your task. Every script is equipped with a property called ant that grants direct access to Ant tasks. In this example, you print out the message "Repeat after me" using the Ant task echo to start the therapy session.

A nifty feature Gradle provides is the definition of dynamic tasks, which specify their name at runtime. Your script creates three new tasks within a loop ❷ using Groovy's times method extension on java.lang.Number. Groovy automatically exposes an implicit variable named it to indicate the loop iteration index. You're using this counter to build the task name. For the first iteration, the task would be called yayGradle0.

Now running gradle groupTherapy results in the following output:

```
$ gradle groupTherapy
:startSession
[ant:echo] Repeat after me...
:yayGradle0
Gradle rocks
:yayGradle1
Gradle rocks
:yayGradle2
Gradle rocks
:groupTherapy
```

As shown in figure 2.10 Gradle executed the tasks in the correct order. You may have noticed that the example omitted the quiet command-line option, which gives more information on the tasks run.

Thanks to your group therapy, you got rid of your deepest fears that Gradle will be just another build tool that can't deliver. In the next chapter, you'll stand up a

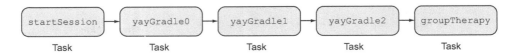

Figure 2.10   Task dependency graph

full-fledged Java application covering a broad range of Gradle's core concepts. For now, let's get more accustomed to Gradle's command line.

2.6   Using the Command line

In the previous sections, you executed the tasks helloWorld and groupTherapy on the command line, which is going to be your tool of choice for running most examples throughout this book. Even though using an IDE may seem more convenient to newcomers, a deep understanding of Gradle's command-line options and helper tasks will make you more efficient and productive in the long run.

2.6.1   Listing available tasks of a project

In the last section I showed you how to run a specific task using the gradle command. Running a task requires you to know the exact name. Wouldn't it be great if Gradle could tell you which tasks are available without you having to look at the source code? Gradle provides a helper task named tasks to introspect your build script and display each available task, including a descriptive message of its purpose. Running gradle tasks in quiet mode produces the following output:

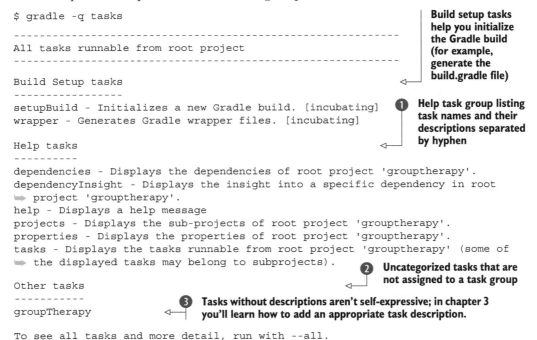

```
$ gradle -q tasks
------------------------------------------------------------
All tasks runnable from root project
------------------------------------------------------------

Build Setup tasks
-----------------
setupBuild - Initializes a new Gradle build. [incubating]
wrapper - Generates Gradle wrapper files. [incubating]

Help tasks
----------
dependencies - Displays the dependencies of root project 'grouptherapy'.
dependencyInsight - Displays the insight into a specific dependency in root
     project 'grouptherapy'.
help - Displays a help message
projects - Displays the sub-projects of root project 'grouptherapy'.
properties - Displays the properties of root project 'grouptherapy'.
tasks - Displays the tasks runnable from root project 'grouptherapy' (some of
     the displayed tasks may belong to subprojects).

Other tasks
-----------
groupTherapy

To see all tasks and more detail, run with --all.
```

Build setup tasks help you initialize the Gradle build (for example, generate the build.gradle file)

1 **Help task group listing task names and their descriptions separated by hyphen**

2 **Uncategorized tasks that are not assigned to a task group**

3 **Tasks without descriptions aren't self-expressive; in chapter 3 you'll learn how to add an appropriate task description.**

There are some things to note about the output. Gradle provides the concept of a task group, which can be seen as a cluster of tasks assigned to that group. Out of the box, each build script exposes the task group Help tasks ❶ without any additional work from the developer. If a task doesn't belong to a task group, it's displayed under Other tasks ❷. This is where you find the task groupTherapy ❸. We'll look at how to add a task to a task group in chapter 4.

You may wonder what happened to the other tasks that you defined in your build script. On the bottom of the output, you'll find a note that you can get even more details about your project's tasks by using the --all option. Run it to get more information on them:

```
$ gradle -q tasks --all

------------------------------------------------------------
All tasks runnable from root project
------------------------------------------------------------

Build Setup tasks
-----------------
setupBuild - Initializes a new Gradle build. [incubating]
wrapper - Generates Gradle wrapper files. [incubating]

Help tasks
----------
dependencies - Displays the dependencies of root project 'grouptherapy'.
help - Displays a help message
projects - Displays the sub-projects of root project 'grouptherapy'.
properties - Displays the properties of root project 'grouptherapy'.
tasks - Displays the tasks runnable from root project 'grouptherapy' (some of
➥ the displayed tasks may belong to subprojects).

Other tasks
-----------
groupTherapy
    startSession
    yayGradle0
    yayGradle1
    yayGradle2
```

❶ **Root task of dependency graph**

Indented names of dependent tasks listed in order of execution

The --all option is a great way to determine the execution order of a task graph before actually executing it. To reduce the noise, Gradle is smart enough to hide tasks that act as dependencies to a root task ❶. For better readability, dependent tasks are displayed indented and ordered underneath the root task.

2.6.2 *Task execution*

In the previous examples, you told Gradle to execute one specific task by adding it as an argument to the command gradle. Gradle's command-line implementation will in turn make sure that the task and all its dependencies are executed. You can also execute multiple tasks in a single build run by defining them as command-line parameters. Running gradle yayGradle0 groupTherapy would execute the task yayGradle0 first and the task groupTherapy second.

Tasks are always executed just once, no matter whether they're specified on the command line or act as a dependency for another task. Let's see what the output looks like:

```
$ gradle yayGradle0 groupTherapy
:startSession
[ant:echo] Repeat after me...
:yayGradle0
Gradle rocks
:yayGradle1
Gradle rocks
:yayGradle2
Gradle rocks
:groupTherapy
```

No surprises here. You see the same output as if you'd just run `gradle groupTherapy`. The correct order was preserved and each of the tasks was only executed once.

TASK NAME ABBREVIATION

One of Gradle's productivity tools is the ability to abbreviate camel-cased task names on the command line. If you wanted to run the previous example in the abbreviated form, you'd just have to type `gradle yG0 gT`. This is especially useful if you're dealing with very long task names or multiple task arguments. Keep in mind that the task name abbreviation has to be unique to enable Gradle to identify the corresponding task. Consider the following scenario:

```
task groupTherapy << {
    ...
}

task generateTests << {
    ...
}
```

Using the abbreviation `gT` in a build that defines the tasks `groupTherapy` and `generateTests` causes Gradle to display an error:

```
$ gradle yG0 gT

FAILURE: Could not determine which tasks to execute.

* What went wrong:
Task 'gT' is ambiguous in root project 'grouptherapy'. Candidates are:
➥ 'generateTests', 'groupTherapy'.

* Try:
Run gradle tasks to get a list of available tasks.

BUILD FAILED
```

EXCLUDING A TASK FROM EXECUTION

Sometimes you want to exclude a specific task from your build run. Gradle provides the command-line option –x to achieve that. Let's say you want to exclude the task `yayGradle0`:

```
$ gradle groupTherapy -x yayGradle0
:yayGradle1
Gradle rocks
:yayGradle2
Gradle rocks
:groupTherapy
```

Gradle excluded the task yayGradle0 and its dependent task startSession, a concept Gradle calls *smart exclusion*. Now that you're becoming familiar with the command line, let's explore some more helpful functions.

2.6.3   Command-line options

In this section, we explore the most important general-purpose options, flags to control your build script's logging level, and ways to provide properties to your project. The gradle command allows you to define one or more options at the same time. Let's say you want to change the log level to INFO using the -i option *and* print out any stack trace if an error occurs during execution with the option -s. To do so, execute the task groupTherapy command like this: gradle groupTherapy -is or gradle groupTherapy -i -s. As you can see, it's very easy to combine multiple options. To discover the full set, run your build with the -h argument or see appendix A of this book. I won't go over all the available options, but the most important ones are as follows:

- *-?, -h, --help*: Prints out all available command-line options including a descriptive message.
- *-b, --build-file*: The default naming convention for Gradle build script is build.gradle. Use this option to execute a build script with a different name (for example, gradle -b test.gradle).
- *--offline*: Often your build declares dependencies on libraries only available in repositories outside of your network. If these dependencies were not stored in your local cache yet, running a build without a network connection to these repositories would result in a failed build. Use this option to run your build in offline mode and only check the local dependency cache for dependencies.

PROPERTY OPTIONS

- *-D, --system-prop*: Gradle runs as a JVM process. As with all Java processes, you can provide a system property like this: -Dmyprop=myvalue.
- *-P, --project-prop*: Project properties are variables available in your build script. You can use this option to pass a property to the build script directly from the command line (for example, -Pmyprop=myvalue).

LOGGING OPTIONS

- *-i, --info*: In the default settings, a Gradle build doesn't output a lot of information. Use this option to get more informative messages by changing Gradle's logger to INFO log level. This is helpful if you want to get more information on what's happening under the hood.

- `-s, --stacktrace`: If you run into errors in your build, you'll want to know where they stem from. The option -s prints out an abbreviated stack trace if an exception is thrown, making it perfect for debugging broken builds.
- `-q, --quiet`: Reduces the log messages of a build run to error messages only.

HELP TASKS

- `tasks`: Displays all runnable tasks of your project including their descriptions. Plugins applied to your project may provide additional tasks.
- `properties`: Emits a list of all available properties in your project. Some of these properties are provided by Gradle's project object, the build's internal representation. Other properties are user-defined properties originating from a property file or property command-line option, or directly declared in your build script.

2.6.4   *Gradle daemon*

When using Gradle on a day-to-day basis, you'll find yourself having to run your build repetitively. This is especially true if you're working on a web application. You change a class, rebuild the web application archive, bring up the server, and reload the URL in the browser to see your changes being reflected. Many developers prefer test-driven development to implement their application. For continuous feedback on their code quality, they run their unit tests over and over again to find code defects early on. In both cases, you'll notice a significant productivity hit. Each time you initiate a build, the JVM has to be started, Gradle's dependencies have to be loaded into the class loader, and the project object model has to be constructed. This procedure usually takes a couple of seconds. Gradle daemon to the rescue!

The daemon runs Gradle as a background process. Once started, the `gradle` command will reuse the forked daemon process for subsequent builds, avoiding the startup costs altogether. Let's come back to the previous build script example. On my machine, it takes about three seconds to successfully complete running the task `groupTherapy`. Hopefully, we can improve the startup and execution time. It's easy to start the Gradle daemon on the command line: simply add the option `--daemon` to your `gradle` command. You may notice that we add a little extra time for starting up the daemon as well. To verify that the daemon process is running, you can check the process list on your operating system:

- *Mac OS X and *nix*: In a shell run the command ps | grep gradle to list the processes that contain the name gradle.
- *Windows*: Open the task manager with the keyboard shortcut Ctrl+Shift+Esc and click the Processes tab.

Give it a shot and try running `gradle groupTherapy --daemon`. Wow, you got your startup and execution time down to about one second! Subsequent invocations of the `gradle` command will need to declare the `--daemon` option explicitly. In practice you might want to configure the daemon with the help of a system properties to reuse an already started daemon process. For more information on the daemon's configuration, check out the online documentation at http://www.gradle.org/docs/current/ userguide/build_environment.html#sec:gradle_configuration_properties. Keep in mind that a daemon process will only be forked once even though you add the command-line option --daemon. The daemon process will automatically expire after a three-hour idle time. At any time you can choose to execute your build without using the daemon by adding the command-line option --no-daemon. To stop the daemon process, manually run gradle --stop. That's the Gradle daemon in a nutshell. For a deep dive into all configuration options and intricacies, please refer to the Gradle online documentation at http://gradle.org/docs/current/userguide/gradle_daemon.html.

2.7 *Summary*

Existing tools can't meet the build needs of today's industry. Improving on the best ideas of its competitors, Gradle provides a build-by-convention approach, reliable dependency management, and support for multiproject builds without having to sacrifice the flexibility and descriptiveness of your build.

In this chapter, we explored how Gradle can be used to deliver in each of the phases of a deployment pipeline in the context of continuous delivery. Throughout the book, we'll pick up on each of the phases by providing practical examples.

Next, you got a first taste of Gradle's powerful features in action. You installed the runtime, wrote a first simple build script, and executed it. By implementing a more complex build script, you found out how easy it is to define task dependencies using Gradle's DSL. Knowing the mechanics of Gradle's command line and its options is key to becoming highly productive. Gradle offers a wide variety of command-line switches for changing runtime behavior, passing properties to your project, and changing the logging level. We explored how running Gradle with the daemon can be a huge time-saver if you have to continuously execute tasks, such as during test-driven development.

In chapter 3, I'll show how to build a full-fledged, web-enabled application with Gradle. Starting out with a simple, standalone Java application, you'll extend the code base by adding a web component and use Gradle's in-container web development support to efficiently implement the solution. We won't stop there. I'm going to show how to enhance your web archive to make it enterprise-ready and make the build transferable across machines without having to install the Gradle runtime.

Building a Gradle project by example

This chapter covers

- Building a full-stack Java project with Gradle
- Practicing efficient web application development
- Customizing default conventions to adapt to custom requirements
- Using the Gradle wrapper

Chapter 2 introduced Gradle's feature set and showed how it compared to other JVM build tools. Some simple examples gave you a first impression of the tool's expressive build language. By running your first build script, you saw how easy it is to become productive on the command line. Now it's time to strengthen this newly acquired knowledge by building a real-world Java project.

When starting a brand-new application, Java doesn't guide you toward a standardized project structure. You may ask yourself where to put source, configuration, and library files. What if you want to separate your application code from your test source files? Gradle provides a build-by-convention approach for certain domains like Java projects by introducing predefined project layouts with sensible defaults. Stuck with a legacy application that has a different directory structure? No problem! Gradle allows for adapting its conventions to your needs.

In this chapter, you'll explore the inner workings of Gradle's standardization paradigm by building a Java project and learning how to tailor it to nonconventional use cases. In the next step, you'll extend your application by a web component and introduce productivity tools for fast development turnarounds. Then we'll round out this chapter by looking at the Gradle wrapper, which allows you to create transferable and reproducible builds without having to install the Gradle runtime.

3.1 Introducing the case study

This section introduces a simple application to illustrate the use of Gradle: a To Do application. Throughout the book, we'll apply the content to demonstrate Gradle's features in each phase of the build pipeline. The use case starts out as a plain Java application without a GUI, simply controlled through console input. Over the course of this chapter, you'll extend this application by adding components to learn more advanced concepts.

The To Do application will act as a vehicle to help you gain a broad knowledge of Gradle's capabilities. You'll learn how to apply Gradle's standard plugins to bootstrap, configure, and run your application. By the end of this chapter, you'll have a basic understanding of how Gradle works that you can apply to building your own web-based Java projects with Gradle.

3.1.1 The To Do application

Today's world is busy. Many of us manage multiple projects simultaneously, both in our professional and private lives. Often, you may find yourself in situations where you feel overwhelmed and out of control. The key to staying organized and focused on priorities is a well-maintained to-do list. Sure, you could always write down your tasks on a piece of paper, but wouldn't it be convenient to be able to access your action items everywhere you go? Access to the internet is almost omnipresent, either through your mobile phone or publicly available access points. You're going to build your own web-based and visually appealing application, as shown in figure 3.1.

3.1.2 Task management use cases

Now that you know your end goal, let's identify the use cases the application needs to fulfill. Every task management system consists of an ordered list of action items or tasks. A task has a title to represent the action needed to complete it. Tasks can be added to the list and removed from the list, and marked active or completed to indicate their status. The list should also allow for modifying a task's title in case you want

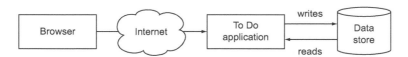

Figure 3.1 The To Do application is accessible through the internet and manages action items in a data store.

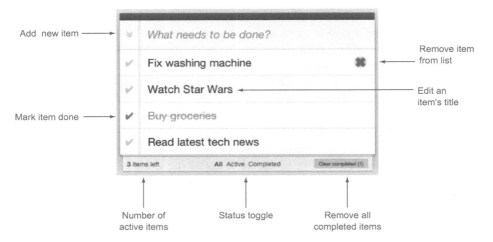

Figure 3.2   Web-based user interface of To Do application and its actions

to make the description more accurate. Changes to a task should automatically get persisted to a data store.

To bring order to your list of tasks, you'll include the option to filter tasks by their status: active or completed. For now, we'll stick with this minimal set of features. Figure 3.2 shows a screenshot of the user interface rendered in a browser.

Let's take a step back from the user interface aspect and build the application from the ground up. In its first version, you'll lay out its foundation by implementing the basic functionality controlled through the command line. In the next section, we're going to focus on the application's components and the interactions between them.

3.1.3   *Examining the component interaction*

We found that a To Do application implements the typical create, read, update, and delete (CRUD) functionality. For data to be persisted, you need to represent it by a model. You'll create a new Java class called ToDoItem, a plain old Java object (POJO) acting as a model. To keep the first iteration of the solution as simple as possible, we won't introduce a traditional data store like a database to store the model data. Instead, you'll keep it in memory, which is easy to implement. The class implementing the persistence contract is called InMemoryToDoRepository. The drawback is that you can't persist the data after shutting down the application. Later in the book, we'll pick up this idea and show how to write a better implementation for it.

Every standalone Java program is required to implement a main class, the application's entry point. Your main class will be called ToDoApp and will run until the user decides to exit the program. You'll present users with a menu of commands through which they can manage their to-do list by typing in a letter triggering a specific action. Each action command is mapped to an enum called CommandLineInput. The class CommandLineInputHandler represents the glue between user interaction and command

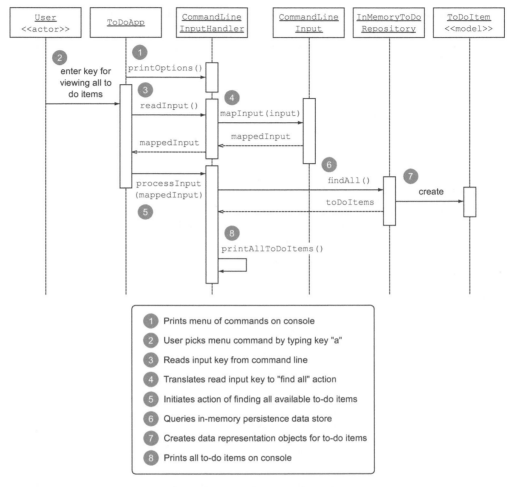

Figure 3.3 Listing all available tasks represented as a sequence diagram

execution. Figure 3.3 illustrates the object interaction arranged in a time sequence for the use case of listing all available tasks.

Now you're ready to implement the application's functionality. In the next section, we'll dive right into the code.

3.1.4 *Building the application's functionality*

In the last section, we identified the classes, their functions, and the interaction between them. Now it's time to fill them with life. First, let's look at the model of a to-do action item.

THE TO DO MODEL CLASS

Each instance of the ToDoItem class represents an action item in your to-do list. The attribute id defines the item's unique identity, enabling you to store it in the in-memory data structure and read it again if you want to display it in the user interface. Additionally, the model class exposes the fields name and completed. For brevity, the getter and setter methods as well as the compareTo method are excluded from the snippet:

```
package com.manning.gia.todo.model;

public class ToDoItem implements Comparable<ToDoItem> {
   private Long id;
   private String name;
   private boolean completed;

   (...)
}
```

Now let's look at the repository implementation for reading and writing the model.

IN-MEMORY PERSISTENCE OF THE MODEL

Storing data in memory is convenient and simplifies the implementation. Later in the book, you may want to provide more sophisticated implementations like database or file persistence. To be able to swap out the implementation, you'll create an interface, the ToDoRepository, as shown in the following listing.

Listing 3.1   The repository interface

```
package com.manning.gia.todo.repository;

import com.manning.gia.todo.model.ToDoItem;
import java.util.Collection;

public interface ToDoRepository {
   List<ToDoItem> findAll();
   ToDoItem findById(Long id);
   Long insert(ToDoItem toDoItem);
   void update(ToDoItem toDoItem);
   void delete(ToDoItem toDoItem);
}
```

The interface declares all the CRUD operations you'd expect. You can find all existing to-do items, look up a specific one by ID, insert new action items, and update or delete them. Next, you'll create a scalable and thread-safe implementation of this interface. The next listing shows the class InMemoryToDoRepository, which stores to-do items in an instance of a ConcurrentHashMap.

Listing 3.2   In-memory persistence of to-do items

```
package com.manning.gia.todo.repository;

import com.manning.gia.todo.model.ToDoItem;
import java.util.ArrayList;
import java.util.Collections;
import java.util.List;
import java.util.concurrent.ConcurrentHashMap;
import java.util.concurrent.ConcurrentMap;
import java.util.concurrent.atomic.AtomicLong;
```

```
public class InMemoryToDoRepository implements ToDoRepository {
    private AtomicLong currentId = new AtomicLong();          ◄── Thread-safe
    private ConcurrentMap<Long, ToDoItem> toDos                   provider for
    ➡ = new ConcurrentHashMap<Long, ToDoItem>();  ◄──┐          identifier
                                            Efficient in-memory  sequence
    @Override                               data structure for  number
    public List<ToDoItem> findAll() {       storing to-do items
        List<ToDoItem> toDoItems = new ArrayList<ToDoItem>(toDos.values());
        Collections.sort(toDoItems);                      ◄──┐
        return toDoItems;                                     Sorting to-do
    }                                                         items by identifier

    @Override
    public ToDoItem findById(Long id) {
        return toDos.get(id);
    }

    @Override
    public Long insert(ToDoItem toDoItem) {
        Long id = currentId.incrementAndGet();
        toDoItem.setId(id);
        toDos.putIfAbsent(id, toDoItem);        ◄──┐ Only puts to-do item into
        return id;                                    Map if it doesn't exist yet
    }

    @Override
    public void update(ToDoItem toDoItem) {
        toDos.replace(toDoItem.getId(), toDoItem);  ◄──┐ Replaces to-do item
    }                                                     if existent in Map

    @Override
    public void delete(ToDoItem toDoItem) {
        toDos.remove(toDoItem.getId());     ◄──┐ Removes to-do item
    }                                             if existent in Map
}
```

So far, you've seen the data structure of a to-do item and an in-memory implementation for storing and retrieving the data. To be able to bootstrap the Java program, you'll need to create a main class.

THE APPLICATION'S ENTRY POINT

The class ToDoApp prints the application's options on the console, reads the user's input from the prompt, translates the one-letter input into a command object, and handles it accordingly, as shown in the next listing.

Listing 3.3 Implementing the main class

```
package com.manning.gia.todo;

import com.manning.gia.todo.utils.CommandLineInput;
import com.manning.gia.todo.utils.CommandLineInputHandler;

public class ToDoApp {
    public static final char DEFAULT_INPUT = '\u0000';

    public static void main(String args[]) {
        CommandLineInputHandler commandLineInputHandler = new
```

```
⇒   CommandLineInputHandler();
char command = DEFAULT_INPUT;

while(CommandLineInput.EXIT.getShortCmd() != command) {          ◁─
    commandLineInputHandler.printOptions();
    String input = commandLineInputHandler.readInput();
    char[] inputChars = input.length() == 1 ? input.toCharArray() : new
    ⇒   char[] { DEFAULT_INPUT };
    command = inputChars[0];
    CommandLineInput commandLineInput =
    ⇒   CommandLineInput.getCommandLineInputForInput(command);   ◁─
    commandLineInputHandler.processInput(commandLineInput);
    }
  }
}
```

**Application
runs as long
as user enters
exit command**

**Executes
CRUD
command**

**Mapping
between
one-letter
prompt
input and a
command
object**

So far, we've discussed the components of the application and their interactions in the context of a specific use case: finding all to-do items of a user. Listing 3.3 should give you a rough idea of the components responsibilities and how they work internally. Don't worry if you don't understand every little implementation detail of the class definitions presented here. What's more important is the automation of the project. We'll look at specific concerns like setting up the project with Gradle, compiling the source code, assembling the JAR file, and running the application in the rest of the chapter. It's time for Gradle to hit the stage.

3.2   Building a Java project

In the last section, we identified the Java classes required to write a standalone To Do application. To assemble an executable program, the source code needs to be compiled and the classes need to be packaged into a JAR file. The Java Development Kit (JDK) provides development tools like `javac` and `jar` that help with implementing these tasks. Unless you're a masochist, you don't want to run these tasks manually each and every time your source code changes.

Gradle plugins act as enablers to automate these tasks. A plugin extends your project by introducing domain-specific conventions and tasks with sensible defaults. One of the plugins that Gradle ships with is the Java plugin. The Java plugin goes far beyond the basic functionality of source code compilation and packaging. It establishes a standard layout for your project and makes sure that tasks are executed in the correct order so they make sense in the context of a Java project. It's time to create a build script for your application and apply the Java plugin.

3.2.1   Using the Java plugin

In chapter 1, you learned that every Gradle project starts with the creation of the build script named `build.gradle`. Create the file and tell your project to use the Java plugin like this:

```
apply plugin: 'java'
```

One line of code is enough to build your Java code, but how does Gradle know where to find your source files? One of the conventions the Java plugin introduces is the location of the source code. By default, the plugin searches for production source code in the directory src/main/java. You'll take all the classes of your To Do application and put them under the appropriate directory.

Automatic project generation

Wouldn't it be great if you didn't have to create the source directories manually? Maven has a concept called *project archetypes*, a plugin to generate a project structure from an existing template. Unfortunately, at the time of writing this functionality hasn't become a Gradle core feature. The plugin Gradle Templates created by the Gradle community proposes a solution to this issue. It's available at https://github.com/townsfolk/gradle-templates. A first attempt at initializing a Gradle project is automatically made by the build setup plugin, which you can use even without a build script. This plugin allows for generating the project file (and other related files you'll learn about later). To generate the Gradle build script, execute gradle setupBuild from the command line.

When creating the source files, keep in mind that the package you used for the classes, com.manning.gia.todo, directly translates into subdirectories under the root source directory. After creating the build script and moving your source code into the correct location, your project structure should look like this:

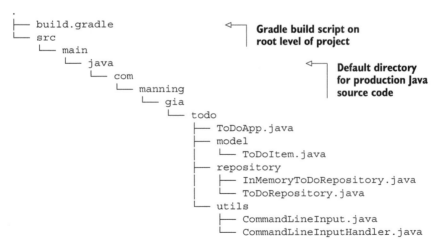

BUILDING THE PROJECT

You're ready to build the project. One of the tasks the Java plugin adds to your project is named build. The build task compiles your code, runs your tests, and assembles the JAR file, all in the correct order. Running the command gradle build should give you an output similar to this:

```
$ gradle build
:compileJava
:processResources UP-TO-DATE
:classes
:jar
:assemble
:compileTestJava UP-TO-DATE
:processTestResources UP-TO-DATE
:testClasses UP-TO-DATE
:test
:check
:build
```

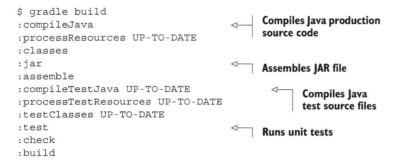

Compiles Java production
source code

Assembles JAR file

Compiles Java
test source files

Runs unit tests

Each line of the output represents an executed task provided by the Java plugin. You may notice that some of the tasks are marked with the message UP-TO-DATE. That means that the task was skipped. Gradle's incremental build support automatically identified that no work needed to be done. Especially in large enterprise projects, this feature proves to be a real timesaver. In chapter 4 you'll learn how to apply this concept to your own tasks. In the command-line output, you can see concrete examples of skipped tasks: compileTestJava and testClasses. As you didn't provide any unit tests in the default directory src/test/java, Gradle happily moves on. If you want to learn how to write tests for your application and integrate them into the build, see chapter 7. Here's the project structure after executing the build:

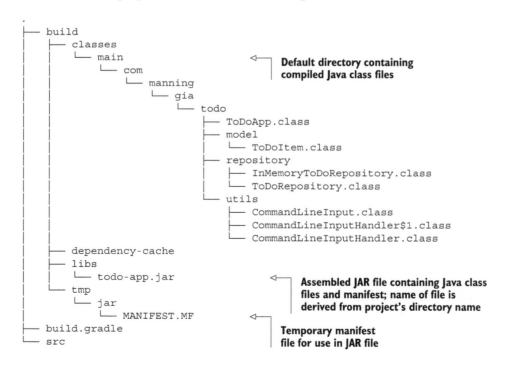

```
.
├── build
│   ├── classes
│   │   └── main
│   │       └── com
│   │           └── manning
│   │               └── gia
│   │                   └── todo
│   │                       ├── ToDoApp.class
│   │                       ├── model
│   │                       │   └── ToDoItem.class
│   │                       ├── repository
│   │                       │   ├── InMemoryToDoRepository.class
│   │                       │   └── ToDoRepository.class
│   │                       └── utils
│   │                           ├── CommandLineInput.class
│   │                           ├── CommandLineInputHandler$1.class
│   │                           └── CommandLineInputHandler.class
│   ├── dependency-cache
│   ├── libs
│   │   └── todo-app.jar
│   └── tmp
│       └── jar
│           └── MANIFEST.MF
├── build.gradle
└── src
```

Default directory containing
compiled Java class files

Assembled JAR file containing Java class
files and manifest; name of file is
derived from project's directory name

Temporary manifest
file for use in JAR file

On the root level of your project, you'll now also find a directory named build, which contains all output of the build run, including class files, test reports, the assembled JAR file, and temporary files like a manifest needed for the archive. If you've previously used the build tool Maven, which uses the standard output directory target, the structure should look familiar. The name of the build output directory is a configurable standard property common to all Gradle builds. You've seen how effortless it is to build a Java project by convention without any additional configuration from your side. The JAR file was created under build/libs and is ready for execution. It's important to understand that the name of the JAR file is derived from the project name. As long as you don't reconfigure it, the directory name of your project is used, which in this case is todo-app. Let's see the To Do application in action.

RUNNING THE PROJECT

Running a Java program is easy. For now, you'll just use the JDK's java command from the root directory of your project:

```
$ java -cp build/classes/main com.manning.gia.todo.ToDoApp

--- To Do Application ---
Please make a choice:
(a)ll items
(f)ind a specific item
(i)nsert a new item
(u)pdate an existing item
(d)elete an existing item
(e)xit
>
```

The Java program starts up, prints a list of all available to-do actions, and awaits your input from the command prompt.

> ### Java standalone application support
> Gradle can simplify building a standalone Java application even further. Another standard Gradle extension worth mentioning is the application plugin. The plugin provides tasks for simplifying the act of running and bundling an application.

That's it—you effortlessly implemented a Java application and built it with Gradle. All it took was a one-liner in your build script as long as you stuck to the standard conventions. Next, we'll look at how to customize the build-by-convention standards.

3.2.2   *Customizing your project*

The Java plugin is a small opinionated framework. It assumes sensible default values for many aspects of your project, like its layout. If your view of the world is different, Gradle gives you the option of customizing the conventions. How do you know what's configurable? A good place to start is Gradle's Build Language Reference, available at http://www.gradle.org/docs/current/dsl/. Remember the command-line option `properties` from chapter 2? Running `gradle properties` gives you a list of configurable standard and plugin properties, plus their default values. You'll customize the project by extending the initial build script.

MODIFYING PROJECT AND PLUGIN PROPERTIES

In the following example, you'll specify a version number for your project and indicate the Java source compatibility. Previously, you ran the To Do application using the `java` command. You told the Java runtime where to find the classes by assigning the build output directory to the classpath command-line option via `-cp build/classes/main`. To be able to start the application from the JAR file, the manifest `MANIFEST.MF` needs to contain the header `Main-Class`. The following listing demonstrates how to configure the default values in the build script and add a header attribute to the JAR manifest.

Listing 3.4   Changing properties and adding a JAR header

```
version = 0.1                                                    ◁────┐  Identifies project's
sourceCompatibility = 1.6      ◁────┐                                    version through a
                                     │  Sets Java version compilation    number scheme
jar {                                │  compatibility to 1.6
   manifest {
      attributes 'Main-Class': 'com.manning.gia.todo.ToDoApp'   ◁────┐  Adds Main-Class
   }                                                                    header to JAR
}                                                                       file's manifest
```

After assembling the JAR file, you'll notice that the version number has been added to the JAR filename. Instead of `todo-app.jar`, it reads `todo-app-0.1.jar`. Now that the generated JAR file contains the main class header, you can run the application with `java -jar build/libs/todo-app-0.1.jar`. Next, we'll look at how to retrofit the project structure to a legacy layout.

RETROFITTING LEGACY PROJECTS

Rarely do enterprises start new software projects with a clean slate. All too often, you'll have to integrate with a legacy system, migrate the technology stack of an existing project, or adhere to internal standards or limitations. A build tool has to be flexible enough to adapt to external constraints by configuring the default settings.

In this section we'll explore examples that demonstrate the customizability of the To Do application. Let's assume you started the project with a different directory layout. Instead of putting source code files into `src/main/java`, you chose to use the directory `src`. The same concept applies if you want to change the default test source directory. Additionally, you'd like to let Gradle render its build output into the directory out instead of the standard value `build`. The next listing shows how to adapt your build to a custom project layout.

Listing 3.5   Changing the project default layout

```
sourceSets {
    main {
        java {
            srcDirs = ['src']
        }
    }
    test {
        java {
            srcDirs = ['test']
        }
    }
}
buildDir = 'out'
```

- Replaces conventional source code directory with list of different directories
- Replaces conventional test source code directory with list of different directories
- Changes project output property to directory out

The key to customizing a build is knowledge of the underlying properties and DSL elements. Next, we'll look at how to use functionality from external libraries.

3.2.3   *Configuring and using external dependencies*

Let's think back to the main method in the class `ToDoApp`. You wrote some code to read the user's input from the console and translate the first character into a to-do command. To do so, you needed to make sure that the entered input string had a length of only one digit. Otherwise, you'd assign the Unicode `null` character:

```
String input = commandLineInputHandler.readInput();
char[] inputChars = input.length() == 1 ? input.toCharArray() : new
    char[] { DEFAULT_INPUT };
command = inputChars[0];
```

I bet you can improve on this implementation by reusing a library that wraps this logic. The perfect match is the class `CharUtils` from the Apache Commons Lang library. It provides a method called `toChar` that converts a `String` to a `char` by using just the first character, or a default character if the string's value is empty. The following code snippet shows the improved version of your input parsing code:

```
import org.apache.commons.lang3.CharUtils;

String input = commandLineInputHandler.readInput();
command = CharUtils.toChar(input, DEFAULT_INPUT);
```

So how do you tell Gradle to reference the Apache Commons Lang library? We'll look at two DSL configuration elements: repositories and dependencies.

DEFINING THE REPOSITORY

In the Java world, dependencies are distributed and used in the form of JAR files. Many libraries are available in a repository, such as a file system or central server. Gradle requires you to define at least one repository to use a dependency. For your purposes, you're going to use the publicly available, internet-accessible repository Maven Central:

```
repositories {
   mavenCentral()          ⤺── Shortcut notation for configuring Maven
}                                Central 2 repository accessible under
                                 http://repo1.maven.org/maven2
```

With a repository in place, you're ready to declare the library. Let's look at the definition of the dependency itself.

DEFINING THE DEPENDENCY

A dependency is defined through a group identifier, a name, and a specific version. You'll use version 3.1 of the library, as shown in this code snippet:

```
dependencies {
   compile group: 'org.apache.commons', name: 'commons-lang3', version: '3.1'
}
```

In Gradle, dependencies are grouped by configurations. One of the configurations that the Java plugin introduces is `compile`. You can probably tell by the configuration's name that it's used for dependencies needed for compiling source code.

> ### How to find a dependency
> Finding out detailed information about a dependency on Maven Central is straight-forward. The repository provides you with an easy-to-use search interface at http://search.maven.org/.

RESOLVING THE DEPENDENCY

Gradle automatically detects new dependencies in your project. If the dependency hasn't been resolved successfully, it downloads it with the next task invocation that requires it to work correctly—in this case, task `compileJava`:

```
$ gradle build
:compileJava
Download http://repo1.maven.org/maven2/org/apache/commons/
➥ commons-lang3/3.1/commons-lang3-3.1.pom              ⤺
Download http://repo1.maven.org/maven2/org/apache/commons/         Metadata
➥ commons-parent/22/commons-parent-22.pom             ⤺   describing library
Download http://repo1.maven.org/maven2/org/apache/apache/9/            and artifact it
➥ apache-9.pom                                        ⤺   depends on
Download http://repo1.maven.org/maven2/org/apache/commons/
➥ commons-lang3/3.1/commons-lang3-3.1.jar    ⤺
:processResources UP-TO-DATE                    Binary artifact: JAR file containing
...                                             Apache Commons Lang classes
:build
```

Chapter 5 will give a deeper coverage of the topic of dependency management. I know that the To Do application in its current form doesn't knock your socks off. It's time to modernize it by adding a visually attractive user interface.

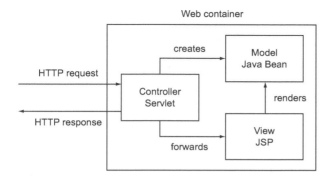

Figure 3.4 Java EE provides components for building a web application based on the MVC architecture pattern.

3.3   *Web development with Gradle*

In Java, server-side web components of the Enterprise Edition (Java EE) provide the dynamic extension capabilities for running your application within a web container or application server. As the name Servlet may already indicate, it serves a client request and constructs the response. It acts as the controller component in a Model-View-Controller (MVC) architecture. The response of a Servlet is rendered by the view component—the Java Server Page (JSP). Figure 3.4 illustrates the MVC architecture pattern in the context of a Java web application.

A WAR (web application archive) file is used to bundle web components, compiled classes, and other resource files like deployment descriptors, HTML, JavaScript, and CSS files. Together they form a web application. To run a Java web application, the WAR file needs to be deployed to the server environment, a web container.

Gradle provides out-of-the-box plugins for assembling WAR files and deploying web applications to a local Servlet container. Before we look at how to apply and configure these plugins, you'll need to turn your standalone Java application into a web application. We focus next on the web components we're going to introduce and how they interact with each other.

3.3.1   *Adding web components*

The Java enterprise landscape is dominated by a wide range of web frameworks, such as Spring MVC and Tapestry. Web frameworks are designed to abstract the standard web components and reduce boilerplate code. Despite these benefits, web frameworks can introduce a steep learning curve as they introduce new concepts and APIs. To keep the example as simple and understandable as possible, we'll stick to the standard Java enterprise web components.

Before jumping into the code, let's see how adding web components changes the interaction between the existing classes from the previous section. The Servlet class you're going to create is called `ToDoServlet`. It's responsible for accepting HTTP requests, executing a CRUD operation mapped to a URL endpoint, and forwarding the request to a JSP. To present the user with a fluid and comfortable experience, you'll implement the to-do list as a single-page application. This means you'll only have to

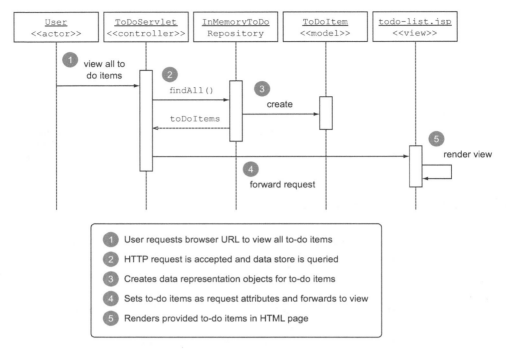

Figure 3.5   **Finding all to-do items use case: the user issues an HTTP request through the browser, which is served by a Servlet and renders the result through a JSP.**

write one JSP, which you'll name `todo-list.jsp`. The page knows how to dynamically render the list of to-do items and provides UI elements like buttons and links for initiating CRUD operations. Figure 3.5 shows the flow through your new system for the use case of retrieving and rendering all to-do items.

As you can see in the figure, you could reuse the class `ToDoItem` to represent the model and the class `InMemoryToDoRepository` to store the data. Both classes work seamlessly with the controller and view components. Let's look at the inner workings of the controller component.

THE CONTROLLER WEB COMPONENT

To make matters simple and centralized, you'll write a single entry point for all URL endpoints you want to expose to the client. The following code snippet shows the most important parts of your controller web component, the class `ToDoServlet`:

```
package com.manning.gia.todo.web;

import com.manning.gia.todo.model.ToDoItem;
import com.manning.gia.todo.repository.InMemoryToDoRepository;
import com.manning.gia.todo.repository.ToDoRepository;
import javax.servlet.*;
import java.io.IOException;
import java.util.List;
```

```
public class ToDoServlet extends HttpServlet {
    private ToDoRepository toDoRepository = new InMemoryToDoRepository();

    @Override
    protected void service(HttpServletRequest request, HttpServletResponse
                            ➥ response) throws ServletException, IOException {
        String servletPath = request.getServletPath();
        String view = processRequest(servletPath, request);
        RequestDispatcher dispatcher = request.getRequestDispatcher(view);
        dispatcher.forward(request, response);
    }

    private String processRequest(String servletPath, HttpServletRequest
                            ➥ request) {
        if(servletPath.equals("/all")) {
            List<ToDoItem> toDoItems = toDoRepository.findAll();
            request.setAttribute("toDoItems", toDoItems);
            return "/jsp/todo-list.jsp";
        }
        else if(servletPath.equals("/delete")) {
            (...)
        }

        (...)

        return "/all";
    }
}
```

Retrieves path of requested URL; path starts with / character — String servletPath = request.getServletPath();

Forwards request from Servlet to JSP — dispatcher.forward(request, response);

Implements CRUD operations for each mapped URL

In case incoming request URL doesn't match any handling, redirect to /all URL — return "/all";

For each of the incoming requests, you get the Servlet path, handle the request in the method `processRequest` based on the determined CRUD operation, and forward it to the JSP `todo-list.jsp` using an instance of `javax.servlet.RequestDispatcher`.

That's it; you converted your task management program into a web application. In the examples I only touched on the most important parts of the code. For a deeper understanding, I encourage you to browse the full source code. Next, we'll bring Gradle into play.

3.3.2 Using the War and Jetty plugins

Gradle provides extensive support for building and running web applications. In this section we'll look at two plugins for web application development: War and Jetty. The War plugin extends the Java plugin by adding conventions for web application development and support for assembling WAR files. Running a web application on your local machine should be easy, enable rapid application development (RAD), and provide fast startup times. Optimally, it shouldn't require you to install a web container runtime environment. Jetty is a popular, lightweight, open source web container supporting all of these features. It comes with an embedded implementation by adding an HTTP module to your application. Gradle's Jetty plugin extends the War plugin, provides tasks for deploying a web application to the embedded container, and runs your application.

> ## Alternative embedded container plugins
> The Jetty plugin works great for local web application development. However, you may use a different Servlet container in your production environment. To provide maximum compatibility between runtime environments early on in the software development lifecycle, look for alternative embedded container implementations. A viable solution that works very similarly to Gradle's standard Jetty extension is the third-party Tomcat plugin.

You already know the drill from the last section. First, you'll apply the plugins and use the default conventions, and then you'll customize them. Let's focus on the War plugin first.

THE WAR PLUGIN

I already mentioned that the War plugin extends the Java plugin. In practice, this means that you don't have to apply the Java plugin anymore in your build script. It's automatically brought in by the War plugin. Note that even if you applied the Java plugin as well, there would be no side effect on your project. Applying plugins is an idempotent operation, and therefore is only executed once for a specific plugin. When creating your `build.gradle` file, use the plugin like this:

```
apply plugin: 'war'
```

What exactly does that mean to your project? In addition to the conventions provided by the Java plugin, your project becomes aware of a source directory for web application files and knows how to assemble a WAR file instead of a JAR file. The default convention for web application sources is the directory src/main/webapp. With all the web resource files in the right location, your project layout should look like this:

```
.
├── build.gradle
└── src
    └── main
        ├── java
        │   └── com
        │       └── manning
        │           └── gia
        │               └── todo
        │                   ├── model
        │                   │   └── ToDoItem.java
        │                   ├── repository
        │                   │   ├── InMemoryToDoRepository.java
        │                   │   └── ToDoRepository.java
        │                   └── web
        │                       └── ToDoServlet.java
        └── webapp
            ├── WEB-INF
            │   └── web.xml
            ├── css
            │   ├── base.css
```

Default directory for web application source files

Web application descriptor file

Directory storing style sheets that describe how to display HTML elements

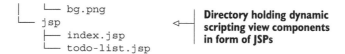

```
        └── bg.png
    └── jsp
        ├── index.jsp
        └── todo-list.jsp
```

Directory holding dynamic scripting view components in form of JSPs

You implemented your web application with the help of classes that aren't part of the Java Standard Edition, such `javax.servlet.HttpServlet`. Before you run the build, you'll need to make sure that you declare those external dependencies. The War plugin introduces two new dependency configurations. The configuration you'll use for the Servlet dependency is `providedCompile`. It's used for dependencies that are required for compilation but provided by the runtime environment. The runtime environment in this case is Jetty. As a consequence, dependencies marked `provided` aren't going to be packaged with the WAR file. Runtime dependencies like the JSTL library aren't needed for the compilation process, but are needed at runtime. They'll become part of the WAR file. The following `dependencies` closure declares the external libraries you need for your application:

```
dependencies {
    providedCompile 'javax.servlet:servlet-api:2.5'
    runtime 'javax.servlet:jstl:1.1.2'
}
```

BUILDING THE PROJECT

Building a web application in Gradle is as straightforward as building a standalone Java application. The assembled WAR file can be found in the directory `build/libs` after running the command `gradle build`. By changing the nature of the project from a standalone application to a web application, the task `jar` was replaced by the task `war`, as shown in the following output:

```
$ gradle build
:compileJava
:processResources UP-TO-DATE
:classes
:war
:assemble
:compileTestJava UP-TO-DATE
:processTestResources UP-TO-DATE
:testClasses UP-TO-DATE
:test
:check
:build
```

Task provided by War plugin for assembling WAR file

The War plugin makes sure that the assembled WAR file adheres to the standard structure defined by the Java EE specification. The `war` task copies the contents of the default web application source directory `src/main/webapp` to the root of the WAR file without modifying the structure. Compiled classes end up in the directory `WEB-INF/classes`, and runtime libraries, defined through the dependencies closure, get put in `WEB-INF/lib`. The following directory structure shows the contents of the assembled WAR file after running `jar tf todo-webapp-0.1.war`:

```
.
├── META-INF
│   └── MANIFEST.MF
├── WEB-INF
│   ├── classes
│   │   └── com
│   │       └── manning
│   │           └── gia
│   │               └── todo
│   │                   ├── model
│   │                   │   └── ToDoItem.class
│   │                   ├── repository
│   │                   │   ├── InMemoryToDoRepository.class
│   │                   │   └── ToDoRepository.class
│   │                   └── web
│   │                       └── ToDoServlet.class
│   ├── lib
│   │   └── jstl-1.1.2.jar
│   └── web.xml
├── css
│   ├── base.css
│   └── bg.png
└── jsp
    ├── index.jsp
    └── todo-list.jsp
```

By default, the WAR filename is derived from the project's directory name. Even if your project doesn't adhere to Gradle's standard conventions, the plugin can be used to build a WAR file. Let's look at some customization options.

CUSTOMIZING THE WAR PLUGIN

You've seen how easy it is to adapt a Java project to custom project structures. The same holds true for unconventional web project layouts. In the following example, we're going to assume that all of your static files sit in the directory static, and that all of your web application content resides under the directory webfiles:

```
.
├── build.gradle
├── src
│   └── main
│       └── java
│           └── ...
├── static
│   └── css
│       ├── base.css
│       └── bg.png
└── webfiles
    ├── WEB-INF
    │   └── web.xml
    └── jsp
        ├── index.jsp
        └── todo-list.jsp
```

The following code snippet shows how to configure the convention properties. The War plugin exposes the convention property webAppDirName. The default value src/main/webapp is easily switched to webfiles by assigning a new value. Directories can be selectively added to the WAR file by invoking the from method, as follows:

```
webAppDirName = 'webfiles'          ⟵┐  Changes web application
                                        source directory
war {
    from 'static'          ⟵┐  Adds directories css and jsp
}                              to root of WAR file archive
```

The previous example only showed an excerpt of the War plugin's configuration options. You can easily include other external JAR files, use a web deployment descriptor from a nonstandard directory, or add another file set to the WEB-INF directory. If you're looking for a configuration parameter, the best place to check is the War plugin DSL guide.

You've seen how to build the WAR file from a web project with a standard structure or customized directory layout. Now it's time to deploy the file to a Servlet container. In the next section, you'll fire up Jetty to run the application on your local development machine.

RUNNING IN AN EMBEDDED WEB CONTAINER

An embedded Servlet container doesn't know anything about your application until you provide the exact classpath and relevant source directories of your web application. Usually, you'd do that programmatically. Internally, the Jetty plugin does all this work for you. As the War plugin exposes all this information, it can be accessed at runtime by the Jetty plugin. This is a typical example of a plugin using another plugin's configuration through the Gradle API. In your build script, use the plugin like this:

```
apply plugin: 'jetty'
```

The task you're going to use to run the web application is jettyRun. It'll start the Jetty container without even having to create a WAR file. The output of running the task on the command line should look similar to this:

```
$ gradle jettyRun
:compileJava
:processResources UP-TO-DATE
:classes
> Building > :jettyRun > Running at http://localhost:8080/todo-webapp-jetty
```

On the last line of the output, the plugin gives you the URL that Jetty listens to for incoming requests. Open your favorite browser and enter the URL. Finally, you can see the To Do web application in action. Gradle will leave the application running until you stop it by pressing Ctrl + C. How did Jetty know what port and context to use for running the application? Again, it's conventions. The default port of a web application run by the Jetty plugin is 8080, and the context path todo-webapp-jetty is derived from your project name. Of course, all of this is configurable.

> ### Rapid application development
> Having to restart the container for every single change you make to your application code is cumbersome and time-consuming. The Jetty plugin allows you to change static resources and JSP files on the fly without having to restart the container. Additionally, bytecode swap technologies like JRebel can be configured to perform hot deployment for class file changes.

CUSTOMIZING THE JETTY PLUGIN

Let's assume you're not happy with the default values the Jetty plugin provides. Another application is already running on port 8080, and you got tired of typing in the long context path. Just provide the following configuration:

```
jettyRun {
    httpPort = 9090
    contextPath = 'todo'
}
```

Great, you achieved what you wanted. Starting the application with this configuration will expose the URL http://localhost:9090/todo. There are many more options for configuring the Jetty plugin. A great place to start is with the API documentation of the plugin. This will help you understand all available configuration options.

3.4   *Gradle wrapper*

You put together a prototype of a task management web application. After you show it to your coworker, Mike, he says he wants to join forces and bring the application to the next level by adding more advanced features. The code has been committed to a version control system (VCS), so he can go ahead, check out the code, and get started working on it.

Mike has never worked with the build tool Gradle, so he asks you how to install the runtime on his machine and which version to use. Because he didn't go through the motions of initially setting up Gradle, he's also concerned about potential differences between setting up Gradle on his Windows machine versus installing it on a Mac. From experience with other build tools, Mike is painfully aware that picking the wrong version of the build tool distribution or the runtime environment may have a detrimental effect on the outcome of the build. All too often, he's seen that a build completes successfully on his machine but fails on another for no apparent reason. After spending hours troubleshooting, he usually discovers that the cause was an incompatible version of the runtime.

Gradle provides a very convenient and practical solution to this problem: the Gradle wrapper. The wrapper is a core feature and enables a machine to run a Gradle build script without having to install the runtime. It also ensures that the build script is run with a specific version of Gradle. It does so by automatically downloading the Gradle runtime from a central location, unpacking it to your local file system, and using it for the build. The ultimate goal is to create reliable and reproducible builds independent of the operating system, system setup, or installed Gradle version.

> **When to use the wrapper**
> Using the wrapper is considered best practice and should be mandatory for every Gradle project. Gradle scripts backed by the wrapper are perfectly prepared to run as part of automated release processes like continuous integration and delivery.

Let's look at how to set up the wrapper for Mike and any other developer who wants to join the team.

3.4.1 Setting up the wrapper

To set up the wrapper for your project, you'll need to do two things: create a wrapper task and execute the task to generate the wrapper files (figure 3.6).

To enable your project to download the zipped Gradle runtime distribution, define a task of type `Wrapper` and specify the Gradle version you want to use through the property `gradleVersion`:

```
task wrapper(type: Wrapper) {
    gradleVersion = '1.7'
}
```

It's not required to name the task `wrapper`—any name will do. However, `wrapper` is used throughout the Gradle online documentation and serves as a helpful convention. Execute the task:

```
$ gradle wrapper
:wrapper
```

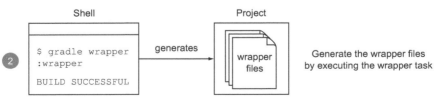

Figure 3.6 Set up the wrapper in two easy steps: add the wrapper task and execute it.

As a result, you'll find the following wrapper files alongside your build script:

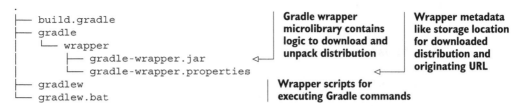

```
.
├── build.gradle
├── gradle
│   └── wrapper
│       ├── gradle-wrapper.jar
│       └── gradle-wrapper.properties
├── gradlew
└── gradlew.bat
```

Gradle wrapper microlibrary contains logic to download and unpack distribution

Wrapper metadata like storage location for downloaded distribution and originating URL

Wrapper scripts for executing Gradle commands

Keep in mind that you'll only need to run `gradle wrapper` on your project once. From that point on, you can use the wrapper's script to execute your build. The downloaded wrapper files are supposed to be checked into version control. For documentation reasons it's helpful to also keep the task in your project. It'll help you to upgrade your wrapper version later by changing the `gradleVersion` and rerunning the `wrapper` task. Instead of creating the wrapper task manually and executing it to download the relevant files, you can use the build setup plugin mentioned earlier. Executing the command `gradle wrapper` will generate the wrapper files with the current version of your Gradle runtime:

```
$ gradle wrapper
:wrapper
```

Next you'll use the generated wrapper scripts to bootstrap the Gradle script.

3.4.2   *Using the wrapper*

As part of the wrapper distribution, a command execution script is provided. For *nix systems, this is the shell script `gradlew`; for Windows operating systems, it's `gradlew.bat`. You'll use one of these scripts to run your build in the same way as you would with the installed Gradle runtime. Figure 3.7 illustrates what happens when you use the wrapper script to execute a task.

Let's get back to our friend Mike. He checked out the application code from the VCS. Included in the source code tree of the project, he'll find the wrapper files. As Mike develops his code on a Windows box, he'll need to run the wrapper batch file to execute a task. The following console output is produced when he fires up the local Jetty container to run the application:

Downloads wrapper distribution from remote server

```
> gradlew.bat jettyRun
Downloading http://services.gradle.org/distributions/gradle-1.7-bin.zip
...
Unzipping C:\Documents and Settings\Mike\.gradle\wrapper\dists\gradle-1.7-
   bin\35oej0jnbfh6of4dd05531edaj\gradle-1.7-bin.zip to C:\Documents and
   Settings\Mike\.gradle\wrapper\dists\gradle-1.7-
   bin\35oej0jnbfh6of4dd05531edaj
Set executable permissions for: C:\Documents and
   Settings\Mike\.gradle\wrapper\dists\gradle-1.7-
   bin\35oej0jnbfh6of4dd05531edaj\gradle-1.7\bin\gradlew.bat
:compileJava
:processResources UP-TO-DATE
:classes
> Building > :jettyRun > Running at http://localhost:9090/todo
```

Unzips compressed wrapper file to predefined local directory

Sets execution permissions for wrapper batch file

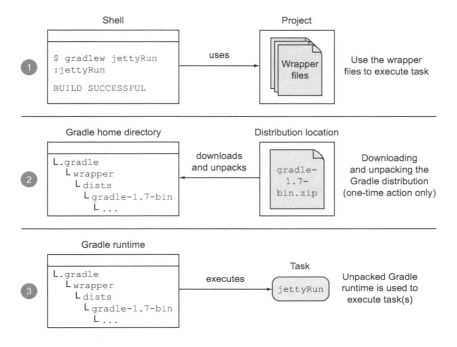

Figure 3.7 When a wrapped task is executed, the Gradle runtime is downloaded, unpacked, and used.

The distribution ZIP file is downloaded from a central server hosted by the Gradle project, stored on Mike's local file system under `$HOME_DIR/.gradle/wrapper/dists`. The Gradle wrapper also takes care of unpacking the distribution and setting the appropriate permissions to execute the batch file. Note that the download only needs to happen once. Subsequent build runs reuse the unpacked installation of the runtime located in your Gradle home directory:

```
> gradlew.bat jettyRun
:compileJava
:processResources UP-TO-DATE
:classes
> Building > :jettyRun > Running at http://localhost:9090/todo
```

What are the key takeaways? A build script executed by the Gradle wrapper provides exactly the same tasks, features, and behavior as it does when run with a local Gradle installation. Again, you don't have to stick with the default conventions the wrapper gives you. Its configuration options are very flexible. We'll look at them in the next section.

3.4.3 Customizing the wrapper

Some enterprises have very restrictive security strategies, especially if you work for a government agency, where access to servers outside of the network is prohibited.

How do you enable your project to use the Gradle wrapper in that case? It's all in the configuration. You'll change the default properties to target an enterprise server hosting the runtime distribution. And while you're at it, you'll also change the local storage directory:

```
task wrapper(type: Wrapper) {
    gradleVersion = '1.2'
    distributionUrl = 'http://myenterprise.com/gradle/dists'
    distributionPath = 'gradle-dists'
}
```

Requested Gradle version

Target URL to retrieve Gradle wrapper distribution

Path where wrapper will be unzipped relative to Gradle home directory

Pretty straightforward, right? There are many more options to explore. Make sure to check out the Gradle wrapper DSL documentation for detailed information at http://gradle.org/docs/current/dsl/org.gradle.api.tasks.wrapper.Wrapper.html.

3.5   Summary

In chapter 2, you learned how to express and execute simple logic by adding tasks to your project. In this chapter we've gone much further. You implemented a full-stack Java application and used Gradle to build it. Many Java projects are similar in nature. They need to compile Java source code, run tests, and bundle a JAR file containing the classes. Luckily, you didn't have to write these tasks yourself to make this happen in your project. Through the use of Gradle plugins, you merely had to write code in your build script.

You started out by using the Java plugin that ships with Gradle. Applying the plugin to your project added preconfigured tasks and a standardized project structure wrapped by an opinionated framework. Custom project requirements call for flexible conventions. We explored the option of customizing the default conventions introduced by the plugin. Key to knowing your options are the Gradle DSL and API documentation.

After a short recap of the fundamentals of Java web application development, we discussed how to extend the example project by Java EE–compatible web components. Gradle helps you with simplifying web development through the War and Jetty plugins. The War plugin assists in assembling a WAR file, and the Jetty plugin provides efficient deployment to a lightweight Servlet container. You saw that the convention-over-configuration paradigm was applied to this dynamic duo as well. You also learned that using the wrapper is a best practice for every Gradle project. Not only does it allow you to run the project on a machine that doesn't have Gradle installed, it also prevents version compatibility issues.

The presented plugins provide far more functionality than we've discussed. For a detailed view on their capabilities, you can go to the online user guide (http://www.gradle.org/docs/current/userguide/standard_plugins.html). This chapter completes part 1 of the book. In part 2, we delve into many of Gradle's core concepts. The next chapter will focus on Gradle's building blocks, the ins and outs of tasks, and the build lifecycle.

Part 2

Mastering
the fundamentals

In part 1, you learned Gradle's core concepts and features by example. Part 2 will boost your knowledge even further. We'll look at more advanced topics like dependency management, testing an application with Gradle, extending your build with plugins, and many more.

Chapter 4 covers Gradle's quintessential building blocks for modeling your build. You'll learn how to declare new tasks, manipulate existing ones, and implement proper abstractions for complex logic. No real-world project can succeed without reusing existing libraries. In chapter 5, you'll learn how to declare and organize dependencies in a build script. We'll also cover dependency reporting and version conflict resolution. Modularized software projects pose an additional layer of complexity for modeling your build. Chapter 6 discusses Gradle's support for multiproject builds.

In chapter 7, we'll turn our attention to the important topic of testing. You'll see how easy it is to write, organize, and execute unit, integration, and functional tests, while at the same time picking and choosing the tooling of your choice. Chapter 8 demonstrates Gradle's extension mechanism by example. You'll learn how to abstract complex logic for deploying your sample application to a cloud service. We'll touch on all facets of the extension model, from custom tasks and script and binary plugins, to exposing your own configuration language. Because Gradle goes hand in hand with popular build tools like Ant and Maven, chapter 9 is dedicated to helping you translate existing build logic from one tool to another, identify integration points, and depict migration strategies.

Once you've finished this part of the book, you'll be able to apply Gradle's core concepts to a real-world project. In part 3, we'll discuss the use of Gradle with other tools of the build and delivery ecosystem.

Build script essentials

This chapter covers

- Gradle's building blocks and their API representation
- Declaring new tasks and manipulating existing tasks
- Advanced task techniques
- Implementing and using task types
- Hooking into the build lifecycle

In chapter 3, you implemented a full-fledged Java web application from the ground up and built it with the help of Gradle's core plugins. You learned that the default conventions introduced by those plugins are customizable and can easily adapt to nonstandard build requirements. Preconfigured tasks function as key components of a plugin by adding executable build logic to your project.

In this chapter, we'll explore the basic building blocks of a Gradle build, namely projects and tasks, and how they map to the classes in the Gradle API. Properties are exposed by methods of these classes and help to control the build. You'll also learn how to control the build's behavior through properties, as well as the benefits of structuring your build logic.

At the core of this chapter, you'll experience the nitty-gritty details of working with tasks by implementing a consistent example. Step by step, you'll build your knowledge from declaring simple tasks to writing custom task classes. Along the way, we'll touch on topics like accessing task properties, defining explicit and implicit task dependencies, adding incremental build support, and using Gradle's built-in task types.

We'll also look at Gradle's build lifecycle to get a good understanding of how a build is configured and executed. Your build script can respond to notifications as the build progresses through the lifecycle phases. In the last part of this chapter, we'll show how to write lifecycle hooks as closure and listener implementations.

4.1 Building blocks

Every Gradle build consists of three basic building blocks: projects, tasks, and properties. Each build contains at least one project, which in turn contains one or more tasks. Projects and tasks expose properties that can be used to control the build. Figure 4.1 illustrates the dependencies among Gradle's core components.

Gradle applies the principles of domain-driven design (DDD) to model its own domain-building software. As a consequence, projects and tasks have a direct class representation in Gradle's API. Let's take a closer look at each component and its API counterpart.

4.1.1 Projects

In Gradle's terminology a project represents a component you're trying to build (for example, a JAR file), or a goal you're trying to achieve, like deploying an application. If you're coming from Maven, this concept should sound pretty familiar. Gradle's equivalent to Maven's pom.xml is the build.gradle file. Each Gradle build script defines at least one project. When starting the build process, Gradle instantiates the class org.gradle.api.Project based on your configuration in build.gradle and makes it implicitly available through the project variable. Figure 4.2 shows the API interface and its most important methods.

Gradle build

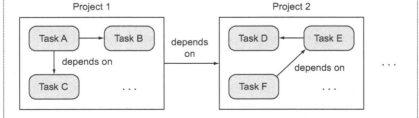

Figure 4.1   Two basic concepts of a Gradle build are projects and tasks. A project can depend on other projects in the context of a multiproject build. Similarly, tasks can form a dependency graph that guarantees their execution order.

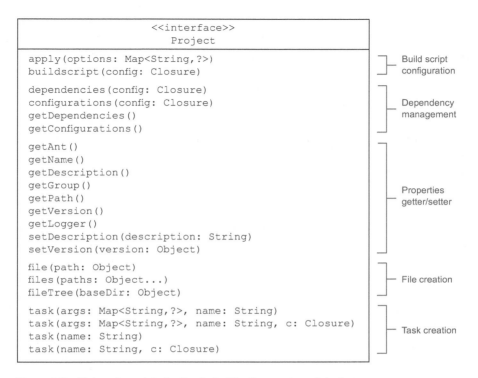

Figure 4.2 Main entry point of a Gradle build—the `Project` interface

A project can create new tasks, add dependencies and configurations, and apply plugins and other build scripts. Many of its properties, like name and description, are accessible via getter and setter methods.

So why are we talking about Gradle's API early on? You'll find that after getting to know Gradle's basics, you'll want to go further and apply the concepts to your real-world projects. The API is key to getting the most out of Gradle.

The `Project` instance gives you programmatic access to all Gradle features in your build, like task creation and dependency management. You'll use many of these features throughout the book by invoking their corresponding API methods. Keep in mind that you're not required to use the project variable when accessing properties and methods of your project—it's assumed you mean the `Project` instance. The following code snippet illustrates valid method invocations on the `Project` instance:

Setting project's description without explicitly using project variable

```
setDescription("myProject")           ◁─┘
println "Description of project $name: " + project.description        ◁─┐
```

Using Groovy syntax to access name and description properties with and without using project variable

In the previous chapters, you only had to deal with single-project builds. Gradle provides support for multiproject builds as well. One of the most important principles of software development is separation of concerns. The more complex a software system becomes, the more you want to decompose it into modularized functionality, in which modules can depend on each other. Each of the decomposed parts would be represented as a Gradle project with its own `build.gradle` script. For the sake of simplicity, we won't go into details here. If you're eager to learn more, feel free to jump to chapter 6, which is fully devoted to creating multiproject builds in Gradle. Next, we'll look at the characteristics of tasks, another one of Gradle's core building blocks.

4.1.2 *Tasks*

You already created some simple tasks in chapter 2. Even though the use cases I presented were trivial, you got to know some important capabilities of a task: task actions and task dependencies. An action defines an atomic unit of work that's executed when the task is run. This can be as simple as printing out text like "Hello world!" or as complex as compiling Java source code, as seen in chapter 2. Many times a task requires another task to run first. This is especially true if the task depends on the produced output of another task as input to complete its own actions. For example, you've seen that you need to compile Java sources first before they can be packaged into a JAR file. Let's look at Gradle's API representation of a task, the interface `org.gradle.api.Task`, as shown in figure 4.3.

The `Task` interface provides even more methods than are shown in the figure. You'll use them one by one as you apply them to concrete examples throughout the book. Now that we've discussed projects and tasks, let's look at different types of properties.

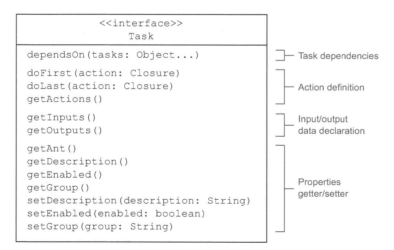

Figure 4.3 `Task` interface in Gradle's API. Tasks can define dependencies on other tasks, a sequence of actions, and conditional execution.

4.1.3 *Properties*

Each instance of `Project` and `Task` provides properties that are accessible through getter and setter methods. A property could be a task's description or the project's version. Later in this chapter, you'll read and modify these values in the context of a practical example. Often, you'll want to define your own properties. For example, you may want to declare a variable that references a file that's used multiple times within the same build script. Gradle allows defining user-defined variables through extra properties.

EXTRA PROPERTIES

Many of Gradle's domain model classes provide support for ad-hoc properties. Internally, these properties are stored as key-value pairs in a map. To add properties, you're required to use the `ext` namespace. Let's look at a concrete example. The following code snippet demonstrates that a property can be added, read, and modified in many different ways:

```
project.ext.myProp = 'myValue'
ext {
    someOtherProp = 123
}
```
Only initial declaration of extra property requires you to use ext namespace

```
assert myProp == 'myValue'
println project.someOtherProp
ext.someOtherProp = 567
```
Using ext namespace to access extra property is optional

Similarly, additional properties can be fed through a properties file.

GRADLE PROPERTIES

Properties can be directly injected into your project by declaring them in a properties file named `gradle.properties` under the directory `<USER_HOME>/.gradle` or a project's root directory. They can be accessed via the project instance. Bear in mind that there can only be one Gradle property file per user under `<USER_HOME>/.gradle`, even if you're dealing with multiple projects. This is currently a limitation of Gradle. Any property declared in the properties file will be available to all of your projects. Let's assume the following properties are declared in your `gradle.properties` file:

```
exampleProp = myValue
someOtherProp = 455
```

You can access both variables in your project as follows:

```
assert project.exampleProp == 'myValue'

task printGradleProperty << {
    println "Second property: $someOtherProp"
}
```

OTHER WAYS TO DECLARE PROPERTIES

Extra properties and Gradle properties are the mechanisms you'll probably use the most to declare custom variables and their values. Gradle offers many other ways to provide properties to your build, such as

- Project property via the -P command-line option
- System property via the -D command-line option
- Environment property following the pattern

```
ORG_GRADLE_PROJECT_propertyName=someValue
```

I won't show you concrete examples for these alternative ways of declaring properties, but you can use them if needed. The online Gradle user guide provides excellent usage examples if you want to go further. For the rest of this chapter, you'll make extensive use of tasks and Gradle's build lifecycle.

4.2   Working with tasks

By default, every newly created task is of type org.gradle.api.DefaultTask, the standard implementation of org.gradle.api.Task. All fields in class DefaultTask are marked private. This means that they can only be accessed through their public getter and setter methods. Thankfully, Groovy provides you with some syntactic sugar, which allows you to use fields by their name. Under the hood, Groovy calls the method for you. In this section, we'll explore the most important features of a task by example.

4.2.1   Managing the project version

To demonstrate properties and methods of the class DefaultTask in action, I'm going to explain them in the context of the To Do application from chapter 3. Now that you have the general build infrastructure in place, features can easily be added. Often, feature sets are grouped into releases. To identify each release, a unique version number is added to the deliverable.

Many enterprises or open source projects have their own versioning strategy. Think back to some of the projects you've worked on. Usually, you assign a specific version numbering scheme (for example, a major and minor version number separated by a dot, like 1.2). You may also encounter a project version that appends a SNAPSHOT designator to indicate that the built project artifact is in the state of development. You've already assigned a version to your project in chapter 3 by setting a string value to the project property version. Using a String data type works great for simple use cases, but what if you want to know the exact minor version of your project? You'll have to parse the string value, search for the dot character, and filter out the substring that identifies the minor version. Wouldn't it be easier to represent the version by an actual class?

You could easily use the class's fields to set, retrieve, and modify specific portions of your numbering scheme. You can go even further. By externalizing the version information to persistent data storage, such as a file or database, you'll avoid having to modify the build script itself to change the project version. Figure 4.4 illustrates the interaction among the build script, a properties file that holds the version information, and the data representation class. You'll create and learn how to use all of these files in the upcoming sections.

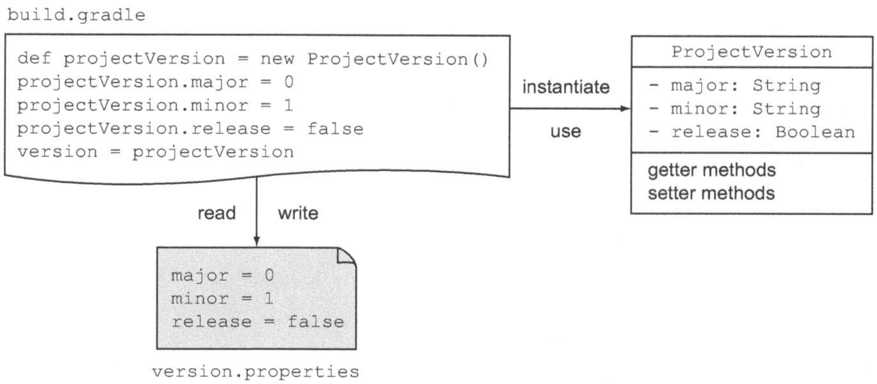

build.gradle

Figure 4.4 The project version is read from a properties file during runtime of the build script. The `ProjectVersion` data class is instantiated. Each of the version classifiers is translated into a field value of the data class. The instance of `ProjectVersion` is assigned to the version property of the project.

Being able to control the versioning scheme programmatically will become a necessity the more you want to automate your project lifecycle. Here's one example: your code has passed all functional tests and is ready to be shipped. The current version of your project is 1.2-SNAPSHOT. Before building the final WAR file, you'll want to make it a release version 1.2 and automatically deploy it to the production server. Each of these steps can be modeled by creating a task: one for modifying the project version and one for deploying the WAR file. Let's take your knowledge about tasks to the next level by implementing flexible version management in your project.

4.2.2 Declaring task actions

An action is the appropriate place within a task to put your build logic. The Task interface provides you with two relevant methods to declare a task action: doFirst(Closure) and doLast(Closure). When a task is executed, the action logic defined as closure parameter is executed in turn.

You're going to start easy by adding a single task named printVersion. The task's purpose is to print out the current project version. Define this logic as the last action of this task, as shown in the following code snippet:

```
version = '0.1-SNAPSHOT'

task printVersion {
   doLast {
      println "Version: $version"
   }
}
```

In chapter 2, I explained that the left shift operator (<<) is the shortcut version of the method doLast. Just to clarify: they do exactly the same thing. When executing the task with gradle printVersion, you should see the correct version number:

```
$ gradle printVersion
:printVersion
Version: 0.1-SNAPSHOT
```

The same result could be achieved as the first action of the task by using the doFirst method instead:

```
task printVersion {
   doFirst {
      println "Version: $version"
   }
}
```

ADDING ACTIONS TO EXISTING TASKS

So far, you've only added a single action to the task printVersion, either as the first or last action. But you're not limited to a single action per task. In fact, you can add as many actions as you need even after the task has been created. Internally, every task keeps a list of task actions. At runtime, they're executed sequentially. Let's look at a modified version of your example task:

```
task printVersion {
   doFirst {
      println "Before reading the project version"
   }

   doLast {
      println "Version: $version"
   }
}
printVersion.doFirst { println "First action" }
printVersion << { println "Last action" }
```

Initial declaration of a task can contain a first and last action

Additive doFirst closures are inserted at beginning of actions list

Using doLast alias to add closure to end of actions list

As shown in the listing, an existing task can be manipulated by adding actions to them. This is especially useful if you want to execute custom logic for tasks that you didn't write yourself. For example, you could add a doFirst action to the compile-Java task of the Java plugin that checks if the project contains at least one Java source file.

4.2.3 Accessing DefaultTask properties

Next you'll improve the way you output the version number. Gradle provides a logger implementation based on the logging library SLF4J. Apart from implementing the usual range of logging levels (DEBUG, ERROR, INFO, TRACE, WARN), it adds some extra levels. The logger instance can be directly accessed through one of the task's methods. For now, you're going to print the version number with the log level QUIET:

```
task printVersion << {
   logger.quiet "Version: $version"
}
```

See how easy it is to access one of the task properties? There are two more properties I want to show you: group and description. Both act as part of the task documentation.

The description property represents a short definition of the task's purpose, whereas the group defines a logic grouping of tasks. You'll set values for both properties as arguments when creating the task:

```
task printVersion(group: 'versioning',
                  ➥ description: 'Prints project version.') << {
   logger.quiet "Version: $version"
}
```

Alternatively, you can also set the properties by calling the setter methods, as shown in the following code snippet:

```
task printVersion {
   group = 'versioning'
   description = 'Prints project version.'

   doLast {
      logger.quiet "Version: $version"
   }
}
```

When running gradle tasks, you'll see that the task shows up in the correct task bucket and is able to describe itself:

```
gradle tasks
:tasks
...

Versioning tasks
----------------
printVersion - Prints project version.

...
```

Even though setting a task's description and grouping is optional, it's always a good idea to assign values for all of your tasks. It'll make it easier for the end user to identify the task's function. Next, we'll review the intricacies of defining dependencies between tasks.

4.2.4 Defining task dependencies

The method dependsOn allows for declaring a dependency on one or more tasks. You've seen that the Java plugin makes extensive use of this concept by creating task graphs to model full task lifecycles like the build task. The following listing shows different ways of applying task dependencies using the dependsOn method.

Listing 4.1 Applying task dependencies

```
task first << { println "first" }
task second << { println "second" }

task printVersion(dependsOn: [second, first]) << {     ⟵ Assigning multiple task dependencies
   logger.quiet "Version: $version"
}
```

```
task third << { println "third" }
third.dependsOn('printVersion')
```
⟵┤ **Referencing task by name when declaring dependency**

You'll execute the task dependency chain by invoking the task third from the command line:

```
$ gradle -q third
first
second
Version: 0.1-SNAPSHOT
third
```

If you take a close look at the task execution order, you may be surprised by the outcome. The task printVersion declares a dependency on the tasks second and first. Wouldn't you have expected that the task second would get executed before first? In Gradle, the task execution order is not deterministic.

TASK DEPENDENCY EXECUTION ORDER
It's important to understand that Gradle doesn't guarantee the order in which the dependencies of a task are executed. The method call dependsOn only defines that the dependent tasks need to be executed beforehand. Gradle's philosophy is to declare *what* should be executed before a given task, not *how* it should be executed. This concept is especially hard to grasp if you're coming from a build tool that defines its dependencies imperatively, like Ant does. In Gradle, the execution order is automatically determined by the input/output specification of a task, as you'll see later in this chapter. This architectural design decision has many benefits. On the one hand, you don't need to know the whole chain of task dependencies to make a change, which improves code maintainability and avoids potential breakage. On the other hand, because your build doesn't have to be executed strictly sequentially, it's been enabled for parallel task execution, which can significantly improve your build execution time.

4.2.5 *Finalizer tasks*

In practice, you may find yourself in situations that require a certain resource to be cleaned up after a task that depends on it is executed. A typical use case for such a resource is a web container needed to run integration tests against a deployed application. Gradle's answer to such a scenario is finalizer tasks, which are regular Gradle tasks scheduled to run even if the finalized task fails. The following code snippet demonstrates how to use a specific finalizer task using the Task method finalizedBy:

```
task first << { println "first" }
task second << { println "second" }
first.finalizedBy second
```
⟵┤ **Declares that one task is finalized by another task**

You'll find executing the task first will automatically trigger the task named second:

```
$ gradle -q first
first
second
```

Chapter 7 covers the concept of finalizer tasks in more depth with the help of a real-world example. In the next section, you'll write a Groovy class to allow for finer-grained control of the versioning scheme.

4.2.6 Adding arbitrary code

It's time to come back to my statement about Gradle's ability to define general-purpose Groovy code within a build script. In practice, you can write classes and methods the way you're used to in Groovy scripts or classes. In this section, you'll create a class representation of the version. In Java, classes that follow the bean conventions are called plain-old Java objects (POJOs). By definition, they expose their fields through getter and setter methods. Over time it can become very tiresome to write these methods by hand. POGOs, Groovy's equivalent to POJOs, only require you to declare properties without an access modifier. Their getter and setter methods are intrinsically added at the time of bytecode generation and therefore are available at runtime. In the next listing, you assign an instance of the POGO `ProjectVersion`. The actual values are set in the constructor.

Listing 4.2 Representing the project version by a POGO

```
version = new ProjectVersion(0, 1)          ⟵┐  Version attribute represented by a
                                               java.lang.Object; Gradle always uses
class ProjectVersion {                         the toString() value of the version
   Integer major
   Integer minor
   Boolean release

   ProjectVersion(Integer major, Integer minor) {
      this.major = major
      this.minor = minor
      this.release = Boolean.FALSE
   }

   ProjectVersion(Integer major, Integer minor, Boolean release) {
      this(major, minor)
      this.release = release
   }
                                                   -SNAPSHOT suffix is
   @Override                                        only added if release
   String toString() {                              property is false
      "$major.$minor${release ? '' : '-SNAPSHOT'}"  ⟵┘
   }
}
```

When running the modified build script, you should see that the task `printVersion` produces exactly the same result as before. Unfortunately, you still have to manually edit the build script to change the version classifiers. Next, you'll externalize the version to a file and configure your build script to read it.

4.2.7 Understanding task configuration

Before you get started writing code, you'll need to create a properties file named `version.properties` alongside the build script. For each of the version categories like major and minor, you'll create an individual property. The following key–value pairs represent the initial version 0.1-SNAPSHOT:

```
major = 0
minor = 1
release = false
```

ADDING A TASK CONFIGURATION BLOCK

Listing 4.3 declares a task named loadVersion to read the version classifiers from the properties file and assign the newly created instance of ProjectVersion to the project's version field. At first sight, the task may look like any other task you defined before. But if you look closer, you'll notice that you didn't define an action or use the left shift operator. Gradle calls this a *task configuration*.

Listing 4.3   Writing a task configuration

```
ext.versionFile = file('version.properties')          ◄──   File method is provided
                                                             by Project interface; it
task loadVersion {                    ◄── Task configuration    creates an instance of
   project.version = readVersion()        is defined without    java.io.File relative to
}                                          left shift operator.  project directory.

ProjectVersion readVersion() {
   logger.quiet 'Reading the version file.'

   if(!versionFile.exists()) {
      throw new GradleException("Required version file does not exist:
                        ➥ $versionFile.canonicalPath")   ◄──┐  If version file
   }                                                          doesn't exist throw
                                                              a GradleException
   Properties versionProps = new Properties()   ┐ Groovy's file  with an
                                                 │ implementation appropriate
   versionFile.withInputStream { stream ->  ◄──  ┤ adds methods to error message.
      versionProps.load(stream)                  │ read it with newly
   }                                             ┘ created InputStream.

   new ProjectVersion(versionProps.major.toInteger(),
   ➥ versionProps.minor.toInteger(), versionProps.release.toBoolean())  ◄──┐
}                                                                            │
                        In Groovy you can omit the return
                        keyword if it's last statement in method.
```

If you run printVersion now, you'll see that the new task loadVersion is executed first. Despite the fact that the task name isn't printed, you know this because the build output prints the logging statement you added to it:

```
$ gradle printVersion
Reading the version file.
:printVersion
Version: 0.1-SNAPSHOT
```

You may ask yourself why the task was invoked at all. Granted, you didn't declare a dependency on it, nor did you invoke the task on the command line. Task configuration blocks are always executed before task actions. The key to fully understanding this behavior is the Gradle build lifecycle. Let's take a closer look at each of the build phases.

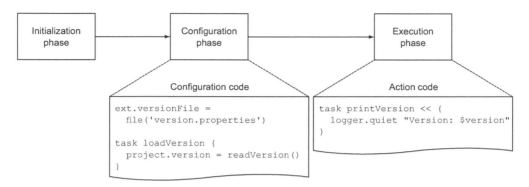

Figure 4.5   Order of build phases in Gradle's build lifecycle

Whenever you execute a Gradle build, three distinct lifecycle phases are run: initialization, configuration, and execution. Figure 4.5 visualizes the order in which the build phases are run and the code they execute.

During the *initialization phase*, Gradle creates a Project instance for your project. Your given build script only defines a single project. In the context of a multiproject build, this build phase becomes more important. Depending on which project you're executing, Gradle figures out which of the project dependencies need to participate in the build. Note that none of your currently existing build script code is executed in this build phase. This will change in chapter 6 when you modularize the To Do application into a multiproject build.

The build phase next in line is the *configuration phase*. Internally, Gradle constructs a model representation of the tasks that will take part in the build. The incremental build feature determines if any of the tasks in the model are required to be run. This phase is perfect for setting up the configuration that's required for your project or specific tasks.

> Keep in mind that any configuration code is executed with every build of your project—even if you just execute gradle tasks.

In the *execution phase* tasks are executed in the correct order. The execution order is determined by their dependencies. Tasks that are considered up to date are skipped. For example, if task B depends on task A, then the execution order would be A → B when you run gradle B on the command line.

As you can see, Gradle's incremental build feature is tightly integrated in the lifecycle. In chapter 3 you saw that the Java plugin made heavy use of this feature. The task compileJava will only run if any of the Java source files are different from the last time the build was run. Ultimately, this feature can improve a build's performance

significantly. In the next section, I'll show how to use the incremental build feature
for your own tasks.

4.2.8   *Declaring task inputs and outputs*

Gradle determines if a task is up to date by comparing a snapshot of a task's inputs and outputs
between two builds, as shown in figure 4.6. A
task is considered up to date if inputs and outputs haven't changed since the last task execution. Therefore, the task only runs if the inputs
and outputs are different; otherwise, it's skipped.

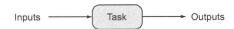

**Figure 4.6   Gradle determines if a task
needs to be executed though its inputs/
outputs.**

An input can be a directory, one or more files, or an arbitrary property. A task's output is defined through a directory or 1...*n* files. Inputs and outputs are defined as fields
in class DefaultTask and have a direct class representation, as shown in figure 4.7.

Let's see this feature in action. Imagine you want to create a task that prepares
your project's deliverable for a production release. To do so, you'll want to change the
project version from SNAPSHOT to release. The following listing defines a new task
that assigns the Boolean value true to the version property release. The task also
propagates the version change to the property file.

Listing 4.4   Switching the project version to production-ready

```
task makeReleaseVersion(group: 'versioning', description: 'Makes project
                      a release version.') << {
    version.release = true
    ant.propertyfile(file: versionFile) {
        entry(key: 'release', type: 'string', operation: '=', value: 'true')
    }
}
```

**Ant task propertyfile provides a convenient
way of modifying the property file.**

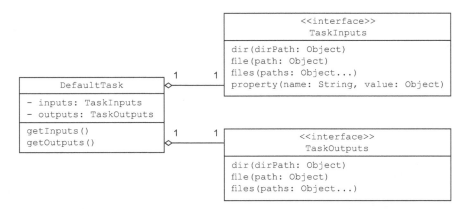

Figure 4.7   The class DefaultTask defines task inputs and outputs.

As expected, running the task will change the version property and persist the new value to the property file. The following output demonstrates the behavior:

```
$ gradle makeReleaseVersion
:makeReleaseVersion

$ gradle printVersion
:printVersion
Version: 0.1
```

The task `makeReleaseVersion` may be part of another lifecycle task that deploys the WAR file to a production server. You may be painfully aware of the fact that a deployment can go wrong. The network may have a glitch so that the server cannot be reached. After fixing the network issues, you'll want to run the deployment task again. Because the task `makeReleaseVersion` is declared as a dependency to your deployment task, it's automatically rerun. Wait, you already marked your project version as production-ready, right? Unfortunately, the Gradle task doesn't know that. To make it aware of this, you'll declare its inputs and outputs, as shown in the next listing.

Listing 4.5   Adding incremental build support via inputs/outputs

```
task makeReleaseVersion(group: 'versioning', description: 'Makes project
                            ➥ a release version.') {
    inputs.property('release', version.release)
    outputs.file versionFile

    doLast {
        version.release = true
        ant.propertyfile(file: versionFile) {
            entry(key: 'release', type: 'string', operation: '=', value: 'true')
        }
    }
}
```

Inputs/outputs are declared during configuration phase

As the version file is going to be modified it's declared as output file property

Declaring version release property as input

You moved the code you wanted to execute into a `doLast` action closure and removed the left shift operator from the task declaration. With that done, you now have a clear separation between the configuration and action code.

Task inputs/outputs evaluation

Remember, task inputs and outputs are evaluated during the configuration phase to wire up the task dependencies. That's why they need to be defined in a configuration block. To avoid unexpected behavior, make sure that the value you assign to inputs and outputs is accessible at configuration time. If you need to implement programmatic output evaluation, the method `upToDateWhen(Closure)` on `TaskOutputs` comes in handy. In contrast to the regular inputs/outputs evaluation, this method is evaluated at execution time. If the closure returns `true`, the task is considered up to date.

Now, if you execute the task twice you'll see that Gradle already knows that the project version is set to release and automatically skips the task execution:

```
$ gradle makeReleaseVersion
:makeReleaseVersion

$ gradle makeReleaseVersion
:makeReleaseVersion UP-TO-DATE
```

If you don't change the release property manually in the properties file, any subsequent run of the task makeReleaseVersion will be marked up to date.

So far you've used Gradle's DSL to create and modify tasks in the build script. Every task is backed by an actual task object that's instantiated for you during Gradle's configuration phase. In many cases, simple tasks get the job done. However, sometimes you may want to have full control over your task implementation. In the next section, you'll rewrite the task makeReleaseVersion in the form of a custom task implementation.

4.2.9   *Writing and using a custom task*

The action logic within the task makeReleaseVersion is fairly simple. Code maintainability is clearly not an issue at the moment. However, when working on your projects you'll notice that simple tasks can grow in size quickly the more logic you need to add to them. The need for structuring your code into classes and methods will arise. You should be able to apply the same coding practices as you're used to in your regular production source code, right? Gradle doesn't suggest a specific way of writing your tasks. You have full control over your build source code. The programming language you choose, be it Java, Groovy, or any other JVM-based language, and the location of your task is up to you.

Custom tasks consist of two components: the custom task class that encapsulates the behavior of your logic, also called the task type, and the actual task that provides the values for the properties exposed by the task class to configure the behavior. Gradle calls these tasks *enhanced tasks.*

Maintainability is only one of the advantages of writing a custom task class. Because you're dealing with an actual class, any method is fully testable through unit tests. Testing your build code is out of the scope of this chapter. If you want to learn more, feel free to jump to chapter 7. Another advantage of enhanced tasks over simple tasks is reusability. The properties exposed by a custom task can be set individually from the build script. With the benefits of enhanced tasks in mind, let's discuss writing a custom task class.

WRITING THE CUSTOM TASK CLASS

As mentioned earlier in this chapter, Gradle creates an instance of type DefaultTask for every simple task in your build script. When creating a custom task, you do exactly that—create a class that extends DefaultTask. The following listing demonstrates how to express the logic from makeReleaseVersion as the custom task class Release-VersionTask written in Groovy.

Listing 4.6   Custom task implementation

```
class ReleaseVersionTask extends DefaultTask {
    @Input Boolean release                          Declaring custom task's inputs/
    @OutputFile File destFile                       outputs through annotations

    ReleaseVersionTask() {
        group = 'versioning'                         Setting task's group and
        description = 'Makes project a release version.'   description properties
    }                                                in the constructor

    @TaskAction                          Annotation declares
    void start() {                       method to be executed
        project.version.release = true
        ant.propertyfile(file: destFile) {
            entry(key: 'release', type: 'string', operation: '=', value: 'true')
        }
    }                                          Writing a custom task that extends Gradle's
}                                              default task implementation
}
```

In the listing, you're not using the DefaultTask's properties to declare its inputs and outputs. Instead, you use annotations from the package org.gradle.api.tasks.

EXPRESSING INPUTS AND OUTPUTS THROUGH ANNOTATIONS

Task input and output annotations add semantic sugar to your implementation. Not only do they have the same effect as the method calls to TaskInputs and Task-Outputs, they also act as automatic documentation. At first glance, you know exactly what data is expected as input and what output artifact is produced by the task. When exploring the Javadocs of this package, you'll find that Gradle provides you with a wide range of annotations.

In your custom task class, you use the @Input annotation to declare the input property release and the annotation @OutputFile to define the output file. Applying input and output annotations to fields isn't the only option. You can also annotate the getter methods for a field.

> **Task input validation**
>
> The annotation @Input will validate the value of the property at configuration time. If the value is null, Gradle will throw a TaskValidationException. To allow null values, mark the field with the @Optional annotation.

USING THE CUSTOM TASK

You implemented a custom task class by creating an action method and exposed its configurable properties through fields. But how do you actually use it? In your build script, you'll need to create a task of type ReleaseVersionTask and set the inputs and outputs by assigning values to its properties, as shown in the next listing. Think of it as creating a new instance of a specific class and setting the values for its fields in the constructor.

Listing 4.7   Task of type `ReleaseVersionTask`

```
task makeReleaseVersion(type: ReleaseVersionTask) {
    release = version.release
    destFile = versionFile
}
```

Defining an enhanced task of type ReleaseVersionTask

Setting custom task properties

As expected, the enhanced task `makeReleaseVersion` will behave exactly the same way as the simple task if you run it. One big advantage you have over the simple task implementation is that you expose properties that can be assigned individually.

APPLIED CUSTOM TASK REUSABILITY

Let's assume you'd like to use the custom task in another project. In that project, the requirements are different. The version POGO exposes different fields to represent the versioning scheme, as shown in the next listing.

Listing 4.8   Different version POGO implementation

```
class ProjectVersion {
    Integer min
    Integer maj
    Boolean prodReady

    @Override
    String toString() {
        "$maj.$min${prodReady? '' : '-SNAPSHOT'}"
    }
}
```

Additionally, the project owner decides to name the version file `project-version`
`.properties` instead of `version.properties`. How does the enhanced task adapt to these requirements? You simply assign different values to the exposed properties, as shown in the following listing. Custom task classes can flexibly handle changing requirements.

Listing 4.9   Setting individual property values for task `makeReleaseVersion`

```
task makeReleaseVersion(type: ReleaseVersionTask) {
    release = version.prodReady
    destFile = file('project-version.properties')
}
```

POGO version representation uses field prodReady to indicate release flag

Assigning different version file object

Gradle ships with a wide range of out-of-the-box custom tasks for commonly used functionality, like copying and deleting files or creating a ZIP archive. In the next section we'll take a closer look at some of them.

4.2.10 *Gradle's built-in task types*

Do you remember the last time a manual production deployment went wrong? I bet you still have a vivid picture in your mind: angry customers calling your support team,

Figure 4.8 Task dependencies for releasing the project

the boss knocking on your door asking about what went wrong, and your coworkers frantically trying to figure out the root cause of the stack trace being thrown when starting up the application. Forgetting a single step in a manual release process can prove fatal.

Let's be professionals and take pride in automating every aspect of the build lifecycle. Being able to modify the project's versioning scheme in an automated fashion is only the first step in modeling your release process. To be able to quickly recover from failed deployments, a good rollback strategy is essential. Having a backup of the latest stable application deliverable for redeployment can prove invaluable. You'll use some of the task types shipped with Gradle to implement parts of this process for your To Do application.

Here's what you're going to do. Before deploying any code to production you want to create a distribution. It'll act as a fallback deliverable for future failed deployments. A distribution is a ZIP file that consists of your web application archive, all source files, and the version property file. After creating the distribution, the file is copied to a backup server. The backup server could either be accessible over a mounted shared drive or you could transfer the file over FTP. Because I don't want to make this example too complex to grasp, you'll just copy it to the subdirectory `build/backup`. Figure 4.8 illustrates the order in which you want the tasks to be executed.

USING TASK TYPES

Gradle's built-in task types are derived classes from `DefaultTask`. As such, they can be used from an enhanced task within the build script. Gradle provides a broad spectrum of task types, but for the purposes of this example you'll use only two of them. The following listing shows the task types `Zip` and `Copy` in the context of releasing the production version of your software. You can find the complete task reference in the DSL guide.

Listing 4.10   Using task types to back up a zipped release distribution

```
task createDistribution(type: Zip, dependsOn: makeReleaseVersion) {
    from war.outputs.files                                          ⟵── Implicit reference to
                                                                        output of War task
    from(sourceSets*.allSource) {          ⟵┐ Takes all source files
        into 'src'                           │ and puts them into src
    }                                        │ directory of ZIP file

    from(rootDir) {
        include versionFile.name    ⟵┐ Adds version
    }                                 │ file to ZIP
}
```

```
task backupReleaseDistribution(type: Copy) {
   from createDistribution.outputs.files
   into "$buildDir/backup"
}
```
Implicit reference to output of createDistribution output

```
task release(dependsOn: backupReleaseDistribution) << {
   logger.quiet 'Releasing the project...'
}
```

In this listing there are different ways of telling the Zip and Copy tasks what files to include and where to put them. Many of the methods used here come from the superclass AbstractCopyTask, as shown in figure 4.9. For a full list of available options, please refer to the Javadocs of the classes.

The task types you used offer far more configuration options than those shown in the example. Again, for a full list of available options, please refer to the DSL reference or the Javadocs. Next, we'll take a deeper look at their task dependencies.

TASK DEPENDENCY INFERENCE

You may have noticed in the listing that a task dependency between two tasks was explicitly declared through the dependsOn method. However, some of the tasks don't model a direct dependency to other tasks (for example, createDistribution to war). How does Gradle know to execute the dependent task beforehand? By using the output of one task as input for another task, dependency is inferred. Consequently, the dependent task is run automatically. Let's see the full task execution graph in action:

```
$ gradle release
:makeReleaseVersion
:compileJava
:processResources UP-TO-DATE
:classes
:war
:createDistribution
:backupReleaseDistribution
:release
Releasing the project...
```

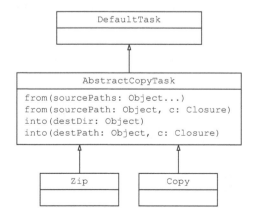

Figure 4.9   Inheritance hierarchy for the task types Zip **and** Copy

After running the build, you should find the generated ZIP file in the directory `build/distributions`, which is the default output directory for archive tasks. You can easily assign a different distribution output directory by setting the property `destination-Dir`. The following directory tree shows the relevant artifacts generated by the build:

```
.
├── build
│   ├── backup
│   │   └── todo-webapp-0.1.zip
│   ├── distributions
│   │   └── todo-webapp-0.1.zip
│   └── libs
│       └── todo-webapp-0.1.war
├── build.gradle
├── src
└── version.properties
```

Task types have incremental build support built in. Running the tasks multiple times in a row will mark them as up-to-date if you don't change any of the source files. Next, you'll learn how to define a task on which the behavior depends on a flexible task name.

4.2.11 Task rules

Sometimes you may find yourself in a situation where you write multiple tasks that do similar things. For example, let's say you want to extend your version management functionality by two more tasks: one that increments the major version of the project and another to do the same work for the minor version classifier. Both tasks are also supposed to persist the changes to the version file. If you compare the `doLast` actions for both tasks in the following listing, you can tell that you basically duplicated code and applied minor changes to them.

Listing 4.11 Declaring tasks for incrementing version classifiers

```
task incrementMajorVersion(group: 'versioning', description: 'Increments
                           ⇥ project major version.') << {
    String currentVersion = version.toString()
    ++version.major
    String newVersion = version.toString()
    logger.info "Incrementing major project version: $currentVersion ->
                ⇥ $newVersion"

    ant.propertyfile(file: versionFile) {                    ⟵── Using Ant task
        entry(key: 'major', type: 'int', operation: '+', value: 1)      propertyfile to
    }                                                                    increment a
}                                                                        specific
                                                                         property within
                                                                         a property file
task incrementMinorVersion(group: 'versioning', description: 'Increments
                           ⇥ project minor version.') << {
    String currentVersion = version.toString()
    ++version.minor
    String newVersion = version.toString()
```

```
    logger.info "Incrementing minor project version: $currentVersion ->
                ➡ $newVersion"
                                                                              ⎫ Using Ant task
    ant.propertyfile(file: versionFile) {                              ◁─┤   propertyfile to
        entry(key: 'minor', type: 'int', operation: '+', value: 1)         │  increment a
    }                                                                       │  specific
}                                                                           │  property within
                                                                           ⎭  a property file
```

If you run `gradle incrementMajorVersion` on a project with version `0.1-SNAPSHOT`, you'll see that the version is bumped up to `1.1-SNAPSHOT`. Run it on the `INFO` log level to see more detailed output information:

```
$ gradle incrementMajorVersion -i
:incrementMajorVersion
Incrementing major project version: 0.1-SNAPSHOT -> 1.1-SNAPSHOT
[ant:propertyfile] Updating property file: /Users/benjamin/books/
➡ gradle-in-action/code/chapter4/task-rule/version.properties
```

Having two separate tasks works just fine, but you can certainly improve on this implementation. In the end, you're not interested in maintaining duplicated code.

TASK RULE-NAMING PATTERN

Gradle also introduces the concept of a task rule, which executes specific logic based on a task name pattern. The pattern consists of two parts: the static portion of the task name and a placeholder. Together they form a dynamic task name. If you wanted to apply a task rule to the previous example, the naming pattern would look like this: `increment<Classifier>Version`. When executing the task rule on the command line, you'd specify the classifier placeholder in camel-case notation (for example, `incrementMajorVersion` or `incrementMinorVersion`).

Task rules in practice

Some of Gradle's core plugins make good use of task rules. One of the task rules the Java plugins define is `clean<TaskName>`, which deletes the output of a specified task. For example, running `gradle cleanCompileJava` from the command line deletes all production code class files.

DECLARING A TASK RULE

You just read about defining a naming pattern for a task rule, but how do you actually declare a task rule in your build script? To add a task rule to your project, you'll first need to get the reference to `TaskContainer`. Once you have the reference, you can call the method `addRule(String, Closure)`. The first parameter provides a description (for example, the task name pattern), and the second parameter declares the closure to execute to apply the rule. Unfortunately, there's no direct way of creating a task rule through a method from `Project` as there is for simple tasks, as illustrated in figure 4.10.

With a basic understanding of how to add a task rule to your project, you can get started writing the actual closure implementation for it. The next listing demonstrates

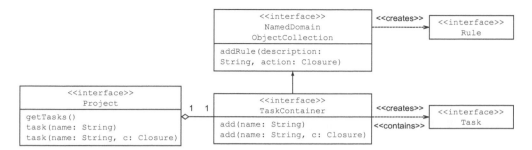

Figure 4.10 Simple tasks can be directly added by calling methods of your project instance. Task rules can only be added through the task container, so you'll need to get a reference to it first by invoking the `getTasks()` method.

how applying a task rule becomes a very expressive tool to implement task actions with similar logic.

Listing 4.12 Merging similar logic into a task rule

```
tasks.addRule("Pattern: increment<Classifier>Version - Increments the
              ⇒ project version classifier.") { String taskName ->
  if(taskName.startsWith('increment') && taskName.endsWith('Version')) {
     task(taskName) << {
        String classifier = (taskName - 'increment' - 'Version')
                            ⇒ .toLowerCase()
        String currentVersion = version.toString()

        switch(classifier) {
           case 'major': ++version.major
                    break
           case 'minor': ++version.minor
                    break
           default: throw new GradleException("Invalid version
                    ⇒ type '$classifier. Allowed types: ['Major', 'Minor']")
        }

        String newVersion = version.toString()
        logger.info "Incrementing $classifier project version:
                    ⇒ $currentVersion -> $newVersion"

        ant.propertyfile(file: versionFile) {
           entry(key: classifier, type: 'int', operation: '+', value: 1)
        }
     }
  }
}
```

Adding a task rule with provided description

Dynamically add a task named after provided pattern with a doLast action

Extracting type string from full task name

Checking task name for predefined pattern

After adding the task rule in your project, you'll find that it's listed under a specific task group called Rules when running the help task tasks:

```
$ gradle tasks
...
```

```
Rules
-----
Pattern: increment<Classifier>Version - Increments project version type
```

Task rules can't be grouped individually as you can do with any other simple or enhanced task. A task rule, even if it's declared by a plugin, will always show up under this group.

4.2.12 *Building code in buildSrc directory*

You've seen how quickly your build script code can grow. In this chapter you already created two Groovy classes within your build script: ProjectVersion and the custom task ReleaseVersionTask. These classes are perfect candidates to be moved to the buildSrc directory alongside your project. The buildSrc directory is an alternative location to put build code and a real enabler for good software development practices. You'll be able to structure the code the way you're used to in any other project and even write tests for it.

Gradle standardizes the layout for source files under the buildSrc directory. Java code needs to sit in the directory src/main/java, and Groovy code is expected to live under the directory src/main/groovy. Any code that's found in these directories is automatically compiled and put into the classpath of your regular Gradle build script. The buildSrc directory is a great way to organize your code. Because you're dealing with classes, you can also put them into a specific package. You'll make them part of the package com.manning.gia. The following directory structure shows the Groovy classes in their new location:

```
.
├── build.gradle
├── buildSrc
│   └── src
│       └── main
│           └── groovy
│               └── com
│                   └── manning
│                       └── gia
│                           ├── ProjectVersion.groovy
│                           └── ReleaseVersionTask.groovy
├── src
│   └── ...
└── version.properties
```

Keep in mind that extracting the classes into their own source files requires some extra work. The difference between defining a class in the build script versus a separate source file is that you'll need to import classes from the Gradle API. The following code snippet shows the package and import declaration for the custom task ReleaseVersionTask:

```
package com.manning.gia

import org.gradle.api.DefaultTask
import org.gradle.api.tasks.Input
```

```
import org.gradle.api.tasks.OutputFile
import org.gradle.api.tasks.TaskAction

class ReleaseVersionTask extends DefaultTask {
    (...)
}
```

In turn, your build script will need to import the compiled classes from `buildSrc` (for example, `com.manning.gia.ReleaseVersionTask`). The following console output shows the compilation tasks that are run before the task you invoked on the command line:

```
$ gradle makeReleaseVersion
:buildSrc:compileJava UP-TO-DATE
:buildSrc:compileGroovy
:buildSrc:processResources UP-TO-DATE
:buildSrc:classes
:buildSrc:jar
:buildSrc:assemble
:buildSrc:compileTestJava UP-TO-DATE
:buildSrc:compileTestGroovy UP-TO-DATE
:buildSrc:processTestResources UP-TO-DATE
:buildSrc:testClasses UP-TO-DATE
:buildSrc:test
:buildSrc:check
:buildSrc:build
:makeReleaseVersion UP-TO-DATE
```

The `buildSrc` directory is treated as its own Gradle project indicated by the path `:buildSrc`. Because you didn't write any unit tests, the compilation and execution tasks for tests are skipped. Chapter 7 is fully dedicated to writing tests for classes in `buildSrc`.

In the previous sections, you learned the ins and outs of working with simple tasks, custom task classes, and specific task types provided by Gradle's API. We examined the difference between task action and configuration code, as well as their appropriate use cases. An important lesson you learned is that action and configuration code is executed during different phases of the build lifecycle. The rest of this chapter will talk about how to write code that's executed when specific lifecycle events are fired.

4.3   *Hooking into the build lifecycle*

As a build script developer, you're not limited to writing task actions or configuration logic, which are evaluated during a distinct build phase. Sometimes you'll want to execute code when a specific lifecycle event occurs. A lifecycle event can occur before, during, or after a specific build phase. An example of a lifecycle event that happens after the execution phase would be the completion of a build.

Suppose you want to get feedback about failed builds as early as possible in the development cycle. A typical reaction to a failed build could be that you send an email to all developers on the team to restore the sanity of your code. There are two ways to write a callback to build lifecycle events: within a closure, or with an implementation of a listener interface provided by the Gradle API. Gradle doesn't steer you toward one

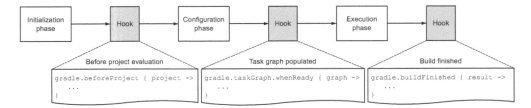

Figure 4.11   Examples of build lifecycle hooks

of the options to listen to lifecycle events. The choice is up to you. The big advantage you have with a listener implementation is that you're dealing with a class that's fully testable by writing unit tests. To give you an idea of some of the useful lifecycle hooks, see figure 4.11.

An extensive list of all available lifecycle hooks is beyond the scope of this book. Many of the lifecycle callback methods are defined in the interfaces `Project` and `Gradle`. Gradle's Javadocs are a great starting point to find the appropriate event call-back for your use case.

> Don't be afraid of making good use of lifecycle hooks. They're not considered a secret backdoor to Gradle's API. Instead, they're provided intentionally because Gradle can't predict the requirements for your enterprise build.

In the following two sections, I'll demonstrate how to receive notifications immediately after the task execution graph has been populated. To fully understand what's happening under the hood when this graph is built, we'll first look at Gradle's inner workings.

INTERNAL TASK GRAPH REPRESENTATION

At configuration time, Gradle determines the order of tasks that need to be run during the execution phase. As noted in chapter 1, the internal structure that represents these task dependencies is modeled as a directed acyclic graph (DAG). Each task in the graph is called a node, and each node is connected by directed edges. You've most likely created these connections between nodes by declaring a `dependsOn` relationship for a task or by leveraging the implicit task dependency interference mechanism. It's important to note that DAGs never contain a cycle. In other words, a task that has been executed before will never be executed again. Figure 4.12 demonstrates the DAG representation of the release process modeled earlier.

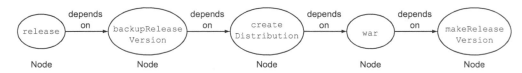

Figure 4.12   Task dependencies represented as Directed Acyclic Graph

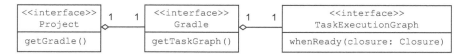

Figure 4.13 `TaskExecutionGraph` **provides the method** `whenReady` **that's called when the task graph has been populated.**

Now that you have a better idea of Gradle's internal task graph representation, you'll write some code in your build script to react to it.

4.3.1 Hooking into the task execution graph

Recall the task `makeReleaseVersion` you implemented that was automatically executed as a dependency of the task `release`. Instead of writing a task to change the project's version to indicate production-readiness, you could also achieve the same goal by writing a lifecycle hook. Because the build knows exactly which tasks will take part in the build before they get executed, you can query the task graph to check for its existence. Figure 4.13 shows the relevant interfaces and their methods to access the task execution graph.

Next you'll put the lifecycle hook in place. Listing 4.13 extends the build script by the method call `whenReady` to register a closure that's executed immediately after the task graph has been populated. Because you know that the logic is run before any of the tasks in the graph are executed, you can completely remove the task `makeRelease-Version` and omit the `dependsOn` declaration from `createDistribution`.

Listing 4.13   Release version functionality implemented as lifecycle hook

```
gradle.taskGraph.whenReady { TaskExecutionGraph taskGraph ->    ⟵ Registers
    if(taskGraph.hasTask(release)) {          ⟵ Checks if task        lifecycle
        if(!version.release) {                   execution graph      hook that
            version.release = true               contains task release gets called
            ant.propertyfile(file: versionFile) {                     when task
                entry(key: 'release', type: 'string', operation: '=', graph is
                ⇨ value: 'true')                                      populated
            }
        }
    }
}
```

Alternatively, you can implement this logic as a listener, which you'll do next.

4.3.2 Implementing a task execution graph listener

Hooking into the build lifecycle via a listener is done in two simple steps. First, you implement the specific listener interface by writing a class within your build script. Second, you register the listener implementation with the build.

The interface for listening to task execution graph events is provided by the interface `TaskExecutionGraphListener`. At the time of writing, you only need to implement one

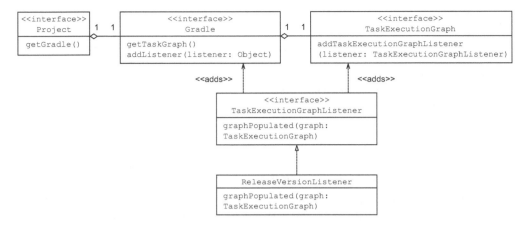

Figure 4.14 Ways to register a `TaskExecutionGraphListener`. A listener can be registered through the generic `addListener` method or through a specific method that only takes an instance of a specialized listener type.

method: `graphPopulated(TaskExecutionGraph)`. Figure 4.14 shows the listener implementation named `ReleaseVersionListener`.

Keep in mind that you don't have direct access to the `Project` instance if you add the listener to your build script. Instead, you can work Gradle's API to its fullest. The following listing shows how to access the project by calling the `getProject()` method on the release task.

Listing 4.14   Release version functionality implemented as lifecycle listener

```
class ReleaseVersionListener implements TaskExecutionGraphListener {
   final static String releaseTaskPath = ':release'

   @Override
   void graphPopulated(TaskExecutionGraph taskGraph) {          Determines whether
      if(taskGraph.hasTask(releaseTaskPath)) {                  release task is included
         List<Task> allTasks = taskGraph.allTasks              in execution graph
         Task releaseTask = allTasks.find {it.path == releaseTaskPath }
         Project project = releaseTask.project
                                                                Every task knows which
         if(!project.version.release) {                        project it belongs to
            project.version.release = true
            project.ant.propertyfile(file: project.versionFile) {
               entry(key: 'release', type: 'string', operation: '=',
                  ➥ value: 'true')
            }
         }
      }
   }
}
def releaseVersionListener = new ReleaseVersionListener()
gradle.taskGraph.addTaskExecutionGraphListener(releaseVersionListener)     Registers listener
                                                                          to task execution
                                                                          graph
```

Filters release task from list of all tasks within execution graph

You're not limited to registering a lifecycle listener in your build script. Lifecycle logic can be applied to listen to Gradle events even before any of your project's tasks are executed. In the next section, we'll explore options for hooking into the lifecycle via initialization scripts to customize the build environment.

4.3.3 Initializing the build environment

Let's say you want to be notified about the outcome of a build. Whenever a build finishes, you'll want to know whether it was successful or failed. You also want to be able to identify how many tasks have been executed. One of Gradle's core plugins, the build-announcements plugin, provides a way

Figure 4.15 Build announcement sent by Growl on Mac OS X

to send announcements to a local notification system like Snarl (Windows) or Growl (Mac OS X). The plugin automatically picks the correct notification system based on your OS. Figure 4.15 shows a notification rendered by Growl.

You could apply the plugin to every project individually, but why not use the powerful mechanisms Gradle provides? Initialization scripts are run before any of your build script logic has been evaluated and executed. You'll write an initialization script that applies the plugin to any of your projects without manual intervention. Create the initialization script under <USER_HOME>/.gradle/init.d, as shown in the following directory tree:

```
.
└── .gradle
    └── init.d
        └── build-announcements.gradle
```

Gradle will execute every initialization script it finds under init.d as long as the file extension matches .gradle. Because you want to apply the plugin before any other build script code is executed, you'll pick the lifecycle callback method that's most appropriate for handling this situation: Gradle#projectLoaded(Closure). The following code snippet shows how to apply the build-announcements plugin to the build's root project:

```
gradle.projectsLoaded { Gradle gradle ->      ◁─┐  Executes closure when
    gradle.rootProject {                            projects of build have
        apply plugin: 'build-announcements'         been created
    }
}
```

An important lesson to learn in this context is that some lifecycle events are only fired if they're declared in the appropriate location. For example, the closure for the lifecycle hook Gradle#projectsLoaded(Closure) wouldn't get fired if you declared it in your build.gradle, because the project creation happens during the initialization phase.

4.4   *Summary*

Every Gradle build script consists of two basic building blocks: one or more projects and tasks. Both elements are deeply rooted in Gradle's API and have a direct class representation. At runtime, Gradle creates a model from the build definition, stores it in memory, and makes it accessible for you to access through methods. You learned that properties are a means of controlling the behavior of the build. A project exposes standard properties out of the box. Additionally, you can define extra properties on many of Gradle's domain model objects (for example, on the project and task level) to declare arbitrary user data.

Later in the chapter, you learned the ins and outs of tasks. As an example, you implemented build logic to control your project's version numbering scheme stored in an external properties file. You started out by adding simple tasks to the build script. Build logic can be defined directly in the action closure of a task. Every task is derived from the class `org.gradle.api.DefaultTask`. As such, it comes loaded with functionality accessible through methods of its superclass.

Understanding the build lifecycle and the execution order of its phases is crucial to beginners. Gradle makes a clear distinction between task actions and task configurations. Task actions, defined through the closures `doFirst` and `doLast` or its shortcut notation `<<`, are run during the execution phase. Any other code defined outside of a task action is considered a configuration and therefore executed beforehand during the configuration phase.

Next, we turned our attention to implementing nonfunctional requirements: build execution performance, code maintainability, and reusability. You added incremental build support to one of your existing task implementations by declaring its input and output data. If the data doesn't change between the initial and subsequent builds task, execution is skipped. Implementing incremental build support is easy and cheap. If done right, it can significantly improve the execution time of your build. Complex build logic is best structured in custom task classes, which give you all the benefits of object-oriented programming. You practiced writing a custom task class by transferring the existing logic into an implementation of `DefaultTask`. You also cleaned up your build script by moving compilable code under the `buildSrc` directory. Gradle comes with a whole range of reusable task types like `Zip` and `Copy`. You incorporated both types by modeling a chain of task dependencies for releasing your project.

Access to Gradle's internals is not limited to the model. You can register build lifecycle hooks that execute code whenever the targeted event is fired. As an example, you wrote a task execution graph lifecycle hook as a closure and listener implementation. Initialization scripts can be used to apply common code like lifecycle listeners across all of your builds.

You already got a first taste of the mechanisms that enable you to declare a dependency on an external library. In the next chapter, we'll deepen your knowledge with a detailed discussion of working with dependencies and how dependency resolution works under the hood.

Dependency management

5

This chapter covers

- Understanding automated dependency management
- Declaring and organizing dependencies
- Targeting various types of repositories
- Understanding and tweaking the local cache
- Dependency reporting and version conflict resolution

In chapter 3, you learned how to declare a dependency on the Servlet API to implement web components for the To Do application. Gradle's DSL configuration closures make it easy to declare dependencies and the repositories to retrieve them from. First, you define what libraries your build depends on with the `dependencies` script. Second, you tell your build the origin of these dependencies using the `repositories` closure. With this information in place, Gradle automatically resolves the dependencies, downloads them to your machine if needed, stores them in a local cache, and uses them for the build.

This chapter covers Gradle's powerful support for dependency management. We'll take a close look at key DSL configuration elements for grouping dependencies and targeting different types of repositories.

Dependency management sounds like an easy nut to crack, but can become difficult when it comes to dependency resolution conflicts. Transitive dependencies, the dependencies a declared dependency relies on, can be a blessing and a curse. Complex dependency graphs can cause a mix-up of dependencies with multiple versions resulting in unreliable, nondeterministic builds. Gradle provides dependency reports for analyzing the dependency tree. You'll learn how to find answers to questions like "Where does a specific dependency come from?" and "Why was this specific version picked?" to resolve version conflicts.

Gradle rolls its own dependency management implementation. Having learned from the shortcomings of other dependency managers like Ivy and Maven, Gradle's special concern is performance, build reliability, and reproducibility.

5.1   A quick overview of dependency management

Almost all JVM-based software projects depend on external libraries to reuse existing functionality. For example, if you're working on a web-based project, there's a high likelihood that you rely on one of the popular open source frameworks like Spring MVC or Play to improve developer productivity. Libraries in Java get distributed in the form of a JAR file. The JAR file specification doesn't require you to indicate the version of the library. However, it's common practice to attach a version number to the JAR filename to identify a specific release (for example, spring-web-3.1.3.RELEASE.jar). You've seen small projects grow big very quickly, along with the number of third-party libraries and modules your project depends on. Organizing and managing your JAR files is critical.

5.1.1   Imperfect dependency management techniques

Because the Java language doesn't provide or propose any tooling for managing versioned dependencies, teams will have to come up with their own strategies to store and retrieve them. You may have encountered the following common practices:

- Manually copying JAR files to the developer machine. This is the most primitive, nonautomated, and error-prone approach to handle dependencies.
- Using a shared storage for JAR files (for example, a folder on a shared network drive), which gets mounted on the developer's machine, or retrieving binaries over FTP. This approach requires the developer to initially establish the connection to the binary repository. New dependencies will need to be added manually, which potentially requires write permissions or access credentials.
- Checking JAR files that get downloaded with the project source code into the VCS. This approach doesn't require any additional setup and bundles source code and all dependencies as one consistent unit. Your team can retrieve changes whenever they update their local copy of the repository. On the downside, binary files unnecessarily use up space in the repository. Changing working copies of a library requires frequent check-ins whenever there's a change to the source code. This is especially true if you're working with projects that depend on each other.

5.1.2 *Importance of automated dependency management*

While all of these approaches work, they're far from being sufficient solutions, because they don't provide a standardized way to name and organize the JAR files. At the very least, you'll need to know the exact version of the library and the dependencies it depends on, the transitive dependencies. Why is this so important?

KNOWING THE EXACT VERSION OF A DEPENDENCY

Working with a project that doesn't clearly state the versions of its dependencies quickly becomes a maintenance nightmare. If not documented meticulously, you can never be sure which features are actually supported by the library version in your project. Upgrading a library to a newer version becomes a guessing game, because you don't know exactly what version you're upgrading from. In fact, you may actually be downgrading without knowing it.

MANAGING TRANSITIVE DEPENDENCIES

Transitive dependencies are of concern even at an early stage of development. These are the libraries your first-level dependencies require in order to work correctly. Popular Java development stacks like the combination of Spring and Hibernate can easily bring in more than 20 additional libraries from the start. A single library may require many other libraries in order to work correctly. Figure 5.1 shows the dependency graph for Hibernate's core library.

Trying to manually determine all transitive dependencies for a specific library can be a real time-sink. Many times this information is nowhere to be found in the library's documentation and you end up on a wild-goose chase to get your dependencies right.

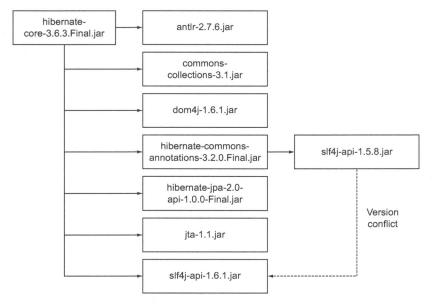

Figure 5.1 Dependency graph of Hibernate core library

As a result, you can experience unexpected behavior like compilation errors and run-time class-loading issues.

I think we can agree that a more sophisticated solution is needed to manage dependencies. Optimally, you'll want to be able to declare your dependencies and their respective versions as project metadata. As part of an automated process, they can be retrieved from a central location and installed for your project. Let's look at existing open source solutions that support these features.

5.1.3   *Using automated dependency management*

The Java space is mostly dominated by two projects that support declarative and automated dependency management: Apache Ivy, a pure dependency manager that's mostly used with Ant projects, and Maven, which contains a dependency manager as part of its build infrastructure. I'm not going to go into deep details of any of these solutions. Instead, the purpose of this section is to explain the concepts and mechanics of automated dependency management.

In Ivy and Maven, dependency configuration is expressed through an XML descriptor file. The configuration consists of two parts: the dependency identifiers plus their respective versions, and the location of the binary repositories (for example, an HTTP address you want to retrieve them from). The dependency manager evaluates this information and automatically targets those repositories to download the dependencies onto your local machine. Libraries can define transitive dependencies as part of their metadata. The dependency manager is smart enough to analyze this information and resolve those dependencies as part of the retrieval process. If a dependency version conflict is recognized, as demonstrated by the example of Hibernate core, the dependency manager will try to resolve it. Once downloaded, the libraries are stored in a local cache. Now that the configured libraries are available on your developer machine, they can be used for your build. Subsequent builds will first check the local cache for a library to avoid unnecessary requests to a repository. Figure 5.2 illustrates the key elements of automated dependency management.

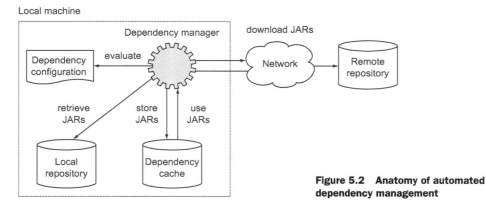

Figure 5.2   Anatomy of automated dependency management

Using a dependency manager frees you from the burden of manually having to copy or organize JAR files. Gradle provides a powerful out-of-the-box dependency management implementation that fits into the architecture just described. It describes the dependency configuration as part of Gradle's expressive DSL, has support for transitive dependency management, and plays well with existing repository infrastructures. Before we dive into the details, let's look at some of the challenges you may face with dependency management and how to cope with them.

5.1.4 Challenges of automated dependency management

Even though dependency management significantly simplifies the handling of external libraries, at some point you'll find yourself dealing with certain shortcomings that may compromise the reliability and reproducibility of your build.

POTENTIAL UNAVAILABILITY OF CENTRALLY HOSTED REPOSITORIES

It's not uncommon for enterprise software to rely on open source libraries. Many of these projects publish their releases to a centrally hosted repository. One of the most widely used repositories is Maven Central. If Maven Central is the only repository your build relies on, you've automatically created a single point of failure for your system. In case the repository is down, you've stripped yourself of the ability to build your project if a dependency is required that isn't available in your local cache.

You can avoid this situation by configuring your build to use your own custom in-house repository, which gives you full control over server availability. If you're eager to learn about it, feel free to directly jump to chapter 14, which talks about how to set up and use open source and commercial repository managers like Sonatype Nexus and JFrog's Artifactory.

BAD METADATA AND MISSING DEPENDENCIES

Earlier you learned that metadata is used to declare transitive dependencies for a library. A dependency manager analyzes this information, builds a dependency graph from it, and resolves all nested dependencies for you. Using transitive dependency management is a huge timesaver and enables traceability for your dependency graph.

Unfortunately, neither the metadata nor the repository guarantees that any of the artifacts declared in the metadata actually exist, are defined correctly, or are even needed. You may encounter problems like missing dependencies, especially on repositories that don't enforce any quality control, which is a known issue on Maven Central. Figure 5.3 demonstrates the artifact production and consumption lifecycle for a Maven repository.

Gradle allows for excluding transitive dependencies on any level of the dependency graph. Alternatively, you can omit the provided metadata and instate your own transitive dependency definition.

You'll find that popular libraries will appear in your transitive dependency graph with different versions. This is often the case for commonly used functionality like logging frameworks. The dependency manager tries to find a smart solution for this problem by picking one of these versions based on a certain resolution strategy to

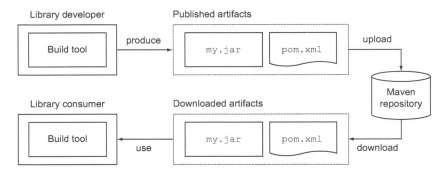

**Figure 5.3   Bad metadata complicates the use of transitive dependencies.
Dependency metadata in Maven repositories is represented by a project object model
(POM) file. If the library developer provides incorrect metadata, the consumer will
inherit the problems.**

avoid version conflicts. Sometimes you'll need to tweak those choices. To do so, you'll
first want to find out which dependencies bring in what version of a transitive dependency. Gradle provides meaningful dependency reports to answer these questions.
Later, we'll see these reports in action. Now let's see how Gradle implements these
ideas with the help of a full-fledged example.

5.2   *Learning dependency management by example*

In chapter 3, you saw how to use the Jetty plugin to deploy a To Do application to an
embedded Jetty Servlet container. Jetty is a handy container for use during development. With its lightweight container implementation, it provides fast startup times.
Many enterprises use other web application container implementations in their production environments. Let's assume you want to build support for deploying your web
application to a different container product, such as Apache Tomcat.

The open source project Cargo (http://cargo.codehaus.org/) provides versatile
support for web application deployment to a variety of Servlet containers and application servers. Cargo supports two implementations you can use in your project. On the
one hand, you can utilize a Java API, which gives you fine-grained access to each and
every aspect of configuring Cargo. On the other hand, you can choose to execute a set
of preconfigured Ant tasks that wrap the Java API. Because Gradle provides excellent
integration with Ant, our examples will be based on the Cargo Ant tasks.

Let's revisit figure 5.1 and see how the components change in the context of a
Gradle use case. In chapter 3 you learned that dependency management for a project is configured with the help of two DSL configuration blocks: `dependencies` and
`repositories`. The names of the configuration blocks directly map to methods of the
interface `Project`. For your use case, you're going to use Maven Central because it
doesn't require any additional setup. Figure 5.4 shows that dependency definitions
are provided through Gradle's DSL in the `build.gradle` file. The dependency manager will evaluate this configuration at runtime, download the required artifacts from

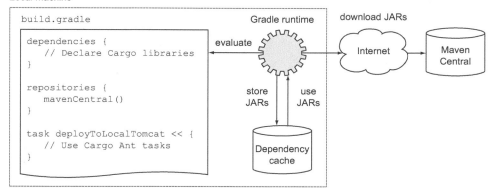

Figure 5.4 Declaring a dependency on the Cargo libraries in a Gradle build

a central repository, and store them in your local cache. You're not using a local repository, so it's not shown in the figure.

The following sections of this chapter discuss each of the Gradle build script configuration elements one by one. Not only will you learn how to apply them to the Cargo example, you'll also learn how to apply dependency management to implement the requirements of your own project. Let's first look at a concept that will become more important in the context of our example: dependency configurations.

5.3   *Dependency configurations*

In chapter 3, you saw that plugins can introduce configurations to define the scope for a dependency. The Java plugin brings in a variety of standard configurations to define which bucket of the Java build lifecycle a dependency should apply to. For example, dependencies required for compiling production source code are added with the `compile` configuration. In the build of your web application, you used the `compile` configuration to declare a dependency on the Apache Commons Lang library. To get a better understanding of how configurations are stored, configured, and accessed, let's look at responsible interfaces in Gradle's API.

5.3.1   *Understanding the configuration API representation*

Configurations can be directly added and accessed at the root level of a project; you can decide to use one of the configurations provided by a plugin or declare your own. Every project owns a container of class `ConfigurationContainer` that manages the corresponding configurations. Configurations are very flexible in their behavior. You can control whether transitive dependencies should be part of the dependency resolution, define the resolution strategy (for example, how to respond to conflicting artifact versions), and even make configurations extend to each other. Figure 5.5 shows the relevant Gradle API interfaces and their methods.

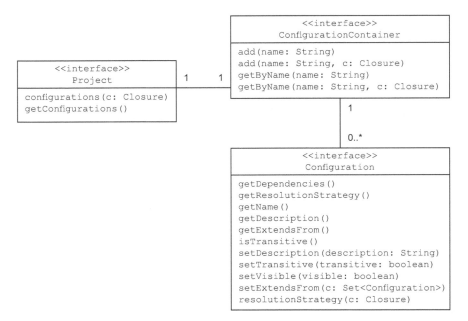

Figure 5.5   Configurations can be added and accessed through the Project instance

Another way of thinking of configurations is in terms of a logical grouping. Grouping dependencies by configuration is a similar concept to organizing Java classes into packages. Packages provide unique namespaces for classes they contain. The same is true for configurations. They group dependencies that serve a specific responsibility.

The Java plugin already provides six configurations out of the box: compile, runtime, testCompile, testRuntime, archives, and default. Couldn't you just use one of those configurations to declare a dependency on the Cargo libraries? Generally, you could, but you'd mix up dependencies that are relevant to your application code and the infrastructure code you're writing for deploying the application. Adding unnecessary libraries to your distribution can lead to unforeseen side effects at runtime and should be avoided at all costs. For example, using the compile configuration will result in a WAR file that contains the Cargo libraries. Next, I'll show how to define a custom configuration for the Cargo libraries.

5.3.2   *Defining a custom configuration*

To clearly identify the dependencies needed for Cargo, you'll need to declare a new configuration with the unique name cargo, as demonstrated in the following listing.

Listing 5.1   Defining a configuration for Cargo libraries

```
configurations {                                    Defines new configuration by name
    cargo {
        description = 'Classpath for Cargo Ant tasks.'    Sets description and
        visible = false                                    visibility of configuration
```

```
        }
    }
```

For now, you're only dealing with a single Gradle project. Limiting the visibility of this configuration to this project is a conscious choice in preparation for a multiproject setup. If you want to learn more about builds consisting of multiple projects, check out chapter 6. You don't want to let configurations spill into other projects if they're not needed. The description that was set for the configuration is directly reflected when you list the dependencies of the project:

```
$ gradle dependencies
:dependencies

------------------------------------------------------------
Root project
------------------------------------------------------------

cargo - Classpath for Cargo Ant tasks.
No dependencies
```

After adding a configuration to the configuration container of a project, it can be accessed by its name. Next, you'll use the `cargo` configuration to make the third-party Cargo Ant task public to the build script.

5.3.3 Accessing a configuration

Essentially, Ant tasks are Java classes that adhere to Ant's extension endpoint for defining custom logic. To add a nonstandard Ant task like the Cargo deployment task to your project, you'll need to declare it using the `Taskdef` Ant task. To resolve the Ant task implementation class, the Cargo JAR files containing them will need to be assigned. The next listing shows how easy it is to access the configuration by name. The task uses the resolved dependencies and assigns them to the classpath required for the Cargo Ant task.

Listing 5.2   Accessing the `cargo` configuration by name

```
task deployToLocalTomcat << {
    FileTree cargoDeps = configurations.getByName('cargo').asFileTree
    ant.taskdef(resource: 'cargo.tasks', classpath: cargoDeps.asPath)

    ant.cargo(containerId: 'tomcat7x', action: 'run',
                output: "$buildDir/output.log") {
        configuration {
            deployable(type: 'war', file: 'todo.war')
        }

        zipUrlInstaller(installUrl: 'http://archive.apache.org/dist/
                            tomcat/tomcat-7/v7.0.32/bin/
                            apache-tomcat-7.0.32.zip')
    }
}
```

Gets all dependencies for cargo configuration as file tree

Uses Cargo Ant task to automatically download a Tomcat 7 distribution, deploy a WAR file, and run it in container

Uses concatenated path of fully qualified dependencies to resolve Cargo Ant task definitions

Don't worry if you don't understand everything in the code example. The important part is that you recognize the Gradle API methods that allow you access to a configuration. The rest of the code is mostly Ant-specific configurations expressed through Gradle's DSL. Chapter 9 will give you the inside scoop on using Ant tasks from Gradle. With the deployment task set up, it's time to assign the Cargo dependencies to the cargo configuration.

5.4   Declaring dependencies

Chapter 3 gave you a first taste of how to tell your project that an external library is needed for it to function correctly. The DSL configuration block dependencies is used to assign one or more dependencies to a configuration. External dependencies are not the only dependencies you can declare for your project. Table 5.1 gives you an overview of the various types of dependencies. In this book we'll discuss and apply many of these options. Some of the dependency types are explained in this chapter, but others will make more sense in the context of another chapter. The table references each of the use cases.

Table 5.1   Dependency types for a Gradle project

Type	Description	Where to Go for More Information
External module dependency	A dependency on an external library in a repository including its provided metadata	Section 5.4.2
Project dependency	A dependency on another Gradle project	Section 6.3.3
File dependency	A dependency on a set of files in the file system	Section 5.4.3
Client module dependency	A dependency on an external library in a repository with the ability to declare the metadata yourself	Not covered—refer to the online manual
Gradle runtime dependency	A dependency on Gradle's API or a library shipped with the Gradle runtime	Section 8.5.7

In this chapter we'll cover external module dependencies and file dependencies, but first let's see how dependency support is represented in Gradle's API.

5.4.1   Understanding the dependency API representation

Every Gradle project has an instance of a dependency handler, which is represented by the interface DependencyHandler. You obtain a reference to the dependency handler by using the project's getter method getDependencies(). Each of the dependency types presented in table 5.1 is declared through a method of the dependency handler within the project's dependencies configuration block. Each dependency is an instance of type Dependency. The attributes group, name, version, and classifier

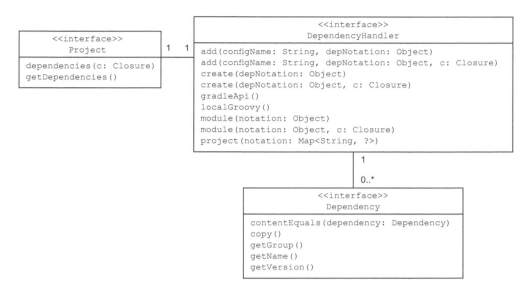

Figure 5.6 Different types of dependencies can be added on the project level.

clearly identify a dependency. Figure 5.6 illustrates the relationship between the project, the dependency handler, and the actual dependencies.

Let's first look at how to declare external module dependencies, their notation, and how to configure them to meet your needs.

5.4.2 *External module dependencies*

In Gradle's terminology, external libraries, usually in the form of JAR files, are called external module dependencies. They represent a dependency on a module outside of the project hierarchy. This type of dependency is characterized by attributes that clearly identify it within a repository. In the following section, we'll discuss each attribute one by one.

DEPENDENCY ATTRIBUTES

When the dependency manager looks for a dependency on a repository, it locates it through the combination of attributes. At a minimum, a dependency needs to provide a name. Let's review the dependency attributes with the help of the Hibernate core library we examined in section 5.1.2:

- *group*: This attribute usually identifies an organization, company, or project. The group may use a dot notation, but it's not mandatory. In the case of the Hibernate library, the group is `org.hibernate`.
- *name*: An artifact's name uniquely describes the dependency. The name of Hibernate's core library is `hibernate-core`.
- *version*: A library may be available in many versions. Many times the version string consists of a major and a minor version. The version you selected for Hibernate core is `3.6.3-Final`.

- *classifier*: Sometimes an artifact defines another attribute, the classifier, which is used to distinguish artifacts with the same group, name, and version, but it needs further specification (for example, the runtime environment). Hibernate's core library doesn't provide a classifier.

Now that we've reviewed some dependency attributes, we can look more closely at how Gradle expects them to be declared in the build script.

DEPENDENCY NOTATION

To declare dependencies in your project, you can use the following syntax:

```
dependencies {
    configurationName dependencyNotation1, dependencyNotation2, ...
}
```

You first state the name of the configuration you want to assign the dependencies to and then a list of dependencies in the notation of your choice. The dependency notation comes in two flavors. You can either provide a map of attribute names and their values, or the shortcut notation as a string that separates each attribute by a colon (see figure 5.7). We'll look at both notations in the example.

Figure 5.7   Dependency attributes in shortcut notation

After defining the configuration, you can easily use it to assign the relevant Cargo dependencies. To use Cargo in your project, you'll need to provide JAR files containing the Cargo API, the core container implementations, and the Cargo Ant tasks. Thankfully, Cargo provides an UberJar, a single JAR file that packages the API and container functionality, which will make the dependency management easier. The following listing shows how to assign the relevant Cargo dependencies to the cargo configuration.

Listing 5.3   Assigning Cargo dependencies to cargo configuration

```
ext.cargoGroup = 'org.codehaus.cargo'
ext.cargoVersion = '1.3.1'

dependencies {
    cargo group: cargoGroup, name: 'cargo-core-uberjar',
        version: cargoVersion
    cargo "$cargoGroup:cargo-ant:$cargoVersion"
}
```

> Dependency declaration using map containing group, name, and version attributes

> Shortcut dependency declaration as a string

If you deal with a lot of dependencies in your project, it's helpful to break out commonly used dependency attributes as extra properties. You do that in the example code by creating and using properties for Cargo's dependency group and version attributes.

Gradle doesn't select a default repository for you. Trying to run the task deployTo-LocalTomcat without configuring a repository would result in an error, as shown in the following console output:

```
$ gradle deployToLocalTomcat
:deployToLocalTomcat FAILED

FAILURE: Build failed with an exception.

* Where: Build file '/Users/benjamin/gradle-in-action/code/
➥ chapter5/cargo-configuration/build.gradle' line: 10

* What went wrong:
Execution failed for task ':deployToLocalTomcat'.
> Could not resolve all dependencies for configuration ':cargo'.
    > Could not find group:org.codehaus.cargo, module:cargo-core-
      ➥ uberjar, version:1.3.1.
      Required by:
          :cargo-configuration:unspecified
    > Could not find group:org.codehaus.cargo, module:cargo-ant,
      ➥ version:1.3.1.
      Required by:
          :cargo-configuration:unspecified
```

So far, we haven't talked about different types of repositories and how to configure them. For the sake of getting this example running, add the following `repositories` configuration block:

```
repositories {
    mavenCentral()
}
```

There's no need to fully understand the intricacies of this code snippet. The important point is that you configured your project to use Maven Central to download the Cargo dependencies. Later in this chapter, you'll learn how to configure other repositories.

INSPECTING THE DEPENDENCY REPORT

When you run the `dependencies` help task, you can now see that the full dependency tree is printed. The tree shows the top-level dependencies you declared in the build script, as well as their transitive dependencies:

```
$ gradle dependencies
:dependencies

------------------------------------------------------------
Root project
------------------------------------------------------------

cargo - Classpath for Cargo Ant tasks.
+--- org.codehaus.cargo:cargo-core-uberjar:1.3.1
|    +--- commons-discovery:commons-discovery:0.4
|    |    \--- commons-logging:commons-logging:1.0.4
|    +--- jdom:jdom:1.0
|    +--- dom4j:dom4j:1.4
|    |    +--- xml-apis:xml-apis:1.0.b2 -> 1.3.03
|    |    +--- jaxen:jaxen:1.0-FCS
|    |    +--- saxpath:saxpath:1.0-FCS
|    |    +--- msv:msv:20020414
|    |    +--- relaxngDatatype:relaxngDatatype:20020414
```

Declared top-level dependencies in build script

Indicates both requested and selected version to resolve version conflict of library

```
|      |     \--- isorelax:isorelax:20020414
|      +--- jaxen:jaxen:1.0-FCS (*)
|      +--- saxpath:saxpath:1.0-FCS (*)
|      +--- msv:msv:20020414 (*)
|      +--- relaxngDatatype:relaxngDatatype:20020414 (*)
|      +--- isorelax:isorelax:20020414 (*)
|      +--- com.sun.xml.bind:jaxb-impl:2.1.13
|      |     \--- javax.xml.bind:jaxb-api:2.1
|      |           +--- javax.xml.stream:stax-api:1.0-2
|      |           \--- javax.activation:activation:1.1
|      +--- javax.xml.bind:jaxb-api:2.1 (*)
|      +--- javax.xml.stream:stax-api:1.0-2 (*)
|      +--- javax.activation:activation:1.1 (*)
|      +--- org.apache.ant:ant:1.7.1
|      |     \--- org.apache.ant:ant-launcher:1.7.1
|      +--- org.apache.ant:ant-launcher:1.7.1 (*)
|      +--- xerces:xercesImpl:2.8.1
|      |     \--- xml-apis:xml-apis:1.3.03 (*)
|      +--- xml-apis:xml-apis:1.3.03 (*)
|      \--- commons-logging:commons-logging:1.0.4 (*)
\--- org.codehaus.cargo:cargo-ant:1.3.1
      \--- org.codehaus.cargo:cargo-core-uberjar:1.3.1 (*)

(*) - dependencies omitted (listed previously)
```

Declared top-level dependencies in build script

Marked transitive dependencies that were excluded from dependency graph

If you examine the dependency tree carefully, you'll see that dependencies marked with an asterisk have been omitted. That means that the dependency manager selected either the same or another version of the library because it was declared as a transitive dependency of another top-level dependency. Interestingly, this is the case for the UberJar, so you don't even have to declare it in your build script. The Ant tasks library will automatically make sure that the library gets pulled in. Gradle's default resolution strategy for version conflicts is newest first—that is, if the dependency graph contains two versions of the same library, it automatically selects the newest. In the case of the library xml-apis, Gradle chooses version 1.3.03 over 1.0.b2, which is indicated by an arrow (->). As you can see, it's very helpful to analyze the information exposed by the dependency report. When you want to find out which top-level dependency declares a specific transitive dependency and why a specific version of a library has been selected or omitted, the dependency report is a good place to start. Next, we'll look at how to exclude transitive dependencies.

EXCLUDING TRANSITIVE DEPENDENCIES

When dealing with a public repository like Maven Central, you may encounter poorly maintained dependency metadata. Gradle gives you full control over transitive dependencies, so you can decide to either fully exclude all transitive dependencies or selectively exclude specific dependencies. Let's say you explicitly want to specify a different version of the library xml-apis instead of using the transitive dependency provided by Cargo's UberJar. In practice, this is often the case when some of your own functionality is built on top of a specific version of an API or framework. The next listing shows how to use the exclude method from ModuleDependency to exclude a transitive dependency.

Listing 5.4   Excluding a single dependency

```
dependencies {
    cargo('org.codehaus.cargo:cargo-ant:1.3.1') {
        exclude group: 'xml-apis', module: 'xml-apis'
    }
    cargo 'xml-apis:xml-apis:2.0.2'
}
```

⟵ **Exclusions can be declared in a shortcut or map notation.**

Notice that the exclusion attributes are slightly different from the regular dependency notation. You can use the attributes group and/or module. Gradle doesn't allow you to exclude only a specific version of a dependency, so the version attribute isn't available.

Sometimes the metadata of a dependency declares transitive dependencies that don't exist in the repository. As a result, your build will fail. This is only one of the situations when you want to have full control over transitive dependencies. Gradle lets you exclude all transitive dependencies using the transitive attribute, as shown in the following listing.

Listing 5.5   Excluding all transitive dependencies

```
dependencies {
    cargo('org.codehaus.cargo:cargo-ant:1.3.1') {
        transitive = false
    }
    // Selectively declare required dependencies
}
```

So far, you've only declared dependencies on specific versions of an external library. Let's see how to resolve the latest version of a dependency or the latest within a range of versions.

DYNAMIC VERSION DECLARATION

Dynamic version declarations have a specific syntax. If you want to use the latest version of a dependency, you'll have to use the placeholder latest.integration. For example, to declare the latest version for the Cargo Ant tasks, you'd use org.codehaus .cargo:cargo-ant:latest-integration. Alternatively, you can declare the part of the version attribute you want to be dynamic by demarcating it with a plus sign (+). The following listing shows how to resolve the latest 1.x version of the Cargo Ant library.

Listing 5.6   Declaring a dependency on the latest Cargo 1.x version

```
dependencies {
    cargo 'org.codehaus.cargo:cargo-ant:1.+'
}
```

Gradle's dependencies help task clearly indicates which version has been picked:

```
$ gradle -q dependencies

------------------------------------------------------------
Root project
------------------------------------------------------------
```

```
cargo - Classpath for Cargo Ant tasks.
\--- org.codehaus.cargo:cargo-ant:1.+ -> 1.3.1
    \--- ...
```

Another option is to select the latest within a range of versions for a dependency. To learn more about the syntax, feel free to check Gradle's online manual.

When should I use dynamic versions?

The short answer is rarely or even never. A reliable and reproducible build is paramount. Choosing the latest version of a library may cause your build to fail. Even worse, without knowing it, you may introduce incompatible library versions and side effects that are hard to find and only occur at runtime of your application. Therefore, declaring the exact version of a library should be the norm.

5.4.3   *File dependencies*

As described earlier, projects that don't use automated dependency management organize their external libraries as part of the source code or in the local file system. Especially when migrating your project to Gradle, you don't want to change every aspect of your build at once. Gradle makes it easy for you to configure file dependencies. You'll emulate this for your project by referencing the Cargo libraries in the local file system. The following listing shows a task that copies the dependencies resolved from Maven Central to the subdirectory `libs/cargo` under your user home directory.

Listing 5.7   Copying the Cargo dependencies to your local file system

```
task copyDependenciesToLocalDir(type: Copy) {
    from configurations.cargo.asFileTree                            <--|  Syntactic sugar provided by
    into "${System.properties['user.home']}/libs/cargo"               |  Gradle API; same as calling
}                                                                     |  configurations.getByName-
                                                                      |  ('cargo').asFileTree.
```

After running the task, you'll be able to declare the Cargo libraries in your `dependencies` configuration block. The next listing demonstrates how to assign all JAR files to the `cargo` configuration as a file dependency.

Listing 5.8   Declaring file dependencies

```
dependencies {
    cargo fileTree(dir: "${System.properties['user.home']}/libs/cargo",
                ➡ include: '*.jar')
}
```

Because you're not dealing with a repository that requires you to declare dependencies with a specific pattern, you also don't need to define a `repositories` configuration block. Next, we'll focus on the various repository types supported by Gradle and how they're configured.

5.5 Using and configuring repositories

Gradle puts a special emphasis on supporting existing repository infrastructures. You've already seen how to use Maven Central in your build. By using a single method call, mavenCentral(), you configured your build to target the most popular Java binary repository. Apart from the preconfigured repository support, you can also assign an arbitrary URL of a Maven or Ivy repository and configure it to use authentication if needed. Alternatively, a simple file system repository can be used to resolve dependencies. If metadata is found for a dependency, it will be downloaded from the repository as well. Table 5.2 shows the different types of repositories and what section to go to next to learn more about it.

Table 5.2   Repository types for a Gradle project

Type	Description	Where To Go for More Information
Maven repository	A Maven repository on the local file system or a remote server, or the preconfigured Maven Central	Section 5.5.2
Ivy repository	An Ivy repository on the local file system or a remote server with a specific layout pattern	Section 5.5.3
Flat directory repository	A repository on the local file system without metadata support	Section 5.5.4

Feel free to jump to the section that describes the repository you want to use in your project. In the next section, we'll look at Gradle's API support for defining and configuring repositories before we apply each of them to practical examples.

5.5.1 Understanding the repository API representation

Central to defining repositories in your project is the interface RepositoryHandler, which provides methods to add various types of repositories. From the project, these methods are invoked within your repositories configuration block. You can declare more than one repository. When the dependency manager tries to download the dependency and its metadata, it checks the repositories in the order of declaration. The repository that provides the dependency first wins. Subsequent repository declarations won't be checked further for the specific dependency. As shown in figure 5.8, each of the repository interfaces exposes different methods specific to the type of repository.

Gradle doesn't prefer any of the repository types. It's up to your project's needs to declare the repository most fitting. In the next section, we'll look at the syntax to declare Maven repositories.

5.5.2 Maven repositories

Maven repositories are among the most commonly used repository types in Java projects. The library is usually represented in the form of a JAR file. The metadata is

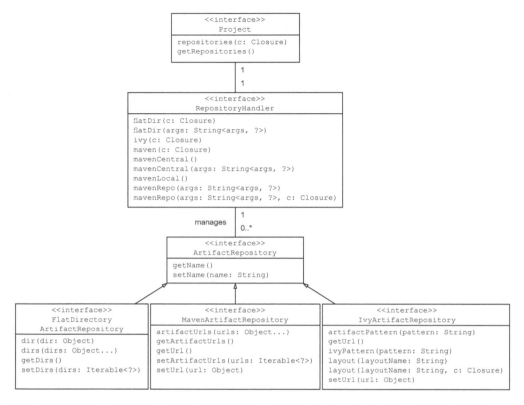

Figure 5.8   Relevant interfaces in Gradle's API for configuring various types of repositories. Gradle supports repository implementations for flat directories, Maven, and Ivy.

expressed in XML and describes relevant information about the library and its transitive dependencies, the POM file. Both artifacts are stored in a predefined directory structure in the repository. When you declare a dependency in your build script, its attributes are used to derive the exact location in the repository. The dot character in the group attribute of a dependency indicates a subdirectory in the Maven repository. Figure 5.9 shows how the Cargo Ant dependency attributes are mapped to determine the location of the JAR and POM files in the repository.

The interface RepositoryHandler provides two methods that allow you to define preconfigured Maven repositories. The method mavenCentral() adds a reference to Maven Central to the list of repositories, and the method mavenLocal() refers to a local Maven repository in your file system. Let's review both repository types and discuss when you'd use them in your project.

ADDING THE PRECONFIGURED MAVEN CENTRAL REPOSITORY

Maven Central is a commonly used repository in a build. Gradle wants to make it as easy for the build developer as possible, and therefore provides you with a shortcut to declare Maven Central. Instead of having to define the URL http://repo1.maven.org/maven2

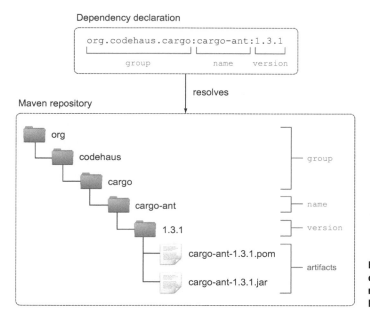

Figure 5.9 How a dependency declaration maps to artifacts in a Maven repository

each and every time, you can just call the method `mavenCentral()`, as shown in the following code snippet:

```
repositories {
    mavenCentral()
}
```

A similar shortcut exists for defining a local Maven repository that by default is available under `<USER_HOME>/.m2/repository`.

ADDING THE PRECONFIGURED LOCAL MAVEN REPOSITORY

When Gradle resolves a dependency, it's located in the repository, downloaded, and then stored in the local cache. The location of this cache in your local file system is different than the directory in which Maven stores artifacts after downloading them. You may wonder when you'd want to use a local Maven repository now that you're dealing with Gradle. This is especially the case if you work in a mixed environment of build tools. Imagine you're working on one project that uses Maven to produce a library, and another project operating with Gradle wants to consume the library. Especially during development, you'll go through cycles of implementing changes and trying out the changes on the consuming side. To prevent you from having to publish the library to a remote Maven repository for every little change, Gradle provides you with the option to target a local Maven repository, as shown in the following repository declaration:

```
repositories {
    mavenLocal()
}
```

Be aware that using a local Maven repository should be limited to this specific use case, as it may cause unforeseen side effects. You're explicitly dependent on artifacts that are only available in the local file system. Running the script on other machines or a continuous integration server may cause the build to fail if the artifacts don't exist.

ADDING A CUSTOM MAVEN REPOSITORY

There are multiple reasons why you'd want to target a repository other than Maven Central. Perhaps a specific dependency is simply not available, or you want to ensure that your build is reliable by setting up your own enterprise repository. One of the options a repository manager gives you is to configure a repository with a Maven layout. This means that it adheres to the artifact storage pattern we discussed before. Additionally, you can protect access to your repository by requiring the user to provide authentication credentials. Gradle's API supports two ways of configuring a custom repository: `maven()` and `mavenRepo()`. The following listing shows how to target an alternative public Maven repository if an artifact isn't available in Maven Central.

Listing 5.9 Declaring a custom Maven repository

```
repositories {
   mavenCentral()
   maven {
      name 'Custom Maven Repository'
      url 'http://repository-gradle-in-action.forge.cloudbees.com/release/'
   }
}
```

I can't discuss every available configuration option in this chapter, so please refer to the online documentation for more information. Let's see how an Ivy repository is different from a Maven repository and its configuration.

5.5.3 Ivy repositories

Artifacts in a Maven repository have to be stored with a fixed layout. Any deviation from that structure results in irresolvable dependencies. On the other hand, even though an Ivy repository proposes a default layout, it's fully customizable. In Ivy, repository dependency metadata is stored in a file named `ivy.xml`. Gradle provides a wide variety of methods to configure Ivy repositories and their specific layout in your build. It goes beyond the scope of this book to cover all options, but let's look at one example. Imagine you want to resolve the Cargo dependencies from an Ivy repository. The following listing demonstrates how to define the repository base URL, as well as the artifact and metadata layout pattern.

Listing 5.10 Declaring an Ivy repository

```
repositories {
   ivy {
      url 'http://repository.myenterprise.com/ivy/bundles/release'   ◁—┐  Ivy
                                                                          repository
                                                                          base URL
```

```
    layout 'pattern', {
        artifact '[organisation]/[module]/[revision]/[artifact]-
                ➥ [revision].[ext]'
        ivy '[organisation]/[module]/[revision]/ivy-[revision].xml'
    }
  }
}
```

Artifact pattern

Metadata pattern

As with the POM in Maven repositories, you're not forced to use the Ivy metadata to resolve transitive dependencies. The Ivy repository is perfect for resolving dependencies that don't necessarily follow the standard Maven artifact pattern. For example, you could decide to place JAR files into a specific directory of a web server and serve it up via HTTP. To complete our discussion about repositories, we'll look at flat directories.

5.5.4 Flat directory repositories

The simplest and most rudimentary form of a repository is the flat directory repository. It's a single directory in the file system that contains only the JAR files, with no metadata. If you're used to manually maintaining libraries with your project sources and planning to migrate to automated dependency management, this approach will interest you.

When you declare your dependencies, you can only use the attributes name and version. The group attribute is not evaluated and leads to an unresolved dependency if you try to use it. The next listing shows how to declare the Cargo dependencies as a map and shortcut notation retrieved from a flat directory repository.

Listing 5.11 Cargo dependencies declaration retrieved from a flat directory repository

```
repositories {
    flatDir(dir: "${System.properties['user.home']}/libs/cargo",
            ➥ name: 'Local libs directory')
}

dependencies {
    cargo name: 'activation', version: '1.1'
    cargo name: 'ant', version: '1.7.1'
    cargo name: 'ant-launcher', version: '1.7.1'
    cargo name: 'cargo-ant', version: '1.3.1'
    cargo name: 'cargo-core-uberjar', version: '1.3.1'
    cargo name: 'commons-discovery', version: '0.4'
    cargo name: 'commons-logging', version: '1.0.4'
    cargo name: 'dom4j', version: '1.4'
    cargo name: 'isorelax', version: '20020414'
    cargo ':jaxb-api:2.1', ':jaxb-impl:2.1.13', ':jaxen:1.0-FCS',
        ➥ ':jdom:1.0', ':msv:20020414', ':relaxngDatatype:20020414',
        ➥ ':saxpath:1.0-FCS', ':stax-api:1.0-2', ':xercesImpl:2.8.1',
        ➥ ':xml-apis:1.3.03'
}
```

Usage of dependency attributes name and version

Usage of dependency shortcut notation without group attribute

This listing also perfectly demonstrates how useful it is to be able to use metadata that automatically declares transitive dependencies. In the case of the flat directory repository, you don't have this information, so you need to declare every single dependency by itself, which can become quite tiring.

5.6   *Understanding the local dependency cache*

So far we've discussed how to declare dependencies and configure various types of repositories to resolve those artifacts. Gradle automatically determines whether a dependency is needed for the task you want to execute, downloads the artifacts from the repositories, and stores them in the local cache. Any subsequent build will try to reuse these artifacts. In this section, we'll dig deeper by analyzing the cache structure, identifying how the cache works under the hood and how to tweak its behavior.

5.6.1   *Analyzing the cache structure*

Let's explore the local cache structure through the example of your Cargo libraries. You know Gradle downloaded the JAR files when you ran the deployment task, but where did it put them? If you check the Gradle forum, you'll find that many users frequently ask for it. You can use Gradle's API to find out. The following listing shows how to print out the full, concatenated path of all dependencies assigned to the configuration cargo.

> **Listing 5.12   Printing the concatenated file path of all Cargo dependencies**

```
task printDependencies << {
    configurations.getByName('cargo').each { dependency ->
        println dependency
    }
}
```

If you run the task, you'll see that all JAR files get stored in the directory /Users/benjamin/.gradle/caches/artifacts-15/filestore:

```
$ gradle -q printDependencies
/Users/benjamin/.gradle/caches/artifacts-15/filestore/
➥ org.codehaus.cargo/cargo-core-uberjar/1.3.1/jar/
➥ 3d6aff857b753e36bb6bf31eccf9ac7207ade5b7/cargo-core-uberjar-1.3.1.jar
/Users/benjamin/.gradle/caches/artifacts-15/filestore/
➥ org.codehaus.cargo/cargo-ant/1.3.1/jar/
➥ a5a790c6f1abd6f4f1502fe5e17d3b43c017e281/cargo-ant-1.3.1.jar
...
```

This path will probably look slightly different on your machine. Let's dissect this path even more and give it some more meaning. Gradle's root directory for storing dependencies in the local cache is <USER_HOME>/.gradle/caches. The next part of the path, artifact-15, is an identifier that's specific to the Gradle version. It's needed to differentiate changes to the way metadata is stored.

Bear in mind that this structure may change with newer versions of Gradle. The actual cache is divided into two parts. The subdirectory filestore contains the raw binaries downloaded from the repository. Additionally, you'll find some binary files that store metadata about the downloaded artifacts. You'll never need to look at them during your day-to-day business. The following directory tree shows the contents from the root level of a local dependency cache:

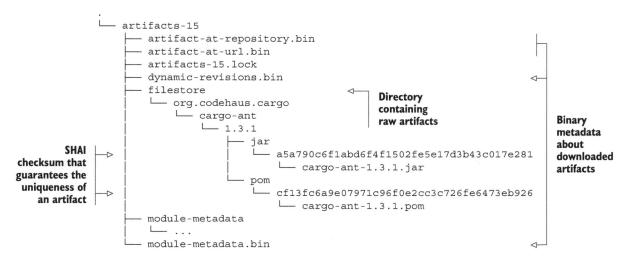

The `filestore` directory is a natural representation of a dependency. The attributes `group`, `name`, and `version` directly map to subdirectories in the file system. In the next section, we'll discuss the benefits Gradle's cache brings to your build.

5.6.2 Notable caching features

The real power of Gradle's cache lies in its metadata. It enables Gradle to implement additional optimizations that lead to smarter, faster, and more reliable builds. Let's discuss the features one by one.

STORING THE ORIGIN OF A DEPENDENCY

Imagine a situation where you declare a dependency in your script. While running the build for the first time, the dependency gets downloaded and stored in the cache. Subsequent builds will happily use the dependency available in the cache. The build is successful. What would happen if the structure of the repository were changed (for example, one of the attributes was renamed or the dependency moved or was simply deleted)—something you as an artifact consumer have no control over? With many other dependency managers like Maven and Ivy, the build would work just fine, because the dependency exists in the local cache and can be resolved. However, for any other developer that runs the build on a different machine, the build would fail. This is a problem and leads to inconsistent builds. Gradle takes a different approach to this situation. It knows the location a dependency originates from and stores this information in the cache. As a result, your build becomes more reliable.

ARTIFACT CHANGE DETECTION

Gradle tries to reduce the network traffic to remote repositories. This is not only the case for dependencies that were already downloaded. If a dependency cannot be resolved in a repository, this metadata is stored in the cache. Gradle uses this information to avoid having to check the repository every time the build runs.

REDUCED ARTIFACT DOWNLOADS AND IMPROVED CHANGE DETECTION

Gradle provides tight integration with Maven's local repository to avoid having to download existing artifacts. If a dependency can be resolved locally, it's reused. The same is true for artifacts that were stored with other versions of Gradle.

Gradle detects if an artifact was changed in the repository by comparing its local and remote checksum. Unchanged artifacts are not downloaded again and reused from the local cache. Imagine the artifact was changed on the repository but the checksum is still the same. This could happen if the administrator of the repository replaces an artifact with the same version. Ultimately, your build will use an outdated version of the artifact. Gradle's dependency manager tries to eliminate this situation by taking additional information into consideration. For example, it can ensure an artifact's uniqueness by comparing the value of the HTTP header parameter content-length or the last modified date. This is an advantage Gradle's implementation has over other dependency managers like Ivy.

OFFLINE MODE

If your build declares remote repositories, Gradle may have to check them for dependency changes. Sometimes this behavior is undesirable; for example, if you're traveling and don't have access to the Internet. You can tell Gradle to avoid checking remote repositories by running in offline mode with the --offline command-line option. Instead of performing dependency resolution over the network, only dependencies from the local cache will be used. If a required dependency doesn't exist in the cache, the build will fail.

5.7   *Troubleshooting dependency problems*

Version conflicts can be a hard nut to crack. If your project deals with many dependencies and you choose to use automatic resolution for transitive dependencies, version conflicts are almost inevitable. Gradle's default strategy to resolve those conflicts is to pick the newest version of a dependency. The dependency report is an invaluable tool for finding out which version was selected for the dependencies you requested. In the following section, I'll show how to troubleshoot version conflict and tweak Gradle's dependency resolution strategy to your specific use case.

5.7.1   *Responding to version conflicts*

Gradle won't automatically inform you that your project dealt with a version conflict. Having to constantly run the dependency report to find out isn't a practical approach to the problem. Instead, you can change the default resolution strategy to fail the build whenever a version conflict is encountered, as shown in the following code example:

```
configurations.cargo.resolutionStrategy {
    failOnVersionConflict()
}
```

Failing can be helpful for debugging purposes, especially in the early phases of setting up the project and changing the set of dependencies. Running any of the project's tasks will also indicate the version conflict, as shown in the following sample output:

```
$ gradle -q deployToLocalTomcat

FAILURE: Build failed with an exception.

* Where:
Build file '/Users/benjamin/Dev/books/gradle-in-action/code/chapter4/
➥ cargo-dependencies-fail-on-version-conflict/build.gradle' line: 10

* What went wrong:
Execution failed for task ':deployToLocalTomcat'.
> Could not resolve all dependencies for configuration ':cargo'.
    > A conflict was found between the following modules:
        - xml-apis:xml-apis:1.3.03
        - xml-apis:xml-apis:1.0.b2
```

> ### Rich API to access resolved dependency graph
>
> In memory, Gradle builds a model of the resolved dependency graph. Gradle's resolution result API gives you an even more fine-grained control over the requested and selected dependencies. A good place to start geting familiar with the API is the interface `ResolutionResult`.

5.7.2 *Enforcing a specific version*

The more projects you have to manage, the more you may feel the need to standardize the build environment. You'll want to share common tasks or make sure that all projects use a specific version of a library. For example, you want to unify all of your web projects to be deployed with Cargo version 1.3.0, even though the dependency declaration may request a different version. With Gradle, it's really easy to implement such an enterprise strategy. It enables you to enforce a specific version of a top-level dependency, as well as a transitive dependency.

The following code snippet demonstrates how to reconfigure the default resolution strategy for the configuration `cargo` to force a dependency on version 1.3.0 of the Ant tasks:

```
configurations.cargo.resolutionStrategy {
    force 'org.codehaus.cargo:cargo-ant:1.3.0'
}
```

Now when you run the dependency report task, you'll see that the requested Cargo Ant version was overruled by the globally enforced module version:

```
$ gradle -q dependencies

------------------------------------------------------------
Root project
------------------------------------------------------------
```

```
cargo - Classpath for Cargo Ant tasks.
\--- org.codehaus.cargo:cargo-ant:1.3.1 -> 1.3.0        ◄─┐  Forced module
    \--- org.codehaus.cargo:cargo-core-uberjar:1.3.0     │  version takes
        +--- ...                                            precedence
```

5.7.3 Using the dependency insight report

A change to the resolution strategy of a configuration, as shown previously, is perfectly placed in an initialization script so it can be enforced on a global level. The build script user may not know why this particular version of the Cargo Ant tasks has been picked. The only thing they saw was that the dependency report indicated that a different version was selected. Sometimes you may want to know what forced this version to be selected.

Gradle provides a different type of report: the dependency insight report, which explains how and why a dependency is in the graph. To run the report, you'll need to provide two parameters: the name of the configuration (which defaults to the com-pile configuration) and the dependency itself. The following invocation of the help task dependencyInsight shows the reason, as well as the requested and selected version of the dependency xml-apis:xml-apis:

```
$ gradle -q dependencyInsight --configuration cargo --dependency
  ➥ xml-apis:xml-apis
xml-apis:xml-apis:1.3.03 (conflict resolution)          ◄─┐  Reason why a particular
+--- org.codehaus.cargo:cargo-core-uberjar:1.3.0         │  dependency was selected
|    \--- org.codehaus.cargo:cargo-ant:1.3.0             │  is shown in brackets
|        \--- cargo
\--- xerces:xercesImpl:2.8.1
     \--- org.codehaus.cargo:cargo-core-uberjar:1.3.0 (*)

xml-apis:xml-apis:1.0.b2 -> 1.3.03                       ◄─┐  Shows requested and
\--- dom4j:dom4j:1.4                                      │  selected version of a
     \--- org.codehaus.cargo:cargo-core-uberjar:1.3.0    │  particular dependency
         \--- org.codehaus.cargo:cargo-ant:1.3.0
             \--- cargo

(*) - dependencies omitted (listed previously)
```

While the dependency report starts from the top-level dependencies of a configuration, the insight report shows the dependency graph starting from the particular dependency down to the configuration. As such, the insight report represents the inverted view of the regular dependency report, as shown in figure 5.10.

5.7.4 Refreshing the cache

To avoid having to hit a repository over and over again for specific types of dependencies, Gradle applies certain caching strategies. This is the case for snapshot versions of a dependency and dependencies that were declared with a dynamic version pattern. Once resolved, they're cached for 24 hours, which leads to snappier, more efficient builds. After the artifact caching timeframe is expired, the repository is checked again and a new version of the artifact is downloaded if it has changed.

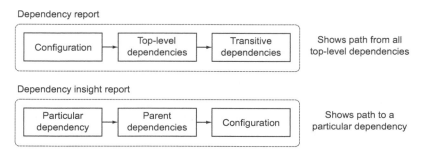

Figure 5.10 View of dependency graph with different report types

You can manually refresh the dependency in your cache by using the command-line option --refresh-dependencies. This flag forces a check for changed artifact versions with the configured repositories. If the checksum changed, the dependency will be downloaded again and replace the existing copy in the cache. Having to add the command-line options can become tiring after a while, or you may forget to tag it on. Alternatively, you can configure a build to change the default behavior of your cache.

Let's say you've always wanted to the get latest 1.x version of the Cargo Ant tasks you declared with org.codehaus.cargo:cargo-ant:1.+. You can set the cache timeout for dynamic dependency versions to 0 seconds, as shown in the following code snippet:

```
configurations.cargo.resolutionStrategy {
    cacheDynamicVersionsFor 0, 'seconds'
}
```

You may have good reasons for not wanting to cache a SNAPSHOT version of an external module. For example, another team in your organization works on a reusable library that's shared among multiple projects. During development the code changes a lot, and you always want to get the latest and (hopefully) greatest additions to the code. The following code block modifies the resolution strategy for a configuration to not cache SNAPSHOT versions at all:

```
configurations.compile.resolutionStrategy {
    cacheChangingModulesFor 0, 'seconds'
}
```

5.8   Summary

Most projects, be they open source projects or an enterprise product, are not completely self-contained. They depend on external libraries or components built by other projects. While you can manage those dependencies yourself, the manual approach doesn't fulfill the requirements of modern software development. The more complex a project becomes, the harder it is to figure out the relationships between dependencies, resolve potential version conflicts, or even know why you need a specific dependency.

With automated dependency management, you declare dependencies by unique identifiers within your project without having to manually touch the artifacts. At runtime, the dependent artifacts are automatically resolved in a repository, downloaded, stored in a local cache, and made available to your project. Automated dependency management doesn't come without challenges. We discussed potential pitfalls and how to cope with them.

Gradle provides powerful out-of-the-box dependency management. You learned how to declare different types of dependencies, group them with the help of configurations, and target various types of repositories to download them. The local cache is an integral part of Gradle's dependency management infrastructure and is responsible for high-performance and reliable builds. We analyzed its structure and discussed its essential features. Knowing how to troubleshoot dependency version conflicts and fine-tune the cache is key to a stable and reliable build. You used Gradle's dependency reporting to get a good understanding of the resolved dependency graph, as well as why a specific version of a dependency was selected and where it came from. I showed strategies for changing the default resolution strategy and cache behavior, as well as appropriate situations that make them necessary.

In the next chapter, you'll take your To Do application to the next level by modularizing the code. You'll learn how to use Gradle's multiproject build support to define dependencies between individual components and make them function as a whole.

Multiproject builds

This chapter covers

- Organizing a project's source code into subprojects
- Modeling the build for a multiproject hierarchy
- Configuring project behavior with the `Project` API
- Declaring dependencies between projects
- Customizing your build with the `Settings` API

The code base of every active software project will grow over time. What started as a small project with a handful of classes may quickly become a collection of packages and classes with different responsibilities. To improve maintainability and prevent tight coupling, you'll want to group code into modules based on particular functionality and logical boundaries. Modules are usually organized hierarchically and can define dependencies on each other. The build tool needs to be able to cope with these requirements.

Gradle provides powerful support for building modularized projects. Because every module in Gradle is a project, we call them multiproject builds (as opposed to Maven's use of multimodule builds). This chapter explains techniques for modeling

133

and executing a multiproject build with Gradle. By the end of the chapter, you'll know how to apply the technique that best fits the needs of your own project and model your build appropriately.

Gradle support for multimodule builds will be explained with the help of your To Do web application. You'll start by deconstructing the existing project structure and break out individual, functional subprojects. This newly created project layout will serve as a basis for modeling the build. Then we'll go over the options for organizing your build logic and you'll get to know the part of the Gradle API that helps define individual and common project behavior. Finally, you'll learn how to control the project execution order by declaring project dependencies, and how to execute a single subproject or the full build for all participating subprojects from the root project. Not only will this chapter teach you the structure of a multiproject build, but you'll also learn how to bring down your build's execution time, something everyone can appreciate. You'll start by refactoring the existing To Do application project structure into a modularized architecture.

6.1   Modularizing a project

In enterprise projects, the package hierarchy and class relationships can become highly complex. Separating code into modules is a difficult task, because it requires you to be able to clearly identify functional boundaries—for example, separating business logic from data persistence logic.

6.1.1   Coupling and cohesion

Two major factors will determine how easy it is to implement separation of concerns for a project: coupling and cohesion. Coupling measures the strength of relationships between specific code artifacts like classes. Cohesion refers to the degree to which components of a module belong together. The less coupled and the higher the cohesion of your code, the easier it will be to perform the restructuring of your project. Teaching good software design practices is beyond the scope of this book, but there are two guidelines you should keep in mind: minimize coupling and maximize cohesion.

An example of a modularized architecture done right is the Spring framework. Spring is an open source framework that provides a wide range of services needed in many enterprise Java applications. For example, the functionality of a service support for a simplified MVC web application development or transaction management is distributed as a JAR file. Services depend on each other if they need the functionality provided by a different module. Figure 6.1 shows all Spring modules of version 3.x and their interrelationships.

Spring's architecture may look scary at first. It defines a lot of components that depend on each other. But in practice, you won't need to import the whole framework with all components into your project. You can pick and choose which service of the framework you want to use. Thankfully, the dependencies between the components

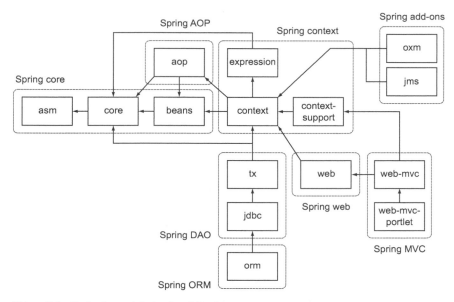

Figure 6.1 Spring's modularized architecture

are specified via metadata. Using Gradle's dependency management makes resolving these transitive dependencies a piece of cake.

In the following sections, you'll modularize the To Do application and use Gradle's multiproject features to build it. With the limited code base you have at the moment, this will be a much easier task than it is for developers of the Spring framework. We'll get started by identifying the modules for your application.

6.1.2 Identifying modules

Let's review the code you already wrote for the To Do application to find its natural boundaries. These boundaries will help you break the application code into modules. The following directory tree demonstrates the existing project structure:

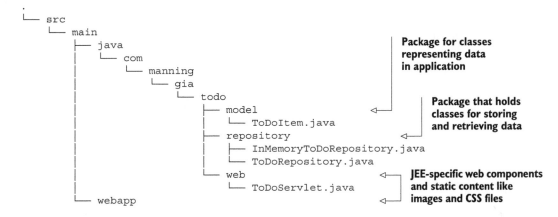

```
   ├── WEB-INF
   │    └── web.xml
   ├── css
   │    ├── base.css
   │    └── bg.png
   └── jsp
        ├── index.jsp
        └── todo-list.jsp
```

You already did a good job of separating the concerns of the application by grouping classes with specific functionality into packages. You're going to use these packages as guidelines for finding the functional boundaries of your application:

- *Model*: Data representation of to-do items
- *Repository*: Storage and retrieval of to-do items
- *Web*: Web components for handling HTTP requests and rendering to-do items and functionality in the browser

Even in your fairly simple application, these modules have relationships between each other. For example, the classes in the Repository module use the Model data classes to transport the data in and out of the data storage. Figure 6.2 gives the full picture of all proposed modules and their relationships.

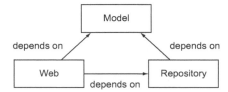

Figure 6.2   Proposed modules for the To Do application

With the identified modules and their relationships in mind, you can get started breaking them out of the single project.

6.1.3   *Refactoring to modules*

It's easy to refactor the existing project structure into the identified modules. For each of the modules, you'll create a subdirectory with the appropriate name and move the relevant files underneath it. The default source directory src/main/java will stay intact for each of the modules. The only module that requires the default web application source directory src/main/webapp is the Web module. The following directory tree shows the modularized project structure:

```
.
├── model                              ◁┐    Model module
│    └── src                            │    containing To Do data
│         └── main                      │    representation classes
│              └── java
│                   └── com
│                        └── manning
│                             └── gia
│                                  └── todo
│                                       └── model
│                                            └── ToDoItem.java
```

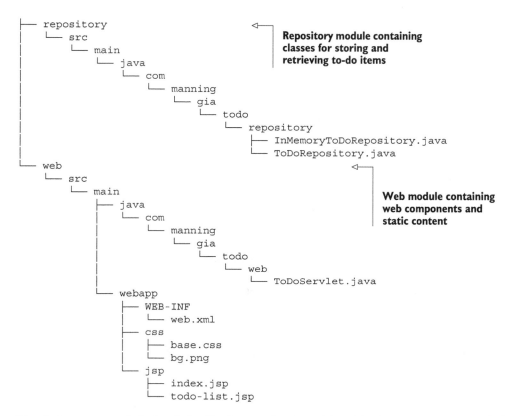

```
├── repository                          ◁──┐   Repository module containing
│   └── src                                │   classes for storing and
│       └── main                           │   retrieving to-do items
│           └── java
│               └── com
│                   └── manning
│                       └── gia
│                           └── todo
│                               └── repository
│                                   ├── InMemoryToDoRepository.java
│                                   └── ToDoRepository.java
└── web                                 ◁──┐
    └── src                                 │   Web module containing
        └── main                            │   web components and
            ├── java                        │   static content
            │   └── com
            │       └── manning
            │           └── gia
            │               └── todo
            │                   └── web
            │                       └── ToDoServlet.java
            └── webapp
                ├── WEB-INF
                │   └── web.xml
                ├── css
                │   ├── base.css
                │   └── bg.png
                └── jsp
                    ├── index.jsp
                    └── todo-list.jsp
```

That's it—you modularized the To Do application. Now it's time to take care of the build infrastructure.

6.2   *Assembling a multiproject build*

In the last section, you defined a hierarchical directory structure for your project. The full project consists of a root directory and one subdirectory per module. In this section, you'll learn how to build such a project structure with Gradle.

Your starting point will be the obligatory `build.gradle` file on the root level of the directory tree. Create an empty build script and check the projects participating in your build by running `gradle projects`:

```
$ gradle projects
:projects

------------------------------------------------------------
Root project
------------------------------------------------------------

Root project 'todo'
No sub-projects
```

Gradle reports that you're only dealing with a single project. When setting up a build with more than one project, Gradle's vocabulary speaks of a multiproject build. The reason is that you'll represent each of the modules as a distinct Gradle project. From this point forward, we won't use the term *module* anymore in keeping with Gradle's syntax; we'll only talk about projects.

The overarching project located in the top-level directory is called the *root project*, and it has its own right to exist in a multiproject build. It coordinates building the subprojects and can define common or specific behavior for them. Figure 6.3 gives you a graphical overview of the hierarchical project structure you're going to achieve.

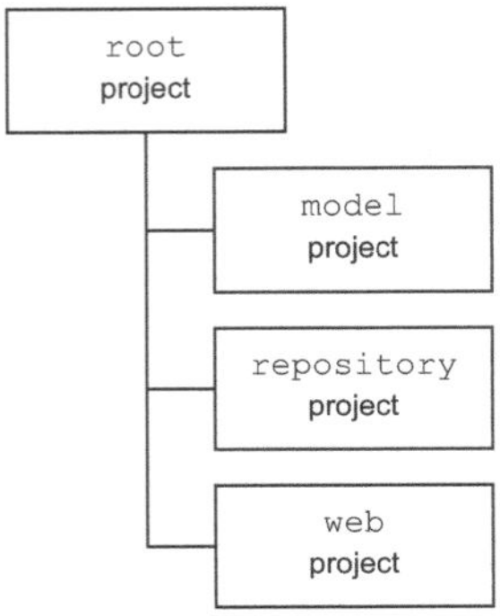

So far we've only dealt with the Gradle configuration of single-project builds. You saw that separating your code into multiple projects wasn't all that hard. What's missing is the build support that represents the root project and its subprojects. The declaration of subprojects in a multiproject build is done via the *settings file*.

Figure 6.3 Hierarchical multiproject structure for To Do application, which defines three subprojects

6.2.1 Introducing the settings file

The settings file declares the configuration required to instantiate the project's hierarchy. By default, this file is named `settings.gradle` and is created alongside the `build.gradle` file of the root project. The following listing shows the contents of the settings file. For each of the subprojects you want to be part of the build, you call the method `include` with the argument of the project's path.

Listing 6.1 Settings file that adds subproject by path

```
include 'model'
include 'repository', 'web'
```
Instead of calling method include for each project individually, pass a String[] of projects to a single call

Adds given subproject to build; argument passed to include method is project path, not file path

The supplied project path in this snippet is the project directory relative to the root directory. Keep in mind that you can also model a deeper project hierarchy. A colon character (`:`) separates each level of the subproject hierarchy. For example, if you wanted to map the directory structure `model/todo/items`, you'd add the subproject via the path `model:todo:items`.

Executing the help task `projects` after adding the settings file will produce a different result:

```
$ gradle projects
:projects

------------------------------------------------------------
Root project
------------------------------------------------------------
```

```
Root project 'todo'
+--- Project ':model'
+--- Project ':repository'
\--- Project ':web'
```

| Subprojects are displayed in the form of an indented, hierarchical tree

By adding a single settings file, you created a multimodule build containing a root project and three subprojects. No additional configuration was needed. Let's go deeper into the details of the settings file. You may have guessed already that there's an API representation for it that you can use to query and modify the configuration of your build.

6.2.2 Understanding the Settings API representation

Before Gradle assembles the build, it creates an instance of type `Settings`. The interface `Settings` is a direct representation of the settings file. Its main purpose is to add the `Project` instances that are supposed to participate in a multiproject build. In addition to assembling your multiproject build, you can do everything you're used to in your `build.gradle` script because you have direct access to the `Gradle` and `Project` interfaces. Figure 6.4 shows the relevant methods of the `Settings` interface and its associations.

The important takeaway here is that you're coding toward an instance of the interface `Settings` in your `settings.gradle` file. Any method of the interface `Settings` can be directly invoked as you did by calling `include`.

Next, we'll discuss when the settings file is executed during the build lifecycle and what rules are applied for resolving the file.

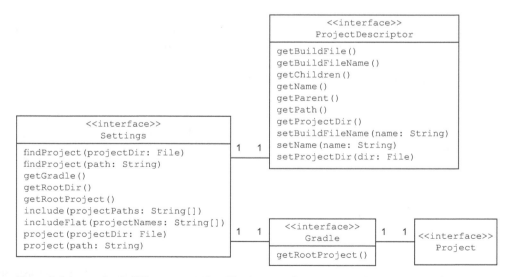

Figure 6.4 `Settings` **API representation. You can use the** `Settings` **instance to retrieve the project descriptor or project instance through the interface** `Gradle`**.**

Accessing Settings from the build file

If you need access to the `Settings` instance from your `build.gradle` file after the settings have been loaded and evaluated, you can register a lifecycle closure or listener. A great place to start is the method `Gradle#settingsEvaluated(Closure)` that provides the `Settings` object as a closure parameter.

6.2.3 *Settings execution*

Think back to chapter 4 when we discussed the three distinct lifecycle phases of a build. You may already have an idea during what phase the code of the settings file is evaluated and executed. It needs to happen during the initialization phase before any of the `Project` instances can be configured, as shown in figure 6.5.

When executing a build, Gradle automatically figures out whether a subproject is part of a single- or multiproject build. Let's examine the set of rules Gradle uses to determine the existence of a settings file.

6.2.4 *Settings file resolution*

Gradle allows you to run your build from the root project directory or any of the subproject directories as long as they contain a build file. How does Gradle know that a subproject is part of a multiproject build? It needs to find the settings file, which indicates whether the subproject is included in a multiproject build. Figure 6.6 shows the two-step process Gradle uses to find a settings file.

In step 1, Gradle searches for a settings file in a directory called `master` with the same nesting level as the current directory. If no settings file is found in step 1, Gradle searches for a settings file in the parent directories, starting from the current directory. In the case of `subproject2`, the search would be `suproject1 > root`.

If one of the steps finds a settings file and the project is included in its definition, the project is considered part of a multiproject build. Otherwise, the project is executed as a single-project build.

Step 2 in the settings file resolution process applies to a hierarchical project layout you set up earlier. Let's step back for a second and also examine the project layout shown in step 1.

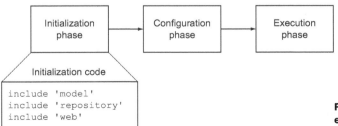

Figure 6.5   The settings file is evaluated and executed during the initialization phase.

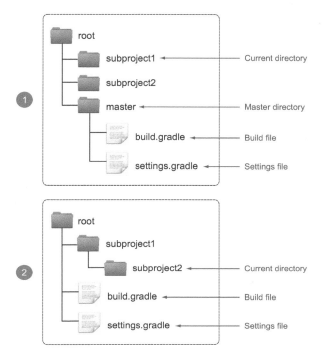

Figure 6.6   Settings file resolution is a two-step process.

Controlling the settings file search behavior

There are two command-line parameters that are helpful in determining the search behavior for a settings file:

- `-u, --no-search-upward`: Tells Gradle not to search for a settings file in parent directories. This option is useful if you want to avoid the performance hit of searching all parent directories in a deeply nested project structure.
- `-c, --settings-file`: Specifies the location of the settings file. You may want to use this option if your settings filename deviates from the standard naming convention.

6.2.5   *Hierarchical versus flat layout*

Gradle projects can be structured hierarchically or with a flat layout, as shown in figure 6.7. We speak of a flat multiproject layout if the participating projects exist on the same directory level as the root project. As a consequence, this means that the nesting level for subprojects can only be one level deep. The layout you choose for your project is up to you. Personally, I prefer the hierarchical project layout, as it gives you a more fine-grained control to model your components.

Figure 6.7 compares the differences between setting up the To Do application project with a hierarchical and a flat layout. Instead of putting the build and settings file on the root level of the project, you'll have to create a dedicated directory alongside

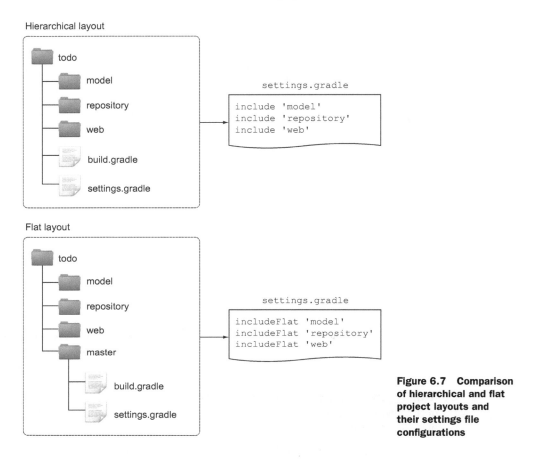

Figure 6.7   Comparison of hierarchical and flat project layouts and their settings file configurations

your other subprojects. Choose the directory name `master` so you can execute the build from your subprojects, as discussed in the previous section. To indicate that you want to include projects on the same project nesting level as the root project, use the method `includeFlat` in the settings file.

In the next section, you'll configure the build logic for each of the projects in your build.

6.3   *Configuring subprojects*

So far, you've split your application code based on functional responsibilities and rearranged it into individual subprojects. Now, you'll take a similar approach to organizing your build logic in a maintainable fashion. The following points represent requirements common to real-world multiproject builds:

- The root project and all subprojects should use the same group and version property value.
- All subprojects are Java projects and require the Java plugin to function correctly, so you'll only need to apply the plugin to subprojects, not the root project.

- The web subproject is the only project that declares external dependencies. The project type derives from the other subprojects in that it needs to build a WAR archive instead of a JAR and uses the Jetty plugin to run the application.
- Model the dependencies between the subprojects.

In this section, you'll learn how to define specific and common behaviors for projects in a multiproject build, a powerful way to avoid having to repeat configuration. Some of the subprojects may depend on the compiled source code of other projects—in your application, the code from the project model is used by the repository project. By declaring project dependencies, you can make sure imported classes are available on the classpath. Before you fill your empty build.gradle file with life, we'll review methods of the Project API I haven't shown you yet but that are relevant in the context of multiproject builds.

6.3.1 *Understanding the Project API representation*

In chapter 4, I explained the properties and methods of the Project API that you'll probably use the most in your day-to-day business. For implementing multiproject builds, you'll need to get to know some new methods, as shown in figure 6.8.

For declaring project-specific build code, the method project is used. At the very least, the path of the project (for example, :model) has to be provided.

Many times, you'll find yourself wanting to define common behavior for all your projects or only the subprojects of your build. For each of these use cases, the Project API provides a specialized method: allprojects and subprojects. Let's say you want to apply the Java plugin to all of your subprojects because you need to compile Java source code. You can do so by defining the code within the subprojects closure parameter.

The default evaluation order of projects in a multiproject build is based on their alphanumeric name. To gain explicit control over the evaluation order at configuration time of the build lifecycle, you can use the project evaluation methods evaluation-DependsOn and evaluationDependsOnChildren. This is especially the case if you need

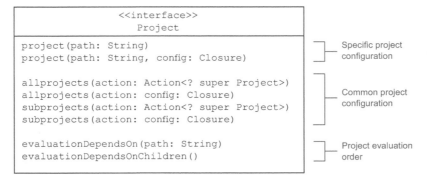

Figure 6.8   Important methods of the `Project` **API for implementing multiproject builds**

to make sure that a property is set for a project before it's used by another project. We won't discuss these methods in this chapter; for specific use cases, refer to Gradle's online manual.

In this chapter, you'll use all of the presented methods to configure your multiproject build. First, you'll take the existing build code and apply it to only specific subprojects.

6.3.2   *Defining specific behavior*

Project-specific behavior is defined with the method `project`. To set up the build infrastructure for your three subprojects—`model`, `repository`, and `web`—you'll create a project configuration block for each of them. The following listing shows the project definition within your single `build.gradle` file.

Listing 6.2   Defining project-specific build logic

```
ext.projectIds = ['group': 'com.manning.gia', 'version': '0.1']   ⟵┐

group = projectIds.group
version = projectIds.version

project(':model') {                       ⟵┐
    group = projectIds.group
    version = projectIds.version
    apply plugin: 'java'
}

project(':repository') {                   ⟵┤
    group = projectIds.group
    version = projectIds.version
    apply plugin: 'java'
}

project(':web') {                          ⟵┘
    group = projectIds.group
    version = projectIds.version
    apply plugin: 'java'
    apply plugin: 'war'
    apply plugin: 'jetty'

    repositories {
        mavenCentral()
    }

    dependencies {
        providedCompile 'javax.servlet:servlet-api:2.5'
        runtime 'javax.servlet:jstl:1.1.2'
    }
}
```

Configures each subproject by project path; actual configuration happens in the closure

Declaration of extra property projectIds as a map that holds the key-value pairs for group and version; property can be used in subprojects

You can see that the solution is far from perfect. Even though you defined an extra property for assigning the group and version for each subproject, you're still left with duplicated code and the Java plugin has to be applied for each subproject individually. For now, just get the project running. You'll improve on that code later.

> **Property inheritance**
>
> Properties defined in a project are automatically inherited by its subprojects, a concept available in other build tools like Maven. In listing 6.2, the extra property `projectIds` declared in the root project is available to the subprojects `model`, `repository`, and `web`.

From the root directory of the multiproject build, you can execute tasks for individual subprojects. All you'll need to do is name the concatenated project path and task name. Remember that paths are denoted by a colon character (:). For example, executing the task `build` for the subproject `model` can be achieved by referencing the full path on the command line:

```
$ gradle :model:build
:model:compileJava
:model:processResources UP-TO-DATE
:model:classes
:model:jar
:model:assemble
:model:compileTestJava UP-TO-DATE
:model:processTestResources UP-TO-DATE
:model:testClasses UP-TO-DATE
:model:test
:model:check
:model:build
```

This works great for the self-contained subproject `model`, because it has no dependencies on code from other subprojects. If you executed the same task for the subproject `repository`, you'd end up with a compilation error. Why is that? The subproject `repository` uses code from the subproject `model`. To function correctly, you'll need to declare a compile-time dependency on the project.

6.3.3 *Declaring project dependencies*

Declaring a dependency on another project looks very similar to declaring a dependency on an external library. In both cases, the dependency has to be declared within the closure of the `dependencies` configuration block. Project dependencies have to be assigned to a particular configuration—in your case, the configuration `compile` provided by the Java plugin. The following listing outlines the project dependency declarations for all of your subprojects.

> **Listing 6.3   Declaring project dependencies**

```
project(':model') {
   ...
}
project(':repository') {
   ...

   dependencies {
```

← **Model subproject doesn't declare any external or project dependencies**

```
        compile project(':model')
    }
}

project(':web') {
    ...

    dependencies {
        compile project(':repository')
        providedCompile 'javax.servlet:servlet-api:2.5'
        runtime 'javax.servlet:jstl:1.1.2'
    }
}
```

Declares compile-time dependency on project with path :model

Declares compile-time dependency on project with path :repository

The subproject repository depends on the subproject model, and the subproject web depends on the sibling project repository. That's all there is to modeling project dependencies. Doing so has three important implications:

- The actual dependency of a project dependency is the library it creates. In the case of the subproject model, it's the JAR file. That's why a project dependency is also called a *lib* dependency.

- Depending on another project also adds its transitive dependencies to the classpath. That means external dependencies and other project dependencies are added as well.

- During the initialization phase of the build lifecycle, Gradle determines the execution order of projects. Depending on another subproject means that it has to be built first. After all, you're depending on its library.

EXECUTING A TASK FROM THE ROOT PROJECT

After passing the initialization phase, Gradle holds an internal model of the project's dependencies in memory. It knows that the subproject repository depends on model and the subproject web depends on repository. You don't have to execute a task from a particular subproject—you can execute one for all projects of the build. Let's say you want to execute the task build from the root project. Given the fact that Gradle knows the order in which the subprojects need to be executed, you'd expect the build to play out as shown in figure 6.9.

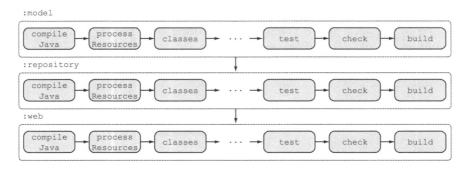

Figure 6.9   Multiproject task execution order when running the task build from the root project

You can prove the hypothesis by executing the task on the root level of your project:

```
$ gradle build
:model:compileJava
:model:processResources UP-TO-DATE
:model:classes
:model:jar
:model:assemble
:model:compileTestJava UP-TO-DATE
:model:processTestResources UP-TO-DATE
:model:testClasses UP-TO-DATE
:model:test
:model:check
:model:build
:repository:compileJava
:repository:processResources UP-TO-DATE
:repository:classes
:repository:jar
:repository:assemble
:repository:compileTestJava UP-TO-DATE
:repository:processTestResources UP-TO-DATE
:repository:testClasses UP-TO-DATE
:repository:test
:repository:check
:repository:build
:web:compileJava
:web:processResources UP-TO-DATE
:web:classes
:web:war
:web:assemble
:web:compileTestJava UP-TO-DATE
:web:processTestResources UP-TO-DATE
:web:testClasses UP-TO-DATE
:web:test
:web:check
:web:build
```

Executing a task from the root project is a real timesaver. Gradle executes the tasks that are required from all subprojects including the support for incremental builds. As much as this behavior is convenient and ensures that you'll always have the latest class files in your classpath, you may want finer-grained control over when to build all dependent subprojects.

6.3.4 Partial multiproject builds

Complex multiproject builds with tens or even hundreds of dependent subprojects will significantly influence the average execution time. Gradle will go through all project dependencies and make sure that they're up to date. During development, oftentimes you know which source files have been changed in what subproject. Technically, you don't need to rebuild a subproject that you didn't change. For these situations, Gradle provides a feature called *partial builds*. Partial builds are enabled through the command-line option -a or --no-rebuild. Suppose you only changed code in the subproject `repository` but don't want to rebuild the subproject `model`. By using partial builds, you can avoid the cost of checking the subproject `model` and bring down your build execution time. If you're working on an enterprise project with hundreds of subproject dependencies, you'll be grateful for every second you can save when executing the build. The following command-line output shows the usage of this option:

```
$ gradle :repository:build -a
:repository:compileJava
:repository:processResources UP-TO-DATE
:repository:classes
:repository:jar
:repository:assemble
:repository:compileTestJava UP-TO-DATE
:repository:processTestResources UP-TO-DATE
:repository:testClasses UP-TO-DATE
:repository:test
:repository:check
:repository:build
```

The `--no-rebuild` option works great if you're only changing files in a single project. As part of your day-to-day development practices, you'll want to pull the latest version of the source code from the repository to integrate changes made by your teammates. To ensure that code didn't break by accident, you'll want to rebuild and test the projects your current project depends on. The regular `build` task only compiles the code of dependent projects, and assembles the JAR files and makes them available as project dependencies. To run the tests as well, execute the task `buildNeeded`, as shown in the following command-line output:

```
$ gradle :repository:buildNeeded
:model:compileJava
:model:processResources UP-TO-DATE
:model:classes
:model:jar
:model:assemble
:model:compileTestJava UP-TO-DATE
:model:processTestResources UP-TO-DATE
:model:testClasses UP-TO-DATE
:model:test UP-TO-DATE
:model:check UP-TO-DATE
:model:build
:model:buildNeeded
:repository:compileJava
:repository:processResources UP-TO-DATE
:repository:classes
:repository:jar
:repository:assemble
:repository:compileTestJava UP-TO-DATE
:repository:processTestResources UP-TO-DATE
:repository:testClasses UP-TO-DATE
:repository:test UP-TO-DATE
```

```
:repository:check UP-TO-DATE
:repository:build
:repository:buildNeeded
```

Any change you make to your project may have side effects on other projects that depend on it. With the help of the task `buildDependents`, you can verify the impact of your code change by building and testing dependent projects. The following command-line output shows its use in action:

```
$ gradle :repository:buildDependents
:model:compileJava
:model:processResources UP-TO-DATE
:model:classes
:model:jar
:repository:compileJava
:repository:processResources UP-TO-DATE
:repository:classes
:repository:jar
:repository:assemble
:repository:compileTestJava UP-TO-DATE
:repository:processTestResources UP-TO-DATE
:repository:testClasses UP-TO-DATE
:repository:test UP-TO-DATE
:repository:check UP-TO-DATE
:repository:build
:web:compileJava
:web:processResources UP-TO-DATE
:web:classes
:web:war
:web:assemble
:web:compileTestJava UP-TO-DATE
:web:processTestResources UP-TO-DATE
:web:testClasses UP-TO-DATE
:web:test UP-TO-DATE
:web:check UP-TO-DATE
:web:build
:web:buildDependents
:repository:buildDependents
```

6.3.5   *Declaring cross-project task dependencies*

In the last section, you saw that executing a specific task from the root project invokes all tasks with the same name across all subprojects, with the execution order for the task `build` determined by the declared compile-time project dependencies. If your project doesn't rely on project dependencies, or defines a task with the same name for the root project and one or more subprojects, the story is different.

DEFAULT TASK EXECUTION ORDER

Let's assume you define a task named `hello` in the root project as well as all subprojects, as shown in the following listing. In each of the `doLast` actions, you print out a message on the console to indicate the project you're in.

Listing 6.4   Cross-project task definition without dependencies

```
task hello << {
    println 'Hello from root project'
}

project(':model') {
    task hello << {
        println 'Hello from model project'
    }
}

project(':repository') {
    task hello << {
        println 'Hello from repository project'
    }
}
```

Declares a task with same name for root project and all subprojects

If you run the task `hello` from the root project, you'll see the following output:

```
$ gradle hello
:hello
Hello from root project
:model:hello
Hello from model project
:repository:hello
Hello from repository project
```

None of the tasks declares a dependency on another task. So how does Gradle know in which order to execute the tasks? Simple: the task on the root level of the multiproject build is always executed first. For the subprojects, execution order is solely determined by the alphanumeric order of the names of the projects: `model` comes before `repository`. Keep in mind that the declaration order of the subprojects within the settings files doesn't play any role in the execution order.

CONTROLLING THE TASK EXECUTION ORDER

You can determine the task execution order by declaring a cross-project task dependency. To do so, you need to reference the path to the task from a different project. The next listing demonstrates how to ensure that the `hello` task from the subproject repository gets executed before the one from the subproject `model`.

Listing 6.5   Declaring cross-project task dependencies

```
task hello << {
    println 'Hello from root project'
}

project(':model') {
    task hello(dependsOn: ':repository:hello') << {
        println 'Hello from model project'
    }
}

project(':repository') {
    task hello << {
```

Declares a task dependency on task from subproject repository

```
        println 'Hello from repository project'
    }
}
```

If you run the task `hello` from the root project, you'll notice that the dependent task is executed in the correct order:

```
$ gradle hello
:hello
Hello from root project
:repository:hello
Hello from repository project
:model:hello
Hello from model project
```

Controlling the execution order between tasks across different projects isn't limited to tasks with identical names. The same mechanics apply if you need to control the execution order for tasks with different names. All you need to do is reference the full path when declaring the task dependency.

You have a basic multiproject build running and a general understanding of how to control the task execution order. Next, we'll discuss methods for defining common behavior to improve your code's readability and reusability.

6.3.6   *Defining common behavior*

In listing 6.2, you needed to apply the Java plugin to each of the subprojects individually. You also created an extra property named `projectIds` to define the group and version. You used that extra property to assign its values to the `Project` properties of the root project and its subprojects. This may not seem like a big problem in this fairly small project, but having to do this in larger projects with more than 10 subprojects can become very tedious.

In this section, you'll improve the existing code by using the `allprojects` and `subprojects` methods. Figure 6.10 provides a visual representation of how each method applies to a multiproject build.

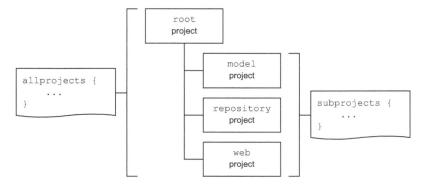

Figure 6.10   Defining common project behavior with the `Project` API

What does this mean for your project? You'll want to use the `allprojects` method for setting the `group` and `version` properties of the root project and subprojects. Because the root project doesn't define any Java code, you don't need to apply the Java plugin. Only the subprojects are Java-specific. You can use the `subprojects` method to apply the plugins to just the subprojects. The following listing demonstrates the usage of the methods `allprojects` and `subprojects` in your multiproject build.

Listing 6.6 Configuring common project behavior

```
allprojects {
    group = 'com.manning.gia'                    ◁——  Sets group and version
    version = '0.1'                                     properties for the root
}                                                        project and all subprojects

subprojects {                                    ◁——
    apply plugin: 'java'                                Applies Java plugin
}                                                        only to subprojects

project(':repository') {
    dependencies {
        compile project(':model')
    }
}

project(':web') {
    apply plugin: 'war'
    apply plugin: 'jetty'

    repositories {
        mavenCentral()
    }

    dependencies {
        compile project(':repository')
        providedCompile 'javax.servlet:servlet-api:2.5'
        runtime 'javax.servlet:jstl:1.1.2'
    }
}
```

Executing this build script will produce the same result as the previous build. However, it'll rapidly become clear that being able to define common project behavior has the potential to reduce duplicated code and improve the build's readability.

6.4 *Individual project files*

The multiproject build you've defined so far only consists of a single `build.gradle` file and the `settings.gradle` file. As you add new subprojects and tasks to your `build.gradle` file, code maintainability will suffer. Having to wade through pages and pages of code to extend or modify your build logic is no fun. You can drive the separation of concerns even further by creating individual `build.gradle` files for each of the projects.

6.4.1 Creating build files per project

You'll get started by setting up the build infrastructure. For each of the subprojects, you'll need to create a build file with the default naming convention. The following directory tree shows the end result:

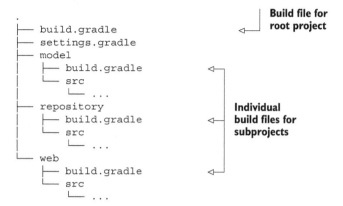

With the project files in place, you can now split up the build logic from the master build file and move it to the appropriate location.

6.4.2 Defining the root project's build code

For your project, the contents of the root-level build file will look fairly simple after stripping subproject-specific code. All you need to keep is the `allprojects` and `subprojects` configuration blocks, as shown in the following listing.

> **Listing 6.7 The root project's `build.gradle` file**

```
allprojects {
    group = 'com.manning.gia'
    version = '0.1'
}

subprojects {
    apply plugin: 'java'
}
```

The remainder of the code will be moved to the build files of your subprojects. Next, we'll focus on defining the build logic of your subprojects.

6.4.3 Defining the subprojects' build code

Remember that the `model` subproject didn't define any project-specific build logic. In fact, you didn't even have to declare a `project` configuration block. As a consequence, you won't have to declare any code in the subproject's `build.gradle` file. Gradle knows that the subproject is part of the multiproject build because you included it in the settings file.

The build files for the subprojects `repository` and `web` won't introduce any new code. You can simply take the existing `project` configuration blocks and copy them into the correct location. Having a dedicated Gradle file per project indicates that you're dealing with a specific project. Therefore, enclosing your code into a `project` closure becomes optional. The following listing shows the contents of the build file for the `repository` subproject.

Listing 6.8 The `build.gradle` file of the repository subproject

```
dependencies {
    compile project(':model')
}
```

The `build.gradle` file for the subproject `web` should look equally familiar, as shown in the next listing.

Listing 6.9 The `build.gradle` file of the `web` subproject

```
apply plugin: 'war'
apply plugin: 'jetty'

repositories {
    mavenCentral()
}

dependencies {
    compile project(':repository')
    providedCompile 'javax.servlet:servlet-api:2.5'
    runtime 'javax.servlet:jstl:1.1.2'
}
```

Running this multiproject build produces the same result as having the same code in one master build file. On the upside, you significantly improved the readability and maintainability of the build code. In the next section, I'll discuss some examples of customizing your projects even more.

6.5   *Customizing projects*

The standard Gradle build filename is `build.gradle`. In a multiproject build with many subprojects, you may want to be more expressive when it comes to naming your build files. Editing multiple `build.gradle` files in parallel and constantly switching between them easily becomes confusing when you're using an IDE. This section will explain how to configure your project to use custom build filenames.

Let's assume you want to build the following project structure: each of the subproject directory names is constructed of the prefix `todo-` and a speaking name for the project. For example, the directory for the subproject `repository` would be named `todo-repository`. The build filename, however, should only be represented by the actual project responsibility. The following directory tree shows the final result you want to accomplish:

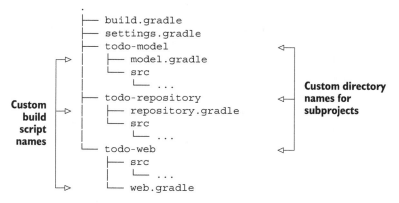

The key to making this project structure work again lies in the settings file. It provides more functionality than just telling your build which of the subprojects should be included. In fact, it's a build script itself that's executed during the initialization phase of the build lifecycle. With the help of the `Settings` API outlined in section 6.2.2, you have direct access to the root project and its children. The following listing shows how to iterate over all subprojects to assign a custom build filename. In addition, you also set a custom name for the root project.

Listing 6.10   Settings file defining custom project script names

```
include 'todo-model', 'todo-repository', 'todo-web'          ⊲─┤ Includes subprojects
                                                                by path

rootProject.name = 'todo'                                    ⊲─┐ Sets root project's name

rootProject.children.each {                                  ⊲──┐ Iterates through
    it.buildFileName = it.name + '.gradle' - 'todo-'      ⊲──┤ all subprojects
}                                                              accessible through
    Sets custom build filename for a subproject by using subprojects' names,  root project
    appending the file extension .gradle and removing the prefix todo-
```

Though this example may not apply to your real-world projects, the possibilities of configuring a multiproject build to your liking are endless. In most cases it can be achieved without much effort. Keep in mind that the `Settings` API is your best friend.

6.6   *Summary*

Modularizing a project improves the quality attributes of your system—that is, reusability, maintainability, and separation of concerns. Two guidelines make it easy to achieve that for your software: minimize coupling and maximize cohesion.

In this chapter, you split the To Do application code base into modules. You created one module that holds the model classes, one that deals with the persistence of the data, and one that exposes the web application capabilities.

Gradle treats every module as a separate project. Every project can declare dependencies on other projects. Gradle's toolbox provides extensive support for modeling and executing multiproject builds either as hierarchical or flat project structures. You learned that the settings file, executed during the initialization phase of the build lifecycle, determines which of the projects should be part of the build.

The `Project` API provides methods for declaring project-specific build code. It also allows for configuring common or subproject-specific build behavior. You learned that dependencies between projects in the current project hierarchy are declared using the same dependency mechanism as external dependencies.

The organization of your multiproject build code is very flexible. You can choose to use a single master build script, individual build scripts per project, or a mixed approach. The route you take depends on the requirements of your project. However, organizing build logic into individual scripts improves maintainability of your code the more subprojects you add to your build.

The `Settings` API available in your settings file can be used to adapt to unconventional multiproject layouts. The example demonstrated how easy it is to use custom build script names that deviate from the standard naming convention.

The next chapter is fully devoted to Gradle's test support. We'll explore the use of different test frameworks for writing unit, integration, and functional tests. We'll also discuss how to write test code for your own build scripts.

Testing with Gradle

This chapter covers

- Understanding automated testing
- Writing and executing tests with different frameworks
- Configuring and optimizing test execution behavior
- Supporting unit, integration, and functional tests in your build

In the previous chapters, you implemented a simple but fully functional web application and learned how to build and run it using Gradle. Testing your code is an important activity of the software development lifecycle. It ensures the quality of your software by checking that it works as expected. In this chapter, we'll focus on Gradle's support for organizing, configuring, and executing test code. In particular, you'll write unit, integration, and functional tests for your To Do application and integrate them into your build.

Gradle integrates with a wide range of Java and Groovy unit testing frameworks. By the end of this chapter, you'll write tests with JUnit, TestNG, and Spock, and execute them as part of the build lifecycle. You'll also tweak the default test execution behavior. You'll learn how easy it is to control the test logging output and to add a hook or listener to react to test lifecycle events. We'll also explore how to improve the performance of big test suites through forked test processes. Integration and functional tests require a more complex tooling setup. You'll learn how to use the third-party tools H2 and Geb to bootstrap your test code.

Before you start exercising tests with your build, let's do a quick refresher on the different types of testing as well as their individual advantages and disadvantages.

7.1   Automated testing

We're not going to cover the details of why an automated testing approach is beneficial to the quality of your project. There are many excellent books that cover this topic. Long story short: if you want to build reliable, high-quality software, automated testing is a crucial part of your development toolbox. Additionally, it'll help reduce the cost of manual testing, improve your development team's ability to refactor existing code, and help you to identify defects early in the development lifecycle.

7.1.1   Types of automated testing

Not all automated tests are alike. They usually differ in scope, implementation effort, and execution time. We categorize three types of automated tests—unit tests, integration tests, and functional tests:

- *Unit testing is performed as a task alongside the implementation of your production code and aims for testing the smallest unit of your code.* In a Java-based project this unit is a method. In a unit test you want to avoid interacting with other classes or external systems (for example, the database or file system). References to other components from within the code under test are usually isolated by test doubles, which is a generic term for a replacement of a component for testing purposes, like a Stub or Mock. Unit tests are easy to write, should execute quickly, and provide invaluable feedback about your code's correctness during development.

- *Integration testing is used to test an entire component or subsystem.* You want to make sure that the interaction between multiple classes works as expected. A typical scenario for an integration test is to verify the interaction between production code and the database. As a result, dependent subsystems, resources, and services have to be accessible during test execution. Integration tests usually take longer to execute than unit tests and are harder to maintain, and the cause of a failure may be harder to diagnose.

- *Functional testing is used to test the end-to-end functionality of an application, including the interaction with all external systems from a user's perspective.* When we talk about the user's perspective, we usually mean the user interface. Functional tests are the hardest to implement and the slowest to run, because they require emulating user interaction. In the case of a web application, the tooling for functional tests will need to be able to click a link, enter data into form fields, or submit a form within a browser window. Because user interfaces can change a lot over time, maintaining functional test code can become tedious and time-consuming.

7.1.2 *Test automation pyramid*

You may wonder which type of testing is the most appropriate for your project and to what extent. In a perfect world, you'd have a good mixture of all of these tests to ensure that your code is working correctly on different layers of architecture. However, the number of tests you write should be driven by the time and effort it takes to implement and maintain them. The easier a test is to write and the quicker it is to execute, the higher the return on investment (ROI). To optimize your ROI, your code base should contain many unit tests, fewer integration tests, and still fewer functional tests. This distribution of tests and their correlation to ROI is best illustrated by the test automation pyramid, introduced by Mike Cohn in his book *Succeeding with Agile: Software Development Using Scrum* (Addison Wesley, 2009). Figure 7.1 shows an adapted version of Cohn's test automation pyramid.

In the rest of this chapter, we'll explore how to automate unit, integration, and functional tests with Gradle. Many of Gradle's out-of-the-box testing capabilities are provided by the Java plugin. Let's start by having a closer look at these features.

7.2 *Testing Java applications*

Traditionally, test code in Java is written in Java. Popular open source testing frameworks like JUnit and TestNG help you write repeatable and structured tests. To execute these tests, you'll need to compile them first, as you do with your production source code. The purpose of test code is solely to exercise its test cases. Because you don't want to ship the compile test classes to production systems, mingling production source and test code isn't a good idea. Optimally, you'll have a dedicated directory in your project that holds test source code and another that acts as a destination directory for compiled test classes.

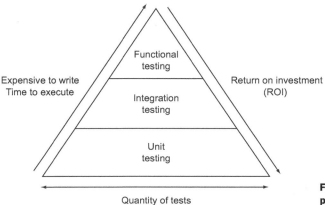

Figure 7.1 Test automation pyramid

Gradle's Java plugin does all of this heavy lifting for you. It introduces a standard directory structure for test source code and required resource files, integrates test code compilation and its execution into the build's lifecycle, and plays well with almost all of the popular testing frameworks. This is a significant improvement over implementing the same functionality in an imperative build tool like Ant. You'd easily have to write 10 to 20 lines of code to set up a testing framework for your code. If that wasn't enough, you'd have to copy the same code for every project that wants to use it.

7.2.1   *Project layout*

In chapter 3 we talked about the default directory structure for placing production source code: `src/main/java` and `src/main/resources`. A similar pattern is followed for test source code. You put test source files into the directory `src/test/java`, and required resources files consumed by your test code into `src/test/resources`. After compiling test source code, the class files end up in the output directory `build/classes/test`, nicely separated from the compiled production class files.

All testing frameworks produce at least one artifact to indicate the results of the test execution. A common format to record the results is XML. You can find these files under the directory `build/test-results`. XML files aren't very human-readable. They're usually intended for further processing by other quality assurance tools that we'll look at in chapter 12. Many testing frameworks allow for transforming the results into a report. JUnit, for example, generates an HTML report by default. Gradle places test reports under the directory `build/reports/test`. Figure 7.2 gives a visual overview of the standard test directories provided by the Java plugin.

With all this talk about testing frameworks, how do you tell Gradle to use a particular one? You'll need to declare a dependency on an external library.

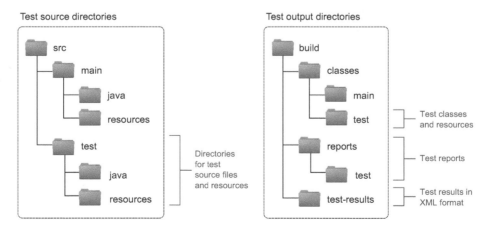

Figure 7.2   Standard test source and output directories

7.2.2 Test configurations

The Java plugin introduces two new configurations that can be used to declare dependencies on libraries required for test code compilation or execution: `testCompile` and `testRuntime`. Let's look at an example that declares a compile-time dependency on JUnit:

```
dependencies {
    testCompile 'junit:junit:4.11'
}
```

The other test configuration, `testRuntime`, is used for dependencies that aren't needed during the compilation phase of your tests, but are needed at runtime during test execution. Keep in mind that dependencies assigned to test configurations don't influence the classpath of your production code. In other words, they're not used for the compilation or packaging process. However, the test configurations extend specific configurations for handling dependencies

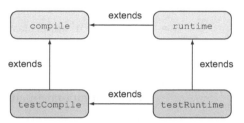

Figure 7.3   Test configuration inheritance hierarchy

needed for your production source code, as shown in figure 7.3. The configuration `testCompile` is automatically assigned the dependencies of the configuration compile. The configuration `testRuntime` extends the runtime and `testCompile` and their configuration parents.

7.2.3 Test tasks

When executing earlier examples, you may have noticed that the task graph contained four tasks that were always up to date and therefore skipped. This is because you hadn't written any test code that Gradle would need to compile or execute. Figure 7.4 shows the test tasks provided by the Java plugin and how they fit into the existing order of tasks.

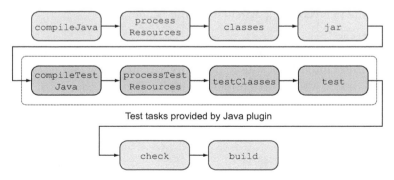

Figure 7.4   Test tasks seamlessly integrate into the build lifecycle.

As shown in the figure, test compilation and execution happen after the production code is compiled and packaged. If you want to avoid executing the test phase, you can run `gradle jar` on the command line or make your task definition depend on the task `jar`.

7.2.4   *Automatic test detection*

Of the compiled test classes in `build/classes/test`, how does Gradle figure out which ones to run? The short answer is that all class files in that directory that match the following descriptions are inspected:

- Any class or superclass that extends either `junit.framework.TestCase` or `groovy.util.GroovyTestCase`.
- Any class or superclass that's annotated with `@RunWith`.
- Any class or superclass that contains at least one method annotated with `@Test`. (The annotation can either be the JUnit or TestNG implementation.)

If none of these rules apply or the scanned class is abstract, it won't be executed. It's time to apply what you've learned in the context of a full example. In the following section, you'll write unit tests with the help of different testing frameworks and execute them with Gradle.

7.3   *Unit testing*

As a Java developer, you can pick from a wide range of testing frameworks. In this section, you'll use the traditional tools JUnit and TestNG, but also look at the new kid on the block, Spock. If you're new to any of these testing frameworks, refer to their online documentation, because we won't cover the basics of how to write a test.

7.3.1   *Using JUnit*

You'll dive right in by writing a JUnit test for the storage implementation of your To Do application: `InMemoryToDoRepository.java`. To highlight commonalities and differences between the testing frameworks and their integration with Gradle, all unit tests will verify the functionality of the same class. However, you'll adapt the test and build code to fit the needs of the particular testing framework.

WRITING THE TEST CLASS
You're going to write a test class for the subproject `repository`. The correct location to put this test is the standard test source directory. Create a new Java test class named `InMemoryToDoRepositoryTest.java` under the directory `src/test/java`:

```
.
├── build.gradle
└── src
    ├── main
    │   └── java
    │       └── com
    │           └── manning
    │
```

```
              └── gia
                  └── todo
                      └── repository
                          ├── InMemoryToDoRepository.java  ◄──┐ Class
                          └── ToDoRepository.java              │ under test
      └── test
          └── java
              └── com
                  └── manning
                      └── gia
                          └── todo
                              └── repository
                                  └── InMemoryToDoRepositoryTest.java  ◄──┐ JUnit
                                                                           │ test
                                                                           │ class
```

In the spirit of test-driven development, you formulate the assertions in such a way that they'll fail first. This gives you confidence later that your assumptions are correct. The following listing shows the JUnit test case implementation that verifies the correctness of the insert functionality.

Listing 7.1   Writing a test class using JUnit

```java
package com.manning.gia.todo.repository;

import com.manning.gia.todo.model.ToDoItem;
import org.junit.Before;
import org.junit.Test;

import java.util.List;

import static org.junit.Assert.*;

public class InMemoryToDoRepositoryTest {
    private ToDoRepository inMemoryToDoRepository;

    @Before
    public void setUp() {                                     ◄── Methods marked with this
        inMemoryToDoRepository = new InMemoryToDoRepository();    annotation are always
    }                                                            executed before every
                                                                 test method of class.
    @Test                                                    ◄── Methods marked with
    public void insertToDoItem() {                               this annotation will be
        ToDoItem newToDoItem = new ToDoItem();                   run as test case.
        newToDoItem.setName("Write unit tests");
        Long newId = inMemoryToDoRepository.insert(newToDoItem);  Wrong assertion put
        assertNull(newId);                                    ◄── there on purpose to
                                                                  provoke a failed test.
        ToDoItem persistedToDoItem = inMemoryToDoRepository.findById(newId);
        assertNotNull(persistedToDoItem);
        assertEquals(newToDoItem, persistedToDoItem);
    }
}
```

With the test class in place, let's look at adding test support to your build.

ADDING THE DEPENDENCY

You already learned about the testCompile configuration. The following listing shows how to assign the JUnit dependency with version 4.11 to the configuration. The testCompile task will now be able to use JUnit on the classpath for compiling the test source files.

Listing 7.2   Declaring a dependency on JUnit in subproject repository

```
project(':repository') {
    repositories {
        mavenCentral()
    }

    dependencies {
        compile project(':model')
        testCompile 'junit:junit:4.11'
    }
}
```

Declares a
dependency on JUnit

That's all there is to it. You enabled your build to use JUnit as a test framework in your project. Next, you'll prove your hypothesis about the failing assertion by executing the task test.

EXECUTING THE TESTS

You learned in the last section that the task test will first compile the production source, and then create the JAR file followed by test sources compilation and test execution. The following command-line output indicates a failed build due to a test assertion error:

```
$ gradle :repository:test
:model:compileJava
:model:processResources UP-TO-DATE
:model:classes
:model:jar
:repository:compileJava
:repository:processResources UP-TO-DATE
:repository:classes
:repository:compileTestJava
:repository:processTestResources UP-TO-DATE
:repository:testClasses
:repository:test

com.manning.gia.todo.repository.InMemoryToDoRepositoryTest
> testInsertToDoItem FAILED
    java.lang.AssertionError at InMemoryToDoRepositoryTest.java:24

1 test completed, 1 failed
:repository:test FAILED

FAILURE: Build failed with an exception.

* What went wrong:
Execution failed for task ':repository:test'.
> There were failing tests. See the report at:
➡ file:///Users/ben/dev/gradle-in-action/code/chapter07/junit-test-
➡ failing/repository/build/reports/tests/index.html
```

Name of failing
test method

Test file and
line of code
where the
exception
occurred

Summary of test
result including
number of completed,
failed, and skipped
test cases

Location of HTML
test report

In the console output, you can see that one of the assertions failed. This is exactly the result you expected. The displayed information doesn't indicate why the test failed. The only thing you know is that an assertion failed on line 24. If you had a huge suite of tests, finding out the cause of any failed test would require you to open the test report. You can make the test output a bit chattier by running the task on the INFO logging level:

```
$ gradle :repository:test -i
...
com.manning.gia.todo.repository.InMemoryToDoRepositoryTest
    > testInsertToDoItem FAILED
      java.lang.AssertionError: expected null, but was:<1>
      at org.junit.Assert.fail(Assert.java:88)
      at org.junit.Assert.failNotNull(Assert.java:664)
      at org.junit.Assert.assertNull(Assert.java:646)
      at org.junit.Assert.assertNull(Assert.java:656)
      at com.manning.gia.todo.repository.InMemoryToDoRepositoryTest
      ➥ .testInsertToDoItem(InMemoryToDoRepositoryTest.java:24)
...
```

Changing the logging level through a command-line option isn't the only way to control the test log output. Later in this chapter, we'll cover options in your build script for configuration test logging.

In the stack trace, you can see that the failing assertion occurred on line 24 in the class `InMemoryToRepositoryTest`. You created the assumption that the value of `newId` should be null. The reality is that every record in a data store should be uniquely identifiable, so the field needs to have a value. You'll fix the assertion in your test method by expecting a non-null ID value:

```
assertNotNull(newId);
```

Running the task `test` again shows that all tests are passing:

```
$ gradle :repository:test
:model:compileJava
:model:processResources UP-TO-DATE
:model:classes
:model:jar
:repository:compileJava
:repository:processResources UP-TO-DATE
:repository:classes
:repository:compileTestJava
:repository:processTestResources UP-TO-DATE
:repository:testClasses
:repository:test
```

Next, we'll look at the generated HTML report.

EXAMINING THE TEST REPORT

Gradle produces a more visually attractive test report than the ones created by Ant or Maven. As you learned earlier, you can find the HTML report under `build/reports/test`.

Test Summary

Figure 7.5   Successful JUnit HTML test report

Opening the index HTML page should render something like the screenshot shown in figure 7.5.

The report gives you a summary of the number of run tests, the failure rate, and the execution duration. You can switch the view between test packages and classes by clicking the tabs. In the case of at least one failed test, another tab is shown that gives you the full stack trace of the unfulfilled assertion.

Clickable report URLs

Navigating to the reports directory and double-clicking the HTML index file can become tedious over time. Sure, you could always bookmark the URL, but Gradle gives you a great shortcut for this manual task. On some operating systems, the outputted file URL in the console is clickable, which opens the HTML report in your primary browser:

- *Linux*: directly clickable in terminal
- *MacOS*: Cmd + double-click
- *Windows*: natively not supported

This feature is not only available to failed test execution. Any task that produces a report file offers a clickable URL in the console.

JUnit is the standard unit testing framework in Gradle; however, Gradle doesn't stand in the way of giving you the option of picking a different solution. Let's discuss how to integrate other unit testing frameworks or even use multiple frameworks together in a single project.

7.3.2   *Using alternative unit testing frameworks*

In your project, you may prefer to use a different unit testing framework than JUnit. The reasons for your choice might vary, but are usually based on the feature set, like out-of-the-box mocking support or the language you use to write the test. In this section, we'll cover how to use two alternatives in your build: TestNG and Spock. We won't go into detail about how to write the test classes with different unit testing frameworks. You'll be able to find examples in the source code of the book, as well as online. Instead, let's focus on the nuts and bolts of integrating these frameworks into your build.

USING TESTNG

Let's assume you wrote the same test class we discussed earlier as the TestNG test class. The package and class name will be the same. Internally, you use TestNG-specific annotations to mark relevant methods. To enable your build to execute TestNG tests, you'll need to do two things:

- Declare a dependency on the TestNG library.
- Specify that TestNG should be used to execute tests by calling the method Test#useTestNG(). Additional options can be configured through the Closure parameter of type org.gradle.api.tasks.testing.testng.TestNGOptions. See the online manual for more information.

The following listing demonstrates TestNG integration in the context of the full build script.

Listing 7.3   Enabling test support for TestNG

```
project(':repository') {
    repositories {
        mavenCentral()
    }

    dependencies {
        compile project(':model')
        testCompile 'org.testng:testng:6.8'      ⟵┐ Declares a
    }                                              dependency
                                                   on TestNG
    test.useTestNG()          ⟵┐ Enables TestNG support
}                              for your project
```

After running `gradle :repository:test` on the example, you'll notice that the task execution order is the same as in the JUnit example. Earlier versions of Gradle produced a different look and feel of the test report than the JUnit report. Starting with version 1.4, the test report looks exactly the same.

USING SPOCK

Spock is a testing and specification framework that follows the concepts of behavior-driven development (BDD). A test case written in a BDD style has a clear title and is formulated in a given/when/then narrative. Spock provides these tests through a Groovy DSL. The result is a very readable and expressive test case.

Spock is fully compatible with JUnit. Every test class needs to extend the base class for Spock specifications, spock.lang.Specification, which is part of the Spock library. This class is marked with the annotation @RunWith that allows running the tests with a specialized JUnit runner implementation.

Let's assume you wrote your test class in Groovy using Spock. To be able to compile Groovy classes in the default source directory `src/test/groovy`, your project will need to apply the Groovy plugin. The Groovy plugin requires you to declare the version of Groovy you'd like to use in your project as a dependency. Because you need to use Groovy for test source code compilation, you'll assign the library to the `testCompile` configuration. In addition to the Groovy library, you'll also declare the version of the Spock library. The next listing illustrates the setup required for compiling and executing Spock tests.

Listing 7.4   Using Spock to write and execute unit tests

```
project(':repository') {
    apply plugin: 'groovy'              ←—┤   Adds Groovy
                                            support to project
    repositories {
        mavenCentral()
    }
                                                Assigns Groovy library for
                                                test code compilation
    dependencies {
        compile project(':model')
        testCompile 'org.codehaus.groovy:groovy:2.0.6'   ←—
        testCompile 'org.spockframework:spock-core:0.7-groovy-2.0'  ←—┤  Declares a
    }                                                                     dependency on
}                                                                        Spock library
```

The produced HTML test report aligns with the look and feel of reports generated for JUnit and TestNG tests. Gradle presents you with a homogeneous reporting approach, no matter which testing framework you pick. You don't have to make one determining decision about which unit testing framework you want to use. All of these frameworks can be incorporated into one project.

7.3.3   *Multiple unit testing frameworks in harmony*

Testing strategies may change over time for long-running projects. It's not unusual for a team to switch from one testing framework to another. Clearly, you don't want to rewrite all of your existing test classes with the new and shiny testing framework you're planning to use. You want to keep them and run them as part of your build. On top of that, you want to generate a single test report that aggregates all test results. So how do you do that?

DEFINING TEST TASKS
In the previous sections, we discussed how to integrate one unit testing framework at a time. Let's assume you want to support the ability to write unit tests in all the frameworks we discussed before. One additional requirement you'll introduce to the project is a naming convention for test classes:

- *JUnit*: All tests class names end with `*Test.java`.
- *TestNG*: All test class names end with `*NGTest.java`.
- *Spock*: All test class names end with `*Spec.groovy`.

Figure 7.6 Additional test tasks integrated into build lifecycle

You've seen that TestNG support needs to be configured by calling the `useTestNG()` method. However, the default `test` task executes either JUnit or TestNG tests. To enable support for both, you'll have to add a new task of class type `Test`. Name that task `testNG`. This new task can easily be integrated into the test lifecycle by making the `test` task depend on it, as shown in figure 7.6.

The result is a build that executes all three test class types. JUnit and Spock tests are executed by the `test` task, and TestNG tests are executed by the `testNG` task. The following listing demonstrates the minor change to your existing build that provides support for multiple frameworks in one build.

Listing 7.5   Configuring build to execute JUnit, TestNG, and Spock tests

```
project(':repository') {
    apply plugin: 'groovy'

    repositories {
        mavenCentral()
    }

    dependencies {
        compile project(':model')
        testCompile 'junit:junit:4.11'
        testCompile 'org.testng:testng:6.8'
        testCompile 'org.codehaus.groovy:groovy:2.0.6'
        testCompile 'org.spockframework:spock-core:0.7-groovy-2.0'
    }

    task testNG(type: Test) {          ⊲──┤ Enhanced task for executing
        useTestNG()                        │ TestNG test classes
    }

    test.dependsOn testNG          ⊲──┤ Creates task dependency
}                                       │ on TestNG test task
```

AGGREGATING THE HTML TEST REPORTS

Executing the build with `gradle :repository:test` reveals one shortcoming: the HTML report index page doesn't contain all test results. This happens because the second run of the report generation overwrites the first one. Therefore, it only contains the JUnit and Spock test results. This can easily be fixed by merging the test results of both test tasks. The next listing shows how to create a new task of type `org.gradle .api.tasks.testing.TestReport` to generate the aggregate report.

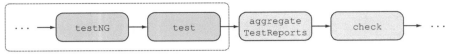

Adds report aggregation as dependency to verification task

Figure 7.7 Test report aggregation within build lifecycle

Listing 7.6 Test report aggregation

```
task aggregateTestReports(type: TestReport) {          ⟵  Adds report aggregation
    destinationDir = test.reports.html.destination         task of type TestReport
    reportOn test, testNG
}
                                                       ⟵  Integrates task into
check.dependsOn aggregateTestReports                       build lifecycle
```

To integrate this task into the build lifecycle, you added it as a dependent task to the verification task check, as shown in figure 7.7. Executing the task build will automatically aggregate the test reports.

After running gradle build, you'll find the aggregated HTML test report under the directory build/reports/test. It should look similar to the screenshot in figure 7.8.

In practice, you'll find yourself tweaking the test execution behavior to fit your needs. The next section explores available configuration options and how to apply them to your build.

7.4   *Configuring test execution*

Test execution is an essential and important phase in the lifecycle of your build. Gradle gives you a wide variety of configuration options in your build script, as well as command-line parameters to control the runtime behavior. How and when you apply

Package com.manning.gia.todo.repository

all > com.manning.gia.todo.repository

Classes

Class	Tests	Failures	Duration	Success rate
InMemoryToDoRepositoryNGTest	1	0	0.005s	100%
InMemoryToDoRepositorySpec	1	0	0.218s	100%
InMemoryToDoRepositoryTest	1	0	0.001s	100%

Figure 7.8   Aggregated HTML test report

these options depends on what you need in your build. This section will give you a short and sweet overview of frequently used functionality and the API classes behind these options. Let's start with some helpful command-line options.

7.4.1 *Command-line options*

Projects with huge test suites call for fine-grained control of the tests you'd like to execute. Every so often, you'll want to run just a single test or tests of a particular package or project. This situation quickly arises if one or more tests fail, and you'd like to fix and rerun them without taking the hit of executing the full test suite.

EXECUTING TESTS BY PATTERN

Gradle provides the following system property for applying a particular test name pattern: `<taskName>.single = <testNamePattern>`. Let's say you'd like to execute Spock tests in all packages. Spock test classes in your project have the naming convention `*Spec.groovy` (for example, `InMemoryToDoRepositorySpec.groovy`). On the command line, express this as follows:

```
$ gradle -Dtest.single=**/*Spec :repository:test
```

This is just one simple example of defining the test name pattern. For the full breadth of pattern options, refer to the online documentation of the Java plugin.

REMOTE DEBUGGING OF TESTS

The root cause of a failing test is sometimes hard to identify, especially if the test doesn't run in isolation as a unit test. Being able to remotely debug your tests with an IDE is an invaluable tool to have in your toolbox. Gradle provides a convenient shortcut for enabling remote debugging: `<taskName>.debug`, which means you can use it for other tasks as well. Using this startup parameter will start a server socket on port 5005 and block task execution until you actually connect to it with your IDE:

```
$ gradle -Dtest.debug :repository:test
...
:repository:test
Listening for transport dt_socket at address: 5005
> Building > :repository:test
```

In the meantime, you can bring up the IDE of your choice, set break points in your code, and connect to the port. Once you're connected, task execution will resume and you'll be able to step through your code. The steps for connecting the remote debugger vary from IDE to IDE. Please consult the documentation for instructions.

While these command-line options come in handy during day-to-day business, you may want to configure test execution in a more permanent way: in your build script.

7.4.2 *Understanding the Test API representation*

The API entry point that enables you to configure specific behavior for your test execution is the class `org.gradle.api.tasks.testing.Test`. The class `Test` extends `DefaultTask` and can be used to create particular test tasks in your build script. In

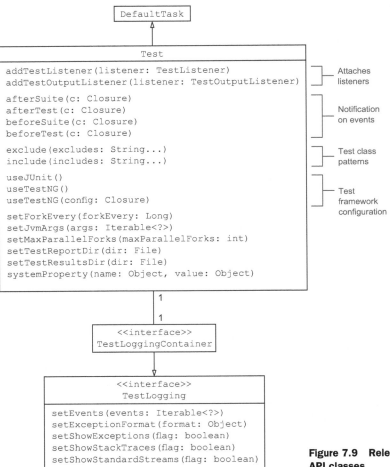

Figure 7.9   Relevant `Test` API classes

fact, the task `test` provided by the Java plugin is a preconfigured enhanced task of type `Test`. You can change the default behavior through its exposed API. Figure 7.9 shows the primary test API and its associated classes. The class diagram mainly shows the methods we'll touch on in this chapter. For a deeper dive into the API, consult the DSL guide or Javadocs.

With this class diagram in mind, you'll start by using some of these configuration options. The following scenarios will give you an idea of how to apply them.

7.4.3   *Controlling runtime behavior*

Gradle runs your tests in a forked JVM process. By doing so, you get all the benefits you usually have when starting up a Java process. You can pass in options to tweak garbage collection and performance tuning, or provide system properties for use in your code.

Let's say you made some minor changes to your test method. Instead of inserting a single to-do item, you make the number of insertable to-do items configurable through a system property named items. The method createAndInsertToDoItems, shown in the following listing, takes the value of the provided system property and determines how well you fill up your list of tasks.

Listing 7.7 Evaluating system property to drive test execution

```
public class InMemoryToDoRepositoryTest {
    ...
    @Test
    public void insertToDoItems() {
        int items = System.getProperty("items") != null ?
                    Integer.parseInt(System.getProperty("items")) : 1;
        createAndInsertToDoItems(items);
        List<ToDoItem> toDoItems = inMemoryToDoRepository.findAll();
        assertEquals(items, toDoItems.size());
    }

    private void createAndInsertToDoItems(int items) {
        System.out.println("Creating " + items + " To Do items.");

        for(int i = 1; i <= items; i++) {
            ToDoItem toDoItem = new ToDoItem();
            toDoItem.setName("To Do task " + i);
            inMemoryToDoRepository.insert(toDoItem);
        }
    }
}
```

Parses system property if provided

Prints number of to-do items about to be created and inserted

Now, how do you tell Gradle to consume a system property that drives the creation of to-do items in your test? You can simply call the method systemProperty on Test and provide a name and value as parameters. You can imagine that the higher the number of items, the easier you'll fill up your memory. While you're at it, you'll also fine-tune the JVM memory settings by calling the method jvmArgs to avoid potential OutOf-MemoryErrors. The following listing demonstrates method calls on the test task.

Listing 7.8 Providing system properties and JVM parameters

```
test {
    systemProperty 'items', '20'
    minHeapSize = '128m'
    maxHeapSize = '256m'
    jvmArgs '-XX:MaxPermSize=128m'
}
```

Sets system property

Provides JVM heap settings

Sets maximum size for JVM's Perm Gen

Depending on the number you provide for the system property items, the time it takes to complete the test might vary. You don't get direct feedback on whether the provided value is actually evaluated correctly. If you examine listing 7.7 closely, you may notice that you print out the provided number of items to the standard output stream. However, when you run the tests, you won't see that output. Let's see how to change this by taking control of test logging.

7.4.4   *Controlling test logging*

Being able to control logging can be tremendously helpful when trying to diagnose problems during test execution. The interface `TestLoggingContainer`, accessible via the property `testLogging`, is central to changing the default configuration. I encourage you to explore the class even further, because we won't cover all options.

LOGGING STANDARD STREAMS

In listing 7.7, you tried to write a message to the standard output stream. One of Gradle's `Test` configuration options is to flip a Boolean flag that prints standard output and error messages to the terminal, as shown in the following listing.

Listing 7.9   Logging standard streams to the terminal

```
test {
    testLogging {
        showStandardStreams = true          Turns on logging of standard
    }                                        output and error streams
}
```

As expected, running `gradle :repository:test` reveals your `System.out.println` statement on the terminal:

```
$ gradle :repository:test
...
:repository:test

com.manning.gia.todo.repository.InMemoryToDoRepositoryTest
    > testInsertToDoItems STANDARD_OUT
        Creating 20 To Do items.
...
```

LOGGING THE EXCEPTION STACK TRACE

Earlier you saw how to print the exception stack trace for a failed test by running the build on the INFO logging level. The drawback to this approach is that your terminal will also fill up with other messages that are irrelevant for diagnosing the cause of a failed test. You can permanently change the format for logging test exceptions via the method `exceptionFormat`. The next listing provides the value `full`, which tells Gradle to print the full stack exception traces independent of the fact that you run your build on the INFO logging level.

Listing 7.10   Displaying exception stack traces

```
test {
    testLogging {
        exceptionFormat 'full'              Shows full exception
    }                                       stack trace
}
```

LOGGING TEST EVENTS

In its default settings, Gradle's test execution doesn't give away any information that would tell you how many tests were run, and which of these passed, failed, or were skipped. Only if at least one of your tests fails will a summary be printed. The method events allows you to pass in a list of event types you'd like to be logged. The following listing demonstrates how to log a message to the terminal every time a test is started, passed, skipped, or failed.

Listing 7.11 Logging specific test events

```
test {
   testLogging {
      events 'started', 'passed', 'skipped', 'failed'   ⟵── Prints specific test events
   }                                                          during test execution
}
```

Executing tests with logging turned on for the events started, passed, skipped, and failed will produce the following result:

```
$ gradle :repository:test
...
:repository:test

com.manning.gia.todo.repository.InMemoryToDoRepositoryTest
   > testInsertToDoItem STARTED
com.manning.gia.todo.repository.InMemoryToDoRepositoryTest
   > testInsertToDoItem PASSED
...
```

Each event is logged on a single line and is color-coded. Events that didn't occur—in this case, skipped and failed—aren't logged. There are even more events to log. Refer to the online documentation to learn about all available options.

7.4.5 *Parallel test execution*

Gradle executes tests in a single, forked process. Executing huge test suites with thousands of test cases may take minutes if not hours, because they run sequentially. Given that today's computers have blazingly fast multicore processors, you should use their computing powers to their fullest.

Gradle provides a convenient way to execute your tests in parallel. All you need to specify is the number of forked JVM processes. In addition, you can set the number of maximum test classes to execute per forked test process. The next listing uses a simple formula to calculate the number of forks by available processors on your machine.

Listing 7.12 Configuring forked test processes

```
test {                                                    Maximum number of test classes
   forkEvery = 5                          ⟵──────────────  to execute in a forked test process
   maxParallelForks = Runtime.runtime.availableProcessors() / 2   ⟵──┐
}                                                        Maximum number for
                                                         test process forks
```

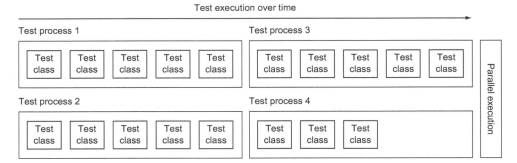

Figure 7.10   Test execution with two forked processes at a time

Let's visualize the execution behavior based on a test suite with 18 test classes. The listing shows that the number of parallel test processes is calculated based on the number of logical cores available to your JVM, either virtual or physical. Let's assume this number is four. Therefore, the assigned value of the property `maxParallel-Forks` is 2. With the property `forkEvery` set to 5, each forked test process will execute a group of five test classes. Figure 7.10 demonstrates how the test execution will play out at runtime.

The assigned numbers in this example are not set in stone. How you configure parallel test execution in your project depends on the target hardware and the type of tests (CPU or I/O bound). Try experimenting with these numbers to find the sweet spot. For more information on how to find the optimal balance on your machine, I recommend reading *Programming Concurrency on the JVM* by Venkat Subramaniam (The Pragmatic Programmers, 2011).

7.4.6   *Reacting to test lifecycle events*

In chapter 4, you learned that you can easily hook into the build lifecycle to execute code whenever an event occurs. Gradle exposes lifecycle methods for any task of type `Test`. In particular, you can listen to the following events:

- `beforeSuite`: before a test suite is executed
- `afterSuite`: after a test suite is executed
- `beforeTest`: before a test class is executed
- `afterTest`: after a test class is executed

Figure 7.11 shows how these events fit into the build lifecycle when they're registered for the default `test` task provided by the Java plugin.

Let's assume you want to find out how long it takes for the tests in your suite to finish. To figure this out, you'll hook into the test lifecycle via the `afterSuite` method. The following listing demonstrates how to use the parameters passed into the closure to calculate the elapsed execution time and send this information as a notification to the desktop.

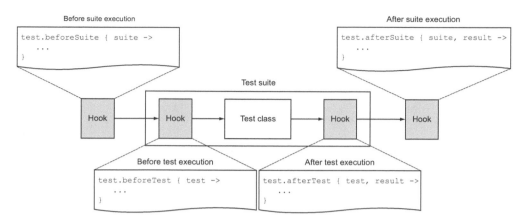

Figure 7.11   Registering test lifecycle hooks

Listing 7.13   Execute code after test suite is executed

```
apply plugin: 'announce'
                                                                    Adds closure to be
test.afterSuite { TestDescriptor suite, TestResult result -> ◁——    notified after test
    if(!suite.parent && result.getTestCount() > 0) {                suite has executed
        long elapsedTestTime = result.getEndTime() - result.getStartTime()
        announce.announce("""Elapsed time for execution of  ◁——
                        ➡ ${result.getTestCount()} test(s):        Checks if
                        ➡ $elapsedTestTime ms""", 'local')          test suite
    }                                                              contains at
}                        Uses announce plugin to show notification least one test
                         informing about test execution time
```

This is a simple and straightforward approach to displaying the test suite execution time. However, you won't have any track record of previously run test suites. You could easily send this data to a database and visualize it in a graph over time.

Registering test event methods is great for ad hoc functionality. The drawback is that you can't easily share it between projects. This is where a `TestListener` implementation comes into play.

7.4.7   *Implementing a test listener*

`TestListener` is an interface for listening to test execution events. You'll implement the same functionality as discussed in the last section. You'll create a new class called `NotificationTestListener` within the build script. The only method you'll need to fill with life is `afterSuite`. All other methods will have empty implementations. The following listing shows the full listener implementation and how to register the class with the `test` task.

Listing 7.14   Adding a test listener to the default `test` task

```
project(':repository') {
    apply plugin: 'announce'
```

```
...

    test.addTestListener(new NotificationTestListener(project))    ⟵——  Adds a test
}                                                                        listener to
                                                                        build

class NotificationTestListener implements TestListener {    ⟵
    final Project project                                          TestListener
                                                                   implementation
    NotificationTestListener(Project project) {                   that notifies user
        this.project = project                                     about test suite
    }                                                              execution time

    @Override
    void afterSuite(TestDescriptor suite, TestResult result) {
        if(!suite.parent && result.getTestCount() > 0) {
            long elapsedTestTime = result.getEndTime() - result.getStartTime()
            project.announce.announce("Elapsed time for execution of
                                ➥ ${result.getTestCount()} test(s):
                                ➥ $elapsedTestTime ms", 'local')
        }
    }

    @Override
    void afterTest(TestDescriptor testDescriptor, TestResult result) {}

    @Override
    void beforeSuite(TestDescriptor suite) {}

    @Override
    void beforeTest(TestDescriptor testDescriptor) {}
}
```

In chapter 4, you learned that you can easily share classes between projects if you put
them into the buildSrc directory. The same is true for TestListener implementations.

In this section, we took a quick flight over the most relevant configuration options.
These options aren't specific to tasks that handle unit tests. They can also be applied
to integration and functional tests. Next, we'll discuss how to write integration tests for
your To Do application and integrate them into your build.

7.5   Integration testing

A unit test verifies that the smallest unit of code in your system, a method, works correctly in isolation. This allows you to achieve a fast-running, repeatable, and consistent
test case. Integration tests go beyond the scope of unit tests. They usually integrate
other components of your system or external infrastructure like the file system, a mail
server, or a database. As a result, integration tests usually take longer to execute.
Oftentimes they also depend on the correct state of a system—for example, an existing file with specific content—making them harder to maintain.

7.5.1   Introducing the case study

A common scenario for integration tests is verifying that your persistence layer works
as expected. Currently, your application only stores objects in memory. You'll change
that by interacting with an SQL database. For your purposes, you'll use an open source

database engine called H2 (http://www.h2database.com/). H2 is easy to set up and provides fast startup times, which makes it a perfect fit for this example.

In chapter 3, you provided an interface for your persistence layer. That makes it easy to provide different implementations of ToDoRepository and interchange them in the web layer. H2 is fully compatible with JDBC. Any interaction with the database is implemented in the new class H2ToDoRepository that implements the interface. I don't want to bore you with repetitive details of a class that uses JDBC, so I won't discuss the code in detail. The downloadable code example contains all the relevant code if you want to dig deeper.

7.5.2   *Writing the test class*

It's not unusual for projects to put all types of tests in the same source directory. Given that integration tests usually take longer to execute than unit tests, you'll want to be able to separate them from each other by a naming convention. Developers will now be able to rerun unit tests on their local machine and get fast feedback about their code changes.

As the naming convention for integration tests in your project, let the test class names end with the suffix IntegTest. The integration test for the H2 repository implementation, H2ToDoRepositoryIntegTest, looks strikingly similar to the unit test. The only big difference is that the class under test is H2ToDoRepository, as shown in the following listing. The integration test code will live alongside the existing unit test class in the same package.

> **Listing 7.15   Testing H2 database persistence code**

```
package com.manning.gia.todo.repository;

import com.manning.gia.todo.model.ToDoItem;
import org.junit.Before;
import org.junit.Test;

import java.util.List;

import static org.junit.Assert.*;                          Integration tests in
                                                           application have naming
public class H2ToDoRepositoryIntegTest {          <─────  convention *IntegTest
    private ToDoRepository h2ToDoRepository;

    @Before
    public void setUp() {
        h2ToDoRepository = new H2ToDoRepository();    <──┐  Creates an instance of
    }                                                    │  H2 data access class

    @Test
    public void testInsertToDoItem() {
        ToDoItem newToDoItem = new ToDoItem();
        newToDoItem.setName("Write integration tests");
        Long newId = h2ToDoRepository.insert(newToDoItem);
        newToDoItem.setId(newId);
        assertNotNull(newId);
```

```
        ToDoItem persistedToDoItem = h2ToDoRepository.findById(newId);
        assertNotNull(persistedToDoItem);
        assertEquals(newToDoItem, persistedToDoItem);
    }
}
```

This test class verifies the same assertions as in the unit tests. In practice, you'd have many more test cases to test the interaction with the database. Next, you'll take care of the build.

7.5.3   *Supporting integration tests in the build*

The test you wrote focuses on testing the integration point between the code and the database. That means you'll need to have an accessible H2 database up and running that hosts the correct schema. It's considered good practice to provide a database instance per environment (for example, development, QA, and production). In the following section, we'll assume that you don't have to deal with managing and configuring the database. It's all set up for you. In your build, you want to support three basic requirements:

- Provide individual tasks for executing unit and integration tests.
- Separate unit and integration test results and reports.
- Make integration tests part of the verification lifecycle task check.

In the previous sections, you already learned the skills to achieve this goal. You use properties and method of the Test API. The following listing demonstrates how to include or exclude test class names with a specific naming pattern. You also override the default directory for test results and report.

Listing 7.16   Defining a task for running integration tests

```
project(':repository') {
    repositories {
        mavenCentral()                                    Adds JDBC driver
    }                                                     as runtime
                                                          dependency to be
    dependencies {                                        able to connect to
        compile project(':model')                         H2 database
        runtime 'com.h2database:h2:1.3.170'    ◁┘
        testCompile 'junit:junit:4.11'
    }                                                     Excludes integration
                                                          tests from default
    test {                                                test task
        exclude '**/*IntegTest.class'          ◁─┘
        reports.html.destination = file ("$reports.html.destination/unit")
        reports.junitXml.destination = file("$reports.junitXml.destination/
                                       ➥ unit")
    }

    task integrationTest(type: Test) {                    Only includes integration
        include '**/*IntegTest.class'          ◁─┤        tests by class naming
                                                          convention
```

Defines output directory for unit test results and report → (annotation pointing to the `reports.html.destination` and `reports.junitXml.destination` lines)

Defines output directory for unit test results and report

```
        reports.html.destination = file("$reports.html.destination/
                                    ➥ integration")
        reports.junitXml.destination = file("$reports.junitXml.destination/
                                                ➥ integration")
    }

    check.dependsOn integrationTest      ◄─┤   Adds integration
                                              tests as dependency
}                                             to check task
```

Running gradle :repository:build on the command line will invoke the test tasks that run unit and integration tests. Mixing different types of tests in the same source folder might sound like a good idea at first. With an increasing number of test classes, the test sources in your project will become hard to navigate and differentiate. You'll also have to teach every developer on your team to stick to the test class naming convention. If this pattern isn't followed meticulously, a test class might be executed in an unintended phase of the build. As you learned, integration tests usually take longer to execute than unit tests, so this would be a significant drawback. With Gradle, you can do better. You can actually enforce your own conventions by separating unit and integration tests into different source sets.

7.5.4 *Establishing conventions for integration tests*

Let's say you want to leave all your unit tests in the directory src/test/java but move the integration tests into the directory src/integTest/java. After creating the new test source directory for integration tests, the project structure should look like this:

```
.
└── src
    ├── integTest
    │   └── java                              ◄─┤   Source directory for
    │       └── com                                integration tests
    │           └── manning
    │               └── gia
    │                   └── todo
    │                       └── repository
    │                           └── H2ToDoRepositoryIntegTest.java
    ├── main
    │   └── java
    │       └── ...
    └── test
        └── java                              ◄─┤   Source directory
            └── com                                for unit tests
                └── manning
                    └── gia
                        └── todo
                            └── repository
                                └── InMemoryToDoRepositoryTest.java
```

Gradle provides a clean solution for separating different types of tests into source directories. In chapter 3, you learned how to reconfigure the default source directories provided by the Java plugin. Adding new source sets is another option. That's what you're going to do for your integration tests.

DEFINING A SOURCE SET FOR INTEGRATION TESTS

Source code in every source set definition needs to be compiled and copied to the correct directory before it can be executed. That's also true for integration tests. Remember the days when you had to implement a similar requirement with Ant? You'd have to write code similar to what you would write for compiling and executing your unit tests. How did you solve this? Usually by copying and pasting the code and modifying the targeting directories, a generally bad practice. Advanced Ant users would consider writing a custom task.

With Gradle, the approach is different. This is where some declarative magic comes into play. In your project, you define *what* you want do: add a new test source code directory. The *how*, compiling the source code, you'll leave to Gradle. In fact, Gradle automatically makes this decision for you and implicitly adds a new compilation task just for that new source set. The following listing shows how to define the new integration test source set in your project.

Listing 7.17   Defining a source set for integration tests

```
sourceSets {
    integrationTest {
        java.srcDir file('src/integTest/java')            ⊲──   Integration test
                                                                 source directory
        resources.srcDir file('src/integTest/resources')  ⊲──   Integration test
                                                                 resources directory
        compileClasspath = sourceSets.main.output
                          ⤳ + configurations.testRuntime   ⊲──   Assigns compilation
        runtimeClasspath = output + compileClasspath       ⊲──   classpath
    }                                                     Assigns runtime
}                                                         classpath
```

You can see in the source code example that the source set needs some additional configuration. It'll require you to assign the compilation classpath, which consists of the production code classes and all dependencies assigned to the configuration testRuntime. You'll also need to define the runtime classpath consisting of the compiled integration test classes directly accessible through the variable output and the compilation classpath.

USING THE SOURCE SET IN THE INTEGRATION TEST TASK

Any task of class type Test will use the default configuration if not configured otherwise. Because the class output directory of your integration test source set deviates from the default directory, you need to point the integrationTest task to it. You also need to take care of reconfiguring the task's classpath. The following code snippet shows the integrationTest task and the assigned property values:

```
                                              Points test task to directory in
                                              which to find the test classes
task integrationTest(type: Test) {
    testClassesDir = sourceSets.integrationTest.output.classesDir   ⊲──
    classpath = sourceSets.integrationTest.runtimeClasspath        ⊲──
}                                             Classpath needed for test execution
```

Give it a shot. The following output shows the result of running the `build` task on the command line:

```
$ gradle :repository:build
...
:repository:assemble
:repository:compileIntegrationTestJava
:repository:processIntegrationTestResources UP-TO-DATE
:repository:integrationTestClasses
:repository:integrationTest
:repository:compileTestJava
:repository:processTestResources UP-TO-DATE
:repository:testClasses
:repository:test
:repository:check
:repository:build
```

By adding a new source set, Gradle automatically adds required tasks to compile and process integration test source code; task names are derived from source set name.

With this build code in place, you have a nice separation of concerns between unit and integration tests. Next, we'll touch on the topic of automatically setting up the database on your local machine as part of the build.

7.5.5 *Bootstrapping the test environment*

There's one drawback to integrating with external systems. They need to be accessible from the machine you're executing the build on. If that isn't the case, your integration tests will fail. To ensure a stable testing environment, you can bootstrap the required resources from your build.

H2 provides lightweight, Java-based tools to manage and control your database, which you can easily integrate into your build. Let's say you want to model the integration test lifecycle by starting H2 first, rebuilding the whole schema through SQL scripts, running the tests against the database instance, and afterwards shutting down H2. The tasks you need to create could look similar to figure 7.12.

Bootstrapping your test environment in your build is very diverse, product-specific, and tailored to the requirements of your project. You may need to stand up a mail server or bring up another application to expose its web services. The important takeaway is that you can make this work if you need to.

It goes beyond the scope of this book to discuss the details of how to make this happen for your H2 database. However, the source code of the book provides a working sample that you can try out and explore. If you run the example, you'll find that the output of the command line looks similar to this:

Bootstraping the required database for integration tests

Figure 7.12 Starting, preparing, and stopping the database for integration testing

```
$ gradle :repository:build
...
:repository:compileTestJava
:repository:processTestResources UP-TO-DATE
:repository:testClasses
:repository:test
:repository:startDatabase
TCP server running at tcp://localhost:9092 (only local connections)
:repository:buildSchema
:repository:startAndPrepareDatabase
:repository:integrationTest
:repository:stopDatabase
Shutting down TCP Server at tcp://localhost:9092
:repository:check
:repository:build
```

Starts up local H2 database on TCP port 9092

Rebuild database schema from scratch

Stops local H2 database after integration tests are run

With a basic understanding on how to write integration tests, we'll turn our attention to the top part of the test automation pyramid: functional testing.

7.6   *Functional testing*

Functional testing is ideal for verifying that the software meets the requirements from the end user's perspective. In the context of your web application, this means simulating the user's interactions with the browser, such as entering values into text fields or clicking links. Historically, functional tests have been hard to write and costly to maintain. You need a tool that automates bringing up the browser, manipulates the data object model (DOM) of the web page, and supports running these tests against different browsers. On top of that, you also need to integrate the functional tests into your build to be able to run them in an automated and repeatable fashion. Let's look at a specific use case and an automation tool that can help you test-drive the tests.

7.6.1   *Introducing the case study*

When designing a functional test on the UI-level, it's helpful to ask yourself the following questions:

- What functionality do you want to test? For example, a to-do list has to support pagination if the number of items reaches more than 10.
- What's the high-level user workflow? For example, the user has to insert 11 to-do items before the list offers pagination.
- What are the technical steps to reach this goal? For example, the user opens a browser and enters the URL /all to view the list of to-do items. To insert a new to-do item, they enter a name for a new to-do Item and press Enter. This UI interaction calls the URL /insert, which adds the to-do item to the list. Repeat this 11 times, and verify that pagination is displayed.

For our purposes, we'll pick a simple use case: open the URL to show the list of to-do items. Insert a new to-do item named "Write functional tests" into the text field and press Enter. Verify that it was successfully added to the list by inspecting its items. This

Figure 7.13   Scripted page workflow

test assumes that the list will start with zero to-do items. Figure 7.13 demonstrates the page workflow you'll need to script.

With these UI interactions in mind, let's look at a tool that can help implement these requirements. An open source tool that can stand up to the challenge of these requirements is Geb (http://www.gebish.org/). Geb is built on top of the popular browser automation framework Selenium and allows you to define your tests with a very readable Groovy DSL. Test classes can be written with frameworks such as JUnit, TestNG, or Spock. This means that if you know any of these testing frameworks and poke through the Geb's DSL documentation, you're perfectly set up to write your first functional tests.

For now, you can assume that test classes for the business workflow described earlier are built with Geb using the test framework JUnit. This book will not teach how to write tests with Geb, as that could easily fill another one or two chapters. I'll leave it to you to explore the provided code examples. All tests are configured to work exclusively against Mozilla Firefox. If you don't have Firefox installed on your machine, now is a good time to do so. It's worth mentioning that Geb allows for executing tests against other browsers as well. For more information, check the Geb online documentation and source code examples. Next, you'll prepare the build for organizing and executing the tests.

7.6.2   *Supporting functional tests in the build*

Your functional tests require an up-and-running instance of the web application. Many organizations provide a specific runtime environment solely for this purpose. Let's say you want to modify your build to support functional tests, given that you have access to such an environment. At first sight, the requirements for the build look similar to the ones you defined for integration tests:

- Define a new source set for functional tests.
- Provide a new task for executing functional tests and generate test results/ reports into dedicated output directories.
- Integrate functional tests as part of the verification lifecycle.

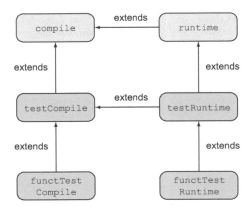

Figure 7.14   Configurations introduced for assigning functional test dependencies

INTRODUCING AND USING CUSTOM FUNCTIONAL TEST CONFIGURATIONS

Geb comes with its own set of dependencies that need to be declared. For compiling the test code, you'll need to assign the Geb JUnit implementation and the Selenium API if needed in the tests. For running the tests, you'll need to provide the Selenium driver for Firefox to remote-control the browser.

You could easily assign these dependencies to the existing testCompile and testRuntime configurations. The drawback is that you'll convolute the classpath for your unit and integration tests, which might cause version conflicts. To keep the classpath for functional tests as clean as possible and separated from other test types, we'll look at two new configurations: functTestCompile and functTestRuntime. Figure 7.14 shows how they fit into the existing configuration hierarchy introduced by the Java plugin.

The Geb tests work against the UI of your application. Therefore, it makes the most sense to add the test definitions to the web project. The following listing shows the basic setup for defining the configurations needed for functional test dependencies.

Listing 7.18   Declaring functional test configurations and dependencies

```
project(':web') {
   apply plugin: 'war'
   apply plugin: 'jetty'
   apply plugin: 'groovy'

   repositories {
      mavenCentral()
   }

   configurations {
      functTestCompile.extendsFrom testCompile          Compile and runtime
      functTestRuntime.extendsFrom testRuntime          configurations for functional tests
   }

   ext.seleniumGroup = 'org.seleniumhq.selenium'
   ext.seleniumVer = '2.32.0'
```

```
                dependencies {
                    compile project(':repository')
                    providedCompile 'javax.servlet:servlet-api:2.5'
   Declared         runtime 'javax.servlet:jstl:1.1.2'
   compile          testCompile 'org.codehaus.groovy:groovy:2.0.6'
dependencies        testCompile 'junit:junit:4.11'
on Geb JUnit        functTestCompile 'org.codehaus.geb:geb-junit4:0.7.2'
   support and      functTestCompile "$seleniumGroup:selenium-api:$seleniumVersion"
Selenium API        functTestRuntime "$seleniumGroup:selenium-firefox-
                                  ➡ driver:$seleniumVersion"      ⊲── Declared runtime
                    }                                                dependency on
                                                                    Selenium driver to
                    ...                                             remote-control Firefox
                }
```

DEFINING THE SOURCE SET AND TEST TASK

You may have noticed in listing 7.18 that the Groovy plugin was applied to your project. Geb tests are written in Groovy and need the assigned external library for compiling and running the tests. The following directory tree shows where the tests live in the example project:

```
.
└── src
     ├── functTest
     │    ├── groovy
     │    │    └── com                       ⊲── Source directory
     │    │         └── manning                  for functional tests
     │    │              └── gia                 written in Groovy
     │    │                   └── todo
     │    │                        └── web
     │    │                             ├── ToDoHomepage.groovy
     │    │                             ├── ToDoInsert.groovy
     │    │                             └── ToDoTest.groovy
     │    └── resources
     │         └── GebConfig.groovy         ⊲── Resources
     ├── main                                   directory for
     │    └── java                              functional tests
     │         └── ...
     └── test
          └── java
               └── ...
```

You'll need to set up a new source set for the functional tests that point to the directories src/functTest/groovy and src/functTest/resources. This can be achieved similarly to the way you did this for the integration test source set. The big difference is that you have to assign the custom configurations to the relevant classpath properties, as shown in the next listing.

Listing 7.19 Functional test source set

```
sourceSets {
   functionalTest {
      groovy.srcDir file('src/functTest/groovy')
      resources.srcDir file('src/functTest/resources')
```

```
    compileClasspath = sourceSets.main.output +
                       ⟿ configurations.functTestCompile   ◁──
    runtimeClasspath = output + compileClasspath +
                       ⟿ configurations.functTestRuntime   ◁──
    }
}
```

Assigning custom functional test configurations to classpath properties

After defining the new source set, you can use its class output directory and runtime classpath in a new enhanced task of class type `Test`. The following listing shows the `functionalTest` task, which writes its results and report to a custom directory.

Listing 7.20   Using the source set in the `functionalTest` task

```
task functionalTest(type: Test) {
    testClassesDir = sourceSets.functionalTest.output.classesDir
    classpath = sourceSets.functionalTest.runtimeClasspath
    reports.html.destination = file("$reports.html.destination/functional")
    reports.junitXml.destination = file("$reports.junitXml.destination/
                                    ⟿ functional")
    systemProperty 'geb.env', 'firefox'
    systemProperty 'geb.build.reportsDir', reporting.file("$name/geb")
}
```

Assigns custom test results and report directory

Mandatory Geb system properties

Geb also requires you to set some mandatory system properties. One of these properties is the name of the browser you want to run tests against. If you want to run your tests against multiple browsers, you'll need to create individual tests tasks and pass in the appropriate value. Please see the Geb documentation for more information.

With these additions to your build script, you can run the functional test against a network-reachable instance of your web application. Next, you'll go the extra mile and provide a way to run the tests exclusively on your local machine.

RUNNING FUNCTIONAL TESTS AGAINST EMBEDDED JETTY

Running the functional tests on your local machine will require you to bring up the web application in an embedded Servlet container. It'll serve up the pages for testing purposes. A benefit of this is that you don't have to rely on a server to run your tests.

You already know how to use the Jetty plugin to deploy your application. By default, the task `jettyRun` will block further build execution until the user stops the process with the keystroke Ctrl + C. This doesn't help you to run functional tests. Thankfully, the Jetty plugin can be configured to execute the embedded container in a background thread with the property `daemon`. For this purpose, you'll create enhanced tasks for starting and stopping the Servlet container, as shown in the next listing.

Listing 7.21   Declaring enhanced Jetty tasks for use with functional tests

```
ext {
    functionalJettyStopPort = 8081
    functionalJettyStopKey = 'stopKey'
}
```

```
task functionalJettyRun(type: org.gradle.api.plugins.jetty.JettyRun) {
    stopPort = functionalJettyStopPort
    stopKey = functionalJettyStopKey
    contextPath = 'todo'
    daemon = true
}
```

Enhanced task for starting an embedded Jetty container

Determines that container should be run in background (task will not be blocked)

```
task functionalJettyStop(type: org.gradle.api.plugins.jetty.JettyStop) {
    stopPort = functionalJettyStopPort
    stopKey = functionalJettyStopKey
}
```

Enhanced task for stopping embedded Jetty container

Now that you have two dedicated tasks for controlling the web application runtime environment, you can sandwich the functionalTest task in between. Figure 7.15 illustrates the order of Gradle tasks you need to model to fully integrate functional tests into the build.

Task dependency chaining is your best friend to help you achieve this goal. The last task in the chain should be the verification task check, as shown in listing 7.22. The check task is a lifecycle task provided by the Java plugin that depends on any of the verification tasks like test. This task is convenient if you want to automatically execute the whole chain of test tasks.

Listing 7.22 Integrating functional test tasks into build lifecycle

```
functionalTest.dependsOn functionalJettyRun
functionalTest.finalizedBy functionalJettyStop
check.dependsOn functionalTest
```

Starts Jetty container before exercising functional tests

Stops Jetty container after exercising functional tests

Executing the command gradle build for the web project commences the following actions: the functional test classes are compiled first, an embedded Jetty container is brought up in the background, and Firefox is automatically started and remote-controlled based on your functional test definitions. After all tests are run, Jetty is shut down. The console output of the command should look as follows:

```
$ gradle :web:build
...
:web:compileFunctionalTestJava UP-TO-DATE
:web:compileFunctionalTestGroovy
:web:processFunctionalTestResources
:web:functionalTestClasses
:web:functionalJettyRun
:web:functionalTest
:web:functionalJettyStop
...
```

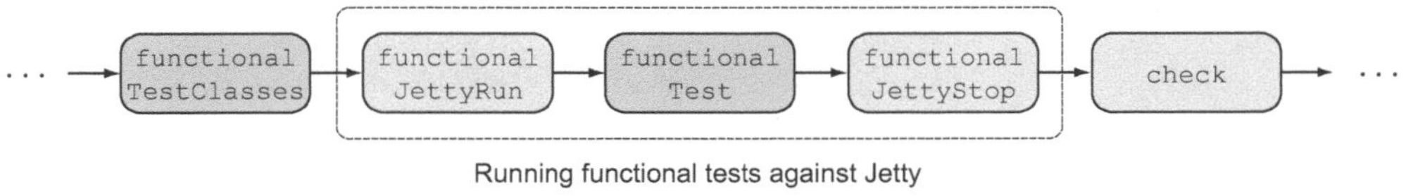

Running functional tests against Jetty

Figure 7.15 Browser test automation tasks

7.7   *Summary*

Automated testing is an essential instrument for ensuring the correctness of your application's functionality, and is a direct enabler for effective refactorings. Unit, integration, and functional tests differ in scope, implementation effort, and execution time. You saw how the test automation pyramid, introduced by Mike Cohn, shows these criteria in relation to the ROI for your project. The easier tests are to implement and the faster they can be executed, the higher the ROI ratio. And the higher the ROI of a test type, the more test cases of this type you should have.

Gradle's Java plugin provides extensive out-of-the-box testing support. By applying the plugin, your project automatically knows where to search for test classes, compiles and executes them as part of the build lifecycle, exposes configurations for assigning required test dependencies, and produces a visually attractive HTML report.

In this chapter, you learned how to implement unit tests with the help of three popular testing frameworks: JUnit, TestNG, and Spock. Gradle's `Test` API plays a significant role in configuring the test execution to your needs. The two examples we discussed in great detail can be directly applied to a real-world project. Being able to have fine-grained control over your test logging is a huge benefit when trying to identify the root cause of a failed test. Test classes that are part of large test suites can be run in parallel to minimize their execution time and utilize your hardware's processing power to its full capacity.

Integration and functional tests are harder to write and maintain than unit tests. Integration tests usually involve calling other components, subsystems, or external services. We discussed how to test an application's data persistence layer in combination with a running SQL database. Functional tests verify the correctness of your application from the user's perspective. With the help of a test automation framework, you remote-controlled the browser and emulated user interaction. You configured your build to provide a source set for different types of tests, provided new test tasks, fully integrated them into the build lifecycle, and even bootstrapped the test environment where needed.

The next chapter will talk about how to extend your build script with a plugin. Not only will you implement a fully functional, real-world plugin and use it in your build, you'll also expand on the topic of testing by verifying its functionality.

Extending Gradle

8

This chapter covers

- Gradle's extension mechanisms by example
- Writing and using script and object plugins
- Testing custom tasks and plugins
- Obtaining configuration from the build script through extension objects

In the previous chapters, we covered a lot of ground discussing how to build a self-contained sample project with Gradle. You added custom logic by declaring simple tasks and custom task classes within your build script. Often, a task becomes so useful that you'll want to share it among multiple projects. Gradle provides various approaches for reusing code, each with its own unique advantages and drawbacks. Plugins take the concept of reusability and extensibility even further. They enhance your project with new capabilities by introducing conventions and patterns for a specific problem domain.

Earlier in the book, you saw how powerful plugins are. In chapter 3, you used the Java, War, and Jetty plugins to implement a task management web application. Applying these plugins to your project was as simple as adding a single line of code and enhanced your build with new capabilities. The Java plugin adds a standardized way of compiling, testing, and bundling Java code. The War plugin allows for building a WAR file, whereas the Jetty plugin deploys in an embedded Servlet container.

All of these plugins are small, opinionated frameworks that introduce default conventions and project layouts. However, your view of the world may be different when it comes to building Java or web applications. Gradle acknowledges that customization is a must-have feature. All core plugins allow for changing the default conventions, which makes it easy to adapt to nonstandard projects.

The plugin implementation described in chapter 8 relies on RUN@Cloud for deploying and hosting a web application. Unfortunately, Cloudbees decided to decommission their service RUN@Cloud on December 31, 2014.

What does this mean for readers of this chapter?

- You cannot create an account on RUN@Cloud anymore as described in section 8.1.
- The business logic implemented by the plugin described in chapter 8 will not work as is.
- The Gradle concepts explained in chapter 8 are still highly relevant for Gradle plugin development and are applicable outside of the context used to demonstrate deployment and web application management functionality.

If you want to follow along with the content and try to run the examples, I'd suggest you select a different PaaS provider with similar capabilities. I won't give any suggestions here as they might get easily outdated as well. A Google should provide you with same valid proviers. If you don't want to rely on an external provide, you could also rewrite the plugin such that it deploys the application to a local instance of Apache Tomcat by making calls to the Tomcat manager.

In this chapter, you'll learn how to structure, implement, test, and build your own custom plugin. Our discussion will touch on topics such as development practices for reusable code, writing flexible tasks, and introducing the concept of convention over configuration. Let's start with a look at the practical application for your plugin.

8.1   Introducing the plugin case study

The running example in this book is a web-based To Do application in Java. Through Gradle's out-of-the-box plugin support, you were able to create a WAR file, deploy it to an embedded Servlet container, and test the application's functionality in the browser. I bet you're eager to show off your hard work to end users by deploying it to an internet-accessible web container. The traditional approach to hosting a web application is to manage your own web servers. Though you have full control over the infrastructure, buying and maintaining servers is expensive. Remember the last time you had to ask your infrastructure team to provide you with a server and the compatible runtime environment for your application? Provisioning the hardware and software delayed your time to market, and in the end, you didn't even have root access to tweak your application's runtime parameters. A quick and easy way to host an application is to use a platform as a service (PaaS), a combination of a deployment platform and a solution

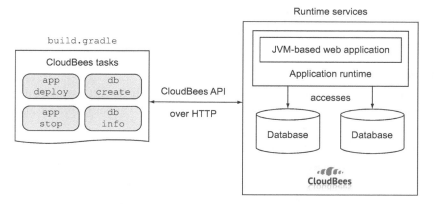

Figure 8.1 Managing CloudBees runtime services through HTTP from a Gradle build script

stack that in many cases is free of charge. A PaaS combines traditional application server functionality with support for scalability, load balancing, and high availability. Let's bring Gradle into the equation.

8.1.1 *Application management in the cloud with Gradle*

Manually deploying an application to a server is a repetitive and error-prone task. Thankfully, many PaaS providers expose an API for managing their platform services and resources programmatically. With the help of Gradle, you can automate the deployment to remote containers and make it part of the project's build lifecycle. Every web application needs to be launched to a runtime environment at some point in the development process, so it makes sense to write the code in a reusable fashion. Unfortunately, you can't fall back to an existing Gradle core plugin, so you'll need to roll your own implementation. This is a great way to practice your build tool's extension mechanism. Before you get started writing code, let's pick a PaaS provider that fulfills your requirements.

In the last couple of years many JVM PaaS providers have sprung up. Some vendors propose a programming model that requires you to conform to their specific software stack and APIs, such as a proprietary data storage implementation. You don't want to lock yourself in, because you'd like to be able to transfer the web application to a different server environment later on. You'll use CloudBees' RUN services, also called RUN@cloud, an infrastructure-agnostic deployment platform and application runtime environment. CloudBees provides a Java-based client library to communicate with runtime services over HTTP. Using the library within a Gradle script is straightforward: define it as a classpath dependency and write tasks to use the API.

Figure 8.1 demonstrates how to interact with RUN@cloud within the microcosm of a single Gradle build script. The CloudBees API provides an HTTP-based programming interface for managing services and applications on the RUN@cloud platform. But what if your coworker wants to use the same tasks in their project? Avoid the urge to just duplicate the code! Friends don't let friends copy and paste code—this maxim is true for build logic as well. The right approach is to formalize the code into a Gradle plugin. You'll start your journey by creating an account on CloudBees.

8.1.2   *Setting up the cloud environment*

Before you can interact with CloudBees' PaaS through its API, you need to provision an account. In this section, I'll walk you through the signup and application setup process.

SIGNING UP FOR A CLOUDBEES ACCOUNT

Signing up a CloudBees account is easy and should take you less than 30 seconds to complete. Open your browser and enter the following URL to render the registration page on CloudBees: https://www.cloudbees.com/signup. Figure 8.2 shows the sign-up form. It requires you to fill out your email address, name, and password, as well as a username and domain. Please note that the value you enter into the input field Domain/Account will be used to construct the service URL for your applications with the following pattern: https://[app-name].[account-name].cloudbees.net.

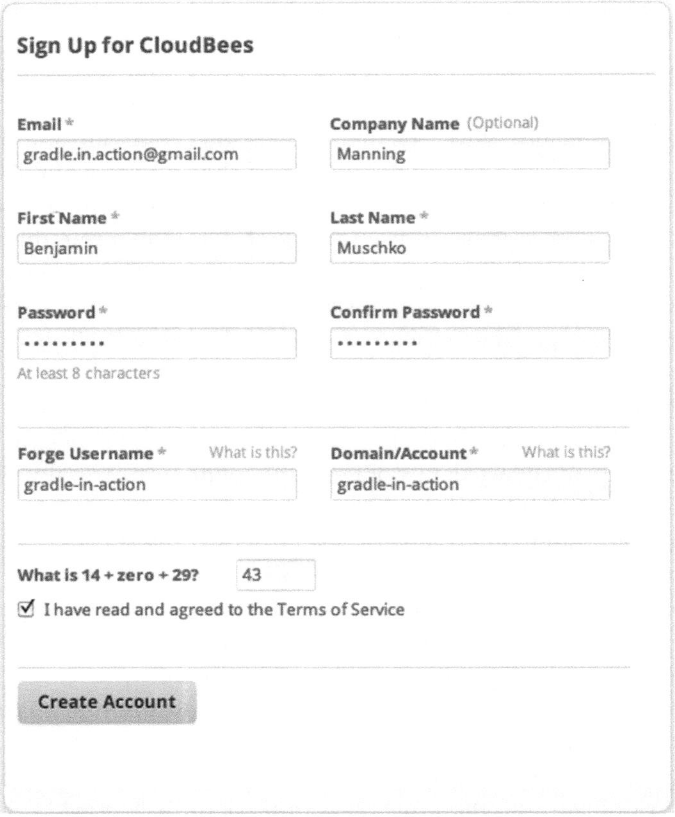

Figure 8.2   Signing up for a CloudBees account

Upon successful submission, you'll receive an email confirming your registration. You can now log in with your credentials. On the CloudBees landing page, you can find the services available to use. In this chapter we'll only concentrate on the application services.

Before you can access any of the application runtime services, you need to select a subscription plan. Click the Applications link shown in figure 8.3 and select the free RUN@cloud plan by clicking the Subscribe button. On the following page add the application service to your account.

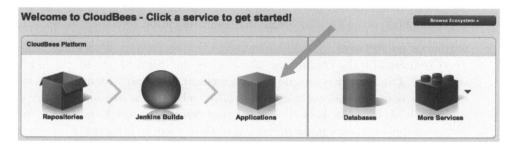

Figure 8.3   CloudBees Grand Central landing page

PROVISIONING THE APPLICATION

With application services set up, you're ready to prepare your application. To create a new application, choose the Apps menu item on top of the page or the Applications link on the landing page. Both links will bring you to the application management page. Before you can deploy any application, you'll need to provision it. Clicking the Create Application button will open a dialog, which should look similar to figure 8.4, that lets you enter the application name and supported runtime environment. Because you'll want to deploy a WAR file, choose the value JVM Web Application (WAR) from the dropdown box and enter todo into the input field to represent the application name. Click the Finish button to initiate the application creation.

That's it—the application is ready to use. You just have to enter the appropriate URL in the browser. Because I chose the account name gradle-in-action in the

Figure 8.4   Provisioning the To Do application on RUN@cloud

registration form, my application URL is http://todo.gradle-in-action.cloudbees.net. Give it a try! The application URL will already resolve even though you haven't deployed a WAR file yet.

In the management page, you can now configure the application, deploy new versions, get an overview of incoming requests, monitor memory usage and server load, and view the log files, all in one place accessible over a central dashboard. Feel free to familiarize yourself with the management functionality by browsing through the tabs.

Even though the application management dashboard is easy to use, you'd probably like to avoid manual labor at any cost. To this end, you'll use the CloudBees API, which enables you to fully automate the communication with the services backend.

SETTING UP THE API KEYS

Every request with the CloudBees API requires the caller to provide an API key and a secret key. The API key is unique to your account and clearly identifies the caller. The secret key is used to securely sign the HTTP web request to the CloudBees services. You can look up both keys under Account Settings > API Keys. Given the private nature of these values, a good practice is to store them in the gradle.properties file. You'll want to avoid checking this file into version control. Making this file public would automatically grant access to your account to everyone that has access to your source code. If you haven't created the file yet, now is a good time to do so. The following terminal commands show how to do this on *nix systems:

```
$ cd $HOME/.gradle
$ vi gradle.properties
```

In the properties file, add the following keys and replace the placeholders with the actual values of your account:

```
cloudbeesApiKey = Your-CloudBees-API-key
cloudbeesApiSecret = Your-CloudBees-API-secret
```

Setting up an account on CloudBees and provisioning an application is really painless. It probably took you less than five minutes to complete the whole process. Imagine how much work it would be to set up a similar runtime environment on a self-hosted server. Next, we'll discuss the step-by-step game plan for building the plugin.

8.2   *From zero to plugin*

Plugin development in Gradle isn't hard. You'll need to get to know some new concepts while at the same time applying techniques you've already learned in previous chapters. Gradle distinguishes two types of plugins: *script* plugins and *object* plugins. A script plugin is nothing more than a regular Gradle build script that can be imported into other build scripts. With script plugins, you can do everything you've learned so far. Object plugins need to implement the interface org.gradle.api.Plugin. The source code for object plugins usually lives in the buildSrc directory alongside your project or a standalone project and is distributed as a JAR file. In this chapter, you'll learn how to use both approaches.

In the spirit of agile development, you'll iteratively build the functionality in digestible pieces. The goal is to get a first version up and running quickly to collect early feedback. From a high-level view, you'll plan to build the CloudBees plugin in three major steps, as shown in figure 8.5. With each of the following iterations, we'll identify the drawbacks of the previous approach and discuss how to improve on it as we go along.

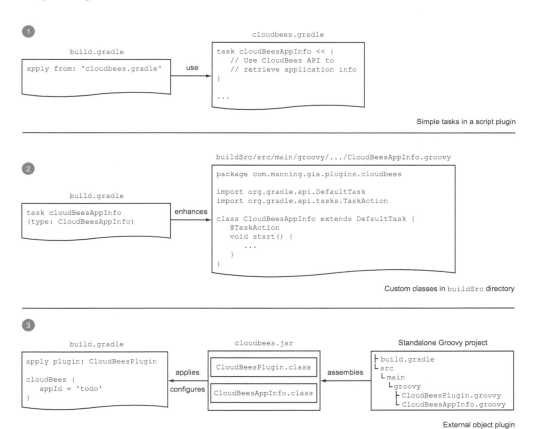

Figure 8.5   Implementing the CloudBees plugin in three steps

In the first step, I want you to become familiar with the CloudBees API and experience its functionality firsthand. You'll write two simple tasks in a script plugin: one for retrieving information on a provisioned application in your CloudBees account, and another one for deploying a WAR file to the cloud.

In step two, you'll transfer the logic you've written in task action closures and encapsulate it into custom task classes. By exposing properties, the behavior of the task classes will become highly configurable and reusable. The property values will be provided by an enhanced task, the consumer of a task class.

In the final step, you'll learn how to create a full-fledged object plugin. You'll set up a standalone Groovy project to produce the plugin JAR file.

With the master plan in place, you'll get started by writing some tasks to interact with the CloudBees client SDK.

8.3   *Writing a script plugin*

A script plugin is no different from your ordinary `build.gradle` file. You can use the same Gradle build language constructs. You'll create a new script named `cloudbees.gradle` that will contain the future CloudBees tasks. Because the build script's filename deviates from the default naming convention, you'll need to use the `-b` command-line option to invoke it. Executing `gradle -b cloudbees.gradle tasks` should only present you with the default help tasks. Before you can write the first task, the build script needs to become aware of the CloudBees API client library.

8.3.1   *Adding the CloudBees API library*

To use an external library directly in a build script, you'll need to declare it in its classpath. For that purpose, Gradle's API class `org.gradle.api.Project` exposes the method `buildscript`. The method expects a single parameter, a closure that defines the dependencies you want to resolve denoted by the `classpath` configuration. The CloudBees API client library is conveniently located on Maven Central. You can target that repository by calling the method `mavenCentral()`. The following listing demonstrates how to add the latest version of the library to the build script's classpath.

Listing 8.1   Adding the CloudBees API library to the build script's classpath

```
buildscript {
    repositories {
        mavenCentral()          Using Maven Central
    }                           to resolve declared
                                dependencies

    dependencies {                                                Adding CloudBees
        classpath 'com.cloudbees:cloudbees-api-client:1.4.0'      client API library
    }                                                             to build script's
}                                                                 classpath
```

Whenever the script is executed for the first time, the CloudBees library is downloaded and put into your local dependency cache. You'll now be able to import and use any of the CloudBees SDK classes directly in your build script. Next, you'll write your first task to interact with your CloudBees account.

8.3.2   *Using the CloudBees API from tasks*

The central class of the CloudBees API is the client implementation: `com.cloudbees.api.BeesClient`. Each of the exposed methods gives you access to a specific RUN@cloud platform service. Upon instantiation, the class expects you to provide the account credentials as well as the API's URL, format, and version. Let's look at an example:

```
BeesClient client = new BeesClient('https://api.cloudbees.com/api',
                    '24HE9X5DFF743671', '24QSXAHS1LAAVWDFAZS3TUFE6FZHK1DBYA=',
                    'xml', '1.0')
```

PREPARING THE CLIENT PROPERTIES

It's unlikely that you'll have to change the API parameters in the near future. For now, you'll define them as extra properties, as shown in the following code block:

```
ext {
    apiUrl = 'https://api.cloudbees.com/api'
    apiFormat = 'xml'
    apiVersion = '1.0'
}
```

You don't want to share the API key and secret or check it into version control. In the last section, you already made an effort to store the values in your local `gradle.properties` file. Read these values and store them in the properties `apiKey` and `secret`:

```
if(project.hasProperty('cloudbeesApiKey')) {
    ext.apiKey = project.property('cloudbeesApiKey')
}

if(project.hasProperty('cloudbeesApiSecret')) {
    ext.secret = project.property('cloudbeesApiSecret')
}
```

RETRIEVING APPLICATION INFORMATION

When setting up the CloudBees account, you provisioned an application with the name `todo`. The CloudBees API can be used to remotely retrieve information about an application without having to log on to the dashboard, as shown in the following listing.

> **Listing 8.2 Writing a task to list an available application on CloudBees account**

```
import com.cloudbees.api.ApplicationInfo
import com.cloudbees.api.BeesClient

task cloudBeesAppInfo(description: 'Returns the basic information about an
                                    application.', group: 'CloudBees') {
    inputs.property('apiKey', apiKey)
    inputs.property('secret', secret)
    inputs.property('appId', appId)

    doLast {
        BeesClient client = new BeesClient(apiUrl, apiKey, secret, apiFormat,
                                           apiVersion)
        ApplicationInfo info

        try {
            info = client.applicationInfo(appId)
        }
```

CloudBees SDK client implementation that exposes access to all services.

Declares input properties for task; if any properties aren't provided the task execution fails.

Retrieving information on application specified through input property appId.

```
        catch(Exception e) {
            throw new GradleException(e.message)
        }
        logger.quiet "Application id : $info.id"
        logger.quiet "          title : $info.title"
        logger.quiet "        created : $info.created"
        logger.quiet "           urls : $info.urls"
        logger.quiet "         status : $info.status"
    }
}
```

Use Gradle logger for printing response data to console.

Any execution failure (e.g., authentication errors from client) bubbles up as exception, which is caught and rethrown as specific Gradle exception.

Before executing the task, you'll create another Gradle script file: build.gradle. The following code snippet demonstrates how an external script can be reused:

```
apply from: 'cloudbees.gradle'
```

Note that the value of the from property in the apply method call can be any kind of URL, such as an HTTP address like http://my.scripts.com/shared/cloudbees.gradle. Script plugins exposed over HTTP(S) are perfect candidates to be shared among departments in an organization. It's time to give the task a spin. The following console output shows how to retrieve information on the application with the ID gradle-in-action/todo:

```
$ gradle -PappId=gradle-in-action/todo cloudBeesAppInfo
:cloudBeesAppInfo
...
Application id : gradle-in-action/todo
        title : todo
      created : Sun Sep 16 10:17:11 EDT 2012
         urls : [todo.gradle-in-action.cloudbees.net]
       status : hibernate
```

The output gives the application's title, when it was created, under what URL it can be reached, and its current status. In this example the status is hibernate. Applications on a free plan will be put to sleep if they have been idle for too long to save resources for other applications. Upon the next request, the application will automatically be reactivated. This may take a few seconds. By successfully querying information about the application, you know that it exists under the given ID. Now, you'll actually deploy a WAR file to it so you can enjoy the fruits of your hard work.

DEPLOYING A WAR FILE

Listing 8.3 demonstrates that writing a task to deploy a WAR file with the CloudBees client API is very similar to retrieving information on an application. The only difference is that you'll need to provide other input parameters, like the WAR file itself and an optional message.

Listing 8.3   Writing a task for deploying a WAR file

```
import com.cloudbees.api.ApplicationDeployArchiveResponse
import com.cloudbees.api.BeesClient
```

```
task cloudBeesDeployWar(description: 'Deploys a new version of an application
                                  ⇥ using a WAR archive file.',
                                  ⇥ group: 'CloudBees') {
    inputs.property('apiKey', apiKey)
    inputs.property('secret', secret)
    inputs.property('appId', appId)
    inputs.file file(warFile)
    ext.message = project.hasProperty('message') ? project.message : null
    inputs.property('message', message)

    doLast {
        logger.quiet "Deploying WAR '$warFile' to application ID '$appId'
                        ⇥ with message '$message'"
        BeesClient client = new BeesClient(apiUrl, apiKey, secret, apiFormat,
                                           ⇥ apiVersion)
        ApplicationDeployArchiveResponse response

        try {
            response = client.applicationDeployWar(appId, null, message,
                                          ⇥ file(warFile), null, null)
        }
        catch(Exception e) {
            throw new GradleException("Error: $e.message")
        }

        logger.quiet "Application uploaded successfully to: '$response.url'"
    }
}
```

In addition to task input properties identified in previous task, make sure WAR file is provided

Method provides extensive list of parameters, most of which aren't important at the moment, so set their values to null

Here we go—the moment of truth. Deploy your To Do application to the cloud:

```
$ gradle -PappId=gradle-in-action/todo -PwarFile=todo.war
⇥ -P=message=v0.1 cloudBeesDeployWar
:cloudBeesDeployWar
...
Deploying WAR 'todo.war' to application ID 'gradle-in-action/todo' with
⇥ message 'v0.1'
Application uploaded successfully to: 'http://todo.gradle-in-
⇥ action.cloudbees.net'
```

As shown in the console output, the deployment was successful. In the CloudBees application dashboard you should see the newly deployed version, as shown in figure 8.6.

Of course, you don't want to miss out on actually trying the application. Open the URL http://todo.gradle-in-action.cloudbees.net/ in the browser. The application is ready to be shown to your customers. You've seen how easy it is to write tasks to interact with the CloudBees API. Because you wrote the code in a shared script, you can manage

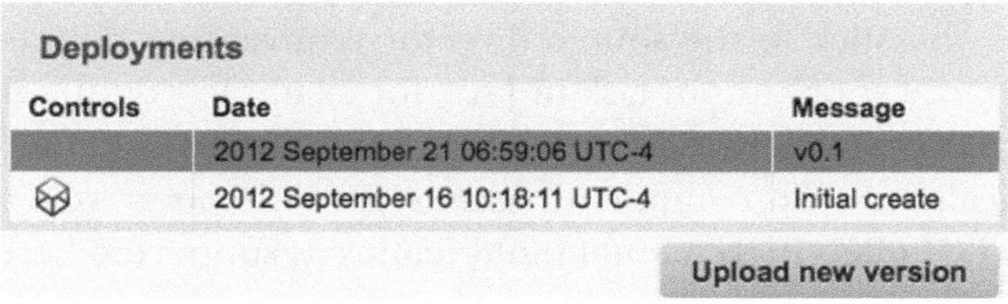

Figure 8.6   Version 0.1 of the To Do application deployed to CloudBees

applications from any other project that applies the script. Let's go a step further and see how to improve your design by turning the simple tasks into custom task classes.

8.4   *Writing custom task classes*

In the last section, you saw how to create a shared script for interacting with a PaaS provider. By applying a script plugin, you provided your project with tasks for managing and deploying your web application in a cloud environment. Let's review the pros and cons of this approach.

Pros:

- Tasks are reusable and can be imported by other projects.
- Tasks are configurable. The consuming script only needs to know about the required inputs.
- Up-to-date checks are available through the task's input and output properties.

Cons:

- The logic of a task is defined through an action closure and therefore cannot be structured into classes and packages.
- The more tasks you add, the longer and less maintainable the build script gets.
- Testability through unit or integration tests is not given.

A simple task is a great solution for developing one-off implementations. Even though you took it to the extreme and provided configurable properties for your tasks, code maintainability and testability fell by the wayside. If you want to go one step further, your best bet is to implement your logic in a custom task. The behavior and properties are defined in a task class implementation. When using the custom task, you define how the task should behave by providing values for the properties. If you see your task code grow, custom tasks can help to structure and encapsulate your build logic.

8.4.1   *Custom task implementation options*

Gradle conveniently provides a default implementation that you can extend your class from: org.gradle.api.DefaultTask. In fact, many tasks of Gradle's standard plugins inherit from DefaultTask.

There are multiple options for where your custom task class can be defined. The easiest way is to put it side by side with existing build code in your build script. The custom task gets compiled automatically and put into the classpath when invoking a task of your script.

Another option is to put it under the buildSrc directory in the root directory of your project. Make sure you stick to the source directory convention defined by the language plugin. If you write your custom task in Java, for example, you'll want to put it under buildSrc/src/main/java. Gradle treats this directory as a default source directory and automatically tries to compile all source files whenever you run your build. Keep in mind that Gradle's incremental build feature is supported here as well.

Custom task classes that live under `buildSrc` are shared among all build scripts of your project and are automatically available in the classpath.

To make custom tasks transferable among projects, you can package them into a JAR file and declare it in your build script's classpath. Figure 8.7 shows the various implementation options for custom tasks.

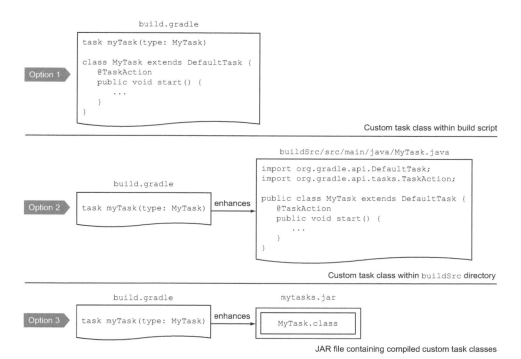

Figure 8.7 Custom task implementation options

8.4.2 Defining a custom task in buildSrc

For now, you'll go with option 2. You'll create custom task source files in the `buildSrc` directory, which is the optimal setup for using them later with an object plugin. All custom task classes will sit in the package `com.manning.gia.plugins.cloudbees.tasks.app`. The build script in the `buildSrc` directory declares the dependency on the CloudBees library. The final directory structure of your project will look as follows:

```
└─ gia
   └─ plugins
      └─ cloudbees
         └─ tasks
            └─ app
                ├─ CloudBeesAppInfo.groovy
                └─ CloudBeesAppDeployWar.groovy
```

**Custom tasks
implemented in Groovy**

To see an example of how one of these custom task classes looks, you'll rewrite your simple task for retrieving application information from CloudBees. The code in the next listing should look familiar.

Listing 8.4 Custom task for retrieving application information

```
package com.manning.gia.plugins.cloudbees.tasks.app

import com.cloudbees.api.ApplicationInfo
import com.cloudbees.api.BeesClient
import org.gradle.api.*
import org.gradle.api.tasks.*

class CloudBeesAppInfo extends DefaultTask {
    @Input String apiUrl
    @Input String apiKey                          Configurable
    @Input String secret                          task
    @Input String apiFormat                       properties
    @Input String apiVersion
    @Input String appId

    CloudBeesAppInfo() {
        description = Returns the basic information about an application.'
        group = 'CloudBees'
    }
                                    Execution method
    @TaskAction    ◁──────────────  indicated by annotation
    void start() {
        BeesClient client = new BeesClient(apiUrl, apiKey, secret,
                                    ⇒ apiFormat, apiVersion)

        ApplicationInfo info

        try {
            info = client.applicationInfo(appId)
        }
        catch(Exception e) {
            throw new GradleException(e.message)
        }

        logger.quiet "Application id : $info.id"
        logger.quiet "         title : $info.title"
        logger.quiet "       created : $info.created"
        logger.quiet "          urls : $info.urls"
        logger.quiet "        status : $info.status"
    }
}
```

**Task group
assignment and
description**

The behavior of the task is encapsulated in the task action. To indicate which action to execute, mark the method start() with the annotation @TaskAction. The name of the task execution method can be picked arbitrarily as long as you don't override the method with signature void execute() from the parent class. The behavior of the task action can be configured through properties—for example, appId for defining the application identifier.

In the custom task implementation you import classes from the CloudBees library. To make sure the classes can be compiled correctly, you'll create a build script dedicated to your buildSrc project and declare the CloudBees library, as shown in the following listing.

Listing 8.5   Build script in `buildSrc` directory

```
repositories {
   mavenCentral()
}

dependencies {
   compile 'com.cloudbees:cloudbees-api-client:1.4.0'
}
```

USING THE CUSTOM TASK

The custom task class can't be executed by itself. To use and configure the behavior defined by the custom task, you'll need to create an enhanced task. The enhanced task declares the type of task it uses, in this case CloudBeesAppInfo, as shown in the next listing.

Listing 8.6   Consuming the custom task

```
import com.manning.gia.plugins.cloudbees.tasks.app.CloudBeesAppInfo   ◁─┐ Imported
                                                                          custom
task cloudBeesAppInfo(type: CloudBeesAppInfo) {   ◁─┐ Use of              task class
   apiUrl = project.apiUrl                            │ custom task
   apiKey = project.apiKey
   secret = project.secret
   apiFormat = project.apiFormat
   apiVersion = project.apiVersion
   appId = project.hasProperty('appId') ? project.appId : null
}
```

Within the task's closure, assign the application identifier. Parse the value from a project property provided as command parameters. The API options and credentials are defined as extra properties within the build script. Executing the enhanced task will first compile all custom classes in the buildSrc project and then retrieve the application information from CloudBees:

```
$ gradle -PappId=gradle-in-action/todo cloudBeesAppInfo
:buildSrc:compileJava UP-TO-DATE
:buildSrc:compileGroovy               ◁─┐ Compiles custom tasks
:buildSrc:processResources UP-TO-DATE     written in Groovy in
:buildSrc:classes                         buildSrc/src/main/groovy
:buildSrc:jar
```

```
:buildSrc:assemble
:buildSrc:compileTestJava UP-TO-DATE
:buildSrc:compileTestGroovy UP-TO-DATE
:buildSrc:processTestResources UP-TO-DATE
:buildSrc:testClasses UP-TO-DATE
:buildSrc:test
:buildSrc:check
:buildSrc:build
:cloudBeesAppInfo
...
```

Enhanced task that retrieves application information from CloudBees

We discussed how to implement and use a single custom task for interacting with the CloudBees backend. The custom task for deploying a WAR file, `CloudBeesAppDeploy-War`, looks similar. You'll find it in the provided code examples for the book.

IMPROVING ON REUSABILITY THROUGH REFACTORING

When you compare both CloudBees custom tasks, you'll find that both implementations look alike in structure. We can identify the following commonalities:

- Both classes create an instance of the CloudBees API client, `BeesClient`.
- They need to be provided with the CloudBees API options and credentials.
- You catch an exception when interacting with the CloudBees API and handle it appropriately.
- All CloudBees custom tasks are assigned to the task group `CloudBees`.

One of the benefits of dealing with actual classes for your task implementation is that you can make good use of principles of object-oriented programming. By creating a parent class, you can significantly simplify the code you have to write for any given CloudBees custom task. The following listing shows that all common characteristics just mentioned became a concern of the parent class.

Listing 8.7 Simplifying CloudBees interaction by introducing a parent task class

```
package com.manning.gia.plugins.cloudbees.tasks

import com.cloudbees.api.BeesClient
import org.gradle.api.*
import org.gradle.api.tasks.*

abstract class CloudBeesTask extends DefaultTask {
   @Input String apiFormat = 'xml'
   @Input String apiVersion = '1.0'
   @Input String apiUrl = 'https://api.cloudbees.com/api'
   @Input String apiKey
   @Input String secret

   CloudBeesTask(String description) {
      this.description = description
      group = 'CloudBees'
   }

   @TaskAction
   void start() {
```

Exposes properties for API credentials

Assigns default task group name

```
                withExceptionHandling {
                    BeesClient client = new BeesClient(apiUrl, apiKey, secret,
                                                    ➡ apiFormat, apiVersion)
                    executeAction(client)
                }
            }

            private void withExceptionHandling(Closure c) {
                try {
                    c()
                }
                catch(Exception e) {
                    throw new GradleException(e.message)
                }
            }

            abstract void executeAction(BeesClient client)
        }
```

Creates instance of CloudBees API client (annotation pointing to `executeAction(client)`)

Catches exception and handles it (annotation pointing to `private void withExceptionHandling(Closure c) {`)

Abstract method required to be implemented by subclass (annotation pointing to `abstract void executeAction(BeesClient client)`)

You'll use the parent CloudBees task for one of your custom tasks. Listing 8.8 demonstrates how easy it is to deal with the CloudBees API. The task infrastructure is already set up for you. No more repetitive creation of the API client or handling of exceptions. You can just concentrate on implementing the business logic.

Listing 8.8 Simplified custom task

```
package com.manning.gia.plugins.cloudbees.tasks.app

import com.cloudbees.api.ApplicationInfo
import com.cloudbees.api.BeesClient
import org.gradle.api.tasks.Input
import com.manning.gia.plugins.cloudbees.tasks.CloudBeesTask

class CloudBeesAppInfo extends CloudBeesTask {
    @Input String appId

    CloudBeesAppInfo() {
        super('Returns the basic information about an application.')
    }

    @Override
    void executeAction(BeesClient client) {
        ApplicationInfo info = client.applicationInfo(appId)
        logger.quiet "Application title : $info.title"
        logger.quiet "          created : $info.created"
        logger.quiet "             urls : $info.urls"
        logger.quiet "           status : $info.status"
    }
}
```

Extends CloudBees parent task (annotation pointing to `class CloudBeesAppInfo extends CloudBeesTask {`)

Exposes property specific to this task's functionality (annotation pointing to `@Input String appId`)

Provides task's description (annotation pointing to `super('Returns the basic information about an application.')`)

Implements task action; the already-created CloudBees API client instance is provided (annotation pointing to `void executeAction(BeesClient client) {`)

You already executed this task and know that it works. The more custom tasks you add to your project, the less you'll feel inclined to manually rerun them each time you change the code to verify that they work. Next, you'll build confidence in your code by writing tests to be prepared for future refactorings.

TESTING A CUSTOM TASK

Gradle's API provides test fixtures that allow you to test custom tasks and plugins under real working conditions. The idea is to hand you a dummy instance of a Gradle `Project` that exposes the same methods and properties as the one you use in your build scripts. This `Project` instance is provided through the method `build()` of the class `org.gradle.testfixtures.ProjectBuilder` and can be used in any of your test classes.

You'll see the `ProjectBuilder` in action by writing a test for the custom task `CloudBeesAppInfo` with the help of the Spock framework, as shown in listing 8.9. You'll start by creating the class `CloudBeesAppInfoSpec.groovy` in the directory `buildSrc/src/test/groovy`. As you can see in the listing, you use the same package as the class under test. Whenever you run the build, this class will automatically be compiled and the test cases will be executed.

> **Listing 8.9 Testing the custom task `CloudBeesAppInfo` using `ProjectBuilder`**

```
package com.manning.gia.plugins.cloudbees.tasks.app

import spock.lang.Specification
import org.gradle.api.*
import org.gradle.api.plugins.*
import org.gradle.testfixtures.ProjectBuilder

class CloudBeesAppInfoSpec extends Specification {
    static final TASK_NAME = 'cloudBeesAppInfo'
    Project project

    def setup() {
        project = ProjectBuilder.builder().build()          ⟵—┘ Creates a dummy
    }                                                            instance of Project

    def "Adds app info task"() {
        expect:
            project.tasks.findByName(TASK_NAME) == null
        when:
      ⟶     project.task(TASK_NAME, type: CloudBeesAppInfo) {
                appId = 'gradle-in-action/todo'
                apiKey = 'myKey'
                secret = 'mySecret'
            }
        then:
            Task task = project.tasks.findByName(TASK_NAME)   ⟵— Verifies that
            task != null                                          task was added
            task.description == 'Returns the basic information about an
                                ➥ application.'                   to project
            task.group == 'CloudBees'
            task.apiFormat == 'xml'
            task.apiVersion == '1.0'
            task.apiUrl == 'https://api.cloudbees.com/api'
            task.appId == 'gradle-in-action/todo'
            task.apiKey == 'myKey'
            task.secret == 'mySecret'
    }
}
```

Creates an enhanced task of type CloudBees AppInfo and assigns property values

```
def "Executes app info task with wrong credentials"() {
    expect:
        project.tasks.findByName(TASK_NAME) == null
    when:
        Task task = project.task(TASK_NAME, type: CloudBeesAppInfo) {
            appId = 'gradle-in-action/todo'
            apiKey = 'myKey'
            secret = 'mySecret'
        }

        task.start()
    then:
        project.tasks.findByName(TASK_NAME) != null
        thrown(GradleException)
    }

    ...
}
```

Creates an enhanced task of type CloudBees AppInfo and assigns property values (annotation pointing to `Task task = project.task(TASK_NAME, type: CloudBeesAppInfo) {`)

Verifies that task was added to project (annotation pointing to `project.tasks.findByName(TASK_NAME) != null`)

The `ProjectBuilder` opens new doors to developing your build code with a test-driven approach, though it's limited in functionality. The `Project` instance produced by the `ProjectBuilder` doesn't behave 100% like the real-world object. Certain behaviors, like the up-to-date checks for input/output annotation or the actual loading of Gradle properties from your home directory, aren't implemented. In most cases, you can work around these shortcomings by writing additional code in your test class. Deep integration testing with a sophisticated toolkit is one of the items on the roadmap and will be available in a future version of Gradle. In the next section, we'll discuss how to turn existing code into an object plugin and apply it from a different project.

8.5 Using and building object plugins

Implementing your logic as custom tasks produces a maintainable and testable solution. Bundled as a JAR file, tasks are fully reusable among independent projects. However, there are limitations to this approach. Let's review the advantages and shortcomings of a packaged custom task implementation:

Pros:

- Custom logic is self-contained in a class and can be configured through enhanced tasks.
- Declarative incremental build support by marking task properties with annotations.
- Custom tasks can be tested through tests.

Cons:

- Custom tasks only expose single units of work. Providing additional boilerplate code, conventions, and lifecycle integration isn't straightforward.
- A custom task can only be configured through an enhanced task. It's lacking an expressive extension mechanism through a self-defined DSL.
- Functionality from other plugins can't easily be used or extended.

Object plugins give you the most flexibility to encapsulate highly complex logic and provide a powerful extension mechanism to customize its behavior within your build script. As with custom task classes, you have full access to Gradle's public API and your project model. Gradle ships with out-of-the-box plugins, called standard plugins, but can be extended by third-party plugins as well. Many plugins are self-contained. This means that they either rely on Gradle's core API or deliver functionality through its packaged code. More complex plugins may depend on features from other libraries, tools, or plugins. Figure 8.8 shows how plugins fit into the overall architecture of Gradle.

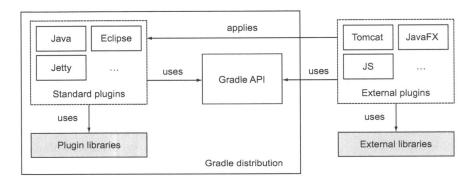

Figure 8.8   Plugin architecture

In the previous chapters, you used various standard plugins covering support for programming languages and smooth integration with software development tools. Think back to chapter 3 and remember how applying the Java plugin extended your project's functionality. As shown in figure 8.9, the plugin can provide a new set of tasks integrated into the execution lifecycle, introduce a new project layout with sensible defaults, add properties to customize its behavior, and expose configurations for dependency management.

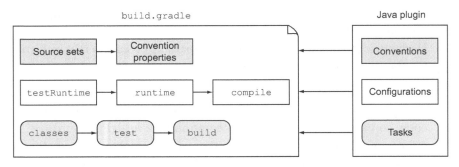

Figure 8.9   Java plugin features

With the addition of a single line of code, your project was able to compile source code, run unit tests, generate a report, and package the project into a JAR file. All of this functionality came with minimal configuration effort from your side.

Standard plugins provide an impressive set of commonly used functionality. Real-world projects are rarely limited to off-the-shelf functionality. Third-party plugins, contributed by the Gradle community or developed and shared among members of an enterprise, can be used to enhance your build scripts with nonstandard capabilities. You may be used to sophisticated plugin portals that let you search for existing plugins, view their documentation, and even rate them. At the time of writing, Gradle doesn't provide a centralized repository for community plugins. How do you know what's out there, you may ask? Gradle provides a curated list of available community plugins on a wiki page: http://wiki.gradle.org/display/GRADLE/Plugins. Feels pretty clunky, doesn't it? Gradleware recognizes the fact that a plugin portal is an important prerequisite for sharing and distributing plugins and has added it as a planned feature to Gradle's development roadmap. For more information on its timeline, please refer to the roadmap's dashboard (http://www.gradle.org/roadmap).

In this section, we'll revisit how to use standard and third-party plugins in your build script. Next, we'll study a plugin's internals to get a deep understanding of its building blocks and mechanics. Finally, you'll apply your knowledge by writing your own object plugin with all the bells and whistles.

8.5.1 Applying object plugins

Let's revisit how to use an object plugin in a project. You've seen that a project can be configured to use a standard plugin by using the `apply` method. I explicitly use the word *method* here to underline that you're calling the method `apply` on the API representation of a Gradle project, an instance of class `org.gradle.api.Project`. The method defines one parameter of type `java.util.Map` called `options`. The specific option you want to use here is `plugin`. A plugin can be applied to a build script by using its name or type.

APPLYING A PLUGIN BY NAME

The identifier of the plugin, the short name, is provided through the plugin meta-information. To apply the Java plugin to a project, pass in the key `plugin` with a value of `java`:

```
apply plugin: 'java'
```

APPLYING A PLUGIN BY TYPE

Alternatively, you can use the class name of the plugin implementation. This is useful if the plugin doesn't expose a name or if there's a naming conflict between two different plugins. Applying a plugin by type makes it explicit but feels a bit more cumbersome:

```
apply plugin: org.gradle.api.plugins.JavaPlugin
```

A convenient side effect of using standard plugins is that they're part of Gradle's runtime. In most cases, the user doesn't have to know about the libraries or the versions the plugin depends on. The Gradle distribution makes sure that all standard plugins are compatible. If you're curious where to find these libraries, look at the directory `lib/plugins` of your Gradle installation.

APPLYING AN EXTERNAL PLUGIN

A build script doesn't know about an external plugin until you add it to its classpath. You can do this by using the `buildscript` method that defines the location of the plugin, the repository, and the plugin dependency. The order in which the `buildscript` and `apply` methods are declared is irrelevant. During the configuration phase, Gradle will build the model of your project and connect the dots between the plugin and the build logic. An external plugin is treated like every other dependency in Gradle. Once it's downloaded and put into the local dependency cache, it's available for subsequent runs of the build. The following listing shows how to apply the external plugin `tomcat` for deploying web applications to an embedded Tomcat container.

Listing 8.10   Applying the `tomcat` plugin available on Maven Central

```
buildscript {
   repositories {
      mavenCentral()
   }
   dependencies {
      classpath 'org.gradle.api.plugins:gradle-tomcat-plugin:0.9.7'
   }
}

apply plugin: 'tomcat'
```

Applying an external plugin is surprisingly easy. The build script only needs to define the plugin dependency and its originating repository. In the following section, we'll dissect the internals of a plugin to get a better understanding of its anatomy.

8.5.2   *Anatomy of an object plugin*

Figure 8.10 shows a high-level overview of the options you have when implementing an object plugin.

There are four basic elements that are important for implementing an object plugin:

- Gradle gives you full flexibility over the *location* in which to place your plugin implementation. The code can live in the build script or the `buildSrc` directory, or it can be developed as a standalone project and in turn distributed as a JAR file.
- Every plugin needs to provide an *implementation class*, which represents the plugin's entry point. Plugins can be written in any JVM language that compiles down to bytecode. I prefer Groovy because you can benefit from its dynamic language features and conciseness. However, you can also use Java or Scala to implement your build logic.
- A plugin applied to a project can be customized through its exposed *extension objects*. This is especially useful if the user wants to override the plugin's default configuration from the consuming build script.

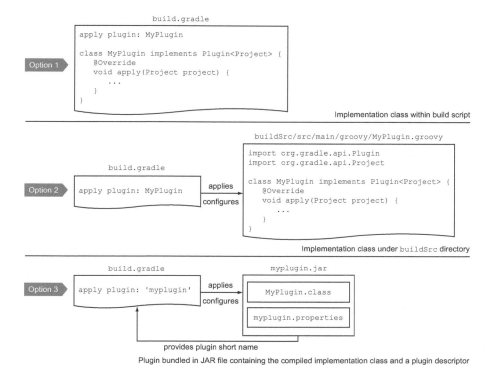

Figure 8.10   Implementation options for object plugins

- The *plugin descriptor* is a property file containing meta-information about the plugin. Usually it contains a mapping between the plugin's short name and the plugin implementation class.

Enough theory—it's time to start building an object plugin. The plugin you're about to create is going to use the custom tasks you implemented before.

8.5.3   *Writing an object plugin*

The minimal requirement for writing a plugin is to provide an implementation of the interface `org.gradle.api.Plugin<Project>`. The interface only defines a single method: `apply(Project)`.

You'll start by creating the plugin implementation class in the `buildSrc` project under the package `com.manning.gia.plugins.cloudbees`. This has several advantages. In the early phases of developing a plugin, you'll want to have a quick feedback loop. Because you don't have to package your plugin code, you can fully concentrate on implementing business logic while having full access to Gradle's API. To represent the intent of the plugin, name the class `CloudBeesPlugin`, as shown in the following listing.

Listing 8.11   Implementing the plugin interface

```
package com.manning.gia.plugins.cloudbees

import org.gradle.api.Plugin
import org.gradle.api.Project
import org.gradle.api.plugins.WarPlugin
import com.manning.gia.plugins.cloudbees.tasks.*

class CloudBeesPlugin implements Plugin<Project> {
    @Override
    void apply(Project project) {
        project.plugins.apply(WarPlugin)          ⟵┐  Applies the
        addTasks(project)                              WAR plugin.
    }

    private void addTasks(Project project) {                        For all CloudBees
        project.tasks.withType(CloudBeesTask) {          ⟵          tasks we automatically
            apiUrl = 'https://api.cloudbees.com/api'                assign the API URL, key
            apiKey = project.property('cloudbeesApiKey')            and secret.
            secret = project.property('cloudbeesApiSecret')
        }

        addAppTasks(project)
    }

    private void addAppTasks(Project project) {
        project.task('cloudBeesAppDeployWar', type: CloudBeesAppDeployWar) {
            appId = project.hasProperty('appId') ? project.appId : null
            message = project.hasProperty('message') ? project.message : null
            warFile = project.hasProperty('warFile') ?
                    ➥ new File(project.getProperty('warFile')) :
                    ➥ project.tasks.getByName(WarPlugin.WAR_TASK_NAME)
                    ➥ .archivePath          ⟵┐
        }                                        If the warFile property is not
        ...                                      provided, we assign path to the
    }                                            WAR file produce by the WAR plugin.
}
```

As shown in the listing, you integrated your custom tasks and preconfigured them with default values. You didn't stop there. Your plugin makes certain assumptions about the nature of the project that consumes the plugin. For example, you automatically apply the War plugin and use the produced artifact as input for the enhanced task `cloudBeesAppDeployWar`.

Plugin capabilities versus conventions

As a plugin developer, you often walk the fine line between capabilities and conventions provided by a plugin. On the one hand, you may want to enhance another project's functionality; for example, through tasks. On the other hand, you may want to introduce conventions that make meaningful decisions for the user; for example, standardized project layouts. If the conventions impose a strong, opinionated view on the structure of the consuming project, it makes sense to separate basic functionality from conventions by creating two different plugins: a base plugin that contains the capabilities, and another one that applies the base plugin and preconfigures these capabilities by convention. This approach was taken by the Java plugin, which derives from the Java base plugin. For more information on their characteristics, please see the online documentation.

You'll apply the plugin to your project. To do so, use the plugin implementation type in build.gradle, as shown in the following code snippet:

```
apply plugin: com.manning.gia.plugins.cloudbees.CloudBeesPlugin
```

To verify that the task has been created, run gradle tasks. You should see the task named cloudBeesAppDeployWar listed. Currently, you're retrieving the inputs for your custom tasks from the command line. You can improve on this design by obtaining this configuration from the consuming build script.

8.5.4 *Plugin extension mechanism*

Parsing command-line parameters to feed your tasks with inputs may not always be desirable. You can establish your own build language by exposing a DSL with its own unique namespace. Let's look at the following listing. The code shows a closure named cloudBees that allows for setting values for properties you need as required input values for tasks from the consuming build script.

Listing 8.12 Providing a plugin DSL for capturing user input

```
cloudBees {
   apiUrl = 'https://api.cloudbees.com/api'
   apiKey = project.apiKey
   secret = project.secret
   appId = 'gradle-in-action/todo'
}
```

Gradle models these language constructs as extensions. An extension can be added to many Gradle objects like the Project or a Task, as long as they're extension-aware. An object is considered to be extension-aware if it implements the interface org.gradle.api.plugins.ExtensionAware. Every extension needs to be backed by a model that captures the values provided in the user's build script. The model can be a simple plain old Java or Groovy Bean. The next listing shows the extension model for the CloudBees plugin that you create in the package as your object plugin implementation.

Listing 8.13 Plugin extension POGO

```
package com.manning.gia.plugins.cloudbees

class CloudBeesPluginExtension {
   String apiUrl
   String apiKey
```

```
    String secret
    String appId
}
```

As shown in listing 8.14, you need to extend the backing `Project` of the build script that applied the CloudBees plugin. Extension-aware objects expose the method `get-Extensions()` that returns a container for registering extension models with a name. The implementing interface of this container is `org.gradle.api.plugins.Extension-Container`. New extensions are registered through the method `create`. That method takes in a name and the model type as parameters. Once an extension is registered, you can query for the model values and assign them to custom task properties.

Extensions versus extra properties

Extensions are used to extend the DSL of an object that is extension-aware. A registered extension model can expose properties and methods that can be used to establish new build language constructs for your build script. The typical use case for an extension is a plugin. Extra properties, on the other hand, are simple variables that can be created through the `ext` namespace. They're meant to be used in the user space, the build script. Try to avoid using them in your plugin implementations.

Using extension values for feeding input properties of custom tasks can be a bit tricky. Remember that custom task properties are set during the configuration phase of the build lifecycle. At that point of time, extension values haven't been populated. You can solve the problem of evaluation order by using the concept of convention mapping. The following listing demonstrates how to register and use your extension of type `CloudBeesPluginExtension` within the plugin implementation class.

Listing 8.14   Registering and using an extension

```
class CloudBeesPlugin implements Plugin<Project> {                    Registers the
    static final String EXTENSION_NAME = 'cloudBees'                    extension
                                                                        container with
    @Override                                                           the name
    void apply(Project project) {                                       cloudBees
        project.plugins.apply(WarPlugin)
        project.extensions.create(EXTENSION_NAME, CloudBeesPluginExtension)  ◁─┘
        addTasks(project)
    }
                                                                    Adds tasks after project is
    private void addTasks(Project project) {                        evaluated to ensure that
        project.tasks.withType(CloudBeesTask) {          ◁─────     extension values are set
            def extension = project.extensions.findByName(EXTENSION_NAME)
            conventionMapping.apiUrl = { extension.apiUrl }
            conventionMapping.apiKey = { extension.apiKey }         Assigning the
            conventionMapping.secret = { extension.secret }        extension property
        }                                                          value wrapped in a
                                                                   closure to the task's
        addAppTasks(project)                                       convention mapping
    }
}
```

Finds the extension container a looks up the configured properties

```
    private void addAppTasks(Project project) {
        project.task('cloudBeesAppInfo', type: CloudBeesAppInfo) {
            conventionMapping.appId = { getAppId(project) }          ◁──
        }

        ...

    }
}
```

Assigning the extension property value wrapped in a closure to the task's convention mapping

Every task of your plugin has a property named `conventionMapping`. To be more specific, every task derived from `DefaultTask` owns this property. You use this property to assign the extension model values to a task's input or output fields. By wrapping the extension model value into a closure, you lazily set these values. This means that the value is only calculated when the task is executed. To retrieve the values of a property stored in convention mapping, you'll need to explicitly use `getter` methods, as shown in the next listing. Keep in mind that trying to access a field directly will result in a `null` value.

Listing 8.15 Using properties set by convention mapping

```
class CloudBeesAppInfo extends CloudBeesTask {
    @Input String appId

    CloudBeesAppInfo() {
        super('Returns the basic information about an application.')
    }

    @Override
    void executeAction(BeesClient client) {
        ApplicationInfo info = client.applicationInfo(getAppId())    ◁──
        logger.quiet "Application title : $info.title"
        logger.quiet "         created : $info.created"
        logger.quiet "            urls : $info.urls"
        logger.quiet "          status : $info.status"
    }
}
```

Properties set by convention mapping need to explicitly use getter methods

Convention mapping is a powerful concept used by many Gradle core plugins to ensure that extension properties are evaluated at runtime. Even though the `convention-Mapping` property isn't part of the public `Task` API, it's your best bet to set a task's input/output property values in combination with extensions.

Next, you'll equip your plugin with a more descriptive name.

Other options for setting configuration-time properties

There are other approaches to dealing with these kinds of situations, each with their own advantages and drawbacks. Usually, they're highly dependent on your use case and the language you use to implement your plugin. Among them are lazy GStrings, `Project#afterEvaluate`, and more. This topic is heavily discussed on the Gradle online forum.

8.5.5   *Assigning a meaningful plugin name*

By default, the name of a plugin is derived from the fully qualified class name that implements the interface org.gradle.api.Plugin. Even though the namespace is less susceptible to naming clashes with other plugins, it would be handy to be able to pick a shorter, more expressive plugin name.

For object plugins, you can provide this information in a property file located under META-INF/gradle-plugins. The name of the property file automatically determines the plugin name. For example, the file META-INF/gradle-plugins/cloud-bees.properties exposes your plugin with the name cloudbees. Within the file, assign the fully qualified class name to the key implementation-class, as shown in the following listing.

Listing 8.16   Assigning a short identifier for plugin

```
implementation-class=com.manning.gia.plugins.cloudbees.CloudBeesPlugin
```

The next listing demonstrates how to apply the plugin with its short identifier in your build script.

Listing 8.17   Using the plugin short identifier

```
apply plugin: 'cloudbees'
```

From now on, you'll only use the short identifier when you want to apply the Cloud-Bees plugin. A plugin can be tested on the level of the implementation class as well. Next, you'll bring your code coverage to 100% by writing a Spock test class for Cloud-BeesPlugin.groovy.

8.5.6   *Testing an object plugin*

Testing your plugin code is as easy as testing custom tasks. The Project instance produced by ProjectBuilder provides the perfect setup for verifying your plugin's functionality. In the following listing, you apply the plugin, set the extension values, and test for the correct behavior of the created tasks.

Listing 8.18   Writing a test for the plugin implementation class

```
package com.manning.gia.plugins.cloudbees

import spock.lang.Specification
import org.gradle.api.*
import org.gradle.api.plugins.*
import org.gradle.testfixtures.ProjectBuilder

class CloudBeesPluginSpec extends Specification {
    static final APP_INFO_TASK_NAME = 'cloudBeesAppInfo'
    static final APP_DEPLOY_WAR_TASK_NAME = 'cloudBeesAppDeployWar'
    Project project

    def setup() {
        project = ProjectBuilder.builder().build()
    }
```

```
def "Applies plugin and sets extension values"() {
    expect:
        project.tasks.findByName(APP_INFO_TASK_NAME) == null
        project.tasks.findByName(APP_DEPLOY_WAR_TASK_NAME) == null
    when:
        project.apply plugin: 'cloudbees'          ◁─┐  Applies plugin by
                                                        │  its short name
        project.cloudBees {          ◁─── Sets extension
            apiKey = 'myKey'                  values
            secret = 'mySecret'
            appId = 'todo'
        }                                              Checks that WAR plugin is
    then:                                          ─┐ automatically applied to project
        project.plugins.hasPlugin(WarPlugin)      ◁─┘
        project.extensions.findByName(CloudBeesPlugin.EXTENSION_NAME) != null

        Task appInfoTask = project.tasks.findByName(APP_INFO_TASK_NAME)
        appInfoTask != null
        appInfoTask.description == 'Returns the basic information about an
                              ➡ application.'
        appInfoTask.group == 'CloudBees'
        appInfoTask.apiKey == 'myKey'
        appInfoTask.secret == 'mySecret'
        appInfoTask.appId == 'todo'
        ...
    }
    ...
}
```

As the next step, you'll set up a standalone project for the plugin so you can build a JAR distribution that can be shared among independent projects.

8.5.7 *Developing and consuming a standalone object plugin*

Implementing a plugin in the buildSrc project is convenient if the code is supposed to be used from the build scripts of the main build; for example, in a multiproject build scenario. If you want to share a plugin across builds, you'll need to develop it as a standalone project and publish the produced artifact to a repository.

PROJECT AND REPOSITORY SETUP

In this section, you'll move the existing plugin code to an independent project. Each time you want to release a new version of the plugin, the produced JAR file will be published to a local Maven repository named repo. The repository will live on the same directory level as the plugin project. The To Do web application will act as a plugin consumer. Its build script will define the local repository, declare the plugin as a dependency, and use the plugin tasks to interact with the CloudBees backend services. The following directory tree shows the final setup:

```
.
├── plugin                    ◁─┐  Standalone plugin project publishing
│   ├── build.gradle             │  to local Maven repository
│   └── src
│         └── ...            ─┐  Local Maven
├── repo                     ◁─┘  repository
```

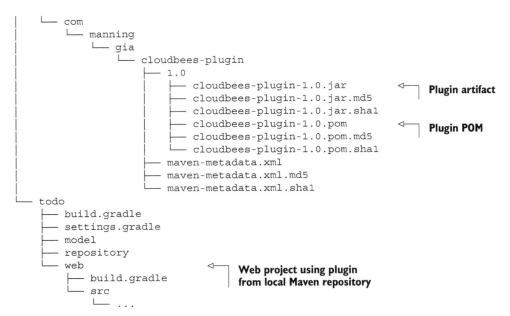

```
│      └── com
│           └── manning
│                └── gia
│                     └── cloudbees-plugin
│                          ├── 1.0
│                          │    ├── cloudbees-plugin-1.0.jar         ◁─┐  Plugin artifact
│                          │    ├── cloudbees-plugin-1.0.jar.md5
│                          │    ├── cloudbees-plugin-1.0.jar.sha1
│                          │    ├── cloudbees-plugin-1.0.pom         ◁─┐  Plugin POM
│                          │    ├── cloudbees-plugin-1.0.pom.md5
│                          │    └── cloudbees-plugin-1.0.pom.sha1
│                          ├── maven-metadata.xml
│                          ├── maven-metadata.xml.md5
│                          └── maven-metadata.xml.sha1
└── todo
     ├── build.gradle
     ├── settings.gradle
     ├── model
     ├── repository
     └── web
          ├── build.gradle        ◁─┐  Web project using plugin
          └── src                     from local Maven repository
               └── ...
```

You'll start by creating a new project for the plugin with the directory named `plugin`. You'll copy the existing structure from the `buildSrc` directory to the new project. The `todo` project is a one-to-one copy from your existing To Do application multiproject build. You won't need to create the directory for the local repository—it's automatically generated at publishing time.

BUILDING THE PLUGIN PROJECT

Writing the build code for the plugin is straightforward. The project doesn't have access to the `buildSrc` infrastructure anymore, so you'll need to declare dependencies on the Groovy and Gradle API libraries. Generating the POM for the plugin and publishing the artifacts to a Maven repository can be easily achieved with the Maven plugin. You'll configure the Maven deployer to upload both files to a local directory. To clearly identify the artifact, assign a value to the plugin's group, name, and version. The following listing shows the full plugin build script.

Listing 8.19   Build script of standalone plugin project

```
apply plugin: 'groovy'                          Applies to Maven plugin for
apply plugin: 'maven'         ◁                  publishing the plugin artifact

archivesBaseName = 'cloudbees-plugin'           Defines artifact group,
group = 'com.manning.gia'                        name, and version
version = '1.0'

repositories {
    mavenCentral()
}

dependencies {                    Declares
    compile localGroovy()         dependencies on
    compile gradleApi()   ◁       Gradle API classes
}
```

```
        compile 'com.cloudbees:cloudbees-api-client:1.4.0'
        testCompile 'org.spockframework:spock-core:0.6-groovy-1.8'
}

uploadArchives {
    repositories {
        mavenDeployer {
            repository(url: "file://$projectDir/../repo")     ◄──┐  Configures Maven
        }                                                          deployer to upload
    }                                                              plugin artifact to a
}                                                                  local directory
```

Before the plugin can be consumed by the To Do web application, you'll upload it with the help of a task from the Maven plugin called `uploadArchives`. Executing the task should produce a similar output to the following:

```
$ gradle uploadArchives
:compileJava UP-TO-DATE
:compileGroovy
:processResources
:classes
:jar
:uploadArchives
Uploading: com/manning/gia/cloudbees-plugin/1.0/cloudbees-plugin-
➡ 1.0.jar to repository remote at file:///Users/ben/gradle-in-
➡ action/code/plugin/../repo
Transferring 32K from remote
Uploaded 32K
```

After publishing the artifact, you'll find a new directory named `repo`. It contains the plugin's JAR and POM files and is ready for consumption. In chapter 14, we'll discuss the Maven plugin in more detail, as well as how to publish artifacts to publicly available repositories.

Using a Maven repository is the most convenient way of preparing an object plugin for consumption. The artifact automatically knows its own dependencies, which are declared in the POM file. Alternatively, the consuming project can also refer to the JAR file directly by declaring a file dependency. If you go with that option, you'll need to handle the plugin's transitive dependencies yourself.

USING THE PLUGIN FROM A PROJECT

It's time to use the plugin in your web project. The next listing demonstrates how easy it is to let your build script depend on the plugin, available in the local Maven repository.

Listing 8.20 Using the object plugin from the web project

```
buildscript {                                                    References local Maven
    repositories {                                               repository containing
        maven { url "file://$projectDir/../../repo" }   ◄──┘     the plugin
        mavenCentral()   ◄──┐  References Maven Central to retrieve
    }                          the plugin's dependencies (namely,
    dependencies {             CloudBees API client library)         Adds plugin to build
        classpath 'com.manning.gia:cloudbees-plugin:1.0'   ◄──┘      script's classpath
    }
}
```

```
project(':web') {
    apply plugin: 'war'
    apply plugin: 'jetty'
    apply plugin: 'cloudbees'          ⟵——  Applies plugin

    ...

    cloudBees {
        apiUrl = 'https://api.cloudbees.com/api'
        apiKey = project.apiKey
        secret = project.secret
        appId = 'gradle-in-action/todo'
    }
}
```

That's it—you've gotten to know all the important development practices that optimally prepare you for writing your own Gradle plugins.

8.6   *Summary*

Gradle provides a rich plugin ecosystem for reusing functionality through out-of-the-box standard plugins and third-party plugins contributed by the community. There are two types of plugins: script plugins and object plugins.

A script plugin is a regular Gradle build script with full access to Gradle's API. Writing a script plugin is very easy, lowers the bar for sharing code, and can be applied to another project by a URL.

Object plugins usually contain more complex logic that requires appropriate structuring into packages and classes. The entry point of every object plugin is the interface `Plugin` that provides direct access to Gradle's `Project` model. Many object plugins that can be shared among independent projects are packaged as JAR files, published to a repository, and consumed by adding them to the build script's classpath.

In this chapter, you built a Gradle plugin for interacting with the CloudBees backend through an API library. For this purpose, we discussed two useful functionalities: deploying a WAR file to a CloudBees web container and retrieving runtime information about this application. You implemented the plugin's functionality build step by step. You wrote simple tasks in a script plugin, translated these tasks into custom tasks located in the `buildSrc` project, and later turned this code into a full-fledged object plugin.

A plugin can expose its own DSL for configuring functionality. Extensions are powerful API elements for introducing the concept of convention over configuration into your plugin. You experienced a typical scenario by registering an extension that serves as a model for capturing user input for overriding default configuration values. Writing test code for your plugin is as important as writing it for application code. Gradle's `ProjectBuilder` allows for creating a `Project` dummy representation that can be used to test custom components. Having tools like this removes impediments to writing tests for build code and encourages developers to aim for high code coverage.

The next chapter will be particularly helpful for users who have existing build infrastructure developed with Ant or Maven and who plan to migrate to Gradle. We'll also talk about upgrading Gradle versions in your project and how to verify its success by comparing the outcomes of the builds before and after the migration.

Integration and migration

Long-running development projects are usually heavily invested in established build tool infrastructure and logic. As one of the first build tools, Gradle acknowledges that moving to a new system requires strategic planning, knowledge transfer, and acquisition, while at the same time ensuring an unobstructed build and delivery process. Gradle provides powerful tooling to integrate existing build logic and alleviate a migration endeavor.

If you're a Java developer, you likely have at least some experience with another build tool. Many of us have worked with Ant and Maven, either by choice or because the project we're working on has been using it for years. If you decide to move to Gradle as your primary build tool, you don't have to throw your existing knowledge overboard or rewrite all the existing build logic. In this chapter, we'll look at how Gradle integrates with Ant and Maven. We'll also explore migration strategies to use if you decide to go with Gradle long-term.

Ant users have the best options by far for integrating with Gradle. The Gradle runtime contains the standard Ant libraries. Through the helper class `AntBuilder`, which is available to all Gradle build scripts, any standard Ant task can be used with a Groovy builder-style markup, similar to the way you're used to in XML. Gradle can also be pointed to an existing Ant build script and can reuse its targets, properties, and paths. This allows for smooth migrations in baby steps as you pick and choose which of your existing Ant build logic you want to reuse or rewrite.

The migration path from Maven to Gradle isn't as easy. At the time of writing, a deep integration with existing Maven project object model (POM) files isn't supported. To get you started, Gradle provides a conversion tool for translating a Maven `pom.xml` into a `build.gradle` file. Whether you're migrating an existing Maven build or starting from scratch, Maven repositories are ubiquitous throughout the build tool landscape. Gradle's Maven plugin allows for publishing artifacts to local and remote Maven repositories.

Migrating a build process from one build tool to another is a strategic, mission-critical endeavor. The end result should be a comparable, functional, and reliable build, without disruption to the software delivery process. On a smaller scale, migrating from one Gradle version to another can be as important. Gradle provides a plugin that compares the binary output of two builds—before and after the upgrade—and can make a deterministic statement about the result before the code is changed and checked into version control. In this chapter, you'll learn how to use the plugin to upgrade your To Do application from one Gradle version to another. Let's start by taking a closer look at Gradle's Ant capabilities.

9.1   Ant and Gradle

Gradle understands Ant syntax on two levels. On the one hand, it can import an existing Ant script and directly use Ant constructs from a Gradle build script as if they're native Gradle language elements. This type of integration between Gradle and Ant doesn't require any additional change to your Ant build. On the other hand, familiar Ant tasks (for example, Copy, FTP, and so on) can be used within your Gradle build script without importing any Ant script or additional dependency. Long-term Ant users will find themselves right at home and can reuse familiar Ant functionality with a convenient and easy-to-learn Groovy DSL notation. Chapter 2 demonstrated how to use the Echo task within a Gradle build.

Central to both approaches is the Groovy `groovy.util.AntBuilder`, a class packaged with the Groovy runtime. It allows for using Ant capabilities directly from Groovy in a concise fashion. Gradle augments the Groovy `AntBuilder` implementation by adding new methods. It does so by providing the class `org.gradle.api.AntBuilder`, which extends Groovy's `AntBuilder` implementation, as shown in figure 9.1.

An instance of the class `org.gradle.api.AntBuilder` is implicitly available to all Gradle projects, as well as to every class that extends `DefaultTask` through the property

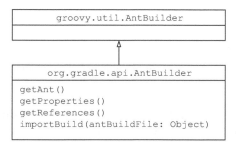

Figure 9.1 Access to Ant functionality from Gradle is provided through the class `AntBuilder`

`ant`. In regular class files that don't have access to a project or task, you can create a new instance. The following code snippet demonstrates how to do that in a Groovy class:

```
def ant = new groovy.util.AntBuilder()
```

Let's look at some use cases for Gradle's `AntBuilder`. You're going to take the Ant build script from chapter 1, import it into a Gradle build script, reuse its functionality, and even learn how to manipulate it.

9.1.1 Using Ant script functionality from Gradle

Importing an Ant script and reusing its functionality from Gradle is dead simple. All you need to do is use the method `importBuild` from Gradle's `AntBuilder` and provide it with the target Ant build script, as shown in figure 9.2.

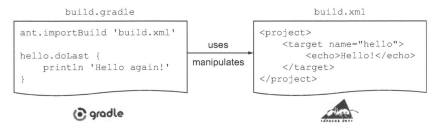

Figure 9.2 Importing an existing Ant script into Gradle

To see the import functionality, you'll take the directory structure of your Ant build from chapter 1 and put it under the directory name `ant`. Parallel to this directory, create another directory named `gradle`, which holds your Gradle build script responsible for importing the Ant script. The end result should look similar to the following directory tree:

```
.
├── ant
│   ├── build.xml
│   ├── lib
│   │   └── commons-lang3-3.1.jar
│   └── src
│       └── main
```

Original Ant build script including multiple properties and tasks

```
|                    └── java
|                        └── com
|                            └── mycompany
|                                └── app
|                                    └── Main.java
|
└── gradle
    └── build.gradle
```

Gradle build script consuming existing Ant build script ⟵

Let's look at the Ant build script shown in listing 9.1. It's a simple script for compiling Java source code and creating a JAR file from the class files. Required external libraries are stored in the directory `lib`. This directory only holds a single library, the Apache Commons language API. The script also defines a target for initializing the build output directory. Another target named `clean` makes sure that existing class and JAR files can be deleted.

Listing 9.1   Original Ant build script

```xml
<project name="my-app" default="dist" basedir=".">
    <property name="src" location="src"/>
    <property name="build" location="build"/>
    <property name="lib" location="lib"/>
    <property name="dist" location="dist"/>
    <property name="version" value="1.0"/>
```

Ant properties for defining directories and the version of your JAR file

Ant tasks for compiling Java source code and creating the JAR file

```xml
    <target name="init">
        <mkdir dir="${build}"/>
    </target>

    <target name="compile" depends="init" description="compile the source">
        <javac srcdir="${src}" destdir="${build}"
               classpath="${lib}/commons-lang3-3.1.jar"
               includeantruntime="false"/>
    </target>

    <target name="dist" depends="compile"
            description="generate the distribution">
        <mkdir dir="${dist}"/>
        <jar jarfile="${dist}/my-app-${version}.jar" basedir="${build}"/>
    </target>

    <target name="clean" description="clean up">
        <delete dir="${build}"/>
        <delete dir="${dist}"/>
    </target>
</project>
```

Now, let's look at the Gradle build file. This is where the `AntBuilder` comes into play. Use the implicit property named `ant`, call the method `importBuild`, and provide the path to the Ant build script, as shown in the following code snippet:

```
ant.importBuild '../ant/build.xml'
```

Listing the tasks available to the Gradle build script reveals that Ant targets are treated as Gradle tasks:

```
$ gradle tasks --all
:tasks

------------------------------------------------------------
All tasks runnable from root project
------------------------------------------------------------

Help tasks
----------
...

Other tasks
-----------
clean - clean up
dist - generate the distribution
compile - compile the source
init
```

Top-level Ant targets are listed.

Ant targets with dependencies are shown in indented form.

As shown in the command-line output, Gradle inspects the available Ant targets, wraps them with Gradle tasks, reuses their description, and even keeps their dependencies intact. You can now execute the translated Ant targets as you're used to in Gradle:

```
$ gradle dist
:init
:compile
:dist
```

After executing the dist Ant target, you'll find that the source code was compiled and the JAR file was created—exactly as if running the script directly from Ant. The following directory tree shows the end result:

```
.
├── ant
│   ├── build
│   │   └── com
│   │       └── mycompany
│   │           └── app
│   │               └── Main.class
│   ├── build.xml
│   ├── dist
│   │   └── my-app-1.0.jar
│   ├── lib
│   │   └── commons-lang3-3.1.jar
│   └── src
│       └── main
│           └── java
│               └── com
│                   └── mycompany
│                       └── app
│                           └── Main.java
└── gradle
    └── build.gradle
```

Java class file

Created JAR file

Accessing imported Ant properties and paths from Gradle

Ant targets translate one-to-one to Gradle tasks and can be invoked from Gradle with exactly the same name. This makes for a very fluent interface between both build tools. The same can't be said about Ant properties or paths. To access them, you'll need to use the methods `getProperties()` and `getReferences()` from Gradle's `AntBuilder` reference. Keep in mind that the Gradle task `properties` won't list any Ant properties.

Importing an Ant script into Gradle can be a first step toward a full migration to Gradle. In section 9.1.3, we'll discuss various approaches in more detail. The command-line output of Gradle tasks wrapping Ant targets is pretty sparse. As an Ant user, you may want to see the information you're used to seeing when executing the targets from Ant. Next, we'll see how to ease that pain.

LOGGING ANT TASK OUTPUT

At any time, you can render the Ant task output from Gradle by executing the Gradle build with the INFO log level (`-i` command-line parameter). As always, this command-line parameter renders more information than you actually want to see. Instead of using this command-line parameter, you can directly change the logging level for the Gradle task that wraps the Ant target. The following assignment changes the logging level to INFO for all Ant targets:

```
[init, compile, dist, clean]*.logging*.level = LogLevel.INFO
```

Listing imported Ant targets manually can be tedious and error-prone. Unfortunately, there's no easy way around it, because you can't distinguish the origin of a task. Run the `dist` task again to see the appropriate output from Ant:

```
$ gradle dist
:init
[ant:mkdir] Created dir: /Users/Ben/books/gradle-in-action/code/
➥ ant-import/ant/build
:compile
[ant:javac] Compiling 1 source file to /Users/Ben/books/
➥ gradle-in-action/code/ant-import/ant/build
:dist
[ant:mkdir] Created dir: /Users/Ben/books/gradle-in-action/code/
➥ ant-import/ant/dist
[ant:jar] Building jar: /Users/Ben/books/gradle-in-action/code/
➥ ant-import/ant/dist/my-app-1.0.jar
```

You'll see the output from Ant that you're familiar with. To indicate that the output originates from Ant, Gradle prepends the message [ant:<ant_task_name>].

Gradle's integration with Ant doesn't stop here. Often you'll want to further modify the original Ant script functionality or even extend it. This could be the case if you're planning a gradual transition from your existing Ant script to Gradle. Let's look at some options.

MODIFYING ANT TARGET BEHAVIOR

When you import an existing Ant script, its targets are effectively treated as Gradle tasks. In turn, you can make good use of all of their features. Remember when we discussed adding actions to existing Gradle tasks in chapter 4? You can apply the same behavior to imported Ant targets by declaring `doFirst` and `doLast` actions. The following listing demonstrates how to apply this concept by adding log messages to Ant target `init` before and after the actual Ant target logic is executed.

Listing 9.2   Adding behavior to existing Ant target functionality

```
init {
    doFirst {                                              ⟵── Adds a Gradle action executed
                                                                before any Ant target code is run
        logger.quiet "Deleting the directory '${ant.properties.build}'."   ⟵┐
    }                                                                        │
                                                          Adds a Gradle action
    doLast {                                        ⟵──   that's executed after
        logger.quiet "Starting from a clean slate."b     Ant target code is run
    }
}                             Renders a message to inform the user about the directory
                              you're about to delete by accessing Ant property build
```

Now when you execute the task `init`, the appropriate messages are rendered in the terminal:

```
$ gradle init
:init
Deleting the directory '/Users/Ben/Dev/books/gradle-in-action/
➥ code/ant-import/ant/build'.
[ant:mkdir] Created dir: /Users/Ben/Dev/books/gradle-in-action/
➥ code/ant-import/ant/build
Starting from a clean slate.
```

Importing Ant targets into a Gradle build is often only the starting point when working in the setting of a conjunct build. You may also want to extend the existing model by functionality defined in the Gradle build script. In listing 9.2, you saw how to access the Ant property `build` via the `AntBuilder` method `getProperties()`. Imported Ant properties aren't static entities. You can even change the value of an Ant property to make it fit your needs. You can also make changes to the task graph by hooking in new tasks. With the regular instruments of Gradle's API, a dependency can be defined between an Ant target and a Gradle task or vice versa.

Let's look at code that pulls together all of these concepts in a concise example. In the next listing, you'll make heavy use of existing Ant properties, change the value of an existing Ant property, and let an imported Ant target depend on a new Gradle task.

Listing 9.3   Seamless interaction between Ant and Gradle builds

```
ext.antBuildDir = '../ant/build'
ant.properties.build = "$antBuildDir/classes"        Changes value of
ant.properties.dist = "$antBuildDir/libs"            an Ant property
```

```
task sourcesJar(type: Jar) {              ◁──┐  Creates JAR file
    baseName = 'my-app'                       │  containing source files
    classifier = 'sources'
    version = ant.properties.version
    destinationDir = file(ant.properties.dist)
    from new File(ant.properties.src, 'main/java')
}                                         ┌──  Adds a task dependency
dist.dependsOn sourcesJar                 ◁──  on Ant target
```

The new task `sourcesJar` shouldn't look foreign. It simply creates a new JAR file containing the Java source files in the destination directory `ant/build/libs`. Because it should be part of your distribution, you declared a dependency on the Ant target `dist`. Executing the build automatically invokes the task as part of the task graph:

```
$ gradle clean dist
:clean
:init
:compile              ┌──  Executes task sourcesJar
:sourcesJar           ◁──  as dependency of task dist
:dist
```

The resulting JAR files can be found in a new distribution directory:

```
.
└── ant
    ├── build                     ┌── Redefined classes      ┌── Redefined
    │   ├── classes      ◁────────┘   output directory        │   distribution
    │   │   └── ...                                           │   directory     ┌── Generated JAR file
    │   └── libs                                              │                 │   containing Java
    │       ├── my-app-1.0-sources.jar    ◁──────────────────┘                 │   source files
    │       └── my-app-1.0.jar    ◁──────────────┐  ◁────────────────────────────┘
    ├── ...                                       │  JAR file containing
                                                     production class files
```

So far, you've learned how to apply Gradle's feature set to simplify the integration with an existing Ant build script. Next you'll apply one of Gradle's unique and powerful features: incremental builds.

ADDING INCREMENTAL BUILD CAPABILITIES TO AN ANT TARGET

The build tool Ant doesn't support incremental build functionality because Ant targets can't determine their own state. Sure, you can always implement it yourself by applying homegrown (and potentially error-prone) techniques to prevent the execution of unnecessary targets (for example, with the help of time-stamped files). But why put in all this effort if Gradle provides a built-in mechanism for it? The following listing demonstrates how to define inputs and outputs for the compilation target imported from the Ant script.

Listing 9.4   Defining inputs and outputs for imported Ant target

```
compile {                                    ┌──  Defines compilation input
    inputs.dir file(ant.properties.src)   ◁──┘  directory ../ant/src
    outputs.dir file(ant.properties.build)   ◁──┐  Defines compilation output
}                                               │  directory ../ant/build/classes
```

This looks pretty straightforward, right? Try it out. First, clean up the existing class and JAR files and run through the whole generation process:

```
$ gradle clean dist
:clean
:init
:compile
:sourcesJar
:dist
```

As expected, the Java source code is compiled and the JAR files are created. When you run the `dist` task again without first deleting the files, Gradle realizes that the source files haven't changed and that output files already exist. The compilation task is automatically marked as `UP-TO-DATE`, as shown in the following command-line output:

```
$ gradle dist
:init
:compile UP-TO-DATE           ◁———   Gradle marks compilation
:sourcesJar UP-TO-DATE               task UP-TO-DATE and
:dist                                doesn't execute it.
```

Being able to add incremental build functionality to an imported Ant target is a big win for Ant users coming to Gradle. It proves to be a huge timesaver, especially in enterprise builds with many dependencies and source files.

Even if you don't import an existing Ant build script, Gradle allows for executing Ant tasks directly from your Gradle build script. In this book, you've already seen some examples. To round out your use case, let's discuss how to incorporate one of Ant's standard tasks into the build.

9.1.2 *Using standard Ant tasks from Gradle*

Gradle's `AntBuilder` provides direct access to all standard Ant tasks within your build script—no additional configuration needed. At runtime, Gradle checks the bundled Ant JAR files available on its classpath for the respective Ant task. Figure 9.3 illustrates the interaction between the use of an Ant task within the Gradle build script, the Gradle runtime, and its included Ant tasks. Using standard Ant tasks in Gradle comes in handy if you don't want to import an existing Ant script, or if you feel more comfortable with the Ant syntax.

Using an Ant task in a Gradle build script isn't hard, as long as you remember some basic rules:

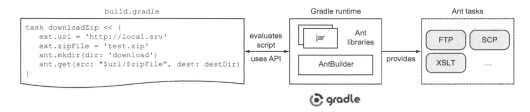

Figure 9.3   Using Ant tasks from Gradle

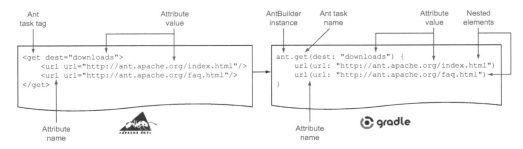

Figure 9.4   Relevant Ant task elements in Gradle

- Use the implicit `AntBuilder` variable `ant` to define an Ant task.
- The Ant task name you use with the `AntBuilder` instance is the same as the tag name in Ant.
- Task attributes are wrapped in parentheses.
- Define a task attribute name and value with the following pattern: `<name>: <value>`. Alternatively, task attributes can be provided as `Map`; for example `[<name1>: <value1>, <name2>: <value2>]`.
- Nested task elements don't require the use of the implicit `ant` variable. The parent task element wraps them with curly braces.

Let's look at a concrete example: the Ant Get task. The purpose of the task is to download remote files to your local disk via HTTP(S). You can find its documentation in the Ant online manual at https://ant.apache.org/manual/Tasks/get.html. Assume that you want to download two files to the destination directory `downloads`. Figure 9.4 shows how to express this logic using the `AntBuilder` DSL.

If you compare the task definition in Ant and Gradle, there are a few differences. You got rid of the pointy brackets and ended up with a more readable task definition. The important point is that you don't have to rewrite existing Ant functionality, and its integration into Gradle is seamless.

Next, you'll use the Get task in the context of your previous code examples. As part of your distribution, you want to bundle a project description file and the release notes. Each file resides on a different server and isn't part of the source code in version control. This is a perfect use case for the Get Ant task. The following listing shows how to apply the Get Ant task to download both files and make them part of the generated JAR file.

Listing 9.5   Using the standard Get Ant task

```
task downloadReleaseDocumentation {
    logging.level = LogLevel.INFO
    ext.repoUrl = 'https://repository-gradle-in-action.forge.cloudbees.com/
                ⇨ release'

    doLast {
        ant.get(dest: ant.properties.build) {          ⟵  Uses implicit AntBuilder
            url(url: "$repoUrl/files/README.txt")           variable to access Get Ant task
            url(url: "$repoUrl/files/RELEASE_NOTES.txt")    Declares nested URL elements
```

```
        }
    }
}
```

```
dist.dependsOn downloadReleaseDocumentation
```

All standard Ant tasks can be used with this technique because they're bundled with the Gradle runtime. Make sure to keep the Ant documentation handy when writing your logic. Optional or third-party Ant tasks usually require you to add another JAR file to the build script's classpath. You already learned how to do that in chapter 5 when you used the external Cargo Ant tasks to deploy your To Do application to a web container. Please refer to the code examples in chapter 5 for more information on how to use optional Ant tasks.

So far, you've learned many ways to interact with existing Ant build scripts or tasks from Gradle. But what if you're planning to move to Gradle long term? How do you approach a step-by-step migration?

9.1.3   *Migration strategies*

Gradle doesn't force you to fully migrate an existing Ant script in one go. A good place to start is to import the existing Ant build script and get familiar with Gradle while using existing logic. In this first step, you only have to invest minimal effort. Let's look at some other measures you may want to take.

MIGRATING INDIVIDUAL ANT TARGETS TO GRADLE TASKS

Later, you'll translate the logic of Ant targets into Gradle tasks, but you'll start small by picking targets with simple logic. Try to implement the logic of the targets "the Gradle way" instead of falling back to an implementation backed by the Ant-Builder. Let's discuss this with the help of an example. Assume you have the following Ant target:

```
<target name="create-manual">
   <zip destfile="dist/manual.zip">
      <fileset dir="docs/manual"/>
      <fileset dir="." includes="README.txt"/>
   </zip>
</target>
```

In Gradle, it's beneficial to implement the same logic with the help of an enhanced task of type org.gradle.api.tasks.bundling.Zip, as shown in the following code snippet:

```
task createManual(type: Zip) {
   baseName = 'manual'
   destinationDir = file('dist')
   from 'docs/manual'
   from('.') {
      include 'README.txt'
   }
}
```

This approach automatically buys you incremental build functionality without actually having to explicitly declare inputs and outputs. If there's no direct Gradle task type for the logic you want to transfer, you can still fall back to the `AntBuilder`. Over time, you'll see that your Ant build script will get smaller and smaller while the logic in your Gradle build will grow.

INTRODUCING DEPENDENCY MANAGEMENT

One of Gradle's many useful features is dependency management. If you're an Ant user and aren't already using Ivy's dependency management, it will relieve you of the burden of having to manually manage external libraries. When migrating to Gradle, dependency management can be used even if you're compiling your sources within an Ant target. All you need to do is move the dependency declaration into your Gradle build script and provide a new property to the Ant script. The next listing demonstrates how to do this for a simple code example.

Listing 9.6 Declaring compilation dependencies

```
configurations {
    antCompile              ←  Custom configuration          Sets a new Ant property to
}                              for Ant compilation           be used for compilation in
                               dependencies                  Ant build script
repositories {
    mavenCentral()
}                                                            Definition of Ant
                                                             dependencies assigned
dependencies {                                               to custom configuration
    antCompile 'org.apache.commons:commons-lang3:3.1'  ←
}
ant.properties.antCompileClasspath = configurations.antCompile.asPath   ←
```

With this code in place, you can use the provided Ant property named `antCompile-Classpath` for setting the classpath in the Ant build script:

```
<target name="compile" depends="init" description="compile the source">
    <javac srcdir="${src}" destdir="${build}"
        classpath="${antCompileClasspath}" includeantruntime="false"/>  ←
</target>
                                                  Using the compile classpath set
                                                       from Gradle build script
```

The change to the Ant build script was minimal. You can now also get rid of the `lib` directory in your Ant build, because Gradle's dependency manager automatically downloads the dependencies. Of course, you could also move the Javac task to Gradle. But why do all of this work when you can simply use the Gradle Java plugin? Introducing the plugin would eliminate the need for the Ant build logic.

TACKLING TASK NAME CLASHES

Sooner or later in your migration, you'll come to a point where you'll want to pull in one or more Gradle plugins. Your example Ant project resembles the typical tasks needed in a Java project: compile the source code, assemble a JAR file, and clean up existing artifacts. Applying the Java plugin works like a charm, as long as your Ant script doesn't define any targets that have the same name as any of the tasks exposed by the plugin. Give it a shot by modifying your Gradle build to have the following content:

```
ant.importBuild '../ant/build.xml'
apply plugin: 'java'
```

Executing any Gradle task will indicate that you have a task namespace clash, as shown in the following command-line output:

```
$ gradle tasks

FAILURE: Build failed with an exception.

* Where:
Build file '/Users/Ben/Dev/books/gradle-in-action/code/migrating-ant-
➡ build/gradle/build.gradle' line: 2

* What went wrong:
A problem occurred evaluating root project 'gradle'.
> Cannot add task ':clean' as a task with that name already exists.
```

You have two choices in this situation. Either exclude the existing Ant target, or wrap the imported Ant target with a Gradle task with a different name. The approach you take depends on your specific use case. The following code snippet demonstrates how to trick `AntBuilder` into thinking that the task already exists:

```
ant.project.addTarget('clean', new org.apache.tools.ant.Target())    ◁──┐  Excludes
ant.importBuild '../ant/build.xml'                                       │  Ant target
apply plugin: 'java'                                                     │  with name
                                                                         └  clean
```

As a result, the original Ant target is excluded; the `clean` task provided by the Java plugin is used instead.

Excluding some of the less complex Ant targets may work for you, but sometimes you want to preserve existing logic because it would require a significant amount of time to rewrite it. In those cases, you can build in another level of indirection, as shown in figure 9.5.

The import of the Ant build script can happen in a second Gradle build script named `importedAntBuild.gradle`:

```
ant.importBuild '../ant/build.xml'
```

The consuming Gradle build script declares an enhanced task of type `GradleBuild` that defines the Ant target you want to use with a new name. You can think of this technique as renaming an existing Ant target. The following code snippet demonstrates its use:

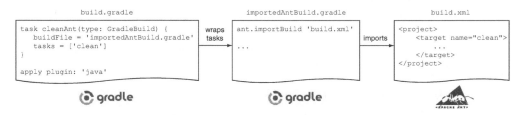

Figure 9.5 Wrapping an imported Ant target by exposing a Gradle task with a new name

```
task cleanAnt(type: GradleBuild) {
    buildFile = 'importedAntBuild.gradle'
    tasks = ['clean']
}
apply plugin: 'java'
```

Preferred task name of type GradleBuild

Tasks from originating build script to be invoked when wrapped task is executed

Originating Gradle build file

With this code in place, the exposed Gradle task name is cleanAnt:

```
$ gradle tasks
:tasks

------------------------------------------------------------
All tasks runnable from root project
------------------------------------------------------------

...
Other tasks
-----------
cleanAnt

...
```

Wrapping task with name cleanAnt that directs the call to imported clean Ant target

If you want to let the standard Gradle clean task depend on the Ant clean-up logic, you can define a task dependency between them:

```
clean.dependsOn cleanAnt
```

We discussed how to approach a migration from Ant to Gradle step by step without completely blocking the build or delivery process. In the next section, we'll compare commonalities and differences between Maven and Gradle concepts. As we did in this section, we'll also talk about build migration strategies.

9.2   *Maven and Gradle*

Gradle's integration with Ant is superb. It allows for importing existing Ant build scripts that translate targets in Gradle tasks, enable executing them transparently from Gradle, and provide the ability to enhance targets with additional Gradle functionality (for example, incremental build support). With these features in place, you can approach migrating from Ant to Gradle through various strategies.

Unfortunately, the same cannot be said about the current Maven integration support. At the time of writing, Gradle doesn't provide any deep imports of existing Maven builds. This means that you can't just point your Gradle build to an existing POM file to derive metadata at runtime and to execute Maven goals. But there are some counter strategies to deal with this situation, and we'll discuss them in this section. Before we dive into migrating from Maven to Gradle, let's compare commonalities and differences between both systems. Then, we'll map some of Maven's core concepts to Gradle functionality.

9.2.1 *Commonalities and differences*

When directly comparing Maven and Gradle, you can find many commonalities. Both build tools share the same concepts (for example, dependency management and convention over configuration) even though they may be implemented differently, use diverging vocabulary, or require specific usage. Let's discuss some important differences frequently asked about on the Gradle forum.

PROVIDED SCOPE

Maven users will feel right at home when it comes to declaring dependencies with Gradle. Many of the Maven dependency scopes have a direct equivalent to a Gradle configuration provided by the Java or War plugin. Please refer to table 9.1 for a quick refresher.

Table 9.1 Maven dependency scopes and their Gradle configuration representation

Maven Scope	Gradle Java Plugin Configuration	Gradle War Plugin Configuration
compile	compile	N/A
provided	N/A	providedCompile, providedRuntime
runtime	runtime	N/A
test	testCompile, testRuntime	N/A

There's one Maven scope that only finds a representation with the War plugin: `provided`. Dependencies defined with the `provided` scope are needed for compilation but aren't exported (that is, bundled with the runtime distribution). The scope assumes that the runtime environment provides the dependency. One typical example is the Servlet API library. If you aren't building a web application, you won't have an equivalent configuration available in Gradle. This is easily fixable—you can define the behavior of the scope as a custom configuration in your build script. The following listing shows how to create a `provided` scope for compilation purposes and one for exclusive use with unit tests.

Listing 9.7 Custom `provided` configuration

```
configurations {
    provided                                    Declares provided
    testProvided.extendsFrom provided           configurations
}
sourceSets {
    main {
        compileClasspath += configurations.provided        Added provided
    }                                                       configurations to
    test {                                                  compilation classpath
        compileClasspath += configurations.testProvided
    }
}
```

DEPLOYING ARTIFACTS TO MAVEN REPOSITORIES

Maven repositories are omnipresent sources for external libraries in the build tool landscape. This is particularly true for Maven Central, the go-to location on the web for retrieving open source libraries.

So far, you've learned how to consume libraries from Maven repositories. Being able to publish an artifact to a Maven repository is equally important because in an enterprise setting a Maven repository may be used to share a reusable library across teams or departments. Maven ships with support for deploying an artifact to a local or remote Maven repository. As part of this process, a `pom.xml` file is generated containing the meta-information about the artifact.

Gradle provides a 100% compatible plugin that resembles Maven's functionality of uploading artifacts to repositories: the Gradle Maven Publishing plugin. We won't discuss the plugin any further in this chapter. If you're eager to learn more about it, jump directly to chapter 14.

SUPPORT FOR MAVEN PROFILES

Maven 2.0 introduces the concept of a build *profile*. A profile defines a set of environment-specific parameters through a subset of elements in a POM (the project `pom.xml`, `settings.xml`, or `profiles.xml` file). A typical use case for a profile is to define properties for use in a specific deployment environment. If you're coming to Gradle, you'll want to either reuse an existing profile definition or to emulate this functionality.

I'm sorry to disappoint you, but Gradle doesn't support the concept of profiles. Don't let this be a downer. There are two ways to deal with this situation. Let's first look at how you can read an existing profile file. Assume that you have the `settings.xml` file shown in the following listing located in your Maven home directory (`~/.m2`).

Listing 9.8   Maven profile file defining application server home directories

```xml
<?xml version="1.0" encoding="UTF-8"?>
<settings>
    <profiles>
        <profile>
            <id>appserverConfig-dev</id>
            <activation>
                <property>
                    <name>env</name>             Development
                    <value>dev</value>          environment property
                </property>
            </activation>
            <properties>                                                       Application
                                                                              server home
                <appserver.home>/path/to/dev/appserver</appserver.home>  ⊲── directory for
            </properties>                                                   development
        </profile>                                                          environment
        <profile>
            <id>appserverConfig-test</id>
            <activation>
                <property>
                    <name>env</name>             Test environment
                    <value>test</value>         property
                </property>
            </activation>
            <properties>
```

```
            <appserver.home>/path/to/test/appserver</appserver.home>    ◁─┐
        </properties>
      </profile>                                    Application server home
    </profiles>                                    directory for test environment
  ...
</settings>
```

The settings file declares two profiles for determining the application server home directory for deployment purposes. Based on the provided environment value with the key env, Maven will pick the appropriate profile.

It's easy to implement the same functionality with Gradle. The next listing shows how to read the settings file, traverse the XML elements, and select the requested profile based on the provided property env.

Listing 9.9   Reading environment-specific property from settings file

```
def getMavenSettingsCredentials = {
    String userHome = System.getProperty('user.home')
    File mavenSettings = new File(userHome, '.m2/settings.xml')
    XmlSlurper xmlSlurper = new XmlSlurper()          Parse settings file with
    xmlSlurper.parse(mavenSettings)                   Groovy's XmlSlurper
}

task printAppServerHome << {                                          Parse provided
    def env = project.hasProperty('env') ? project.getProperty('env')  environment
              ➥  : 'dev'                                              property
    logger.quiet "Using environment '$env'"
    def settings = getMavenSettingsCredentials()
    def allProfiles = settings.profiles.profile         Traverse XML
    def profile = allProfiles.find {                    elements to find
                    it.activation.property.name == 'env' &&    the application
                    ➥  it.activation.property.value == env }   server property
    def appServerHome = profile.properties.'appserver.home'    value
    println "The $env server's home directory: $appServerHome"
}
```

To run this example, call the task name and provide the property as a command-line parameter:

```
$ gradle printAppServerHome -Penv=test
:printAppServerHome
Using environment 'test'
The test server's home directory: /path/to/test/appserver
```

This works great if you want to stick with the settings file. However, at some point you may want to get rid of this artifact to cut off any dependency on Maven concepts. You have many options for defining values for a specific profile:

- Put them into the gradle.properties file. Unfortunately, property names are flat by nature, so you'll need to come up with a naming scheme; for example, env.test.app.server.path.
- Define them directly in your build script. The benefit of this approach is that you're able to use any data type available to Groovy to declare properties.

- Use Groovy's `ConfigSlurper` utility class for reading configuration files in the form of Groovy scripts. Chapter 14 uses this method and provides a full-fledged example.

GENERATING A SITE FOR THE PROJECT

A frequently requested feature from Maven users interested in using Gradle is the ability to generate a site for their projects. Maven's site plugin allows for creating a set of HTML files by running a single goal. A site usually exposes a unified view on general information about the project extracted from the POM, as well as aggregated reporting on test and static code analysis results.

At the time of writing, this functionality isn't available to Gradle users. A standard Gradle plugin that started down that road is `build-dashboard`. The plugin was introduced with Gradle 1.5 and exposes a task for building a dashboard HTML report that contains references to all reports generated during the build. Make sure to check the Gradle online documentation for more information.

9.2.2 *Migration strategies*

In the previous section, we discussed major differences between the build tools Maven and Gradle. The illustrated approaches for bridging the gap between certain functionality will give you a head start on a successful migration. Because Gradle doesn't offer importing Maven goals into the Gradle model at runtime, a migration will have to take place in parallel to the existing Maven setup. This procedure ensures a smooth migration without disrupting the build and delivery process.

Let's see how this can be done with the sample Maven POM file from chapter 1. For a quick refresher on the code, look at the following listing.

Listing 9.10 Original Maven POM file

```
<project xmlns="http://maven.apache.org/POM/4.0.0"
       ⮡ xmlns:xsi="http://www.w3.org/2001/XMLSchema-instance"
       ⮡ xsi:schemaLocation="http://maven.apache.org/POM/4.0.0
                           ⮡ http://maven.apache.org/xsd/maven-4.0.0.xsd">
   <modelVersion>4.0.0</modelVersion>
   <groupId>com.mycompany.app</groupId>
   <artifactId>my-app</artifactId>                    ◁── Maven's artifactId
   <packaging>jar</packaging>                              element value maps to
   <version>1.0</version>                                  a Gradle project name

   <dependencies>
      <dependency>
         <groupId>org.apache.commons</groupId>
         <artifactId>commons-lang3</artifactId>
         <version>3.1</version>
         <scope>compile</scope>
      </dependency>
   </dependencies>
</project>
```

Thankfully, you don't have to manually convert the Maven build logic to a Gradle script. If you're a user of Gradle ≥ 1.6, you're offered a little bit of help: the build

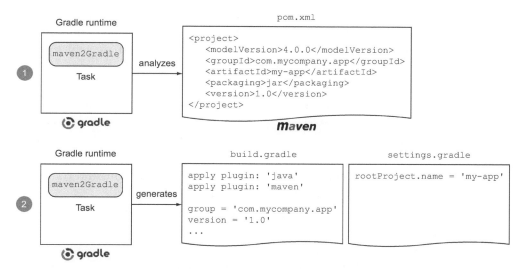

Figure 9.6 Generating Gradle build scripts from a Maven POM

setup plugin. The plugin supports generating `build.gradle` and `settings.gradle` files by analyzing a Maven `pom.xml` file, as shown in figure 9.6.

Let's take a closer look at how to use the plugin.

USING THE MAVEN2GRADLE TASK

The build setup plugin is automatically available to all Gradle builds independent from the build script's configuration. You learned in chapters 2 and 3 that the plugin can be used to generate a new Gradle build script or to add the wrapper files to your project. There's another task provided by the plugin that we haven't looked at yet: `maven2Gradle`. This task is only presented if your current directory contains a `pom.xml` file. Create a new directory, create a `pom.xml` file, and copy the contents of listing 9.10 into it. The directory should look as follows:

```
.
└── pom.xml
```

Now, navigate to this directory on the command line and list the available Gradle tasks:

```
$ gradle tasks --all
:tasks

------------------------------------------------------------
All tasks runnable from root project
------------------------------------------------------------

Build Setup tasks
----------------
setupBuild - Initializes a new Gradle build. [incubating]
maven2Gradle - Generates a Gradle build from a Maven POM.        Maven POM
➥ [incubating]                                                   converter task
setupWrapper - Generates Gradle wrapper files. [incubating]

...
```

Executing the maven2Gradle task will analyze the effective Maven POM configuration. When I talk about the effective POM, I mean the interpolated configuration of the pom.xml file, any parent POM, and any settings provided by active profiles. Even though the task is at an early stage of development, you can expect the following major conversion features:

- Conversion of single-module and multimodule Maven projects
- Translation from declared Maven dependencies and repositories
- Support for converting Maven projects for building plain Java projects as well as web projects
- Analyzing project metadata like ID, description, version, and compiler settings, and translating it into a Gradle configuration

In most cases, this converter task does a good job of translating the build logic from Maven to Gradle. One thing to remember is that the converter doesn't understand any third-party plugin configuration, and therefore can't create any Gradle code for it. This logic has to be implemented manually. You'll execute the task on your pom.xml file:

```
$ gradle maven2Gradle
:maven2Gradle
Maven to Gradle conversion is an incubating feature. Enjoy it and let
➥ us know how it works for you.
Working path:/Users/Ben/Dev/books/gradle-in-action/code/maven2gradle

This is single module project.
Configuring Maven repositories... Done.
Configuring Dependencies... Done.
Adding tests packaging...Generating settings.gradle if needed...
Done.
Generating main build.gradle... Done.
```

After executing the task, you'll find the expected Gradle files in the same directory as the POM file:

```
.
├── build.gradle
├── pom.xml            ◁┐  Generated
└── settings.gradle    ◁┘  Gradle files
```

Let's take a closer look at the generated build.gradle file, as shown in the next listing. The file contains all necessary DSL elements you'd expect: plugins, project metadata, repositories, and dependencies.

Listing 9.11 Generated Gradle build script

```
apply plugin: 'java'
apply plugin: 'maven'

group = 'com.mycompany.app'
version = '1.0'

description = """"""
```

```
sourceCompatibility = 1.5
targetCompatibility = 1.5

repositories {
    mavenRepo url: "http://repo.maven.apache.org/maven2"   ◁──┐
}
```

**Generates URL for
Maven Central instead
of mavenCentral()
shortcut**

```
dependencies {
    compile group: 'org.apache.commons', name: 'commons-lang3', version:'3.1'
}
```

The project name can only be set during Gradle's initialization phase. For that reason, the `maven2Gradle` task also generates the settings file shown in the following listing.

Listing 9.12　Generated Gradle settings file

```
rootProject.name = 'my-app'
```

The generated Gradle files will give you a good start in migrating your complete Maven. Without compromising your existing build, you can now add on to the generated Gradle logic until you've fully transferred all functionality. At that point, you can flip the switch and continue to use Gradle as the primary build tool and start building confidence. Should you encounter any impediments, you can always fall back to your Maven build.

Wouldn't it be great if you could automatically determine that the build artifacts between the Maven and Gradle build are the same? That's the primary goal of the Gradle build comparison plugin.

9.3　*Comparing builds*

The build comparison plugin was introduced with Gradle 1.2. It has the high goal of comparing the outcomes of two builds. When I speak of an outcome, I mean the binary artifact produced by a build—for example, a JAR, WAR, or EAR file. The plugin aims to support the following comparisons:

- Gradle build compared to an Ant or Maven build in the case of a build tool migration
- Comparing the same Gradle build with two different versions in the case of an upgrade
- Comparing a Gradle build with the same version after changing build logic

I know you're excited because this plugin could be extremely helpful in comparing the build outcomes after migrating from Ant or Maven. Unfortunately, I have to disappoint you. At the time of writing, this functionality hasn't been implemented. What you can do, though, is compare a Gradle build after upgrading the version. Figure 9.7 demonstrates such a use case in the context of your To Do application.

Your sample project creates three binary artifacts: two JAR files produced by the projects `model` and `repository`, and one WAR file produced by the `web` project. The WAR file includes the two other JAR files. A comparison between two builds would

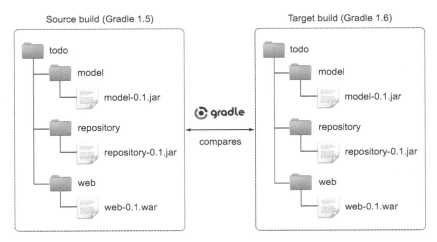

Figure 9.7   Comparing build outcomes of two different Gradle versions

have to take into account these files. Let's say you want to upgrade your project from Gradle 1.5 to 1.6. The following listing shows the necessary setup required to compare the builds.

Listing 9.13   Upgrading the Gradle runtime

```
apply plugin: 'compare-gradle-builds'

compareGradleBuilds {
   sourceBuild {                                    Source build definition
      projectDir = rootProject.projectDir           pointing to root project
      gradleVersion = '1.5'
   }

   targetBuild {                                     Target build definition
      projectDir = sourceBuild.projectDir            pointing to root project
      gradleVersion = '1.6'                          of source build definition
   }
}
```

If you want to initiate a build comparison, all you need to do is execute the provided task compareGradleBuilds. The task will fail if the outcome of the compared build is different. Because the command-line output of this task is lengthy, I won't show it here. What's more interesting is the reporting structure produced by the task. The following directory tree shows the build outcome files used to compare the build and HTML report:

```
.
└── build
     └── reports
          └── compareGradleBuilds
               ├── files                     Build outcome files
               │    ├── source               generated with Gradle 1.5
```

```
|    |    ├── _model_jar
|    |    |    └── model_0.1.jar
|    |    ├── _repository_jar
|    |    |    └── repository_0.1.jar
|    |    └── _web_war
|    |         └── web_0.1.war                    Build outcome files
|    └── target                                   generated with Gradle 1.6
|         ├── _model_jar
|         |    └── model_0.1.jar
|         ├── _repository_jar
|         |    └── repository_0.1.jar
|         └── _web_war
|              └── web_0.1.war                    Build comparison
└── index.html                                    HTML report
```

The report file `index.html` gives detailed information about the compared builds, their versions, the involved binary artifacts, and the result of the comparison. If Gradle determines that the compared builds aren't identical, it'll be reflected in the reports, as shown in figure 9.8.

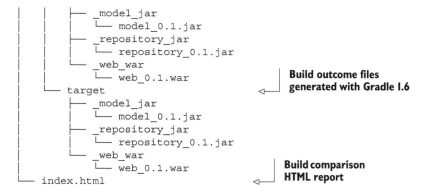

Gradle Build Comparison

The build outcomes were not found to be identical.

Comparison host details

Project: /Users/Ben/Dev/books/gradle-in-action/code/chapter09/todo-build-comparison
Task: :compareGradleBuilds
Gradle version: 1.5
Executed at: 5/11/13 7:45 PM

Compared builds

	Source Build	Target Build
Project	/Users/Ben/Dev/books/gradle-in-action/code/chapter09/todo-build-comparison	/Users/Ben/Dev/books/gradle-in-action/code/chapter09/todo-build-comparison
Gradle version	1.5	1.6
Tasks	clean assemble	clean assemble
Arguments		

Figure 9.8   Sample build comparison HTML report for upgrading a Gradle version

I think it becomes apparent how helpful the functionality of this plugin can be in making a determination whether an upgrade can be performed without side effects. The plugin has a lot of future potential, especially if you're interested in comparing existing builds backed by other build tools within the scope of a migration.

9.4   Summary

In this chapter, we discussed how the traditional Java-based build tools Ant and Maven fit into the picture of integration and migration. As an Ant user, you have the most options and the most powerful tooling. Gradle allows for deep imports of an Ant build script by turning Ant targets into Gradle tasks. Even if you don't import existing Ant builds, you can benefit from reusing standard and third-party Ant tasks. You learned that migrating from Ant to Gradle can be done in baby steps: first import the existing build, then introduce dependency management, and then translate targets into tasks using Gradle's API. Finally, make good use of Gradle plugins.

Maven and Gradle share similar concepts and conventions. If you're coming from Maven, the basic project layout and dependency management usage patterns should look strikingly familiar. We discussed some Maven features that are missing from Gradle, such as the `provided` scope and the concept of profiles. You saw that Gradle (and ultimately its underlying language Groovy) is flexible enough to find solutions to bridge the gap. Unfortunately, Gradle doesn't support importing Maven goals from a POM at runtime, which makes migration less smooth than for Ant users. With Gradle's `maven2Gradle` conversion task, you can get a head start on a successful migration by generating a `build.gradle` file from an effective POM.

Upgrading a Gradle build from one version to another shouldn't cause any side effects or even influence your ability to compile, assemble, and deploy your application code. The build comparison plugin automates upgrade testing by comparing the outcomes of a build with two different versions. With this information in hand, you can mitigate the risk of a failed upgrade.

Congratulations, you got to know Gradle's most essential features! This chapter concludes part 2 of the book. In part 3, we'll shift our focus to using Gradle in the context of a continuous delivery process. First, let's discuss how to use Gradle within popular IDEs.

Part 3

From build
to deployment

Building an application on the developer's machine is only part of the story. In times of increased pressure to deliver software quickly and frequently, automating the deployment and release process is extremely important. In part 3, you'll learn how to use Gradle to its fullest in the context of continuous delivery.

Many developers live and breathe their IDEs, which are key to being highly productive. Chapter 10 delves into the nitty-gritty details of generating IDE project files with the Gradle's core plugins, importing a Gradle project from scratch, and using IDE features to manage and operate a build from the IDE.

Software projects in today's world rarely concentrate on using a single programming language to get the work done. Instead, developers bring in suited languages to make their lives easier. In chapter 11, we'll discuss the use of Gradle as a single solution to build polyglot projects.

Continuous delivery describes a build pipeline that orchestrates the end-to-end process for getting software from the developer's machine into the production environment. The last four chapters of the book are devoted to implementing a pipeline with Gradle and third-party tools. We'll start by looking at continuous integration, the backbone of every build pipeline. In chapter 13, you'll use Jenkins, an open source continuous integration server, to model a chain of build steps. Between each of these steps, you'll build in quality gates with the help of code analysis tools discussed in chapter 12. Chapters 14 and 15 discuss how to assemble and publish an artifact produced by your project. Later on, you'll take this artifact and deploy it to different environments.

By the end of part 3, you'll be able to use your Gradle skills to take your own projects to the next level. Being able to automate the full delivery process will save your organization lots of money and vastly improve your time-to-market ratio.

IDE support and tooling

This chapter covers
- Using IDE plugins to generate project files
- Managing Gradle projects in popular IDEs
- Embedding Gradle with the tooling API

While Gradle's target runtime environment is the command line, editing build scripts happens in a text editor. The types of editors that developers use range from simple screen-oriented editors like vi or Emacs, to full-blown integrated development environments (IDEs) like Eclipse and IntelliJ IDEA. IDEs can boost a developer's productivity tremendously. Functionality like syntax highlighting, navigation through keyboard shortcuts, refactoring, and code completion generation save valuable time during development and make implementing code a more enjoyable experience. Developing Gradle code should be no different.

IDEs store the configuration data for projects in *project files*. The format of these files, usually described in XML, is different from vendor to vendor. Historically, popular IDEs didn't incorporate integration support for Gradle, so Gradle had to provide plugins to generate these files. In this chapter, we'll look at the plugins provided by Gradle to generate project metadata for popular Java IDEs. These plugins are effective tools in deriving most of this metadata from your build script definition. While the generated project files are usually a good start, you often need more fine-grained control to customize the metadata. We'll discuss how to use the DSL exposed by these plugins to adjust this metadata to your individual needs.

With the increasing popularity of Gradle, IDE vendors have provided first-class, built-in support for managing Gradle projects. We'll explore how to import existing projects backed by Gradle build scripts, navigate these projects, and execute Gradle tasks directly in the IDE. The breadth of this functionality is dependent on the IDE product. In this chapter, we'll compare the feature sets provided by Eclipse, IntelliJ IDEA, NetBeans, and Sublime Text.

Most IDE vendors use the tooling API to embed Gradle into their products. The tooling API is part of Gradle's public API and is used to execute and monitor a build. While the API's main focus is to embed Gradle into third-party applications, it can also be used in other situations. You'll get to know one of these use cases and apply the API in practice. You'll start by using Gradle's IDE plugins to generate project files for your To Do application.

10.1   Using IDE plugins to generate project files

IDEs describe organizational units with the notation of a project, similarly to a Gradle project. A project defines a type (for example, web versus desktop application), external dependencies (for example, JAR, source, and Javadoc files), plus individual settings. With the help of project files, a project can be opened in an IDE and can allow for sharing configuration data with other developers. Unfortunately, the formats of these project files are not unified across IDE products. Among the most common formats are XML and JSON.

Gradle allows for generating IDE project files with the help of plugins. The standard Gradle distribution provides two out-of-the-box plugins: Eclipse and IDEA. Each plugin understands how to model IDE-specific project files. The plugins also expose a powerful DSL for customizing the generated project settings. To generate project files, you'll need to apply the IDE plugin to your build script, execute the task provided by the plugin, and import the generated project files into your IDE, as shown in figure 10.1.

To be able to share project files, you'd usually check them into your VCS alongside your source code. When another developer checks out the project from the VCS, they

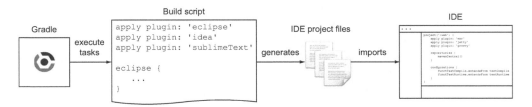

Figure 10.1   IDE project generation with Gradle

can directly open the project in the IDE and start working. Using the Gradle IDE plugins makes this step redundant because you describe the project settings using the plugin's DSL. The project files can be regenerated at any time, similarly to the process of compiling source code to class files.

In this chapter, you'll model project files to enable your To Do application to be loaded in the IDEs Eclipse, IntelliJ IDEA, and Sublime Text. Therefore, Gradle's IDE plugins need to be able to translate the individual needs of your build into the IDE's configuration data. In this book, you added very specific configuration elements that stand out from a simple Gradle project:

- Multiproject build definition including compile-time project dependencies
- Custom configurations used to declare external dependencies
- Custom source sets for integration and functional tests

You'll learn how to describe these rules with the help of the DSL exposed by the Gradle plugins. You'll start by generating Eclipse project files.

10.1.1 *Using the Eclipse plugins*

Eclipse (http://www.eclipse.org/) is probably the most popular and widely used IDE for Java projects. It's completely open source and can be extended by plugins to add specialized functionality, such as support for Groovy projects and the use of version control systems like Git. You need a good understanding of the format of Eclipse project files before you start generating them because the plugin's DSL elements target specific files.

PROJECT FORMAT AND FILES

Eclipse stores configuration data per project. This means that every project participating in a multiproject build contains its own set of Eclipse project files and directories. All configuration data is described in XML. There are three types of files/directories:

- `.project`: The name of this file is self-explanatory—it stores the basic information about a project. It contains the name, description, references of other projects or resources, and the type of project.
- `.classpath`: This file describes the classpath entries to referenced external libraries and other projects.
- `.settings`: This directory is optional for a project. It contains workspace-specific settings. The file within the directory stores settings like the Java compiler version and source code version compliance.

In the setting of your To Do application, the generated project files will look similar to figure 10.2.

Each project in the hierarchy, root project, and subprojects has its own set of project files. Next, you'll apply the relevant Gradle plugins to your project and generate the project files.

Eclipse project files

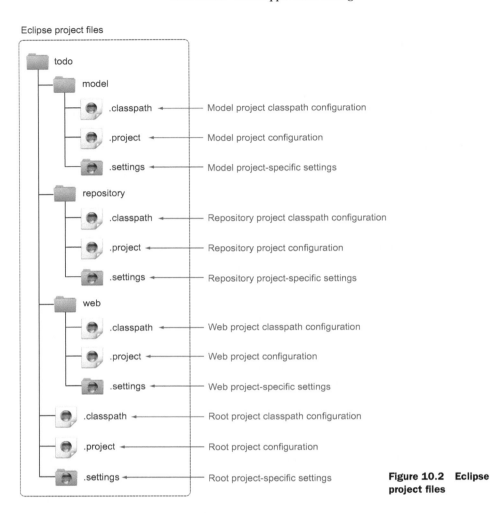

Figure 10.2 **Eclipse project files**

APPLYING AND EXECUTING THE PLUGINS

The Gradle distribution comes with two Eclipse plugins: `eclipse` and `eclipse-wtp`. The `eclipse` plugin is responsible for generating standard Eclipse configuration data. The plugin named `eclipse-wtp` builds on top of the `eclipse` plugin and generates configuration files to be used with Eclipse's Web Tools Platform (WTP). WTP provides tools for developing Java EE applications and can be installed as an optional Eclipse plugin. The WTP plugin simplifies the creation of typical web artifacts like web descriptors, Servlets, and JSP files. It also provides support for deploying WAR files to various web containers, which can come in handy if you need to debug your running application from your IDE.

At its core, your To Do application is a web application, which makes it a good candidate to apply both Gradle Eclipse plugins. First, apply the `eclipse` plugin to all Gradle projects of your application:

```
allprojects {
    apply plugin: 'eclipse'
}
```

Applying the plugin to the `allprojects` configuration block will create project files for the root project and all subprojects. The only project that you need to generate WTP configuration files for is the `web` project. You can apply the plugin as shown in the following code snippet:

```
project(':web') {
    apply plugin: 'eclipse-wtp'
}
```

With these two plugins in place, you're ready to generate Eclipse project files by executing their provided tasks. Two tasks are of high importance: `eclipse` and `cleanEclipse`. The task `eclipse` generates all Eclipse project files, including `.project`, `.classpath`, and the settings files under the directory `.settings`. The task `cleanEclipse` removes all existing Eclipse project files. Try executing the task `eclipse` on the root level of your multiproject hierarchy:

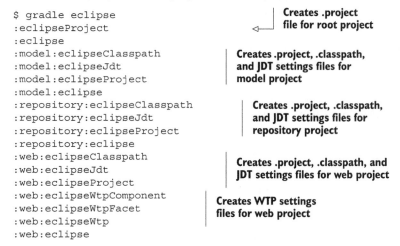

```
$ gradle eclipse
:eclipseProject                          Creates .project
:eclipse                                 file for root project
:model:eclipseClasspath
:model:eclipseJdt                        Creates .project, .classpath,
:model:eclipseProject                    and JDT settings files for
:model:eclipse                           model project
:repository:eclipseClasspath
:repository:eclipseJdt                   Creates .project, .classpath,
:repository:eclipseProject               and JDT settings files for
:repository:eclipse                      repository project
:web:eclipseClasspath
:web:eclipseJdt                          Creates .project, .classpath, and
:web:eclipseProject                      JDT settings files for web project
:web:eclipseWtpComponent
:web:eclipseWtpFacet                     Creates WTP settings
:web:eclipseWtp                          files for web project
:web:eclipse
```

The task `eclipse` automatically executes many dependent tasks. Each of these dependent tasks is responsible for generating a specific type of project file. For example, the task `eclipseClasspath` generates the content of the file `.classpath`. The following directory tree shows the end result:

```
.
├── .project
├── model
│   ├── .classpath
│   ├── .project
│   └── .settings
│       └── org.eclipse.jdt.core.prefs
├── repository
│   ├── .classpath
```

```
|   ├── .project
|   └── .settings
|       └── org.eclipse.jdt.core.prefs
└── web
    ├── .classpath
    ├── .project
    └── .settings
        ├── org.eclipse.jdt.core.prefs
        ├── org.eclipse.wst.common.component
        └── org.eclipse.wst.common.project.facet.core.xml
```

We already discussed the purpose of the configuration files .project and .class-path. Let's take a closer look at one of the generated settings files. A prominent settings file available to all subprojects is org.eclipse.jdt.core.prefs. This file stores configuration data specific to Java projects provided by Eclipse's Java development tools (JDT). One example of a JDT setting is the Java compiler version.

If you open the generated project files in Eclipse right now, what would you have achieved with the default Gradle plugin configuration? All of the projects would be recognized as Java or Groovy projects (in Eclipse this is described as project *nature*), the correct source paths would be set, and dependencies for default configurations defined by the Gradle Java plugin would be linked. The prep work for using Eclipse WTP tooling would be done. This is a lot of configuration that the Gradle plugins provide out of the box without any additional customization from your side. So what's missing? Any custom configurations aren't recognized automatically. In this case, these are functTestCompile and functTestRuntime, two configurations you defined for declaring functional test dependencies. You'll fix this by customizing the generation of the project files.

CUSTOMIZING THE CONFIGURATION

The Gradle Eclipse plugins expose an extensive DSL for customizing almost every aspect of the project file generation process. Table 10.1 shows the important key properties that provide access to the Eclipse generation model.

Table 10.1 Eclipse plugin configuration properties

Property Name	Gradle API Class	Plugin	Description
project	EclipseProject	eclipse	Configures project information
classpath	EclipseClasspath	eclipse	Configures classpath information
jdt	EclipseJdt	eclipse	Configures JDT information
wtp.component	EclipseWtpComponent	eclipse-wtp	Configures WTP component information
wtp.facet	EclipseWtpFacet	eclipse-wtp	Configures WTP facet information

Each concern is nicely separated and can be configured individually by using the dedicated property. In the following section, you'll see each of these properties in action. Project setups are different and can be very specific. It's likely that you won't find your use case covered by the example. If you feel that you need to dig deeper, the best place to start is the Gradle DSL guide. Also keep in mind that it's a good idea to delete existing project files whenever you change the configuration and want to regenerate the project files. You can easily achieve this by executing the task `cleanEclipse`:

```
$ gradle cleanEclipse eclipse
```

The Gradle Eclipse plugin derives many configuration values for Eclipse project files from the implicit or explicit build script configuration. For example, the Eclipse project name is taken from the Gradle property `project.name`. All of the preconfigured values can be reconfigured.

You'll start by fine-tuning the project details of your root project. You can easily override the default value of the Eclipse project by assigning a new value to the property `eclipse.project.name`, as shown in the following listing. You'll also set various other properties.

Listing 10.1 Setting root project properties

```
eclipse {
    project {
        name = 'todo'                                              ← Sets project name
        comment = 'A task management application'                  ← Sets project description
        referencedProjects 'model', 'repository', 'web'           ← Indicates referenced
    }                                                                subprojects
}
```

If you just want to assign properties to the subprojects of your application, you can put the specific configuration into the `subprojects` configuration block. The next listing shows how to set values for JDT properties and how to influence the classpath generation.

Listing 10.2 Setting JDT and classpath properties for all subprojects

```
subprojects {
    apply plugin: 'java'

    eclipse {
        jdt {
            sourceCompatibility = 1.6         Sets compiler and source
            targetCompatibility = 1.6         compatibility version
        }

        classpath {
            downloadSources = true            Indicates whether source code and Javadocs
            downloadJavadoc = false           for external dependencies should be
        }                                     downloaded and linked to project sources
    }
}
```

Eclipse configuration to individual subprojects is applied on top of already existing configuration data. All you need to do is add another `eclipse` configuration block in the build script of the subproject. This method can also be used if you want to redefine an already set configuration value. The following listing demonstrates how to set the project description, add the custom Gradle configurations, and individualize WTP configuration data.

Listing 10.3   Fine-tuning the Eclipse properties of the `web` subproject

```
project(':web') {
    eclipse {                                                    Sets project description
        project {
            comment = 'Web components for managing To Do items in the browser'
        }

        classpath {
            plusConfigurations << configurations.functTestCompile      Adds custom
            plusConfigurations << configurations.functTestRuntime      configurations to
        }                                                              Eclipse classpath

        wtp {
            component {
                contextPath = 'todo'          Sets URL context path for
            }                                 web application in WTP
        }
    }
}
```

These examples give you an idea of how easy it is to customize the generated configuration by the properties exposed through the Gradle plugin DSL. The exposed properties cover many of the commonly used configuration options. However, it's impossible for the DSL to reflect configuration options for third-party Eclipse plugins or personalized user customizations. For that purpose, the DSL provides hooks into the model generation that allow you to manipulate the resulting XML project files.

MANIPULATING THE GENERATED CONFIGURATION

There are two ways to customize the generated project files. One is to directly reach into the XML domain object model (DOM) using the `withXml` hook. The other is to register the merge hook `beforeMerged` or `whenMerged`, which allows for working directly with the domain object representing the Eclipse metadata model. Let's see the usage of these hooks by implementing a practical example.

When applying the Gradle `eclipse-wtp` plugin to your `web` project, you can generate project files for basic functionality in Eclipse WTP. Unfortunately, the basic plugin settings don't preconfigure support for editing JavaScript files (including syntax highlighting and code completion).

In Eclipse, a unit of functionality is called a *facet*. One example of a facet is the JavaScript editing functionality. To configure the JavaScript facet, you'll need to specify the value `wst.jsdt.web` as the facet key. The next listing shows how to append a node to the XML DOM representation that adds the JavaScript facet with version 1.0.

Listing 10.4   Adding the WTP JavaScript facet using the XML hook

```
project(':web') {
    eclipse {
        wtp {
            facet {
                file {                              Adds hook for
                    withXml { xml ->               manipulating
                        def node = xml.asNode()    generated XML
                        node.appendNode('installed', [facet: 'wst.jsdt.web',
                                                      version: '1.0'])
                    }
                }                                              Appends node
            }                                                  for adding
        }                                                    JavaScript facet
    }
}
```

After adding this configuration and regenerating the project files, you'll see that the file `web/.settings/org.eclipse.wst.common.project.facet.core.xml` contains an entry for your JavaScript facet.

The same configuration can be achieved using the merge hooks. You'll use the hook `whenMerged`. When applying the hook in the context of the WTP facet element, the closure is provided with an instance of `WtpComponent`. In the next listing, you'll instantiate a new instance of type `Facet`, provide the data you need in the constructor, and add it to the list of facets.

Listing 10.5   Adding the WTP JavaScript facet using a merge hook

```
import org.gradle.plugins.ide.eclipse.model.Facet

project(':web') {
    eclipse {
        wtp {                                    Adds hook for manipulating
            facet {                              WTP component file after
                file {                           Gradle populates its build
                    whenMerged { wtpComponent -> information
                        wtpComponent.facets << new Facet('wst.jsdt.web', '1.0')
                    }
                }                                       Adds JavaScript facet to list
            }                                            of facets registered with
        }                                                     WTP component
    }
}
```

Choosing the "right" type of hook

You may ask yourself, which of these hooks should be used in what situation, or is there even a best practice? In short, there isn't. Gradle provides a variety of flexible options. The option you choose for your project is often subjective.

(continued)

My personal preference is to go with merge hooks because I can directly work with domain objects that represent my configuration data. These domain objects usually describe the data they need to work correctly. If you're unsure about what data needs to be provided, you can easily answer this question by looking at the Javadocs of the Eclipse plugin.

If you need to add a configuration that isn't backed by domain objects available in the Gradle API, you can always fall back to the XML hook. The XML hook doesn't run any validation on the data you provide, which makes it easy to provide unconventional configuration data. To find out the structure of available Eclipse XML configuration elements, please refer to the Eclipse documentation.

It's time to see the results of your hard work. Next, you'll import the generated project files in Eclipse.

IMPORTING THE PROJECTS

The Eclipse distribution comes in various packages targeted for the type of projects you're working on. Because you're working on a Java Enterprise project, the package best suited is Eclipse IDE for Java EE Developers. The package contains many useful plugins you'll want to use. If you haven't already done so, download the package from the Eclipse homepage and install it on your machine.

The standard Eclipse distribution doesn't provide an easy way of importing hierarchical projects. Instead, you'll need to import each project individually. To import a single project, choose the menu item File > Import... > General > Existing Projects into Workspace. Press the Next button and browse to the root directory of the project you want to import. If Eclipse can find a valid project file, it'll display it in the list of projects ready to be imported. After pressing the Finish button, you'll find the project in the Package Explorer tab. If you repeat this process for the root project and all subprojects, your Eclipse workspace should look similar to figure 10.3.

Congratulations—if you're an Eclipse user, you successfully set up your project for yourself and your peers in a reproducible manner. At any time, you can regenerate the project files. Later, we'll also touch on a more sophisticated Eclipse distribution called the SpringSource Tool Suite (STS) that provides out-of-the-box support for importing hierarchical Gradle projects. In the next section, you'll learn how to achieve the same for users of IntelliJ IDEA.

10.1.2 *Using the IDEA plugin*

IntelliJ IDEA (http://www.jetbrains.com/idea/) is a commercial IDE for working with JVM-based projects. It provides extensive support for popular frameworks and is backed by a suite of integrated developer tools. While many of its features are preinstalled with the core product, it can be extended by plugins. Let's start with a quick tour of IntelliJ's project files.

Figure 10.3   Imported projects in Eclipse

PROJECT FORMAT AND FILES

IntelliJ stores project files in the root directory of a project. The actual data is formatted in XML. We differentiate between project files with the following file extensions:

- `.ipr`: The file with this extension stores the core project information. In a multiproject setting, referenced subprojects are stored here.
- `.iml`: In IntelliJ, a unit of functionality (a.k.a. a module) is stored in an `.iml` module file. A module file holds configuration data about source code, build scripts, and relevant descriptors. Each Gradle project in a multiproject build maps to one module file.
- `.iws`: The `.iws` file contains workspace-specific settings. There's only one settings file per single project or multiproject setting.

Your To Do application would be based on the project files shown in figure 10.4.

Every project—root and subproject—contains at least the module file. The file with the extension `.ipr` and the workspace settings file are stored on the level of the root project. Next, you'll apply and execute the Gradle IDEA plugin to generate these files.

APPLYING AND EXECUTING THE PLUGIN

The Gradle standard distribution ships with the core plugin `idea`. You can use this plugin to generate all required IntelliJ project files previously discussed. To generate the project files for all projects of your To Do application, apply it in the `allprojects` configuration block of the root build script:

```
allprojects {
    apply plugin: 'idea'
}
```

IntelliJ IDEA project files

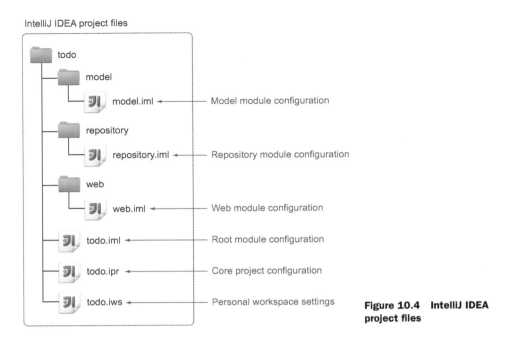

Figure 10.4   IntelliJ IDEA
project files

The main task provided by the plugin is called `idea`. On execution, it generates all project files shown in figure 10.4. The command-line output of the task looks like the following:

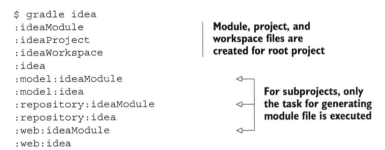

```
$ gradle idea
:ideaModule
:ideaProject
:ideaWorkspace
:idea
:model:ideaModule
:model:idea
:repository:ideaModule
:repository:idea
:web:ideaModule
:web:idea
```

Module, project, and workspace files are created for root project

For subprojects, only the task for generating module file is executed

You can already open the full IntelliJ project with the generated project files. For now, hold off on that, because the IDEA plugin doesn't recognize custom source sets and configuration. This can only be achieved by customizing the configuration. Next, you'll learn how to fine-tune the generated configuration data.

CUSTOMIZING THE CONFIGURATION

The IDEA Gradle plugin exposes a rich DSL for setting properties to tweak the generation of project, module, and workspace files. Table 10.2 shows the relevant DSL configuration blocks that give you access to the internal model.

Table 10.2 IDEA plugin configuration properties

Property Name	Gradle API Class	Plugin	Description
project	IdeaProject	idea	Configures project information
module	IdeaModule	idea	Configures module information
workspace	IdeaWorkspace	idea	Configures workspace information

We'll explore each of the configuration elements in the context of your To Do application. If at any time you want to set a property that isn't mentioned in the examples, make sure to have the Gradle DSL guide handy. After changing the configuration, it's a good idea to fully replace the existing project files with the `cleanIdea` command:

```
$ gradle cleanIdea idea
```

The usage of the main IDE tasks is uniform among the Eclipse and IDEA plugins. This makes it easy for a user to switch between IDEs or provide support for both. You'll start by customizing the project file. The following listing demonstrates how to set project properties on the root level of a multiproject build.

Listing 10.6 Setting root project properties

```
idea {
    project {
        jdkName = '1.6'              │  Sets a specific JDK
        languageLevel = '1.6'       │  and language level
    }
}
```

If you want to customize the configuration for all subprojects participating in a multiproject build, use the `subprojects` configuration block. Next, you'll provide instructions to download the source files for all external dependencies in your Java projects. The following listing shows how to make the sufficient configuration for all module files.

Listing 10.7 Setting module properties for all subprojects

```
subprojects {
    apply plugin: 'java'

    idea {                                          Downloads the source for
        module {                                    external dependencies of
            downloadSources = true      ◁───────    all subprojects
            downloadJavadoc = false     ◁─┐
        }                                  │  Avoids downloading
    }                                      │  Javadocs for all subprojects
}
```

As mentioned earlier, the IDEA plugin doesn't recognize custom source sets right off the bat. You can easily change that by modifying the build scripts for the `repository` and web subprojects. Start with the source set integrationTest defined by the subproject repository. Thankfully, you don't have to repeat the directory path again. Gradle allows for accessing the path directly via its API. The following listing demonstrates a perfect example of how Gradle's Java plugin DSL can be used to retrieve the required information to apply the IDEA module DSL.

Listing 10.8   Adding the custom source set for the repository subproject

```
project(':repository') {
    idea {
        module {
            sourceSets.integrationTest.allSource.srcDirs.each {   ⟵──   Iterates over all
                testSourceDirs += it              ⟵                    directories of
            }                                                          source set
        }                                                              integrationTest
    }
}
```

Iterates over all directories of source set integrationTest

Adds each of the directories to list of test source directories recognized by IntelliJ

You'll want to apply the same type of customization to the web module. Listing 10.9 shows how to add the test source set functionalTest. In addition to this customization, the listing also demonstrates how to add dependencies defined by your custom configurations to the IDE's test compilation scope.

Listing 10.9   Adding custom source set and configurations for the web subproject

```
project(':web') {
    idea {
        module {
            sourceSets.functionalTest.allSource.srcDirs.each {   ⟵──
                testSourceDirs += it

            scopes.TEST.plus += configurations.functTestCompile
            scopes.TEST.plus += configurations.functTestRuntime
        }
    }
}
```

Iterates over all directories of source set functionalTest

Adds each of the directories to list of test source directories recognized by IntelliJ

Adds custom configurations to module's classpath

After creating this configuration setup, you can regenerate the IntelliJ project files and open the project without any problems in the IDE. Before you do, let's also look at the XML and merge hooks provided by the plugin.

MANIPULATING THE GENERATED CONFIGURATION

The IDEA plugin provides the same kind of low-level customization hooks as the Eclipse plugin. In fact, they even follow the identical naming convention. XML modifications can be achieved with the withXml hook to merge modifications with the methods beforeMerge and afterMerge.

While the IDEA plugin does a good job of deriving a default configuration from the build script, it certainly doesn't pick up every desirable setting you need to get started right away as an end user. Let's discuss an example. Gradle comes with the Jet-Gradle plugin preinstalled to support executing Gradle build scripts. To be able to use any functionality of the plugin, a Gradle build script has to be selected first. The IDEA plugin doesn't make this selection for you when generating the project metadata. Thankfully, you can use the XML and merge hooks to generate this configuration.

Let's see how to use the XML hook for this purpose. In the next listing, you first gain access to the XML root node, then append a new component XML tag as its child node, and finally assign the required configuration to point to your root project's build script.

Listing 10.10   Preconfiguring project settings with the XML hook

```
idea {
    project {
        ipr.withXml { provider ->              Adds hook for manipulating
            def node = provider.asNode()       generated XML
            def gradleSettings = node.appendNode('component',
                                [name: 'GradleSettings'])
            gradleSettings.appendNode('option', [name: 'linkedProjectPath',
                                value: '$PROJECT_DIR$/build.gradle'])
        }
    }
}
```

Creates a new XML component tag that preselects the root build script for use with IntelliJ's Gradle IDE support

Unfortunately, you can't achieve the same customization with a merge hook. In comparison to the domain model exposed by the Eclipse plugin, the API of the IDEA plugin comes with fewer domain model representations. Your best bet is to implement the desired functionality with the XML hook, which provides you with maximum flexibility.

To give you an idea of the usefulness of the merge hooks, let's look at an example. Instead of using the properties exposed by `idea.project`, you can also use the plugin's project domain models. The following listing demonstrates how to set the JDK name and language level of your IntelliJ project using the `whenMerged` hook.

Listing 10.11   Preconfiguring project settings using a merge hook

```
import org.gradle.plugins.ide.idea.model.IdeaLanguageLevel
import org.gradle.plugins.ide.idea.model.Jdk

idea {                                          Adds hook for manipulating
    project {                                   project domain model
        ipr.whenMerged { project ->
            project.jdk = new Jdk('1.6', new IdeaLanguageLevel('1.6'))
        }
    }
}
```

Assigns JDK name and language level using domain classes

IMPORTING THE PROJECTS

To take full advantage of all features provided by IntelliJ, download the Ultimate Edition. If you don't buy a license key for it, you can still test it for 30 days. After installing IntelliJ on the local machine, you're ready to import the project hierarchy. In IntelliJ, you can directly import the full multiproject hierarchy by pointing it to the root-level project file. In the menu bar, choose File > Open... and pick the generated .ipr file from the directory browser. You should end up with a project setup similar to figure 10.5.

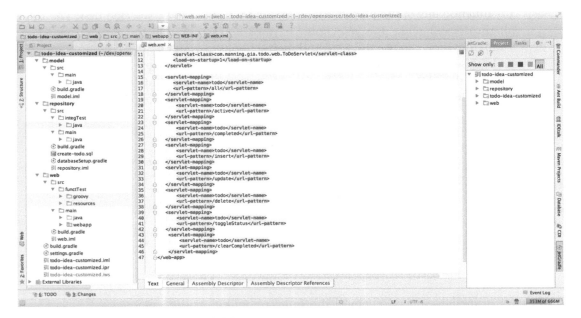

Figure 10.5   Imported projects in IntelliJ IDEA

Eclipse and IntelliJ IDEA are among the major players when it comes to feature-rich IDEs for JVM language development. If you're a NetBeans user, you're out of luck. At the time of writing, there's no published plugin that allows for generating project files with a customizable DSL approach.

IDEs provide the best support for frameworks and tooling. However, some developers prefer a more minimalistic editing environment: plaintext editors or power editors. They're lightweight and can be extremely effective with the right key bindings. In recent times, the power editor Sublime Text has become extremely popular. In the next section, we'll discuss how to generate project files for this editor by using a third-party plugin.

10.1.3   *Using the Sublime Text plugin*

Sublime Text (http://www.sublimetext.com/) is a sophisticated text editor with support for a wide range of programming languages including Java, Groovy, and Scala. The basic functionality of the tool can be extended by custom plugins. Sublime Text can be downloaded and evaluated for free. Continued use requires you to buy a license.

PROJECT FORMAT AND FILES

Sublime's set of project files is simple and easy to understand. It differentiates between two types of files, each of which stores configuration data as JSON:

- `.sublime-project`: The file with this extension contains the project definition consisting of source paths, the classpath, and build tool commands.
- `.sublime-workspace`: The workspace file stores user-specific data, such as currently open files and modified settings.

Sublime Text project files

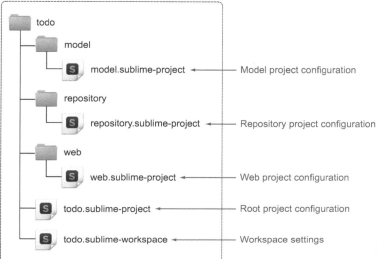

Figure 10.6 Sublime Text project files

In the context of your To Do application, a typical project setup would consists of one `.sublime-project file` per Gradle project. After working with the project in the editor, Sublime Text will automatically create the workspace file. A workspace file can exist for any of the projects, not just the root project. Figure 10.6 illustrates the project files in the directory tree.

Similar to the Eclipse and IDEA Gradle plugins bundled with the Gradle distribution, you can generate Sublime Text project files with the help of a third-party plugin. Next, you'll explore its functionality by using it for your application.

APPLYING AND EXECUTING THE PLUGIN

At the time of writing, the Sublime Text Gradle plugin (https://github.com/phildopus/gradle-sublimetext-plugin) is at an early stage of development and only provides limited functionality. Its core feature is generating and customizing project files. As an add-on, it allows for preparing the project to execute Gradle tasks for Java projects from within the IDE.

The following listing shows the content of your root project build script that declares the plugin and adds it to the classpath. Because you want to generate Sublime Text project files for all projects of your application, apply the plugin within the `allprojects` configuration block.

Listing 10.12   Applying the Sublime Text plugin to all projects of your build

```
buildscript {
    repositories {
        maven { url 'http://phildop.us/m2repo' }        Declares custom
    }                                                    repository
                                                         containing plugin
```

```
dependencies {
    classpath 'us.phildop:gradle-sublimetext-plugin:0.5'
}
}
```
Declares plugin dependency that makes plugin available to build script's classpath

```
allprojects {
    apply plugin: 'sublimeText'
}
```
Applies plugin to all projects of the build

It's time to generate the project files. If you execute the task `sublimeText` from your root project, you should end up with the following command-line output:

```
$ gradle sublimeText
:sublimeText
:model:sublimeText
:repository:sublimeText
:web:sublimeText
```
Generates Sublime Text project file for root project

Generates Sublime Text project file for subprojects

With the default settings of the plugin, the generated project files contain mere pointers to the directory path. You can open the project and edit the files, but you won't be able to compile the code with Gradle. Next, you'll customize the configuration a bit more.

CUSTOMIZING THE CONFIGURATION

Customization options are limited. Listing 10.13 shows how to exclude unwanted directories and set up the project's source directories and classpath. By default, the plugin doesn't make the selection for you, even though these directories aren't necessarily relevant for working with your project within Sublime Text.

Listing 10.13   Tweaking the configuration of Sublime Text project files

```
allprojects {
    sublimeText {
        defaultFolderExcludePatterns = ['.gradle', 'build']
        addGradleCompile = true
    }
}

subprojects {
    apply plugin: 'java'

    sublimeText {
        generateSublimeJavaClasspath = true
        generateSublimeJavaSrcpath = true
    }
}
```
Excludes patterns for unwanted files and directories

Adds the task compileJava to Sublime's build tool support

Generates source path and classpath for Java projects

The Gradle plugin doesn't define a `clean` task to delete existing project files. To regenerate the changed metadata, run the task `sublimeText` again. The task will override existing project files. You're ready to open the project in Sublime Text.

IMPORTING THE PROJECTS

Sublime Text is easy to download and install. Because you're working with a multi-project build, you'll want to see the full project hierarchy in the user interface. To import

Figure 10.7 Imported projects in Sublime Text

the project, choose Project > Open Project... and pick the root project's `.sublime-project` file. The rendered To Do application project hierarchy should look similar to figure 10.7. Choosing Tools > Build System > Gradle triggers a Gradle build. At the time of writing, only an installed Gradle runtime can be used; your provided Gradle Wrapper is omitted.

This concludes our discussion of generating project files for prominent IDEs and text editors. In the next section, you'll take the inverse approach by letting the IDE analyze your build scripts to generate the project files.

10.2 Managing Gradle projects in popular IDEs

A couple of years ago, Gradle was the newcomer among the top dogs Ant and Maven. None of the IDE vendors provided any significant Gradle support. To import a project built by Gradle, you had to generate the project files using the provided Eclipse and IDEA plugins. If you used a different IDE (for example, NetBeans), you had no tooling support.

With Gradle's increasing popularity, this has changed. Tooling vendors realized the need for first-class Gradle support. Figure 10.8 shows how the IDE acts as the middleman between the build script and Gradle runtime.

You may ask yourself which method of generating project files should be preferred: generating project files via the build, or letting the IDE analyze your build code. My personal preference is to let the IDE do the heavy lifting. It'll usually give you a good start. If you need fine-grained control over your configuration, you can bring in the Gradle IDE plugin support. You may have to be careful, though, not to directly override the existing configuration produced by the IDE. In practice, it sometimes takes a bit of playing around to get the desired result.

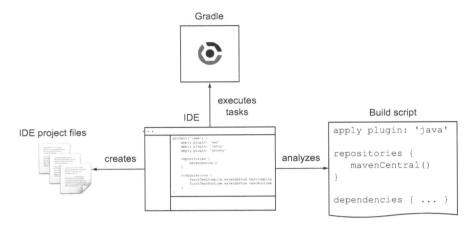

Figure 10.8   Built-in Gradle support in IDEs

The following features are particularly important to IDE end users:

- Opening a project by analyzing the existing Gradle build script and automatically setting up the correct source directories and classpath
- Generating project files from an existing Gradle build script
- Synchronizing project settings whenever there's a change to the build script (for example, adding a new external dependency)
- Executing Gradle tasks from the IDE's user interface
- Code completion and syntax highlighting for Gradle DSL configuration elements

In this section, we'll compare Gradle support for three products: SpringSource STS, IntelliJ IDEA, and NetBeans. As you'll learn, the feature sets and their effectiveness differ slightly. Let's start by taking a closer look at SpringSource's Tool Suite.

10.2.1 *Gradle support in SpringSource STS*

Earlier in this chapter, you learned how to generate project files for Eclipse. With the help of the generated project metadata, you were able to import the project into the IDE. So far, we haven't discussed how to work with a Gradle project after importing it. The standard distribution of Eclipse doesn't come with any Gradle integration. You'll need to manually install the Groovy and Gradle plugins. For more information, see the relevant Eclipse marketplace pages (such as http://marketplace.eclipse.org/content/gradle-integration-eclipse) for the Gradle integration.

But why install these plugins manually, when you can do it the easy and convenient way using the Spring Tool Suite (STS) (http://www.springsource.org/sts)? STS is an Eclipse-based development environment mainly targeted for building applications using the Spring framework. The IDE also provides excellent support for importing and managing applications powered by Gradle. In this section, you'll use its built-in Gradle support.

INSTALLING STS WITH GRADLE SUPPORT

Installing STS is as simple as downloading the distribution from the homepage and running the installer. Alternatively, you can modify your existing Eclipse instance by stacking STS's features on top of it. You'll find the required installation instructions on SpringSource's web page. The following description is based on STS version 3.2.0.

A central dashboard is integrated in STS. The dashboard contains sections for creating new projects, accessing tutorials and documentation, and installing extensions. The core idea of an extension is to give you a preconfigured Eclipse plugin for a particular language, framework, or tool. We're mainly interested in installing extensions for Groovy and Gradle.

If you open the IDE for the first time, the dashboard is rendered in the main panel. At any time, you can also render the dashboard panel from the menu with Help > Dashboard. Click on the Extensions panel, scroll to the section Language and Framework Tooling, and tick the checkboxes next to the extensions named Gradle Support and Groovy-Eclipse, as shown in figure 10.9. You can initiate the installation process by pressing the Install button on the bottom of the dashboard panel. After successfully installing both extensions, the STS must be restarted. After the IDE restarts, you can now use full Gradle support, like importing multiproject builds, managing dependencies, DSL code completion, and integrated task execution. Let's see these features in action.

IMPORTING A GRADLE PROJECT

STS provides a wizard for importing Gradle projects. The wizard doesn't require an application to contain existing project files. During the import process, STS analyzes the Gradle build script, derives the configuration data from the internal model, and generates the project files for you. You can bring up the wizard by choosing the menu

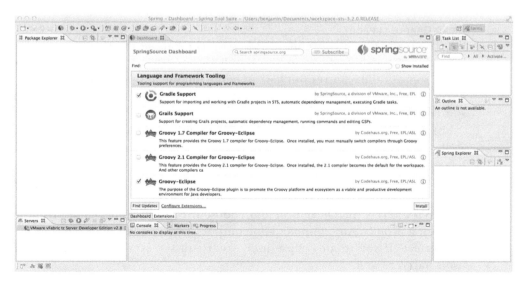

Figure 10.9   Installing the Groovy and Gradle plugins from the dashboard

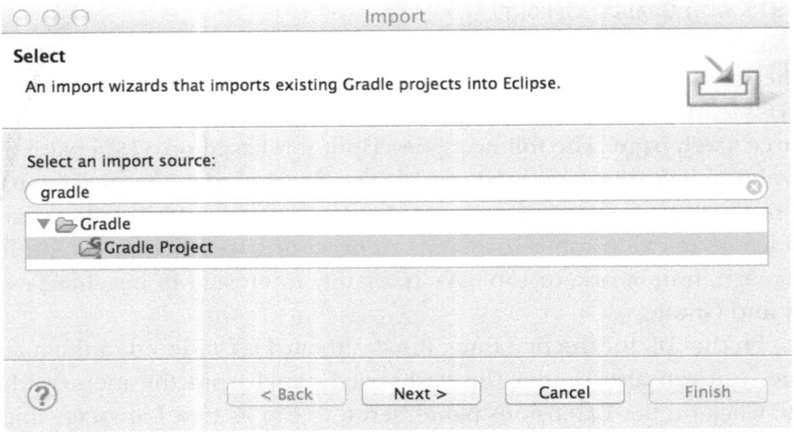

Figure 10.10   Gradle project import wizard

item Import... under File, as shown in figure 10.10. In the filter text input field, type "gradle" to indicate that you want to import a Gradle project.

Pressing the Next button will present you with the dialog shown in figure 10.11. In this dialog, you can select the root directory of your To Do project and build the STS project hierarchy from it by pressing the Build Model button.

STS will correctly identify the root project and all subprojects of your application. Select all Gradle projects, as well as the relevant import options for enabling dependency management, enabling DSL support, and running Gradle Eclipse plugin tasks. Press the Finish button, and the projects are imported and will show up in the workspace as a flat folder hierarchy. As a result, the Eclipse project files are created.

USING GRADLE SUPPORT

You're now ready to conveniently work on your application without ever having to leave the STS again—of course, this is only for the IDE-purists among us. Figure 10.12 shows some of the features you have at hand. On the left side, you can see the Package Explorer. It holds all of your projects. If you open one of them, you can examine the source directories and external dependencies.

In the editor pane, you can modify your build script. As you can see in the screenshot, you're making good use of the DSL code completion feature (type in the first letters of a keyword and press CTRL + space).

Gradle tasks can be executed from the Gradle view. To add the view to your IDE, select the menu item Window > Show View > Other.... This will bring up the dialog Show View. Press the OK button and choose the task to be executed from the list of tasks for a project. Any command-line output is displayed in the Console tab.

Perfect! If you're an Eclipse user, you're all set. Next, you'll make your IntelliJ users happy as well.

Figure 10.11   **Importing a multiproject Gradle build**

10.2.2   *Gradle support in IntelliJ IDEA*

Starting with version 12.1, IntelliJ has a feature set for Gradle that's comparable to STS's feature set. With the help of the preinstalled Gradle plugin, you can import a project by pointing to a Gradle build script, generate the IDE metadata, execute Gradle tasks directly from the IDE, and make use of code completion in the editor. Let's look at IntelliJ's Gradle support by showing how to import your To Do application.

IMPORTING A GRADLE PROJECT

IntelliJ understands how to render and manage hierarchical, multiproject applications. This is a big advantage over Eclipse, because the physical structure of your project is directly reflected in the IDE. All you need to do to import a multiproject application is open IntelliJ, choose the menu item File > Import Project..., and pick the root project's Gradle build script, as shown in figure 10.13.

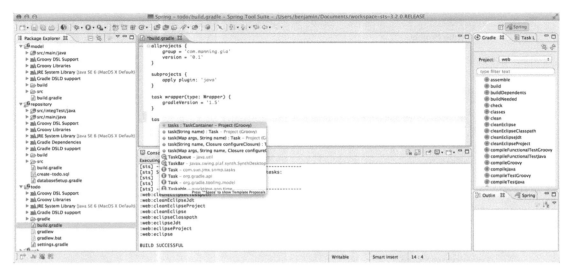

Figure 10.12   Imported Gradle project in use in STS

Pressing the OK button will bring you to the next dialog, shown in figure 10.14. In the dialog, you can choose the Gradle runtime and some other configuration parameters, like its home directory. If the project comes with a Gradle wrapper, IntelliJ automatically recognizes it. Not only should you use the wrapper on the command line, you also want to use it in the IDE to ensure a consistent runtime environment. Move on to the next wizard dialog by pressing the Next button.

Figure 10.13   Selecting the Gradle build script to import

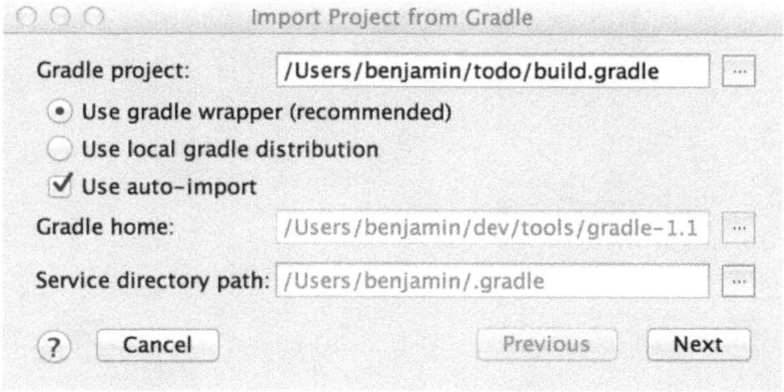

Figure 10.14　Gradle runtime configuration

The dialog shown in figure 10.15 is all about the details for generating the project files. On the left side, you can see the project structure that IntelliJ will generate for you. On the right side of the dialog, you can change important settings of your project. The initial values presented here are derived from the configuration of your build script. If you decide to change the location of your project files or change the JDK, you can do it here. Stick to the default settings and let IntelliJ generate the project files by pressing the Finish button.

You may be surprised by the format of the generated project files. A closer look at the project structure reveals that IntelliJ created a new directory named .idea to store IDE metadata. This is a different format for project files than the one we saw in section 10.1.1. Newer versions of IntelliJ favor the use of this directory-based format

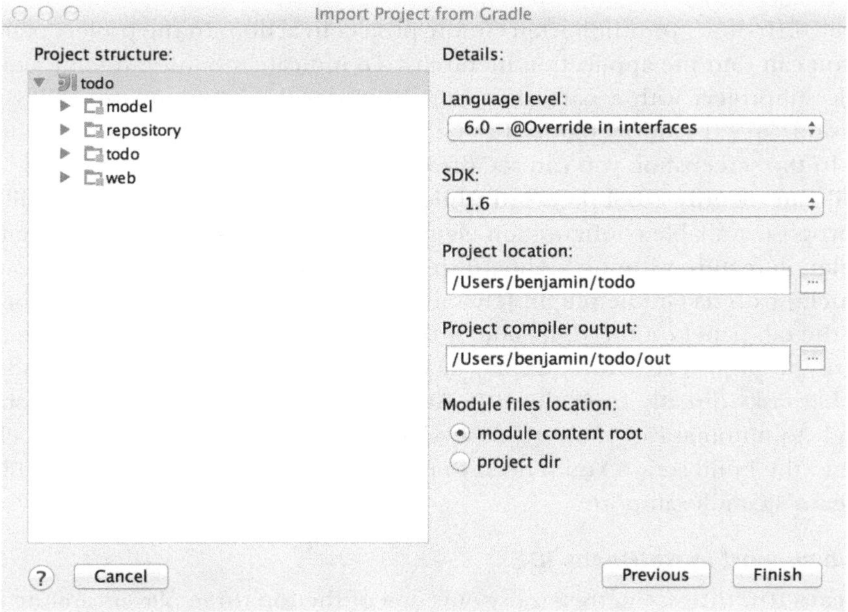

Figure 10.15　Setting project details

Figure 10.16   Imported Gradle project in use in IntelliJ

(.idea) over the file-based approach (.ipr, .iml, .iws). After importing the application, you can start working on the code.

USING GRADLE SUPPORT

Figure 10.16 shows your imported Gradle project in action. In the project pane on the left, you can find the application hierarchy. To indicate modules, IntelliJ marks every Gradle subproject with a particular icon (folder with a blue square). Files with the extension .gradle are recognized as Gradle build scripts, as indicated by the Gradle icon. In the screenshot, you can see the code completion feature for Gradle's DSL. If IntelliJ can identify a DSL keyword while typing text, the context menu will pop up and propose available configuration elements. Alternatively, you can activate the code completion feature with the keyboard shortcut CTRL + space.

IntelliJ calls its Gradle plugin JetGradle. You can open the JetGradle functionality from the tab panel on the right side of the editor. One of its features is the ability to analyze the project structure, display its dependencies, download them, and execute available tasks directly from the IDE. At the time of writing, the plugin isn't smart enough to automatically import newly defined dependencies whenever a change is made to the build script. You'll need to manually trigger a refresh. Next, we'll look at NetBeans's Gradle support.

10.2.3   *Gradle support in NetBeans IDE*

NetBeans IDE (https://netbeans.org/) is one of the top three players among the popular Java IDEs. It supports implementing Java and Groovy applications out of the box, along with the typical functionality you can expect of a first-class IDE, like refactoring

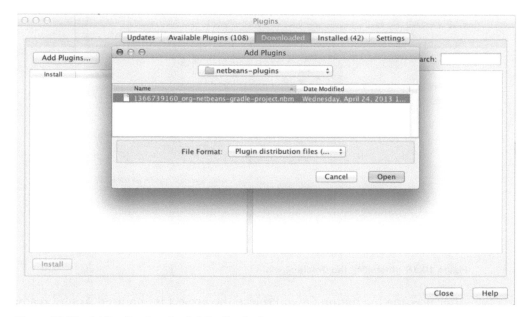

Figure 10.17   Adding the downloaded Gradle plugin

capabilities, code completion, and integration with popular frameworks and tools. The IDE's functionality can be extended by plugins.

INSTALLING NETBEANS WITH GRADLE SUPPORT
Installing the NetBeans IDE is straightforward. Download the distribution for your OS (at the time of writing, this is version 7.3) and run the installer. After a couple of minutes, the IDE is set up and you're ready to take care of adding Gradle support.

To install Gradle support, you'll need to download a third-party plugin from http:// plugins.netbeans.org/plugin/44510/gradle-support. You can place the plugin file anywhere in your file system. In NetBeans IDE, choose the menu item Tools > Plugins. This brings up a new dialog for managing plugins. On the tab Downloaded, press the button Add Plugins.... Select your downloaded Gradle plugin file, as shown in figure 10.17.

After pressing the Open button, you're presented with details about the plugin. In figure 10.18, you can see the version you're about to install, the source of the plugin, and a description of its functionality. Make sure the checkbox next to the plugin name is checked and press the Install button to initiate the installation process. After a successful install, NetBeans IDE needs to be restarted.

IMPORTING A GRADLE PROJECT
Next you'll import your To Do application into NetBeans IDE. With the help of the menu item File > Open Project you can open a new dialog that allows you to select a Gradle project. The displayed file browser conveniently displays the Gradle icon for every folder containing a Gradle build script. Navigate to the To Do project and select the root folder, as shown in figure 10.19.

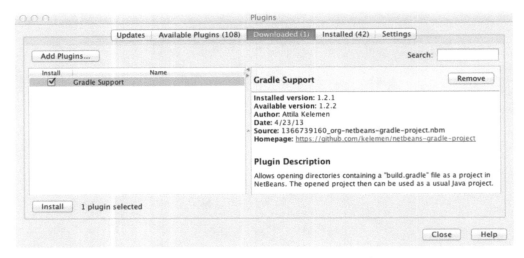

Figure 10.18   Installing the Gradle plugin

After pressing the button Open Project, the project is imported. You're ready to work with it in the IDE.

USING GRADLE SUPPORT

The project is initially opened in a tab on the left side marked Projects view. All you'll see is the root project. Subprojects are aligned under the tree node. For convenience, expand the Subprojects node and click each of the subproject names. This will automatically add the subprojects to the top level of the Projects view, as shown in figure 10.20.

Gradle tasks can be executed by clicking a project node, bringing up the context menu, and choosing a task from the list. Every project node groups source and test packages, dependencies, and build scripts. This is great if you prefer a logical grouping of important Gradle elements. If you need to change individual files, you can

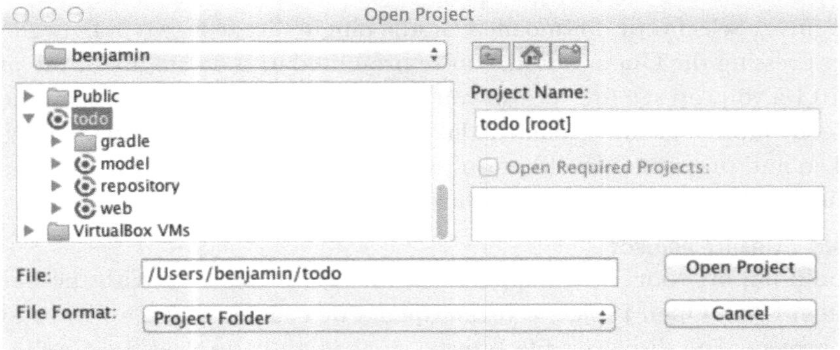

Figure 10.19   Importing the Gradle project

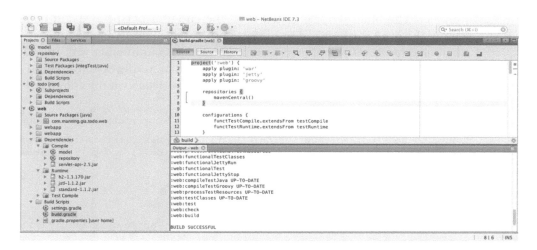

Figure 10.20   Imported Gradle project in use in NetBeans IDE

switch to the Files tab at any time. In the screenshot, you can also see an opened Gradle build script in the editor. Unfortunately, the Gradle plugin doesn't come with any support for DSL code completion.

This concludes our discussion of Gradle support within IDEs. Next up, we'll look at Gradle's tooling API, the API that makes it possible for all of these IDEs to provide a smooth Gradle integration.

10.3   *Embedding Gradle with the tooling API*

The main purpose of the tooling API is to embed Gradle into an application. Without knowing it, you already used the tooling API, because it's the main driver for Gradle support in IDEs. The tooling API is good for achieving three main goals:

- Executing the build with a specific version of Gradle (either via the wrapper or an installed Gradle runtime).
- Querying the build for runtime information and its internal model (for example, tasks, dependencies, and the command-line output).
- Listening to build events to react to them. One example is automatically downloading external dependencies in an IDE whenever the declaration is changed.

Many developers aren't working for tool vendors—we usually work on Enterprise or open source applications that use Gradle as the build system. Why would we care about the tooling API? The tooling API is very versatile and can be applied to other use cases. Let's explore one of them to see the API in action. In the following section, you'll use the tooling API to implement integration testing by actively executing a build script. To verify its correct behavior, you can query for the runtime information available through the tooling API. When you integration-test a build script with the tooling API, you don't have to use the `ProjectBuilder` class to emulate the creation of a project. The build script is tested from the end-user perspective and behaves as if you ran the `gradle` command from the console. Let's look at an example.

In chapter 8, you developed various Gradle tasks to interact with the CloudBees backend. The following listing shows the task that retrieves information about a deployed application on RUN@cloud and prints the details on the command line.

Listing 10.14 CloudBees task for retrieving application information

```
task cloudBeesAppInfo(description: 'Returns the basic information about an
                              application.', group: 'CloudBees') {
    inputs.property('apiKey', apiKey)
    inputs.property('secret', secret)
    inputs.property('appId', appId)

    doLast {
        BeesClient client = new BeesClient(apiUrl, apiKey, secret, 'xml',
                                     '1.0')
        ApplicationInfo info

        try {
            info = client.applicationInfo(appId)
        }
        catch(Exception e) {
            throw new GradleException(e.message)
        }

        logger.quiet "Application id : $info.id"
        logger.quiet "         title : $info.title"
        logger.quiet "       created : $info.created"
        logger.quiet "          urls : $info.urls"
        logger.quiet "        status : $info.status"
    }
}
```

> **Application information rendered on command line**

There's no easy way to fully test this task under real-world conditions because it uses properties provided on the command line and in the file `gradle.properties`. Let's see how the tooling API can help you to verify its correct behavior by using the build script.

First, set up the directory structure. Put the CloudBees task into a regular Gradle build script in a directory named script-under-test. Your testing code will live in a directory named `tooling-api-integ-test` on the same nesting level. It holds a Gradle build script that sets up Spock as its testing framework and pulls in the tooling API dependencies. The test class implementation is called `CloudBeesSpec.groovy`. The final setup looks as follows:

```
.
├── script-under-test
│   └── build.gradle
└── tooling-api-integ-test
    ├── build.gradle
    └── src
        └── test
```

> **Build script containing task for retrieving application information from CloudBees**

> **Sets up integration test dependencies**

```
└── groovy
    └── com
        └── manning
            └── gia
                └── CloudBeesSpec.groovy    ◄──┐
```
                                            Spock integration test using tooling API

Let's take a quick peek at the integration test build script shown in listing 10.15. Because you're using Spock to write your tests, you'll need to apply the Groovy plugin. All dependencies use the `testCompile` configuration because you're only planning to write tests.

Listing 10.15   Preparing the integration tests

```
apply plugin: 'groovy'

repositories {
    mavenCentral()
}
                                            Adds a dependency on
                                            Gradle API for pulling
                                            in tooling API
dependencies {                                                    Declares Spock
    testCompile localGroovy()                                     for integration
    testCompile gradleApi()                    ◄──┘               tests
    testCompile 'org.spockframework:spock-core:0.7-groovy-1.8'  ◄──┘
}
```

Listing 10.16 shows the content of the test class `CloudBeesSpec.groovy`. It defines a single test method that uses the Gradle tooling API to execute the CloudBees task named `cloudBeesAppInfo`. Not only do you want to execute the task, you also want to make sure it behaves as expected. The task only produces command-line output, so you'll need to parse the standard output stream to see if the correct application information is printed. This functionality is testable in a unit test because a Gradle task doesn't allow for setting a mock object for the logger instance.

Listing 10.16   Integration testing using the tooling API

```
package com.manning.gia

import org.gradle.tooling.*
import spock.lang.Specification                    Points to project directory
                                                   of script under test
class CloudBeesSpec extends Specification {
    static final String GRADLE_VERSION = '1.5'
    static final File PROJECT_DIR = new File('../script-under-test')  ◄──┘

    def "CloudBees application information is rendered on the command line"() {
        given:
            String[] tasks = ['cloudBeesAppInfo'] as String[]
            String arguments = '-PappId=gradle-in-action/todo'
        when:
            ByteArrayOutputStream stream = executeWithGradleConnector(
                            ➡ GRADLE_VERSION, PROJECT_DIR, tasks, arguments)
            String output = stream.toString('UTF-8')
```

Executes script under test with Gradle connector and parses its command-line output

```
                          then:
Asserts                       output != null
expected                      output.contains('Application id : gradle-in-action/todo')
values from                   output.contains('title : todo')
task output                   output.contains('urls : [todo.gradle-in-action.cloudbees.net]')
                          }

                          private ByteArrayOutputStream executeWithGradleConnector(String
                                                  ➡ gradleVersion, File projectDir,
                                                  ➡ String[] tasks, String arguments) {
Creates                       GradleConnector connector = GradleConnector.newConnector()
instance of                   ProjectConnection connection                                    Sets Gradle
GradleConnector                                                                               version and
                              try {                                                           project
                                  connection = connector.useGradleVersion(gradleVersion)      directory
                                      ➡ .forProjectDirectory(projectDir).connect()
                                  BuildLauncher buildLauncher = connection.newBuild()
Sets target                       buildLauncher.forTasks(tasks).withArguments(arguments)       Creates a new
tasks,                            ByteArrayOutputStream stream = new ByteArrayOutputStream()   instance of
arguments,                        buildLauncher.setStandardOutput(stream).run()               BuildLauncher
and output                        return stream
stream to run                 }
build script                  finally {
                                  connection.close()          Closes connection
                              }                               of GradleConnector
                          }
                      }
```

The intention of the test method should be clear. Let's also analyze how you use the Gradle tooling API within the test class `CloudBeesSpec`. As shown in the listing, you defined a method named `withGradleConnector` that does the heavy lifting. The tooling API is used in five steps:

1 Create an instance of the class `GradleConnector`—the main entry point to invoking a build script.
2 Configure the `GradleConnector` instance by setting the expected Gradle version, installation location, and the project directory containing the build script to invoke. By default, the wrapper is automatically downloaded and used.
3 Connect to the target build script by invoking the `connect()` method.
4 Provide build parameters, such as the tasks, command-line arguments, and the output stream you want to write to.
5 After the build script task is executed, the connection should be closed to free up the resource by calling the method `close()`.

This is the tooling API in a nutshell. There are many more options to explore, but this example should give you an idea of how powerful the tooling API is. You can find more information on usage patterns and configuration options in the user guide at http://www.gradle.org/docs/current/userguide/embedding.html.

10.4 *Summary*

Gradle's main runtime environment is the command line. While this feature makes the build portable, many developers are most productive in a visual editor or IDE. Having to switch between a command-line tool and editor can slow down the development process.

Gradle doesn't leave you hanging. With the help of plugins, you can generate project files for various IDEs and editors. The generated project files contain the metadata needed to conveniently open a project in an IDE with the correct setup. We discussed how to use these plugins in the context of your To Do application to create project files for Eclipse, IntelliJ IDEA, and Sublime Text. This metadata is mainly derived from the default build script configuration but can be customized to fit individual needs.

Popular Java IDE vendors realized the need for first-class Gradle support. The IDEs SpringSource STS, IntelliJ IDEA, and NetBeans provide sufficient tooling for opening a Gradle project by pointing them to a build script. Once the project is opened in the tool, a developer is able to manage dependencies, use Gradle DSL code completion, and execute tasks from within the IDE.

The tooling API forms the foundation for integrating Gradle with many of the IDEs we discussed. It allows for executing Gradle tasks, while at the same time monitoring and querying the running build. You learned that the tooling API can be used for implementing integration tests for a Gradle build script under real-world conditions.

Building polyglot projects

This chapter covers

- Managing JavaScript with Gradle
- Building a Gradle project with Java, Groovy, and Scala
- Exploring plugin support for other languages

In recent years, the interest in polyglot programming and its application in real-world, mission-critical software stacks has skyrocketed. The term *polyglot programming* was coined to describe projects that incorporate more than one language. That's particularly true for the Java world. For web developers, the world can no longer do without a potpourri of JavaScript, corresponding frameworks, libraries, and CSS. Backend code or desktop applications are no longer built with Java alone. Other JVM-based languages like Groovy or Scala are added to the mix. It's all about picking the right tool for the job. In this chapter, we'll discuss how Gradle faces the challenge of organizing and building polyglot projects by using your To Do application as an example.

As Java developers, we're spoiled by extensive tooling and build automation support. Concepts like build-time dependency management of external libraries and convention over configuration for project layouts have been around for years and are part of our day-to-day vocabulary. In JavaScript land, commonly accepted patterns and techniques for build automation are in their early stages of development. Gradle doesn't provide first-class support for JavaScript and CSS, but we'll discuss how to use its API to implement typical usage scenarios, like combining and minifying JavaScript files.

In past chapters, we mainly concentrated on building Java projects. Software stacks that incorporate a wide range of languages are a reality for many organizations. JVM-based languages are well supported by Gradle. We'll drill into the details of using the core language plugins for building Java, Groovy, and Scala code. Along the way, we'll touch on topics like compiler daemons and joint compilation.

In addition, many enterprises have to integrate with software written in non-JVM languages like C or C++. This chapter will give an overview of how to incorporate heterogeneous software infrastructure into a build. Let's start by looking at build automation for modern web architectures.

11.1 Managing JavaScript with Gradle

A rich user experience has become the key to success for any application. This holds true for desktop, mobile, and web applications. Today, users demand the same look and feel for web applications as they do for native applications. Long gone are the days when customers were happy with static HTML pages and synchronous server roundtrips.

JavaScript has become the most popular programming language for the web that can meet this demand. Developers no longer have to depend on plain JavaScript to implement their features. Many application development frameworks and libraries (like jQuery, Prototype, and Backbone, to name just a few) are available to simplify the use of JavaScript development and to smooth the rough edges this language introduces.

JavaScript has moved far beyond client-side runtime environments. Platforms like Node.js (http://nodejs.org/) use JavaScript for implementing server-side applications as well. As a result, JavaScript is ubiquitous and grows in relevance.

11.1.1 Typical tasks when dealing with JavaScript

When dealing with JavaScript, various tasks come to mind that may be part of your workflow. In fact, some of them should sound familiar, because we discussed them in the context of your Java web application:

- *Minification*: JavaScript is often included in an HTML page as an external file. This means it has to be downloaded to the browser before it can be used to render the page. The smaller the byte footprint of such a file, the faster the page can be loaded. Minification aims to decrease the size of an original JavaScript file by applying smart optimizations such as removing comments, spaces, and tabs. One tool that helps you minify your JavaScript files is the Google Closure compiler (https://developers.google.com/closure/compiler/).
- *Merging*: The size of a JavaScript file isn't the only factor playing a role in the loading performance of a page. Another problem is the number of HTTP

requests needed for each JavaScript file included in your page. The more external JavaScript files requested, the longer the user has to wait until the page is rendered. Combining multiple JavaScript files into one can solve this problem.

- *Testing*: Similar to writing test code for server-side code, you also want to be able to verify the correct behavior of your JavaScript implementation. Testing frameworks like Jasmine (http://pivotal.github.io/jasmine/) let you write test code in JavaScript.

- *Code analysis*: JavaScript source code can be analyzed to find potential bugs and problems, structural issues, and abnormal style conventions. JSLint (http://www.jslint.com/lint.html), a program written in JavaScript, aims to spot these problems in an automated fashion.

- *Transpiling*: Some client-side programming languages like CoffeeScript or Dart provide their own syntax and language constructs. Unfortunately, these kinds of languages do not run in a browser. Transpiling, a specific kind of compilation, translates this source code into JavaScript to make it executable in the target environment.

If you try to incorporate all of these tasks in your To Do project without proper automation, there are many manual and repetitive steps that need to be performed before you can assemble the WAR file. For the same reasons laid out in chapter 1, you'll want to avoid this situation under all circumstances. In this chapter, we won't cover solutions to all tasks presented, but you'll learn how to generally automate them with Gradle.

11.1.2   *Using JavaScript in the To Do application*

Let's assume you start to modernize your To Do application. Instead of submitting the data to the server for each operation and rerendering the page, you change the functionality to exchange data via asynchronous JavaScript calls (AJAX) in the background. If the HTML user interface needs to be updated, you directly modify the document object model (DOM). As a result, the To Do application will behave similar to a desktop application with no page reload required.

To simplify the use of JavaScript, your application will use an external JavaScript library. Out of the many available libraries, pick JQuery (http://jquery.com/), an established, feature-rich, easy-to-use API for handling AJAX calls and manipulating the HTML DOM.

With the help of JQuery, you'll implement updating the name of an existing To Do item in your list. This functionality requires two actions. Double-clicking the item's name will bring the item name into edit mode by offering an input field to change its value. Pressing the Enter key while in editing mode will send the modified item name to the server, update the value in the data store, and exit the edit mode. These actions are implemented in the JavaScript files `edit-action.js` and `update-action.js`. We won't discuss the content of these files here. Feel free to check out their implementation in the book's source code examples. The following directory structure shows both JavaScript files, as well as the minified JQuery library in your web project:

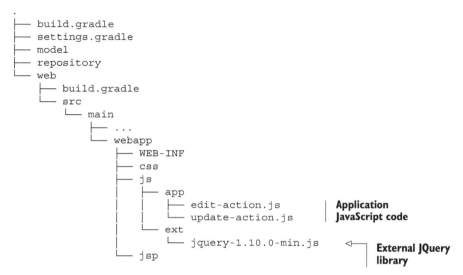

```
.
├── build.gradle
├── settings.gradle
├── model
├── repository
└── web
       ├── build.gradle
       └── src
              └── main
                     ├── ...
                     └── webapp
                            ├── WEB-INF
                            ├── css
                            ├── js
                            │      ├── app
                            │      │      ├── edit-action.js          Application
                            │      │      └── update-action.js        JavaScript code
                            │      └── ext
                            │             └── jquery-1.10.0-min.js    External JQuery
                            └── jsp                                    library
```

Now, you could just download the JQuery library manually and put it into the directory `src/main/webapp/js/ext`. Many projects do that. Remember when we talked about dependency management for external Java libraries in chapter 5? You can apply the same concept for automatically resolving and downloading JavaScript files. Let's see how this can be done.

11.1.3 Dependency management for JavaScript libraries

Historically, JavaScript developers didn't bother with the concept of dependency management. We used to throw in external libraries with our application sources. As our code base grew, we had no way of knowing what JavaScript dependencies the project required and with what version. If we were lucky, the filename of the JavaScript library would indicate that.

If you exclusively work with JavaScript, this problem can be tackled by using the node package manager (NPM). Dependencies between JavaScript files can be modeled by using RequireJS (http://requirejs.org/). But what if you want to use JavaScript dependency management from Gradle? No problem; you can just use the standard Gradle dependency declaration and resolution mechanism.

There are some challenges we face with this approach, though. As JVM developers, we're used to having access to all possible libraries we'd ever want to use. We pointed our build script to Maven Central and that was that. For JavaScript libraries, there's no established hosting infrastructure. One of the hosting providers with a reasonable collection of popular, open source JavaScript libraries is Google Hosted Libraries (https://developers.google.com/speed/libraries/). Alternatively, you can directly use the hosted versions of a specific library if the project provides them.

On top of an insufficient JavaScript hosting infrastructure, you can't depend on a unified descriptor format for libraries, similar to the pom.xml file for Maven repositories. This means that transitive JavaScript libraries, CSS, and even required images need to be declared explicitly.

Let's look at how to retrieve the minified version of the library from JQuery's download page. You'll see a familiar pattern here. First, you define a custom configuration, and then you declare the library with the specific version in the dependencies configuration block. For downloading the library to your source code directory, create a new task of type Copy that uses your custom configuration. The following listing demonstrates how to wire this task up with other important tasks of your project to ensure that you fetch the JavaScript before running the application in Jetty or assembling the WAR file.

Listing 11.1   Using dependency management for consuming JavaScript libraries

```
repositories {
    ivy {
        name 'JQuery'                                              ⟵ Declares JQuery
        url 'http://code.jquery.com'                                 download URL as
        layout 'pattern', {                                          Ivy repository
            artifact '[module]-[revision](.[classifier]).[ext]'
        }
    }
}
configurations {
    jquery                          ⟵ Declares a custom
}                                     configuration for
                                      JavaScript dependencies

dependencies {                                                    ⟵ Declares JQuery
    jquery group: 'jquery', name: 'jquery', version: '1.10.0',      library as
        ⟹ classifier: 'min', ext: 'js'                            ⟵ dependency
}
task fetchExternalJs(type: Copy) {          Task for downloading JavaScript
    from configurations.jquery              dependencies to directory
    into "$webAppDir/js/ext"                src/main/webapp/js/ext
}                                                                   Task requiring
[jettyRun, jettyRunWar, war]*.dependsOn fetchExternalJs   ⟵         JavaScript library
                                                                    will download it first
```

Give the task a shot. You'll run it from the root directory of your Gradle project:

```
$ gradle :web:fetchExternalJs
:web:fetchExternalJs
Download http://code.jquery.com/jquery-1.10.0.min.js
```

As expected, the JavaScript library is downloaded and ends up in the specified directory src/main/webapp/js/ext. You can now directly link to this library in your JSPs and HTML files. After its initial download, the task fetchExternalJs automatically knows that it doesn't have to run again:

```
$ gradle :web:fetchExternalJs
:web:fetchExternalJs UP-TO-DATE
```

Your application source directory now contains all required JavaScript files. Feel free to check out the working application by running `gradle :web:jettyRun`. You'll see that the application is fully functional.

You may ask yourself why the downloaded JavaScript file was put directly in your project's source tree. Good point! Usually, you don't want to mix versioned files with downloaded dependencies. This was done to support in-place web application deployment with the Jetty plugin using the `jettyRun` task. Unfortunately, the plugin doesn't allow pointing to a secondary web application directory. Therefore, the jQuery JavaScript file needs to sit in the target web application location. There are ways to deal with this shortcoming. For example, you could exclude the file from versioning (please consult your VCS documentation).

You laid the groundwork for implementing additional automation tasks for your JavaScript code. In the next two sections, we'll talk about how to build your own JavaScript automation with the help of standard Gradle tooling. In particular, we'll look at how to implement minification and how to generate code quality metrics.

11.1.4 Merging and minifying JavaScript using a third-party Ant task

There are two essential optimizations every large JavaScript project needs to embrace: merging multiple JavaScript files into one and minifying its content. A tool that provides support for both of these tasks is the Google Closure Compiler (https://developers.google.com/closure/compiler/). One of its distributions is a Java library that can be directly included in a Gradle build, as shown in the following listing.

Listing 11.2 Declaring dependency on Google Closure Compiler library

```
repositories {
    mavenCentral()
}

configurations {
    googleClosure          ◁──┐  Custom configuration for
}                              │  assigning Google Closure
                               │  Compiler library

dependencies {
    googleClosure 'com.google.javascript:closure-compiler:v20130603'  ◁──┐ Declared
}                                                                          Google
                                                                           Closure
                                                                           Compiler
                                                                           dependency
```

Apart from the plain Java API classes, this library includes an Ant task wrapping the provided functionality. It's a matter of personal taste which of these approaches you use in your Gradle build—both of them work. For further examples, you'll use the Ant task because it conveniently wraps the API. The next listing demonstrates a custom task written in Groovy that you'll put into the directory `buildSrc/src/main/groovy` of your project. If you need a quick refresher on how to use an Ant task from Gradle, cross-reference chapter 9.

Listing 11.3   Calling Google Closure Compiler Ant task

```
package com.manning.gia.js

import org.gradle.api.DefaultTask
import org.gradle.api.file.FileCollection
import org.gradle.api.tasks.InputFiles
import org.gradle.api.tasks.OutputFile
import org.gradle.api.tasks.TaskAction

class GoogleClosureMinifier extends DefaultTask {
    @InputFiles
    FileCollection inputFiles

    @OutputFile
    File outputFile

    @TaskAction
    void minify() {
        ant.taskdef(name: 'jscomp', classname:
                'com.google.javascript.jscomp.ant.CompileTask', classpath:
                project.configurations.googleClosure.asPath)

        ant.jscomp(compilationLevel: 'simple', warning: 'verbose', debug:
                'false', output: outputFile.canonicalPath) {
            inputFiles.each { inputFile ->
                ant.sources(dir: inputFile.parent) {
                    ant.file(name: inputFile.name)
                }
            }
        }
    }
}
```

Declared Ant task from dependency

Ant task usage

Declaration of input files

For the custom task to function, an enhanced task of type GoogleClosureMinifier needs to set a list of input JavaScript files and the target output file, which will contain the combined and minified JavaScript code. The following listing uses the project's fileTree method to derive the list of your application's JavaScript files as input. The output file is defined as all-min.js and is created in the directory build/js.

Listing 11.4   Using custom task for minifying JavaScript

```
import com.manning.gia.js.GoogleClosureMinifier

ext {
    jsSourceDir = "$webAppDir/js/app"
    jsOutputDir = "$buildDir/js"
}

def jsSourceFiles = fileTree(jsSourceDir).include('*.js')

task minifyJs(type: GoogleClosureMinifier) {
    inputFiles = jsSourceFiles
    outputFile = file("$jsOutputDir/all-min.js")
}
```

Declares a set of JavaScript files in given directory

Sets input JavaScript files

Sets minified JavaScript output file

Executing the task `minifyJs` will first compile your minification custom task under `buildSrc`, and then produce a single, optimized JavaScript file:

```
$ gradle :web:minifyJs
:buildSrc:compileJava UP-TO-DATE
:buildSrc:compileGroovy
:buildSrc:processResources UP-TO-DATE
:buildSrc:classes
:buildSrc:jar
:buildSrc:assemble
:buildSrc:compileTestJava UP-TO-DATE
:buildSrc:compileTestGroovy UP-TO-DATE
:buildSrc:processTestResources UP-TO-DATE
:buildSrc:testClasses UP-TO-DATE
:buildSrc:test
:buildSrc:check
:buildSrc:build
:web:minifyJs
```

Being able to create an optimized JavaScript file is great, but now you have to change the references in your dynamic and static web page files. Of course, this process should be fully automated and integrated in your development process. In the next section, we'll discuss one way to implement this.

11.1.5 *JavaScript optimization as part of the development workflow*

In production environments performance is key. That's why many organizations choose to deploy optimized JavaScript files. The downside is that single-line, optimized JavaScript files are hard to read and not very useful for debugging or even diagnosing an issue. Therefore, you don't want to package and run your application with only minified files. During development or in testing environments, you still want to use plain old JavaScript files. Obviously, at build time you need to be able to control whether your application JavaScript files need to be optimized and used.

There are many approaches to tackle this problem. Here, we'll only discuss one of them. For your project, we'll discuss a new project property named `jsOptimized`. If it's provided on the command line, you indicate that optimizations should happen. If it's not provided, use the original JavaScript files. Here's an example of how to use it:
`gradle :web:war -PjsOptimize`.

Gradle is flexible enough to support this requirement. Based on this optimization flag, you can configure your `war` task to trigger the minification, exclude the original JavaScript files, include the produced minified file, and change the JSP file to reference it. The following listing shows how to make this happen for your To Do application.

> **Listing 11.5   Conditional packaging and use of optimized JavaScript files**

```
ext.jsOptimize = project.hasProperty('jsOptimize')

war {
    if(jsOptimize) {                             ⊲──┤  Only optimize JavaScript
        dependsOn minifyJs                            if requested by property
```

```
    exclude 'js/app/*'

    from(jsOutputDir) {                     Exclude original
        into 'js/app'                       JavaScript files; include
        include 'all-min.js'                minified ones instead
    }
                                                       Exclude JSP, which
    exclude 'jsp/app-js.jsp'                           applies original
                                                   ◁—┘ JavaScript files
    from("$webAppDir/jsp") {
        include 'todo-list.jsp'
        into 'jsp'                                     Replace JSP
        filter { String line ->                        import file
            if(line.contains('<c:import url="app-js.jsp"/>')) {   with minified
                return '<c:import url="app-js-min.jsp"/>'          version for file
            }                                                      todo-list.jsp

            line
        }
    }
}
}
```

The trickiest part of this configuration is the replacement of the JavaScript import in
the JSP file `todo-list.jsp`. To make life easier, you created two new JSP files that reference either the original JavaScript files or the minified file. At build time, you only
need to replace the JSTL import statement if you decide to go with the optimized version. Keep in mind that the original source file isn't touched. The file is changed on
the fly when building up the WAR file.

This example covers one of the most common use cases for JavaScript developers.
Let's also look at introspecting JavaScript source files for code quality purposes.

11.1.6 JavaScript code analysis using an external Java library

Detecting issues and potential problems before the code gets deployed to production
should be of concern to every JavaScript developer. JSHint is a popular tool written in
JavaScript for detecting errors and potential issues in JavaScript code. To run JSHint,
you'll need to be able to execute it from Gradle. So how do you execute JavaScript
from Gradle?

Rhino is an open source implementation of JavaScript written in Java. With the
help of this library, you can run JavaScript files and therefore use JSHint in your build.
In the next listing, you'll retrieve Rhino from Maven Central and the JSHint JavaScript
file from a hosted download URL.

> **Listing 11.6   Declaring Rhino and JSHint dependencies**

```
repositories {
    mavenCentral()

    ivy {
        name 'JSHint'                            Declares JSHint download
        url 'http://www.jshint.com/get'          URL as Ivy repository
        layout 'pattern', {
```

```
        artifact '[module]-[revision](.[classifier]).[ext]'
      }
    }
  }
}
```
⌐ Declares JSHint
| download URL
| as Ivy repository

```
configurations {
   rhino
   jshint
}
```
| **Custom configurations**
| **for Rhino and JSHint**

Declares Rhino
dependency

```
dependencies {
   rhino 'org.mozilla:rhino:1.7R4'
   jshint 'jshint-rhino:jshint-rhino:2.1.4@js'
}
```

Declares JSHint JavaScript
dependency indicated by
@js file extension

You declared Rhino as a dependency—now let's see it in action. Instead of using an Ant task, invoke the main method by assigning it to an enhanced Gradle task of type JavaExec. JSHint requires you to define a list of JavaScript files as arguments that it should examine. Under the hood, a Java invocation of Rhino for your application looks as follows:

```
java -jar rhino-1.7RC4.jar jshint-rhino-2.1.4.js edit-action.js update-
➥ action.js
```

The following listing demonstrates how to build this argument list and write the enhanced task for invoking the Rhino main class.

Listing 11.7 Executing the JSHint JavaScript with Rhino from Gradle

```
ext.jsSourceDir = "$webAppDir/js/app"
def jsSourceFiles = fileTree(jsSourceDir).include('*.js')
def jsHintArgs = configurations.jshint + jsSourceFiles

task jsHint(type: JavaExec) {
   classpath configurations.rhino
   main 'org.mozilla.javascript.tools.shell.Main'
   args jsHintArgs
}
```
Puts together
arguments for Rhino
executable with JSHint,
JavaScript being the first

Declares enhanced task
for executing Rhino as
Java process

Executing the task for your fully functional application doesn't report any issues:

```
$ gradle jsHint
:web:jsHint
```

However, try emulating a bug in your JavaScript by removing a semicolon at the end of a line in the file edit-action.js. You can see that JSHint rightfully complains about it and fails the build:

```
$ gradle :web:jsHint
:web:jsHint
Missing semicolon. (/Users/Ben/gradle-in-action/code/chapter11/todo-
➥ js-code-quality/web/src/main/webapp/js/app/edit-action.js:2:46)
> $("#toDoItem_" + row).addClass("editing")

:web:jsHint FAILED
```

11.1.7 *Using a third-party Gradle JavaScript plugin*

We saw that it's really easy to incorporate third-party libraries to create sufficient tooling for JavaScript in your Gradle build. This can be accomplished by reusing Ant tasks, by executing Java applications with the help of the task type `JavaExec`, or even by calling external shell scripts. All it takes is a little bit of research and the eagerness to find the best tool for the job.

We all know that good developers are lazy—lazy because they hate doing monotonous and repetitive tasks. Most developers prefer to reuse existing functionality. There's a community Gradle plugin that provides most of the functionality you've implemented and even more (for example, generating API documentation with JSDoc). Enter the Gradle JavaScript plugin (https://github.com/eriwen/gradle-js-plugin). The plugin is a good starting point for every project that incorporates JavaScript and doesn't require you to implement your own tasks.

In this section, we'll discuss how to use the plugin and its exposed DSL to optimize your JavaScript—that is, by combining and minifying it. First, pull in the plugin from Maven Central and apply it to your web project, as shown in the next listing.

Listing 11.8   Adding the JavaScript plugin to the build script's classpath

```
buildscript {
    repositories {
        mavenCentral()
    }

    dependencies {
        classpath 'com.eriwen:gradle-js-plugin:1.5.1'
    }
}

apply plugin: com.eriwen.gradle.js.JsPlugin
```

The plugin describes JavaScript source directories with a dedicated name. This named JavaScript source set can then be used as input for one of the tasks the plugin defines. The following listing shows the JavaScript DSL in more detail. This code should look similar to what you've built so far, but is more readable and easier to understand.

Listing 11.9   Configuring the JavaScript plugin

```
ext {
    jsSourceDir = "$webAppDir/js/app"
    jsOutputDir = "$buildDir/js"
}

javascript.source {
    app {
        js {
            srcDir jsSourceDir          Defines the directory
            include '*.js'              src/main/webapp/jsp/app
            exclude '*.min.js'          as source directory
        }
                                        Only includes nonminified
                                        JavaScript files
```

```
    }
}
combineJs {
    source = javascript.source.dev.js.files      ◁─┐  Uses JavaScript source set
    dest = file("$jsOutputDir/all.js")                as input for combining
}                                                     JavaScript files

minifyJs {                                            Uses output from task
    source = combineJs                          ◁─┐  combineJs as input for
    dest = file("$jsOutputDir/all-min.js")            task minifyJs
}
```

The task usage is very similar to what you've experienced so far. To run minification on your files, execute the task minifyJs. This task first calls the combineJs task to merge your application JavaScript files before shrinking their size.

> **What about CSS?**
>
> Requirements for optimizing CSS are in many cases no different from JavaScript. Similar tasks can be implemented to combine and minify CSS, except with other tools. For a quick start, check out the Gradle CSS plugin: https://github.com/eriwen/gradle-css-plugin.

Great, there's third-party plugin support for JavaScript in Gradle. But what if your frontend team already implemented build automation that doesn't use Gradle? Do you need to rewrite all their existing logic? Thankfully, you don't. You can directly invoke other build automation tools from Gradle. Let's examine this by the example of Grunt.

11.1.8 Executing Grunt from Gradle

If you're deeply involved in the JavaScript community, you may know the build tool Grunt (http://gruntjs.com/). Grunt is targeted toward implementing common tasks like minifying, merging, and testing of JavaScript code in an automated fashion. With its plugin system and rapidly growing community, you'll need to take into consideration existing JavaScript automation workflows.

To get started with Grunt, you first need to install the executable via NPM, the Node.js package manager. Please check the Grunt documentation for detailed information on how to install it. Based on your operating system, you'll either end up with a batch script named grunt.cmd (Windows) or a shell script named grunt (*nix). This executable is used to evaluate and run a Grunt build. A Grunt build requires two mandatory files: the file Gruntfile.js defines the tasks and their configuration, and the file package.json defines the project metadata and required external dependencies (for example, plugins).

In this section, we'll discuss how to call Grunt tasks from Gradle. This is a valuable approach for two reasons: either you already have an automation process in place and

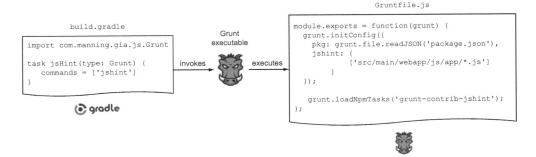

Figure 11.1   Invoking the Grunt executable from Gradle

don't want to rewrite this code in Gradle, or you want to drive build automation from a single tool that allows you to cover the full application stack. Figure 11.1 illustrates how executing the Grunt executable looks in practice.

Let's see this setup in action. Grunt doesn't automatically install dependencies defined in package.json. If a user forgets about this step, the Grunt build will fail. To install these dependencies, navigate to the directory that contains the file and run the NPM with the command npm install. The NPM installs dependencies to the directory node_modules.

Of course, we, as automation specialists, want to make this happen automatically. Before running a Grunt task from Gradle, run the Node install command. The following listing demonstrates how to wrap this call with a Gradle task.

Listing 11.10   Task that installs Grunt dependencies via npm

```
task installGruntDependencies(type: Exec) {          Grunt package file that declares
    inputs.file 'package.json'                       required dependencies
    outputs.dir 'node_modules'
                                                     Output directory npm
    executable 'npm'          Executed command       used to store downloaded
    args 'install'            npm install            dependencies
}
```

If you take a closer look at figure 11.1, you'll notice a task of type Grunt. Listing 11.11 shows the Groovy task Grunt, a class defined under buildSrc/src/main/groovy, which acts as a simple wrapper for invoking the Grunt executable. All you need to provide to the enhanced task are the commands (the Grunt tasks) defined in the Grunt build file.

Listing 11.11   Custom task for calling Grunt executable

```
package com.manning.gia.js

import org.gradle.api.DefaultTask
import org.gradle.api.tasks.Input
import org.gradle.api.tasks.TaskAction
```

```
class Grunt extends DefaultTask {
    @Input
    List<String> commands

    @TaskAction
    void callGrunt() {
        project.exec {
            executable isWindows() ? 'grunt.cmd' : 'grunt'
            args commands
        }
    }
    boolean isWindows() {
        System.properties['os.name'].toLowerCase().contains('windows')
    }
}
```

Using exec method from Project to invoke Grunt executable

Provides Grunt tasks as command-line arguments

Determines Grunt executable based on operating system

Let's assume you have an existing Grunt build that applies the JSHint plugin. The JSHint task is named `jshint`. To invoke this Grunt task, you create a new task of type `Grunt` and provide the Grunt task name as the command, as shown in the next listing.

Listing 11.12   Enhanced task executing the Grunt JSHint plugin

```
import com.manning.gia.js.Grunt

task jsHint(type: Grunt, dependsOn: installGruntDependencies) {
    commands = ['jshint']
}
```

Installs Grunt project dependencies before executing task

Executes a list of GruntJS tasks

Run the task `jsHint` on your To Do application. The following command-line output shows the output from Grunt discovering an erroneous JavaScript file that's missing a semicolon:

```
$ gradle :web:jsHint
:buildSrc:compileJava UP-TO-DATE
:buildSrc:compileGroovy
...
:buildSrc:build
:web:installGruntDependencies
npm WARN package.json my-project-name@0.1.0 No README.md file found!
npm http GET https://registry.npmjs.org/grunt
...
grunt@0.4.1 node_modules/grunt
├── dateformat@1.0.2-1.2.3
├── ...
...
grunt-contrib-jshint@0.6.0 node_modules/grunt-contrib-jshint
└── jshint@2.1.4 (console-browserify@0.1.6, underscore@1.4.4, shelljs@0.1.4,
➥ minimatch@0.2.12, cli@0.4.4-2)
:web:jsHint
Running "jshint:all" (jshint) task
Linting src/main/webapp/js/app/edit-action.js...ERROR
[L2:C46] W033: Missing semicolon.
    $("#toDoItem_" + row).addClass("editing")
```

```
Warning: Task "jshint:all" failed. Use --force to continue.

Aborted due to warnings.
:web:jsHint FAILED
```

After this extensive discussion about JavaScript integration with Gradle, we'll look at Gradle support for JVM languages other than Java.

11.2   *Building polyglot, JVM-based projects*

The days when Java was the one and only language used for writing applications are over. Today, when we think about Java, we also refer to it as a mature development platform: the Java Virtual Machine (JVM). There's a wide range of languages running on the JVM that are suitable for enterprise or server-side development. Among them are popular languages likes Groovy, Scala, Clojure, and JRuby. Why would you even want to use a different language than Java or mix them within a single project? Again, it's all about the right tool for the job. You may prefer Java for its statically typed nature and library support to implement your business logic. However, Java's syntax isn't a natural fit for producing DSLs. This is where other, more suitable languages like Groovy come into play.

So far, we've discussed how to build Java applications, but there's more to Gradle. It has first-class support for other JVM languages. In this section, we'll look at how to organize and build Groovy and Scala projects and how to bring them all under one umbrella within a single project. Before we dive into the details, let's take a step back and review some of the inner workings of the Java plugin, which to an extent builds the foundation for other language plugins.

11.2.1   *Base capabilities of JVM language plugins*

In chapter 8, we talked about a guiding principle for separating concerns in plugins: capabilities versus conventions. Let's quickly recap this concept. A plugin that provides a capability oftentimes introduces new concepts or tasks, and a plugin that provides conventions imposes opinionated defaults for these concepts. What might sound very abstract becomes strikingly clear by dissecting the inner workings of the Java plugin.

CAPABILITIES VERSUS CONVENTIONS IN JAVA PROJECTS

What you see as a Gradle user when you apply the Java plugin to one of your projects is the full gamut of functionality. Your project is automatically equipped with the concept of source sets and Java-specific configurations, and exposes tasks as well as properties. This baseline Java support builds the foundation for every JVM language-based project. These capabilities are

- *Configurations*: compile, runtime
- *Tasks per source set*: compileJava, processResources, classes
- *Lifecycle tasks*: check, build, buildNeeded, buildDependents
- *Properties*: sourceCompatibility, targetCompatibility

Gradle also preconfigured your project with sensible default configurations, also called conventions—for example, production source code sits in the directory `src/main/java`, and test source code in `src/test/java`. These conventions aren't set in stone and can be reconfigured, but they paint an initial opinioned view of your project. Some of the tasks in a Java project are based on the preconfigured source sets. The following list describes the opinionated bits of the Java plugin:

- *Configurations*: `testCompile`, `testRuntime`
- *Source sets*: `main`, `test`
- *Tasks*: `jar`, `test`, `javadoc`

THE JAVA BASE PLUGIN

The Java plugin separates capabilities and conventions. How does it do it? Capabilities are extracted into another plugin: the Java base plugin. Internally, the Java plugin applies the Java base plugin and adds the conventions on top, as shown in figure 11.2.

This separation of concerns has various implications. First of all, if your Java project doesn't fit the default conventions introduced by the Java plugin, you can instead apply the Java base plugin and define your own conventions. Second, the Java base plugin can be used as the basis for building other JVM language plugins because they require similar concepts. This is a perfect example of code reuse and is applied to the core plugins for building Groovy and Scala projects. Before we look at how these base capabilities are applied, let's explore another useful optimization you can use when compiling Java sources.

SPEEDING UP JAVA COMPILATION WITH THE COMPILER DAEMON

By default, Gradle will fork a new JVM for every Java compilation task. Especially in large Java-based multiproject builds, this causes unnecessary overhead. You can speed up the compilation process by reusing an already-forked instance of a Java compilation process. In the following listing, you configure every task of type `Java-Compile` to run in fork mode, while at the same time using Gradle's own Java compiler integration.

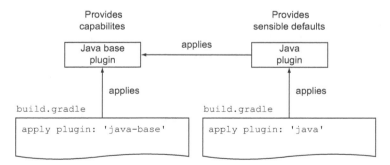

Figure 11.2   Java plugin automatically applies the Java base plugin

```
subprojects {
    apply plugin: 'java'

    tasks.withType(JavaCompile) {
        options.useAnt = false
        options.fork = true
    }
}
```

Uses Gradle's direct compiler integration, bypassing Ant javac task

Runs compilation in a separate process

When executing the multiproject build on the root level with `gradle clean build`, notice that the total time of your build is faster than without this modification. Internally, Gradle reuses the compiler daemon process across tasks even if they belong to a different subproject. After the build is finished, the compiler daemon process(es) are stopped. This means that they don't outlast a single build. Next, we'll focus on building and configuring Groovy projects.

11.2.2 *Building Groovy projects*

Groovy works nicely in conjunction with its older brother Java. It builds on top of Java, but has a more concise syntax and adds dynamic language features to the mix. Introducing Groovy to a Java project is as simple as adding the Groovy JAR file to its classpath.

In this book, you already used Groovy to write project infrastructure code. You used the Spock framework to write unit tests for your production application code. We also looked at how Groovy can be used to implement custom Gradle tasks. For conservative organizations, these are suitable use cases for incorporating Groovy, because the code isn't deployed to a production environment. There are many good reasons why you may also want to use Groovy instead of Java for implementing production code. Groovy is a great match for writing DSLs with the help of its meta-programming features. This is something Gradle does itself. It uses Java to implement the core logic, but wraps it with Groovy to expose the powerful DSL you're now accustomed to. Groovy support in Gradle is provided by the Groovy plugin. Let's look at its features and see where the Java base plugin comes into play.

GROOVY BASE AND GROOVY PLUGIN

The Groovy plugin ecosystem imposes an analogous concept to separate capabilities and conventions as the Java plugin. To get a quick overview on how they play together, look at figure 11.3.

Central to the figure are the Groovy base plugin and the Groovy plugin. The Groovy base plugin inherits all the capabilities of the Java base plugin and imposes its own conventions on top of it. Check out its feature list:

- *Source set*: `groovy`
- *Tasks per source set*: `compileGroovy`, `compileTestGroovy`

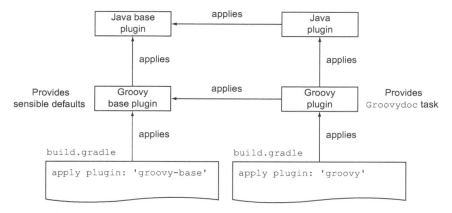

Figure 11.3 Groovy plugin inherits capabilities from the Java base plugin

The Groovy plugin builds upon the Groovy base plugin and the Java plugin. The additional benefit that the plugin adds to the equation is a task of type Groovydoc. Executing this task generates the HTML API documentation for the Groovy source code. Next, you'll convert one of the projects in your To Do application from a Java project into a Groovy project.

MINIMAL SETUP TO GET STARTED

Turning a self-contained Java project into a Groovy project is easy. We'll examine the conversion process by the example of your model project. Currently, this project only defines a single Java class file: ToDoItem.java. Before you turn this class into a Groovy class, you'll add the build infrastructure code to the script model/build.gradle, as shown in the following listing.

> **Listing 11.14 Using Groovy to manage production source code**

```
apply plugin: 'groovy'          ⟵┐  Applies Groovy
                                   │  plugin
repositories {
   mavenCentral()
}
                                              Declares Groovy
dependencies {                                JAR file as compile
   compile 'org.codehaus.groovy:groovy-all:2.1.5'  ⟵┘  dependency
}
```

By applying the Groovy plugin, you equipped your project with the capabilities to compile Groovy source code and the default source sets that define where the compiler looks for the source code files.

Remember that the Groovy plugin automatically applies the Java plugin as well. This means that your project now contains a source set for Java sources and one for Groovy sources. Figure 11.4 shows the default project layout with the applied Groovy plugin.

Default project layout

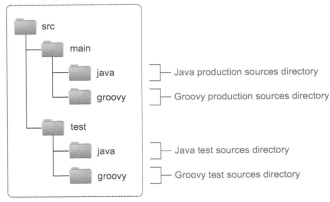

Figure 11.4   **Default source directories for projects applying the Groovy plugin**

Which Groovy distribution do I pick?

You may be aware that there are multiple distributions of the Groovy library. The file `groovy-all` contains all external dependencies (for example, Antlr and Apache Commons CLI) in a single JAR file archive to ensure compatibility between them. The file with the name `groovy` doesn't contain these dependencies. You're responsible for declaring these dependencies in your build script. No matter which distribution you choose, both will enable your project to compile Groovy source code.

Keep in mind that this doesn't mean that you're required to have Java source files in your project. However, it enables you to mix Java and Groovy files in a single project. For now, just rename the existing Java class to `ToDoItem.groovy` and move the file under `src/main/groovy` with the package directory `com.manning.gia.todo.model`. It's time to convert the bulky POJO class implementation into Groovy. The next listing demonstrates to what extreme the code could be condensed.

Listing 11.15   `ToDoItem` model class written in Groovy

```
package com.manning.gia.todo.model

import groovy.transform.Canonical

@Canonical
class ToDoItem implements Comparable<ToDoItem> {
    Long id
    String name
    boolean completed

    @Override
    int compareTo(ToDoItem toDoItem) {
        this.id.compareTo(toDoItem.id)
    }
}
```

Groovy annotation that auto-generates methods equals, hashCode, and toString

Try out the build of your Groovy project. You can see that the task `compileJava` is marked `UP-TO-DATE` because you don't have any Java source files under `src/main/java`. The task `compileGroovy` finds the file `ToDoItem.groovy` and compiles it. The following command-line output demonstrates this behavior:

```
$ gradle :model:build
:model:compileJava UP-TO-DATE
:model:compileGroovy
Download http://repo1.maven.org/maven2/org/codehaus/groovy/groovy-
➥ all/2.1.5/groovy-all-2.1.5.pom
Download http://repo1.maven.org/maven2/org/codehaus/groovy/groovy-
➥ all/2.1.5/groovy-all-2.1.5.jar
:model:processResources UP-TO-DATE
:model:classes
:model:jar
:model:assemble
:model:compileTestJava UP-TO-DATE
:model:compileTestGroovy UP-TO-DATE
:model:processTestResources UP-TO-DATE
:model:testClasses UP-TO-DATE
:model:test
:model:check
:model:build
```

CUSTOMIZING THE PROJECT LAYOUT

If the default conventions introduced by the Groovy base plugin don't fit your needs, you can redefine them in the same way as you can for Java projects. The underlying concept that enables you to reconfigure the default source directories is a `SourceSet`. In the following listing, you'll say that the Groovy production source files should sit under `src/groovy`, and Groovy test source files should reside under `test/groovy`.

Listing 11.16   Customizing the default Groovy source set directories

```
sourceSets {
    main {
        groovy {
            srcDirs = ['src/groovy']
        }
    }
    test {
        groovy {
            srcDirs = ['test/groovy']
        }
    }
}
```

JAVA AND GROOVY JOINT COMPILATION

I mentioned before that a single Gradle project can contain Java and Groovy files. To a developer, it feels natural to use Java classes from Groovy classes and vice versa. In the end, shouldn't both source file types be compiled to bytecode? There's a catch. Groovy can depend on Java, but Java can't depend on Groovy.

To demonstrate this behavior, you'll apply the Groovy plugin to the repository project. You'll also turn the class ToDoRepository from a Java interface into a Groovy interface, as shown in the next listing.

Listing 11.17   Repository interface written in Groovy

```
package com.manning.gia.todo.repository

import com.manning.gia.todo.model.ToDoItem

interface ToDoRepository {
    List<ToDoItem> findAll()
    List<ToDoItem> findAllActive()
    List<ToDoItem> findAllCompleted()
    ToDoItem findById(Long id)
    Long insert(ToDoItem toDoItem)
    void update(ToDoItem toDoItem)
    void delete(ToDoItem toDoItem)
}
```

This interface has two implementations, both of which are still Java classes: InMemory-ToDoRepository.java and H2ToDoRepository.java. Now, if you compile the repository project, you'll end up with a compilation error:

```
$ gradle :repository:classes
:model:compileJava UP-TO-DATE
:model:processResources UP-TO-DATE
:model:classes UP-TO-DATE
:model:jar UP-TO-DATE
:repository:compileJava
/Users/Ben/gradle-in-action/chapter11/todo-mixed-java-groovy/
➥ repository/src/main/java/com/manning/gia/todo/repository/
➥ H2ToDoRepository.java:9: cannot find symbol
symbol: class ToDoRepository
public class H2ToDoRepository implements ToDoRepository {
                                         ^

/Users/Ben/gradle-in-action/code/chapter11/todo-mixed-java-groovy/
➥ repository/src/main/java/com/manning/gia/todo/repository/
➥ InMemoryToDoRepository.java:12: cannot find symbol
symbol: class ToDoRepository
public class InMemoryToDoRepository implements ToDoRepository {
                                               ^

...
16 errors
:repository:compileJava FAILED
```

Does this mean you can never depend on Groovy classes from Java classes? No. The key to making this work is called *joint compilation*, which allows you to freely mix Java and Groovy source code with bidirectional dependencies on each other. One way to address this issue is to put the Java source code together with the Groovy source code under the directory src/main/groovy. Alternatively, you can configure the Groovy compiler to enable joint compilation. The following listing shows what needs to be configured in your build to use this feature.

Listing 11.18   Reconfiguring source sets for joint compilation

Removes source directories for Java source set

```
sourceSets.main.java.srcDirs = []          ◄──┘
sourceSets.main.groovy.srcDirs = ['src/main/java', 'src/main/groovy']    ◄─┐
```

Includes Java and Groovy source
directory for Groovy compiler

After you add this code snippet to the `build.gradle` file of the repository project, joint compilation works as expected:

```
$ gradle :repository:classes
:model:compileJava UP-TO-DATE
:model:processResources UP-TO-DATE
:model:classes UP-TO-DATE
:model:jar UP-TO-DATE
:repository:compileJava UP-TO-DATE
:repository:compileGroovy
:repository:processResources UP-TO-DATE
:repository:classes
```

For the compiler nerds among us, let's look at what happens under the hood:

1 The compiler parses the Groovy source files and generates stubs for them.
2 The Groovy compiler invokes the Java compiler and generates the stubs for Java source files.
3 With the Java stubs in the Groovy source path, the Groovy compiler can compile both.

With the techniques presented in this chapter, you should be able to set up your own project to incorporate Groovy, either as a standalone Groovy project or as a mixed Java and Groovy project. Next, we'll explore Gradle's support for Scala projects.

11.2.3   Building Scala projects

Scala is another language running on the JVM that has become increasingly popular in the past few years. The language is statically typed, combines object-oriented programming with support for functional programming, and is designed to express logic in an elegant, concise way. As with Groovy, Scala can use all Java libraries that a Java developer already knows. Scala has seen quite a bit of real-world adoption. Twitter reimplemented their backend services with Scala, and Foursquare moved on to Scala as well.

Scala support in Gradle is as sophisticated as the support for Groovy. In this section, we'll explore the corresponding Scala language plugins. You'll take an approach similar to what you did for Groovy to transform parts of your To Do application to Scala and build them with Gradle.

SCALA BASE AND SCALA PLUGIN

The Scala plugins are designed with the same concepts in mind as the Groovy plugins. The basic idea is to separate capabilities from conventions. In figure 11.5, you can see that Gradle provides two Scala plugins.

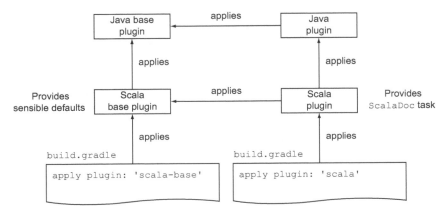

Figure 11.5   Scala plugin inherits capabilities from the Java base plugin

The Scala base plugin automatically applies the Java base plugin. You learned before that the Java plugin provides the capabilities for building Java-based projects. The Scala base plugin uses these capabilities and preconfigures default conventions for Scala projects, as shown in the following list:

- *Source set*: scala
- *Tasks per source set*: compileScala, compileTestScala

The Scala plugin internally applies not only the Scala base plugin, but also the Java plugin. This allows you to build Java and Scala source code within a single project. The feature the Scala plugin provides on top of the Scala base plugin is the ability to generate HTML API documentation for Scala source code. If you're building a full-fledged Scala project, applying the Scala plugin is your best choice. Let's see Scala in action.

MINIMAL SETUP TO GET STARTED

To demonstrate the use of Scala within your To Do application, you'll convert a Java class into a Scala class. The project in your build with the least complex source code is the model project. At the moment, this project's build.gradle file doesn't define any logic. The following listing applies the Scala plugin and declares the Scala library to get a hold on the Scala compiler.

Listing 11.19   Using Scala to manage production source code

```
apply plugin: 'scala'          ⟵┐ Applies Scala
                                 │ plugin
repositories {
   mavenCentral()
}

                                              ┌ Declares Scala library
dependencies {                                │ JAR file as compile
   compile 'org.scala-lang:scala-library:2.10.1'  ⟵┘ dependency
}
```

Default project layout

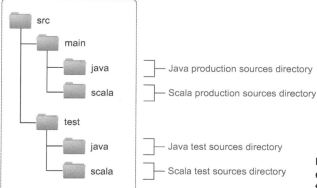

Figure 11.6   Default source directories for projects applying the Scala plugin

After applying the Scala plugin, your project can compile any Scala source code found in the directories src/main/scala and src/test/scala. Figure 11.6 shows the groovy source set directories alongside the source directory conventions introduced by the Java plugin.

Next, you'll transform the existing Java file ToDoItem.java into a Scala file. Every Scala source code file has the extension .scala. Go ahead and rename the file and move it under the directory src/main/scala. It's time to change the source code to Scala, as shown in the next listing.

Listing 11.20   ToDoItem model class written in Scala

```
package com.manning.gia.todo.model

class ToDoItem extends Ordered[ToDoItem] {
   var id: Long = _
   var name: String = _
   var completed: Boolean = _

   def getId: Long = {
      id
   }

   def setId(id: Long) = {
      this.id = id
   }

   ...

   override def compare(that: ToDoItem) = this.id compare that.id

   override def equals(that: Any) = {
      that match {
         case t: ToDoItem => t.id == id && t.name == name
                            ➥ && t.completed == completed
         case _ => false
      }
   }
}
```

Even though you may not be well versed in Scala, the language syntax is relatively easy to decipher. In fact, the class doesn't introduce any additional logic and works exactly like its Java counterpart. Executing the build for the `model` project produces the following output:

```
$ gradle :model:build
:model:compileJava UP-TO-DATE
:model:compileScala
Download http://repo1.maven.org/maven2/org/scala-lang/scala-library/
➥ 2.10.1/scala-library-2.10.1.pom
Download http://repo1.maven.org/maven2/org/scala-lang/scala-library/
➥ 2.10.1/scala-library-2.10.1.jar
Download http://repo1.maven.org/maven2/org/scala-lang/scala-compiler/
➥ 2.10.1/scala-compiler-2.10.1.pom
Download http://repo1.maven.org/maven2/org/scala-lang/scala-reflect/
➥ 2.10.1/scala-reflect-2.10.1.pom
Download http://repo1.maven.org/maven2/org/scala-lang/scala-compiler/
➥ 2.10.1/scala-compiler-2.10.1.jar
Download http://repo1.maven.org/maven2/org/scala-lang/scala-reflect/
➥ 2.10.1/scala-reflect-2.10.1.jar
:model:processResources UP-TO-DATE
:model:classes
:model:jar
:model:assemble
:model:compileTestJava UP-TO-DATE
:model:compileTestScala UP-TO-DATE
:model:processTestResources UP-TO-DATE
:model:testClasses UP-TO-DATE
:model:test
:model:check
:model:build
```

We can see that the `compileScala` task initiates the download of the Scala library to be able to invoke the Scala compiler. As a result, your project compiles the Scala code, which can be used as a dependency for other projects in your build.

CUSTOMIZING THE PROJECT LAYOUT
If you're unhappy with the default Scala source directories, feel free to redefine them. By now, you've used this concept various times, so the code in the next listing should come as no surprise. In this example, you'll point the production source directory to src/scala and the test source directory to test/scala.

Listing 11.21 Customizing the default Scala source set directories

```
sourceSets {
    main {
        scala {
            srcDirs = ['src/scala']
        }
    }

    test {
        scala {
```

```
        srcDirs = ['test/scala']
      }
    }
}
```

JAVA AND SCALA JOINT COMPILATION

Mixing Java and Scala source code within one Gradle project follows the same rules as for mixing Java and Groovy. What it boils down to is that Scala can depend on Java, but Java can't depend on Scala. Bidirectional dependencies between these source code file types can only be achieved by joint compilation. You can either put the Java code into the Scala source directory (by default, `src/main/scala`) or reconfigure the source directory sets, as shown in the following listing.

> **Listing 11.22 Reconfiguring source sets for joint compilation**

Removes source directories for Java source set
```
sourceSets.main.scala.srcDirs                                          ⟵┘
sourceSets.main.groovy.srcDirs = ['src/main/java', 'src/main/scala']   ⟵┐
```
Includes Java and Scala source directory for Scala compiler

What happens when you configure Scala joint compilation? Joint compilation for Scala code works slightly differently than for Groovy code. The Scala compiler doesn't directly invoke the Java compiler. The following steps should make this clear:

1. The Scala compiler parses and analyzes the Scala source code to figure out the dependencies on Java classes. The Scala compiler understands Java syntax, but doesn't invoke the Java compiler.
2. The Scala sources are compiled. The compiler also produces a class file for each Java source file. However, these files don't contain bytecode. They're used for type checking between Java and Scala sources.
3. The Java compiler compiles the Java source code.

We covered the most basic skills required to build Scala projects. Optimizations like incremental compilation can reduce the compilation time even more. Please see the online documentation for more details. In the next section, we'll go over the Gradle compilation and packaging support for some other languages, JVM-based and native.

11.3 *Other languages*

There are far more languages out there than we could possibly discuss in this book. Some of these languages are directly supported by a core plugin; others can be integrated with your build through a plugin developed by the Gradle community. Table 11.1 lists some of the more popular language plugins.

Table 11.1 Gradle plugins for popular programming languages

Language Name	Language Homepage	Gradle Plugin
C++	http://www.cplusplus.com	Gradle core plugin
Clojure	http://clojure.org	https://bitbucket.org/clojuresque/clojuresque
Golo	http://golo-lang.org	https://github.com/golo-lang/gradle-golo-plugin
Kotlin	http://kotlin.jetbrains.org	http://repository.jetbrains.com/kotlin/org/jetbrains/kotlin/kotlin-gradle-plugin
R	http://www.programmingr.com	https://github.com/jamiefolson/gradle-plugin-r

Even if you don't find an appropriate plugin for the language you're trying to incorporate into your build, you're not out of luck. You learned that Ant tasks and Java APIs can be wrapped with a Gradle task. The same technique is used by the Groovy plugin, for example, which internally invokes the `groovyc` Ant task. Alternatively, you can always execute a compiler from the command line by creating an enhanced task of type `Exec`.

11.4 *Summary*

Today's software projects embrace a wide range of programming languages, technologies, and libraries. It's all about the right tool for the job. Whatever works best, increases productivity, or solves a problem in a more elegant way should be preferred. This maxim became increasingly important for projects that incorporate more than a single programming language, so-called polyglot projects. In this chapter, we discussed how to configure, manage, and build three different languages with Gradle: JavaScript and the two JVM-based languages, Groovy and Scala.

JavaScript has been the dominant language for creating dynamic web experiences for over a decade. Obviously, page-loading times influenced by the size of the JavaScript files play a significant role for end users. JavaScript files can be merged and minified to improve the page rendering performance. You learned that Gradle can help automate otherwise manual steps to perform these actions and integrate them with the development lifecycle of your To Do application. We didn't stop there. We also explored how to simplify the required configuration of your JavaScript build code by using the community JavaScript plugin. Later, you wrapped existing Grunt build code with Gradle to provide a single, unified control unit for automating all components of your application.

The JVM-based languages Groovy and Scala are directly supported within a Gradle build. Gradle ships with first-class plugin support for both languages. Each language plugin builds on top of the Java base plugin to enforce a separation of capabilities from conventions. You transformed some of the existing To Do application Java classes into Groovy and Scala equivalents to demonstrate the use of these plugins. Source set conventions aren't set in stone. You learned how to reconfigure them in case your project needs to adapt to a legacy project layout. Groovy and Scala source code can coexist with Java source code in a single project. Bidirectional dependencies between Java and Groovy or Scala require the use of joint compilation. We discussed how to prepare the compiler for handling such a scenario. In the last part of this chapter, we touched on other programming languages supported by Gradle.

The next chapter will focus on measuring the code quality of your project by integrating external tooling into the build process.

Code quality management and monitoring

The end product of most commercial projects is a binary. Unless your deliverable doesn't ship with the source code or is the source code itself, users are usually not concerned about the quality of your code. They're happy as long as the software fulfills the functional requirements and has no defects. So why would you as the software development and delivery team care? In a nutshell, high-quality code results in fewer bugs and influences nonfunctional requirements like maintainability, extensibility, and readability, which have a direct impact on the ROI for your business. In this chapter, we'll focus on tools that measure code quality and visualize the results to help you pinpoint problem areas in your code. By the time you finish this chapter, you'll know how to integrate code quality tools with your build.

Earlier, you learned how to write unit, integration, and functional tests to verify the correctness of your To Do application code. Code coverage analysis (also called test coverage analysis) is the process of finding the areas in your code that are not exercised by test cases. Empirical studies show that reasonable code coverage has an indirect impact on the quality of your code.

Measuring code quality doesn't stop with code coverage analysis. Coding standards define agreed-on source code conventions within a team or organization, and can range from simple code formatting aspects, such as the use of whitespaces and indentation, to programming best practices. By following these guidelines, you'll make the code base more readable for other team members, improve its maintainability, and prevent potential bugs. But despite all these benefits, code analysis doesn't replace a code review by an experienced peer; rather, it complements it.

It's impossible for a single person to manually keep track of all of these metrics in a large and ever-changing software project. Therefore, it's essential to be able to easily identify problem areas from a 10,000-foot view and track the progress over time. Code quality tools help you to automatically analyze your software and provide sufficient reporting. In the Java space, you can choose from a wide range of open source and commercial solutions, such as Checkstyle, PMD, Cobertura, FindBugs, and Sonar. Many of these tools are already available in the form of Gradle core or third-party plugins and can be seamlessly integrated into your build. In this chapter, you'll use many of these plugins to measure the code quality of your To Do application.

12.1 *Integrating code analysis into your build*

Let's step back for a minute and think back to the build pipeline stages introduced in chapter 2. Where do we stand? So far you've learned how to compile your code and implement and execute various types of tests. These tasks cover the first two phases of the commit stage. If any of these tasks fail, the build will automatically fail.

Though the outcome of code compilation and testing gives you a basic idea of your project's health status, it doesn't provide you with any feedback about code quality characteristics such as maintainability and code coverage. Code analysis tools help you produce metrics that make a statement about these characteristics. Some of these metrics produced by code analysis include

- Code coverage
- Adherence to coding standards
- Bad coding practices and design problems
- Overly complex, duplicated, and strongly coupled code

In the context of a build pipeline, code analysis is performed after the first two phases of the commit stage, as shown in figure 12.1.

Similar to running integration and functional tests, the process of performing code analysis can take a long time depending on the size of your code base and the number of exercised code quality tools. For that reason, it's helpful to create a dedicated set

Commit stage

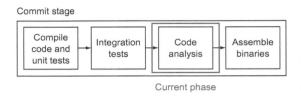

Current phase

Figure 12.1 Code analysis phase in the context of the deployment pipeline

of Gradle tasks for invoking code quality tools. These tasks are usually provided by a plugin, so you won't need to create them yourself. In practice, you'll want to run particular code quality tasks independently from others. For example, during development you may want to know whether you've improved the code coverage of the class you're currently refactoring without having to run other lengthy code quality processes.

Code quality tasks shouldn't depend on each other, which makes them perfect candidates to be executed in parallel. In the overall build lifecycle of a Java project, it's helpful to make the verification task `check` depend on all the code quality tasks, as shown in figure 12.2. Bear in mind that the given task names in the figure are only representative names.

Projects may consist of multiple source sets for separating code with different concerns. You learned how to do this in chapter 7, when you defined an additional source set solely for integration tests. To get a clear, comprehensive picture of code quality, you'll need to be able to selectively perform code analysis on individual source sets or even on all of them. You'll start by measuring the code coverage of your To Do application.

12.2 *Measuring code coverage*

Code coverage doesn't determine code quality per se. It uncovers execution paths in your code that aren't exercised by tests. A frequently discussed metric is the overall percentage of tests covering the production code. While achieving 100% code coverage is an honorable goal, it rarely pays off, nor can it give you the ultimate confidence that the logic is correct or bug-free. A good rule of thumb, though it shouldn't be followed dogmatically, is to aim for 70 to 80% code coverage with meaningful assertions.

When I talk about code coverage metrics, what exactly do I mean? The following list should give you some basic coverage criteria:

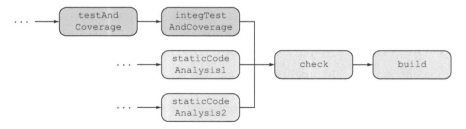

Figure 12.2 Code analysis tasks in relation to the standard Java plugin tasks

- *Branch coverage*: Measures which of the possible execution paths (for example, in if/else branching logic) is executed by tests
- *Statement coverage*: Measures which statements in a code block have been executed
- *Method coverage*: Measures which of the methods were entered during test execution
- *Complexity metrics*: Measures cyclomatic complexity (the number of independent paths through a block of code) of packages, classes, and methods

Let's look at available code coverage tools and their respective Gradle plugins.

12.2.1 Exploring code coverage tools

The Java ecosystem created several tools, free as well as commercial, for producing code coverage metrics. The feature set usually differs by performance to generate the metrics, the type of metric that can be produced, the coverage quality, and how these metrics are produced at runtime (called the *instrumentation*). Many of these tools originated as Ant tasks, which makes them easily wrapped by Gradle tasks in your build. A plugin abstraction is available for some of these tools. At the time of writing, none of these plugins have made it into the Gradle core code base. Table 12.1 gives an overview of some popular coverage tools and their support in Gradle.

Table 12.1 Popular code coverage tools for Java and Groovy projects

Name	License	Type of Instrumentation	Gradle Support
Cobertura	Free	Offline bytecode instrumentation	https://github.com/eriwen/gradle-cobertura-plugin
Clover	Commercial, free for open source projects	Source code instrumentation	https://github.com/bmuschko/gradle-clover-plugin
Emma	Free	Offline bytecode instrumentation	No sophisticated plugin support; Ant tasks available
JaCoCo	Free	On-the-fly bytecode instrumentation	https://github.com/ajoberstar/gradle-jacoco

COMPARING CODE COVERAGE TOOL FEATURES

With all these options, how do you pick the tool that's right for you? First of all, you'll want a tool that's still maintained in case you need a bug to be fixed. With Clover, you have a good chance of getting support, because it's a commercial tool that you pay for. Among the free tools, JaCoCo is the most active, whereas Emma and Cobertura haven't been updated in years.

Two other compelling reasons for choosing a tool are the produced metrics and their quality. Usually, the coverage percentage doesn't deviate very much among the tools (at a maximum by ~3–5%). What's more important is the metrics feature set. Emma, for example, doesn't produce any branch coverage. When comparing performance, JaCoCo is the clear winner. You can find an insightful comparison of these criteria on the SonarSource homepage (http://www.sonarsource.org/pick-your-code-coverage-tool-in-sonar-2-2/).

The method for producing code coverage metrics is different from tool to tool. The job of instrumentation is to inject instructions that are used to detect whether a particular code line or block is hit during test execution. Let's look at the following scenario. You have a single class named ToDoItem that represents a To Do item:

```
public class ToDoItem {
    public final static int MAX_PRIORITY = 3;
    private int priority = 1;                          Initial priority
                                                       start with I
    public int getPriority() {
        return priority;
    }

    public void setMaxPriority() {
        priority = MAX_PRIORITY;
    }
                                                Priority of an item can only be
                                                increased if it isn't already set
    public void bumpUpPriority() {              to highest priority
        if(priority < MAX_PRIORITY) {
            priority++;
        }
    }
}
```

For the ToDoItem class, you want to determine the test coverage. For that purpose, you create a unit test class named ToDoItemTest. The class defines a test method that verifies that the set priority of an item cannot be higher than the maximum priority:

```
public class ToDoItemTest {
    @Test
    public void testBumpUpPriorityIfAlreadyMaxPriority() {
        ToDoItem toDoItem = new ToDoItem();          Sets item's
        toDoItem.setMaxPriority();                    priority to 3
        assertEquals(toDoItem.getPriority(), ToDoItem.MAX_PRIORITY);
        toDoItem.bumpUpPriority();                    Tries to
        assertEquals(toDoItem.getPriority(), ToDoItem.MAX_PRIORITY);  increase
    }                                                 item's
}                                                     priority
```

Item's priority is already 3 and therefore wasn't increased

If you generate code coverage for this class, you'll see that all methods are covered, because you called all of them from your test class. The only line of code that isn't covered is priority++. This is because your test method assumed an initial priority of 3 before you tried to increase the priority of the To Do item. To achieve 100% code coverage for the class ToDoItem, you'd have to write another test method that uses the initial priority.

As shown in table 12.1, this is achieved through source code, offline bytecode, or on-the-fly bytecode instrumentation. What's the difference between these methods? Source code instrumentation adds instructions to the source code before compiling it to trace which part of the code has been executed. Offline bytecode instrumentation applies these instructions directly to the compiled bytecode. On-the-fly instrumentation adds these same instructions to the bytecode, but does this when it's loaded by the JVM's class loader.

While all of these methods do their job and the produced metrics don't exhibit a huge difference, why does it matter which we choose? In the context of a continuous delivery pipeline, where bundling the deliverable is done after executing the code analysis phase, you want to make sure that the source or bytecode isn't modified after the compilation process to avoid unexpected behavior in the target environment. Therefore, on-the-fly instrumentation should be preferred. In the next chapter, I'll also demonstrate ways to avoid problems with other instrumentation methods.

In the following sections, you'll learn how to use two plugins for generating code coverage: the JaCoCo and the Cobertura plugins. Let's start with the JaCoCo plugin.

12.2.2 Using the JaCoCo plugin

JaCoCo (http://www.eclemma.org/jacoco/), short for Java Code Coverage, is an open source toolkit for measuring code coverage through on-the-fly bytecode instrumentation. To achieve this, JaCoCo attaches a Java agent to the JVM class loader, which collects execution information and writes it to a file. JaCoCo produces line and branch coverage metrics. Furthermore, it fully supports analyzing projects that are based on Java 7.

Separating different aspects of software functionality is a best practice. The same principle applies to build code. To separate your main build logic from code coverage logic, you'll create a new build script named `jacoco.gradle` in the directory `gradle` on the root level of your project hierarchy. Later, you'll add other Gradle build files to this directory. After creating the script, your project's directory tree should look like this:

```
.
├── build.gradle
├── gradle                          Script plugin that
│   └── jacoco.gradle          ◄─── configures and applies
├── model                           JaCoCo plugin
├── repository
└── web
```

This script will serve as a container for declaring and configuring the JaCoCo plugin for your project. Remember when you added your own plugin to the classpath of the consuming build script in chapter 8? Here you do the same by assigning a repository and the plugin dependency. The following listing illustrates the basic setup.

> **Listing 12.1 Defining the JaCoCo plugin as script plugin**

```
buildscript {
    repositories {                       Adds JaCoCo plugin to build
        mavenCentral()             ◄─── script's classpath by retrieving
    }                                    it from Maven Central
```

```
    dependencies {                                                    Adds JaCoCo plugin to build
        classpath 'org.ajoberstar:gradle-jacoco:0.3.0'    ◁—         script's classpath by retrieving
    }                                                                 it from Maven Central
}

apply plugin: org.ajoberstar.gradle.jacoco.plugins.JacocoPlugin  ◁—┤  Applies plugin
                                                                      by type
jacoco {                                                          Declares task name for integration
    integrationTestTaskName = 'integrationTest'  ◁—┤              tests to produce code coverage metrics
}                                                                for integration test source set
```

You can now easily apply the script plugin `jacoco.gradle` to other projects. In the context of your multiproject build, this is achieved by declaring a reference on it in the `subprojects` configuration block in the build script of the root project, as illustrated in the following listing. In addition to applying the script plugin, you'll also need to tell the JaCoCo plugin where to retrieve its transitive dependencies. For now, you'll settle on declaring Maven Central as the repository.

> **Listing 12.2   Applying the JaCoCo script plugin to all subprojects**

```
subprojects {
    apply plugin: 'java'                                    Applies JaCoCo
    apply from: "$rootDir/gradle/jacoco.gradle"    ◁—┘      script plugin.

    repositories {                                      Transitive dependencies needed
        mavenCentral()                     ◁—┤          by JaCoCo plugin are retrieved
    }                                                   from Maven Central.
}
```

Your project is prepared for generating code coverage reports with JaCoCo. When executing tasks of type `Test`, JaCoCo's agent will collect runtime information based on the exercised test classes. Keep in mind that you won't see any additional tasks that would indicate that code coverage data is created.

Give it a spin. Executing the full build will produce the execution data file with the extension exec in the directory `build/jacoco` of each subproject. The following directory tree shows the produced execution data files for the subproject `repository`:

```
.
├── build.gradle
├── gradle
│   └── jacoco.gradle
├── model
├── repository
│   └── build
│       └── jacoco
│           ├── integrationTest.exec        JaCoCo execution data for
│           └── test.exec                   unit and integration tests
└── web
```

JaCoCo execution data is stored in a binary, non-human-readable file. To be able to visualize the code coverage, you'll need to generate an HTML report. The JaCoCo plugin automatically registers a report task per test source set for each subproject. In

InMemoryToDoRepository

Element	Missed Instructions ⬇	Cov. ⬍	Missed Branches ⬍	Cov. ⬍	Missed ⬍	Cxty ⬍	Missed ⬍	Lines ⬍	Missed ⬍	Methods ⬍
⊙ findAllActive()	▬▬▬▬	87%	▬▬▬▬	75%	1	3	0	7	0	1
⊙ findAllCompleted()	▬▬▬▬	87%	▬▬▬▬	100%	0	3	0	7	0	1
⊙ insert(ToDoItem)	▬▬	100%		n/a	0	1	0	4	0	1
⊙ InMemoryToDoRepository()	▬	100%		n/a	0	1	0	3	0	1
⊙ findAll()	▬	100%		n/a	0	1	0	3	0	1
⊙ update(ToDoItem)	▬	100%		n/a	0	1	0	2	0	1
⊙ delete(ToDoItem)	▬	100%		n/a	0	1	0	2	0	1
⊙ findById(Long)	▬	100%		n/a	0	1	0	1	0	1
Total	10 of 139	93%	1 of 8	88%	1	12	0	29	0	8

Created with JaCoCo 0.6.2.201302030002

Figure 12.3   Sample JaCoCo HTML report

your `repository` project, these tasks are called `jacocoTestReport` and `jacocoInte-grationTestReport`. Figure 12.3 shows the HTML report for the test source set produced by the task `jacocoTestReport`.

Each method in the HTML report is clickable and brings you directly to a new page that marks the coverage line by line. A line marked in green indicates that it was exercised by tests, and a line marked in red means that it lacks test coverage.

With the default setup of the plugin, you'll have one report for unit test coverage and one for integration test coverage. If you want to get a full picture of the project's overall coverage across test source sets or even across all projects of a multiproject build, you can write a new task of type `JaCoCoMerge`. We won't discuss this task further. For more details, please see the plugin's documentation.

Many enterprises use the established code coverage tool Cobertura. To get an idea of how Cobertura's report compares to the one produced by JaCoCo, you'll configure Cobertura for your build.

12.2.3   *Using the Cobertura plugin*

Cobertura (http://cobertura.sourceforge.net/) is a Java code coverage tools that needs to instrument the bytecode after it's compiled. A report produced by Cobertura contains the percentage of line and branch coverage, as well as the cyclomatic complexity for each package. Unlike JaCoCo, Cobertura doesn't support projects based on Java 7.

You'll prepare the same setup as you did for integrating the JaCoCo plugin. First, you'll create a new script called `cobertura.gradle`, which applies and configures the Cobertura plugin. Then, you'll apply the script plugin to all subprojects of your build. The following project structure shows the new script under the directory `gradle`:

```
.
├── build.gradle
├── gradle
│   └── cobertura.gradle          ◁─┤  Script plugin that
├── model                            configures and applies
├── repository                       Cobertura plugin
└── web
```

The following listing shows the contents of the script plugin cobertura.gradle. You'll retrieve the plugin from Maven Central and apply it by type.

Listing 12.3   Defining the Cobertura plugin as script plugin

```
buildscript {
    repositories {
        mavenCentral()
    }

    dependencies {
        classpath 'com.eriwen:gradle-cobertura-plugin:1.0'
    }
}
apply plugin: org.gradle.api.plugins.cobertura.CoberturaPlugin
```

Adds Cobertura plugin to the build script's classpath by retrieving it from Maven Central

Applies plugin by type

Similar to the JaCoCo script plugin, you can now apply the Cobertura script plugin to all subprojects of your To Do application. The next listing shows the relevant code changes.

Listing 12.4   Applying the Cobertura script plugin to all subprojects

```
subprojects {
    apply plugin: 'java'
    apply from: "$rootDir/gradle/cobertura.gradle"

    repositories {
        mavenCentral()
    }
}
```

Applies Cobertura script plugin

Transitive dependencies needed by Cobertura plugin are retrieved from Maven Central

The plugin adds one task for inserting instrumentation instructions into the compiled class files and another for generating the code coverage report. These tasks are fully integrated into the build lifecycle of a Java project. A build that executes the verification task check will perform the necessary work to generate the code coverage. To do so, the plugin copies the class files from build/classes to build/cobertura, instruments the files, and serializes coverage information to a file named cobertura.ser. The resulting report is written to the directory build/reports/cobertura. The following directory tree shows the relevant files after executing the build:

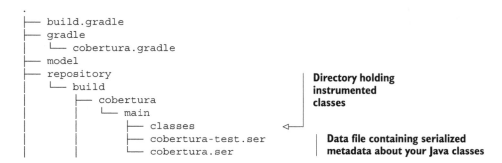

Directory holding instrumented classes

Data file containing serialized metadata about your Java classes

```
    |          └── reports
    |               └── cobertura
    |                    └── main                              Cobertura HTML
    |                         ├── index.html    ◁              report index page
    |                         └── ...
    |
    └── web
```

The task `testCoberturaReport` is responsible for creating the code coverage report. By default, the task produces an HTML report but can also be reconfigured to create code coverage formatted as XML. Figure 12.4 shows a sample HTML report created for the unit tests of the `repository` project.

We'll stop at this point in our discussion of code coverage tools. Later in this chapter, you'll reuse the reports you generated to track your code coverage quality over time with Sonar. JaCoCo and Cobertura are the most widely used open source coverage tools today. If you're planning to use a different tool, please refer to the links provided in table 12.1. In the next section, we'll explore various static code analysis tools.

12.3 Performing static code analysis

Members of the software development team perform code reviews to identify architectural problems, security defects, and potential bugs. While this kind of review is extremely helpful in mitigating the risk of technical debt, this process easily becomes expensive and unmanageable for large software projects.

How many of us have had to toil away at code reviews? Sure, they're useful—you identify problems, security defects, and bugs—but it can easily get expensive and unwieldy. A cheap and automated way of finding issues in code is static code analysis.

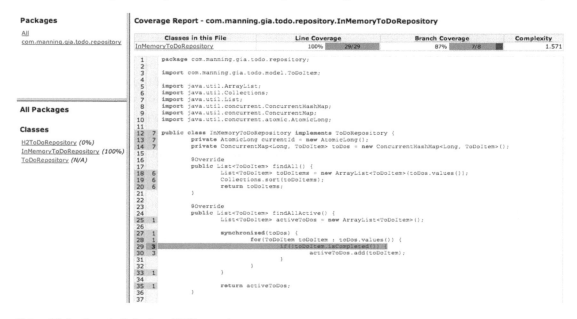

Figure 12.4 Sample Cobertura HTML report

Static code analysis is the task of analyzing source code without actually executing the software to derive quality metrics. Metrics that can be extracted range from potential bugs and adherence to coding standards, to unnecessary code complexity and bad coding practices. Let's look at a list of tools producing these metrics.

12.3.1 *Exploring static code analysis tools*

There are a lot of open source tools for identifying poor code quality. In this section, we'll concentrate on the ones that are directly supported by Gradle through a standard plugin. Because they're shipped with Gradle's runtime distribution, it's easy to integrate them into your build and make them part of the build pipeline. Table 12.2 shows these code analysis tools, the metrics they produce, and the name of the Gradle plugins for applying them to the build.

Table 12.2   Standard Gradle static code analysis plugins

Tool Name	Gradle Plugin	Report Formats	Description
Checkstyle	`checkstyle`	Only XML	Enforces coding standards; discovers poor design problems, duplicated code, and bug patterns
PMD	`pmd`	XML and HTML	Finds unused, overly complex, and inefficient code
CodeNarc	`codenarc`	Text or XML or HTML	PMD equivalent for Groovy projects
FindBugs	`findbugs`	XML or HTML	Discovers potential bugs, performance issues, and bad coding practices
JDepend	`jdepend`	Text or XML	Measures design quality metrics like extensibility, reusability, and maintainability

This list of plugins and their feature sets may look overwhelming at first. To be able to differentiate their metrics, you'll apply and configure each of them to determine the code quality of your To Do application. In the next couple of sections, you'll work your way from the top to the bottom of the table, with the exception of CodeNarc.

PREPARING THE SUBPROJECTS

As you did with the code coverage tools, you'll write a script plugin for each static code analysis tool to achieve a clean separation of concerns. Many of these Gradle plugins require a configuration file located in a directory config/<toolname> that defines the rules for the analysis. To be optimally prepared, you'll create the directory config on the root level of your multiproject build and define a property that can be used in all subprojects:

```
.
├── build.gradle
├── config              ◁── Default configuration
│   ├── checkstyle          directory used by code
│   │   └── ...             quality plugins
```

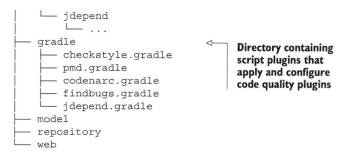

Directory containing
script plugins that
apply and configure
code quality plugins

The dependencies of each tool aren't included in the Gradle distribution. At runtime, they're automatically retrieved from a repository. You'll configure Maven Central for that purpose. The following listing shows the changes you'll need to make to the root project's build script.

Listing 12.5 Preparing subprojects for the integration of static code analysis plugins

```
subprojects {
    ext.configDir = new File(rootDir, 'config')

    // Apply static code analysis script plugin

    repositories {
        mavenCentral()
    }
}
```

Extra property pointing to
configuration directory
(directory can have any
arbitrary name)

Configures Maven
Central for retrieving
plugin dependencies

GENERATING HTML REPORTS

The default format for reports generated by these plugins is XML. While XML is a useful format for postprocessing the results from other tools like Sonar, it's not convenient to read. An easier-to-consume format is HTML. Unfortunately, not all of the plugins you'll use provide such a report output. However, you can easily produce them yourself via an XML-to-HTML transformation. For that purpose, you'll create a reusable custom task in the buildSrc directory of your project that uses the Ant XSLT task, as show in the next listing.

Listing 12.6 Task for generating HTML reports via XSLT

```
package com.manning.gia

import org.gradle.api.DefaultTask
import org.gradle.api.tasks.*

class XsltReport extends DefaultTask {
    @InputFile @Optional File inputFile
    @InputFile File xslStyleFile
    @Input @Optional Map<String, String> params = [:]
    @OutputFile File outputFile

    XsltReport() {
        onlyIf {
            inputFile.exists()
```

Only run HTML generation
if input file exists; if not,
task will be skipped

```
      }
   }

   @TaskAction
   void start() {
      ant.xslt(in: inputFile, style: xslStyleFile, out: outputFile) {   ⤙
         params.each { key, value ->
            ant.param(name: key, expression: value)
         }
      }
   }
}
```

Using Ant XSLT task to generate an HTML report

You're prepared for applying the static code analysis tools to your build. You'll start by using the Checkstyle plugin.

12.3.2 *Using the Checkstyle plugin*

In enterprise projects, it's helpful to introduce a coding standard to define how source code should be formatted, structured, and annotated to form a uniform picture. As a by-product, you'll receive more readable and maintainable source code. This is where Checkstyle (http://checkstyle.sourceforge.net/) comes into play. The project started out as a tool for finding areas in your source code that don't comply with your coding rules. Over time, the feature set was expanded to also check for design problems, duplicate code, and common bug patterns.

You'll start by creating a new script file called checkstyle.gradle in the directory gradle. It'll serve as your Checkstyle script plugin. In that script plugin, you'll need to apply the standard Gradle Checkstyle plugin and configure the version of the tool you'd like to use and its runtime behavior. The following listing demonstrates how to use the Sun coding standards, defined by the rule set in the file config/sun_checks.xml, which is available from the Checkstyle distribution.

Listing 12.7 Applying and configuring the Checkstyle plugin as script plugin

```
apply plugin: 'checkstyle'                                       ⤙ Applies Gradle standard
                                                                    Checkstyle plugin
ext.checkstyleConfigDir = "$configDir/checkstyle"

checkstyle {                                                     ⤙ Declares dependencies
   toolVersion = '5.6'                                              on Checkstyle 5.6
   configFile = new File(checkstyleConfigDir, 'sun_checks.xml')
   ignoreFailures = true
   showViolations = false      ⤙
}
```

Defines rule set to be used

Prevents Gradle from printing out every violation on command line

Changes default behavior of failing build if at least one rule violation is discovered

With the basic Checkstyle definitions in place, you can apply the encapsulating script plugin to all subprojects of your multiproject build, as shown in the next listing.

Listing 12.8   Applying Checkstyle to all subprojects

```
subprojects {
    apply plugin: 'java'

    ext.configDir = new File(rootDir, 'config')            Applies Checkstyle
    apply from: "$rootDir/gradle/checkstyle.gradle"   ◁─┘  script plugin

    repositories {
        mavenCentral()
    }
}
```

Executing a full build will now produce the default Checkstyle XML report for all source sets of the project in the directory `build/reports/checkstyle` of each subproject. The following command-line output shows the relevant bits for the repository subproject:

Checkstyle task and violations notification for integration test source set

```
$ gradle build
...
:repository:checkstyleIntegrationTest
Checkstyle rule violations were found. See the report at:
➡ file:///Users/Ben/checkstyle/repository/build/reports/checkstyle/
➡ integrationTest.xml
:repository:checkstyleMain
Checkstyle rule violations were found. See the report at:
➡ file:///Users/Ben/checkstyle/repository/build/reports/checkstyle/main.xml
:repository:checkstyleTest
Checkstyle rule violations were found. See the report at:
➡ file:///Users/Ben/checkstyle/repository/build/reports/checkstyle/test.xml
...
```

Checkstyle task and violations notification for main source set

Checkstyle task and violations notification for test source set

Of course, the default report directory can be reconfigured to point to a custom directory. For more information on this and other configuration options, please see the DSL documentation of the Checkstyle plugin.

The Checkstyle plugin is one of the candidates that doesn't currently provide the generation of HTML reports. Listing 12.9 shows how to create report tasks of type `XsltReport` for each of your source sets. By declaring a dependency on the default Checkstyle task, you can ensure that the HTML report task is executed after the initial XML Checkstyle report generation. You can add this code snippet directly to `checkstyle.gradle` as needed.

Listing 12.9   Generating a Checkstyle HTML report for all source sets

Only executes the logic the Checkstyle plugin applied to project

```
import com.manning.gia.XsltReport            Makes sure all source        Iterates
                                             sets have been               through all
afterEvaluate {                          ◁── evaluated for a project      source sets
    plugins.withType(CheckstylePlugin) {                                  of a project
        sourceSets.each { sourceSet ->                            ◁──
            String capitalizedSourceSetName = sourceSet.name.capitalize()
            String reportTaskName = "checkstyle${capitalizedSourceSetName}Report"
```

Declares an enhanced HTML report task for each source set and configures it

```
String reportDir = "$reporting.baseDir/checkstyle"
XsltReport reportTask = tasks.create(reportTaskName, XsltReport)

reportTask.with {
    description = "Generates a Checkstyle HTML report for
                     ➥ ${sourceSet.name} classes."
    dependsOn tasks."checkstyle${capitalizedSourceSetName}"
    inputFile = new File(reportDir, "${sourceSet.name}.xml")
    xslStyleFile = new File(checkstyleConfigDir,
                                'checkstyle-noframes.xsl')
    outputFile = new File(reportDir,
                     ➥ "checkstyle_${sourceSet.name}.html")
}
check.dependsOn reportTaskName          ⟵┐ Makes verification
    }                                       │ task depend on
  }                                         │ report task
}
```

For the transformation from XML to HTML, you used an XSL file provided with the Checkstyle distribution. It generates a single HTML report with no frames. Executing the build with `gradle build` again will produce a report similar to figure 12.5.

12.3.3 *Using the PMD plugin*

PMD (http://pmd.sourceforge.net/) is similar to Checkstyle, though it exclusively focuses on coding problems like dead or duplicated code, overly complex code, and possible bugs. PMD's distribution comes with a wide range of specialized rule sets—for

CheckStyle Audit

Designed for use with CheckStyle and Ant.

Summary	
Files	Errors
3	132

Files	
Name	Errors
/Users/Ben/Dev/books/gradle-in-action/code/chapter12/checkstyle/repository/src/main/java/com/manning/gia/todo/repository/H2ToDoRepository.java	98
/Users/Ben/Dev/books/gradle-in-action/code/chapter12/checkstyle/repository/src/main/java/com/manning/gia/todo/repository/InMemoryToDoRepository.java	24
/Users/Ben/Dev/books/gradle-in-action/code/chapter12/checkstyle/repository/src/main/java/com/manning/gia/todo/repository/ToDoRepository.java	10

File /Users/Ben/Dev/books/gradle-in-action/code/chapter12/checkstyle/repository/src/main/java/com/manning/gia/todo/repository/H2ToDoRepository.java	
Error Description	Line
File does not end with a newline.	0
Missing package-info.java file.	0
Using the '.*' form of import should be avoided - java.sql.*.	5
Missing a Javadoc comment.	9
File contains tab characters (this is the first instance).	10
Method 'findAll' is not designed for extension - needs to be abstract, final or empty.	10
Line has trailing spaces.	16

Figure 12.5   Sample Checkstyle HTML report

example, JEE components, web frameworks like JSF, and mobile technologies such as Android.

You'll take the same approach you took for setting up the Checkstyle plugin. First, you'll create a script plugin named `pmd.gradle` that applies the PMD plugin. Then, you'll configure it and apply it to all subprojects of your To Do application. The following listing demonstrates how to use the default version and rule set of PMD.

Listing 12.10   Applying and configuring the PMD plugin as script plugin

```
apply plugin: 'pmd'         ⟵┐   Applies Gradle standard
pmd {                            PMD plugin
    ignoreFailures = true   ⟵┐   Changes default behavior of
}                                failing the build if at least one
                                 rule violation is discovered
```

We won't explore exactly how to apply the script plugin to your subprojects, because it looks very similar to the way you integrated the Checkstyle plugin. The PMD Gradle plugin generates an XML and HTML report out of the box, so you don't need to do any extra work. The following command-line output shows how PMD metrics are produced for all source sets of the project `repository`:

```
$ gradle build
...
:repository:pmdIntegrationTest
:repository:pmdMain
3 PMD rule violations were found. See the report at:
➥   file:///Users/Ben/pmd/repository/build/reports/pmd/main.html
:repository:pmdTest
...
```

The rendered HTML report in `build/reports/pmd` should look similar to figure 12.6.

PMD 4.3 Report. Generated on 2013-03-17 - 12:38:29							

Summary							
Files	Total	Priority 1	Priority 2	Priority 3	Priority 4	Priority 5	
1	3	0	0	3	0	0	

Rules		
Rule	Violations	Severity
[Basic Rules] EmptyCatchBlock	3	3

Files					
File	5	4	3	2	1
/Users/Ben/Dev/books/gradle-in-action/code/chapter12/pmd/repository/src/main/java/com/manning/gia/todo/repository/H2ToDoRepository.java	0	0	3	0	0

File /Users/Ben/Dev/books/gradle-in-action/code/chapter12/pmd/repository/src/main/java/com/manning/gia/todo/repository/H2ToDoRepository.java		
Violation	Error Description	Line
3	[Basic Rules.EmptyCatchBlock] - Avoid empty catch blocks	226 - 226
3	[Basic Rules.EmptyCatchBlock] - Avoid empty catch blocks	235 - 235
3	[Basic Rules.EmptyCatchBlock] - Avoid empty catch blocks	244 - 244

Back to top

Figure 12.6   Sample PMD HTML report

Sometimes you may just want to generate a single type of report. This need arises especially if you want to verify your progress during development. The PMD task can be configured to enable or disable particular types of report formats, as shown in the next listing. The same method can be applied to other code quality tasks where applicable.

Listing 12.11 Configuring the generated PMD report type

```
tasks.withType(Pmd) {          Applies to all tasks of type
    reports {                  org.gradle.api.plugins.quality.Pmd
        xml.enabled = false       Disables the XML report generation,
        html.enabled = true       but enables HTML report generation
    }
}
```

12.3.4 *Using the FindBugs plugin*

FindBugs (http://findbugs.sourceforge.net/) is a static code analysis tool for finding potential bugs and bad coding practices. The bugs identified include problems like `equals/hashCode` implementations, redundant null checks, and even performance issues. Unlike the other analyzers presented earlier, FindBugs operates on the Java bytecode, rather than the source code. You'll find that operating on bytecode makes the analysis slower than source code analysis. For bigger projects, be prepared for it to take minutes.

Listing 12.12 shows that the FindBugs plugin is as easy to integrate into your build as the other code quality plugins. For a good overview of the available configuration options, see the Gradle DSL guide. Currently, the plugin only supports the generation of an XML or HTML report.

Listing 12.12 Applying and configuring the FindBugs plugin as script plugin

```
apply plugin: 'findbugs'          Applies Gradle standard
                                  FindBugs plugin
findbugs {
    toolVersion = '2.0.1'
    ignoreFailures = true         Defines analysis effort level;
    effort = 'max'                the higher the precision, the
}                                 more meticulous the analysis

tasks.withType(FindBugs) {
    reports {
        xml.enabled = false       Configures org.gradle.api.plugins.quality.FindBugs
        html.enabled = true       task to generate an HTML report
    }
}
```

Executing the full build on all subprojects will produce the expected reports for all available source sets. The following command-line output shows the representative tasks for the `repository` subproject:

FindBugs Report

Project Information

Project:

FindBugs version: 2.0.1

Code analyzed:

- /Users/Ben/Dev/books/gradle-in-action/code/chapter12/findbugs/repository/build/classes/main/com/manning/gia/todo/repository/H2ToDoRepository.class
- /Users/Ben/Dev/books/gradle-in-action/code/chapter12/findbugs/repository/build/classes/main/com/manning/gia/todo/repository/InMemoryToDoRepository.class
- /Users/Ben/Dev/books/gradle-in-action/code/chapter12/findbugs/repository/build/classes/main/com/manning/gia/todo/repository/ToDoRepository.class

Metrics

208 lines of code analyzed, in 3 classes, in 1 packages.

Metric	Total	Density*
High Priority Warnings		0.00
Medium Priority Warnings	3	14.42
Total Warnings	**3**	**14.42**

(* Defects per Thousand lines of non-commenting source statements)

Figure 12.7 Sample FindBugs HTML report

```
$ gradle build
...
:repository:findbugsIntegrationTest
:repository:findbugsMain
FindBugs rule violations were found. See the report at:
➥ file:///Users/Ben/findbugs/repository/build/reports/findbugs/main.html
:repository:findbugsTest
...
```

After executing the FindBugs tasks, you'll find an HTML report for each source set in the directory build/reports/findbugs. Figure 12.7 illustrates the report for the main source set.

12.3.5 Using the JDepend plugin

The static code analysis tool JDepend (http://clarkware.com/software/JDepend.html) produces metrics that measure the design quality of your code. It scans all packages of your Java code, counts the number of classes and interfaces, and determines their dependencies. This information will help you identify hot spots of unwanted or strong coupling.

Listing 12.13 shows how to apply and configure the standard Gradle JDepend plugin. You can choose a report that's formatted either as XML or plain text. The default value is XML and doesn't require any additional configuration. The listing also shows you how to easily switch between the report formats.

Listing 12.13   Applying and configuring the JDepend plugin as script plugin

```
apply plugin: 'jdepend'                              ⟵ ⌐ Applies Gradle standard
                                                         │ JDepend plugin
def configDir = new File(rootDir, 'config')
ext.jdependConfigDir = "$configDir/jdepend"

jdepend {
    toolVersion = '2.9.1'
    ignoreFailures = true
}

tasks.withType(JDepend) {
    reports {
        text.enabled = false        ⌐ Configures org.gradle.api.plugins.quality.JDepend
        xml.enabled = true          │ task to generate an XML report
    }
}
```

After the code is applied to the subprojects configuration block, an XML report is generated for all source sets of a project. The following command-line output illustrates the executed JDepend tasks required to produce the reports:

```
$ gradle build
...
:repository:jdependIntegrationTest
:repository:jdependMain
:repository:jdependTest
...
```

Unfortunately, you can't generate an HTML report out of the box, but you can use the custom XSTL task introduced in section 12.3.1 to produce the desired result. An XSL file is available through the JDepend distribution. You can find an example in the source code of the book. After executing the HTML report generation, your build/reports/ jdepend directory will contain at least one file that renders similarly to figure 12.8.

Another great feature of JDepend is the ability to visualize the dependencies between packages as a graph. Part of the JDepend distribution is an XSL style sheet file that transforms an XML report into a Graphviz DOT file. You'll find a full-fledged example in the source code of the book.

12.4   Integrating with Sonar

You've seen how to generate code metrics for your project using different code analysis tools. Each of these tools produces reports that need to be checked individually. With every build, the existing report is potentially deleted and a new one is created, so you have no idea whether the code quality has improved or decayed over time. What you need is a centralized tool that monitors, visualizes, and aggregates your metrics. A tool that provides this functionality is Sonar (http://www.sonarsource.org/).

Sonar is an open source, web-based platform for managing and monitoring code quality metrics like coding rules compliance, unit tests and their coverage, and source

JDepend Analysis

Designed for use with JDepend and Ant.

Summary

[summary] [packages] [cycles] [explanations]

Package	Total Classes	Abstract Classes	Concrete Classes	Afferent Couplings	Efferent Couplings	Abstractness	Instability	Distance
com.manning.gia.todo.repository	3	1	2	0	6	0.33	1	0.33
com.manning.gia.todo.model	No stats available: package referenced, but not analyzed.							
java.lang	No stats available: package referenced, but not analyzed.							
java.sql	No stats available: package referenced, but not analyzed.							
java.util	No stats available: package referenced, but not analyzed.							
java.util.concurrent	No stats available: package referenced, but not analyzed.							
java.util.concurrent.atomic	No stats available: package referenced, but not analyzed.							

Packages

[summary] [packages] [cycles] [explanations]

com.manning.gia.todo.repository

Afferent Couplings: 0	Efferent Couplings: 6	Abstractness: 0.33	Instability: 1	Distance: 0.33

Abstract Classes	Concrete Classes	Used by Packages	Uses Packages
com.manning.gia.todo.repository.ToDoRepository	com.manning.gia.todo.repository.H2ToDoRepository com.manning.gia.todo.repository.InMemoryToDoRepository	None	com.manning.gia.todo.model java.lang java.sql java.util java.util.concurrent java.util.concurrent.atomic

Cycles

[summary] [packages] [cycles] [explanations]

There are no cyclic dependancies.

Figure 12.8   Sample JDepend HTML report

code documentation, as well as architectural aspects like maintainability and technical debt. It integrates well with most of the tools we discussed earlier, including JaCoCo, Checkstyle, and PMD. If the need arises to support an unconventional tool or language, Sonar can be extended by plugins.

Sonar uses a central database to collect code quality metrics over time. In its default configuration, Sonar comes with an embedded H2 instance, which doesn't require any additional setup. While H2 is a great way to get started and explore Sonar's functionality, it's recommended to configure a more scalable solution for a production setting like MySQL or Oracle. Gradle integrates well with Sonar through its Sonar Runner plugin. The Sonar Runner is a launcher that analyzes your project and pushes the gathered metrics to the Sonar database via JDBC. You can directly open your project's dashboard and view aggregated quality metrics over time. Figure 12.9 shows the interaction between Gradle and Sonar.

As the figure shows, Sonar can be fed metrics from the outside. The rule set for these metrics is defined in *quality profiles*. A quality profile, which is directly configured on Sonar, defines the code analysis tools you'd like to run on your source code and their acceptance criteria. For example, you could say, "A class must have a documented API greater than 70%."

This means that Sonar not only gives you the option to apply specific metric rule sets and thresholds per project, but also allows you to decide whether you want to use the analysis tools provided by Sonar to generate metrics. Let's take the default, pre-configured quality profile called Sonar way, for example. It automatically analyzes your project through Checkstyle and PMD with 119 rules without having to configure the standard Gradle plugins.

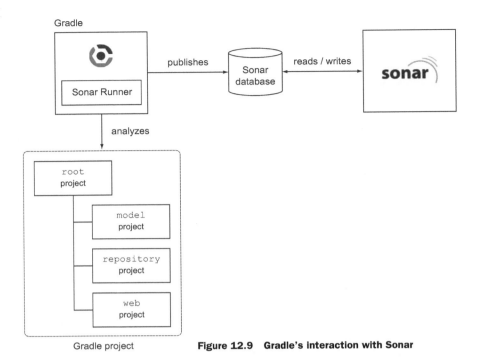

Figure 12.9   Gradle's interaction with Sonar

Reusing existing code analysis reports

Earlier, you configured your build to produce metrics through Gradle's static code analysis plugins. You might ask yourself if you can configure the Sonar Runner plugin to reuse these reports. At the time of writing, Sonar doesn't provide a mechanism to publish these reports to Sonar's database. Instead, you'll need to rely on the embedded Checkstyle, PMD, and FindBugs plugins that are configured by a quality profile. The only exception to this rule is code coverage metrics. You can find a discussion of this topic later in this chapter.

12.4.1 Installing and running Sonar

Installing Sonar is straightforward. Go to Sonar's homepage, download the latest version (at the time of writing this is 3.5), and extract the ZIP file anywhere in your local file system. Depending on your operating system, you can start up the Sonar web server through the provided startup scripts in the directory $SONARHOME/bin. Let's assume you want to start Sonar on a Mac OS X 64-bit machine. From the command line, navigate to the dedicated `bin` directory and start up the server:

```
$ cd $SONARHOME/bin/macosx-universal-64
$ ./sonar.sh start
Starting sonar...
Started sonar.
```

Figure 12.10 Central Sonar dashboard

Starting up Sonar for the first time takes about 30 seconds. You can check on the startup progress in the log file `<SONARHOME>/logs/sonar.log`. After successfully bringing up Sonar, the dashboard can be opened in the browser under the URL http://localhost:9000, as shown in figure 12.10.

In the upper-right corner of the screenshot, you'll see a panel named Projects. Because you didn't publish any metrics for a project, the list doesn't contain any data. Next, you'll change that by configuring your Gradle build to use the Sonar Runner plugin.

12.4.2 Analyzing a project with Sonar Runner

The Sonar Runner plugin is the recommended way of analyzing source code in a single-project or multiproject build. The plugin is fully compatible with Sonar version ≥ 3.4 and only requires minimal setup if you stick to the default Sonar configuration.

Using Sonar version < 3.4

If you need to support an already existing Sonar instance with a version before 3.4, you'll need to rely on the standard Gradle Sonar plugin. Because this chapter will only discuss the Sonar Runner plugin, I'll refer you to the Gradle documentation for more information: http://www.gradle.org/sonar_plugin.

Listing 12.14 shows the relevant changes to your build from using Sonar Runner. It applies the plugin to the root project of your build and configures basic properties like the project's name and description, as well as the source code encoding for all subprojects. If you don't set the properties `sonar.projectName` and `sonar.project-Description`, this information is derived from the Gradle project properties `name` and `description`.

Listing 12.14 Applying and configuring the Sonar Runner plugin

```
apply plugin: 'sonar-runner'          ⟵ Applies Sonar Runner
                                          standard Gradle plugin
sonarRunner {
    sonarProperties {
        property 'sonar.projectName', 'todo'                                    Sets Sonar project
        property 'sonar.projectDescription', 'A task management application'    and description
```

```
    }
}

subprojects {
    ...

    sonarRunner {
        sonarProperties {
            property 'sonar.sourceEncoding', 'UTF-8'    ◁─┐  Changes source file
        }                                                  │  encoding from system
    }                                                      │  encoding to UTF-8
}
```

This is all you need to get started with Sonar. Analyze your project using the default quality profile and publish the reports to the Sonar database. You can initiate this process by executing the task named `sonarRunner` provided by the plugin:

```
$ gradle sonarRunner
...
:sonarRunner
07:01:25.468 INFO   .s.b.b.BatchSettings - Load batch settings
07:01:25.572 INFO      o.s.h.c.FileCache - User cache:
➡ /Users/Ben/.sonar/cache
07:01:25.577 INFO   atchPluginRepository - Install plugins
07:01:26.645 INFO   .s.b.b.TaskContainer - ------------ Executing
➡ Project Scan
07:01:27.235 INFO   b.b.JdbcDriverHolder - Install JDBC driver
07:01:27.238 INFO   .b.ProjectExclusions - Apply project exclusions
07:01:27.242 WARN   .c.p.DefaultDatabase - H2 database should be used
➡ for evaluation purpose only
07:01:27.243 INFO       o.s.c.p.Database - Create JDBC datasource for
➡ jdbc:h2:tcp://localhost/sonar
...
07:01:38.122 INFO   .b.p.UpdateStatusJob - ANALYSIS SUCCESSFUL, you
➡ can browse http://localhost:9000
...
```

A lot of information is rendered. It gives you sufficient insight into which projects and directories have been analyzed and what code quality tools have been used. If you refresh the Sonar dashboard after executing the task, you'll find your project named `todo`, with some basic information like lines of code, a percentage of rules compliance, and the last date of analysis. Clicking on the project name will bring you to a more detailed view of the project's metrics, as shown in figure 12.11.

The project dashboard gives you an informative, condensed summary of metrics like code complexity, rules violations, and code coverage. You can drill into each of these metrics even further by clicking on them.

The plugin lets you set properties to change every aspect of your Sonar configuration. One set of properties is dedicated to pointing to a different database to host your Sonar metrics. I'll leave it up to you to work with the plugin documentation to make this happen in your environment. Another set of properties I want to discuss, though, is directly relevant to your project. To let Sonar take into account your integration test

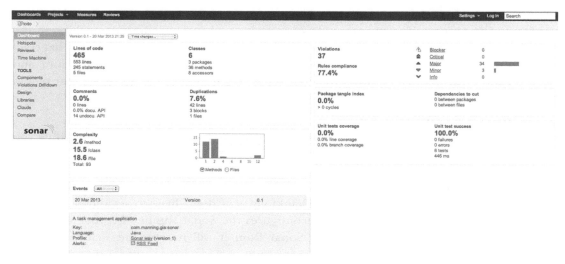

Figure 12.11 Sonar project dashboard

source set, you'll have to tell Sonar about it. The following listing demonstrates how to add the source set directory to the appropriate Sonar property.

Listing 12.15 Adding custom source sets for analysis

```
project(':repository') {
    ...

    sonarRunner {
        sonarProperties {
            properties['sonar.tests'] += sourceSets.integrationTest.
                                          allSource.srcDirs    ◁─┐  Adds integration test
        }                                                        │  source set to default
    }                                                            │  analysis source sets
}
```

12.4.3 Publishing code coverage metrics to Sonar

If you took a deeper look at the Sonar dashboard, you may notice that the Sonar unit test coverage widget shown in figure 12.12 reports a 100% success rate for unit tests, but the code coverage rate is noted as 0%. Code coverage is an extremely helpful metric to have in the Sonar dashboard. If available, you can directly walk through each class and see a visual representation of coverage metrics.

Unit tests coverage	Unit test success
0.0%	**100.0%**
0.0% line coverage	0 failures
0.0% branch coverage	0 errors
	8 tests
	446 ms

Figure 12.12 Unit test coverage widget in Sonar

Earlier in this chapter, we discussed how to generate code coverage reports with JaCoCo and Cobertura. You can reuse these coverage reports by feeding them through the Sonar Runner plugin. Sonar supports this functionality for coverage reports that comply with the JUnit XML format generated by the tools JaCoCo, Emma, Cobertura, and Clover. All you need to do is to add some configuration to the Sonar Runner plugin configuration. You'll start with integrating the JaCoCo report.

REUSING THE JACOCO REPORT

JaCoCo is supported as the default code coverage tool in Sonar. The only thing you need to do is tell Sonar Runner where to find the JaCoCo report files. Sonar requires you to provide two properties for setting the path of the report files: one for unit tests (sonar.jacoco.reportPath), and another for integration tests (sonar.jacoco.itReportPath). Thankfully, you don't have to set these properties manually. The JaCoCo plugin preconfigures the Sonar Runner for you. You'll find that the command-line output of Sonar Runner will register the analyzed JaCoCo report files:

```
$ gradle build sonarRunner
...
07:28:20.300 INFO  o.s.p.j.JaCoCoPlugin - Analysing /Users/Ben/sonar-
    jacoco/repository/build/jacoco/integrationTest.exec
07:28:23.812 INFO  o.s.p.j.JaCoCoPlugin - Analysing /Users/Ben/sonar-
    jacoco/repository/build/jacoco/test.exec
...
```

Now that the additional data has been sent to Sonar, you can refresh the project dashboard page and see the correct reporting on code coverage in the unit test coverage widget. To get insight into the integration test coverage, you need to add the integration test widget to your dashboard. Figure 12.13 shows both code coverage widgets side by side.

At the time of writing, Sonar doesn't provide a dedicated widget for functional test coverage. To work around this shortcoming, you could register your functional code coverage as integration test coverage. To complete our discussion of reusing code coverage metrics, we'll also look at the configuration for integrating Cobertura reports into Sonar.

Figure 12.13   Populated unit and integration test code coverage widgets in Sonar

REUSING THE COBERTURA REPORT

When you initially generated code coverage reports with Cobertura, you chose to format them as HTML. Sonar can only process XML-formatted report files, so you'll need to reconfigure the Cobertura plugin. In the `cobertura.gradle` file, set the following extension property:

```
cobertura {
    format = 'xml'
}
```

To tell Sonar Runner to reuse a different coverage processing mechanism, you'll need to set a new property: `sonar.core.codeCoveragePlugin`. Keep in mind that you'll only need to provide this property if you wish to reuse reports produced by a tool other than JaCoCo. In addition to this property, you'll also need to point Sonar Runner to the Cobertura report files. The following listing demonstrates how to reuse the Cobertura unit test report.

Listing 12.16   Configuring Sonar Runner plugin to reuse Cobertura reports

```
subprojects {
    ...

    sonarRunner {
        sonarProperties {
            property 'sonar.sourceEncoding', 'UTF-8'
            property 'sonar.core.codeCoveragePlugin', 'cobertura'    ⟵ Changes default Sonar coverage tool to Cobertura

            tasks.withType(SourceTask) { task ->
                if(task.name == 'testCoberturaReport') {
                    property 'sonar.cobertura.reportPath',
                             new File(task.reportDir, 'coverage.xml')    ⟵ Sets Sonar property for declaring JaCoCo unit test report file
                }
            }
        }
    }
}
```

The task `sonarRunner` will give you concrete information about the parsed report files:

```
$ gradle build sonarRunner
...
12:10:42.895 INFO  p.PhasesTimeProfiler - Sensor CoberturaSensor...
12:10:42.896 INFO  .p.c.CoberturaSensor - parsing /Users/Ben/sonar-
    cobertura/repository/build/reports/cobertura/main/coverage.xml
12:10:42.949 INFO  p.PhasesTimeProfiler - Sensor CoberturaSensor
    done: 54 ms
...
```

Integrating other third-party coverage reports produced by tools like Emma or Clover follows the same pattern. The key is to look up the required property from the Sonar online documentation.

12.5   *Summary*

Poor code quality and technical debt inevitably lead to developer productivity losses, missed deadlines, and a higher bug rate. In addition to design and code reviews through peers, it's important to introduce coding standards and start monitoring your project's code quality with the help of static code analysis tools in the early stages of your product. The Java ecosystem offers many open source tooling options to produce code quality metrics. Gradle simplifies the integration of many of these tools into the build process by providing standard or third-party plugins.

Code coverage measures the percentage of code that's exercised by tests and reveals obvious areas that aren't covered by tests. A high code coverage rate significantly improves your ability to refactor, maintain, and enhance your code base. We looked at how to apply and configure two code coverage plugins: JaCoCo and Cobertura. While both tools do their jobs in generating adequate coverage reports, JaCoCo shines through better flexibility, performance, and developer support.

Static code analysis tools help you enforce coding standards and uncover bad coding practices and potential bugs. Gradle offers a wide range of standard plugins for you to pick and choose from. We discussed how to apply, configure, and execute these plugins in a reusable way.

Tracking, evaluating, and improving code quality over time can be achieved with Sonar. Sonar provides a set of static code analysis tools out of the box and defines quality rules and thresholds on a central platform. Sonar should be the preferred solution if you have to manage more than one project and need a central place for aggregating quality metrics. You saw that integrating Sonar into a build process required minimal effort.

In the next chapter, we'll discuss how to install and configure a continuous integration server that automatically builds your project whenever a code change is pushed to the VCS.

Continuous integration

This chapter covers

- The benefits of continuous integration
- Using Jenkins to build a Gradle project
- Exploring cloud-based CI solutions
- Modeling a build pipeline with Jenkins

If you're working as a member of a software development team, you inevitably will have to interface with code written by your peers. Before working on a change, a developer retrieves a copy of the code from a central source code repository, but the local copy of this code on the developer's machine can quickly diverge from the version in the repository. While working on the code, other developers may commit changes to existing code or add new artifacts like resource files and dependencies. The longer you wait to commit your source code into the shared code repository, the harder it'll become to avoid merge conflicts and integration issues.

Continuous integration (CI) is a software development practice where source code is integrated frequently, optimally multiple times a day. With each change, the source code is compiled and tested by an automated build, which leads to significantly less integration headaches and immediate feedback about the health status of your project.

In this chapter, we'll discuss the principles and architecture of continuous integration. We'll also explore the tooling that enables continuous integration, called *CI servers* or *platforms*. CI servers automatically schedule and execute a build after a code change is made to the central repository. After learning the basic mechanics of a CI server, you'll put your knowledge into practice. We'll discuss how to install and use the popular open source CI server Jenkins to build your To Do application. As with many development tools, CI server products have been moved to the cloud. We'll explore various offerings and compare their feature sets.

Breaking up a big, monolithic build job into smaller, executable steps leads to faster feedback time and increases flexibility. A build pipeline orchestrates individual build steps by defining their order and the conditions under which they're supposed to run. Jenkins provides a wide range of helpful extensions to model such a pipeline. This chapter will build the foundation for configuring the pipeline steps we've touched on so far in the book. With each of the following chapters, you'll add new steps to the pipeline until you reach deployment into production. Let's first get a basic understanding of how continuous integration ties into the development process.

13.1 *Benefits of continuous integration*

Integrating source code committed to a central VCS by different developers should be a nonevent. Continuous integration is the process of verifying these integrations by building the project in well-defined intervals (for example, every five minutes) or each time a commit is pushed to the VCS. You're perfectly set up with your Gradle build to make this determination. With every commit, you can compile the code, run various types of tests, and even determine if the code quality for your project improved or degraded. What exactly do you gain? Apart from the initial time investment of setting up and configuring a CI server, continuous integration provides many benefits:

- *Reduced risk*: Code is built with every commit to the VCS. Therefore, the code is frequently integrated. This practice reduces the risk of discovering integration issues late in the project's lifecycle; for example, every two to four weeks for a new release. As a side effect, you can also be confident that your build process works because it's constantly exercised.

- *Avoiding environment-specific errors*: Developers usually build software on a single operating system. While you can rule out general build tool runtime issues by using the Gradle Wrapper, you still have a dependency on the machine's setup. On a CI server, you can exercise the build independent of a particular machine setup or configuration.

- *Improved productivity*: While developers run their builds many times a day, it's reasonable for them to concentrate on executing tasks that are essential to their work: compiling the code and running selected tests. Long-running tasks, like generating code quality reports, would reduce their productivity and are better off being run on a CI server.

- *Fast feedback*: If a build fails because of an integration issue, you'll want to know about it as soon as possible so you can fix the root cause. CI servers offer a wide variety of notification methods. A common notification would be an email containing the link to the failed build, the error message, and a list of recent commits.
- *Project visibility*: Continuous integration will give you a good idea of the current health status of your project. Many CI servers come with a web-based dashboard that renders successful and failed builds, aggregates metrics, and provides central reporting.

Despite all of these benefits, introducing continuous integration to a team or organization requires an attitude of transparency, and in extreme cases may even require a complete culture shift. The health status of a project is always visible through a dashboard or notifications. This means that a broken build won't be a secret anymore. To improve project quality, try to foster a culture of intolerance for defects. You'll see that it pays off in the long run. With these benefits in mind, let's see how continuous integration plays out in practice by playing through a typical scenario.

Three components are essential to a CI environment: a central VCS that all developers commit changes to, the CI server, and an executable build script. Figure 13.1 illustrates the interaction between those components.

Let's go over a typical scenario of integrating code changes in a team of three developers:

1 *Committing code*: One or more developers commit a code change to the VCS within a certain timeframe.
2 *Triggering the build*: A CI server can be configured in two different modes to identify if there's a code change in the VCS. The server can either be scheduled to check the VCS for changes in predefined time intervals (pull mode), or it can be configured to listen for a callback from the VCS (push mode). If a change is identified, the build is automatically initiated. Alternatively, you schedule a predefined time interval for triggering a build.

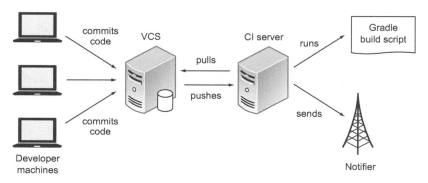

Figure 13.1 Anatomy of a CI environment

3 *Executing the build*: Once a build is triggered, it executes a specific action. An action could be anything from invoking a shell script, to executing a code snippet, to running a build script. In our discussions, this will usually be a Gradle build.

4 *Sending a notification*: A CI server can be configured to send out notifications about the outcome of a build, whether it was successful or failed. Notifications can include emails, IMs, IRC messages, SMS, and many more.

Depending on the configuration of your CI server, these steps are performed for a single code change or for multiple code changes at once. The longer the scheduled intervals for a scheduled build, the more changes are usually picked up.

Over the past 10 years, many open source and commercial CI server products have sprung up. Many of them are downloadable products that are installed and hosted within your company's network. Recently, there's been a lot of hype about CI servers available in the cloud. Cloud-based solutions relieve you from the burden of having to provision infrastructure and lower the barrier of entry. They're usually a good fit for your own open source project. Among the most popular CI servers are Hudson/Jenkins, JetBrains TeamCity, and Atlassian Bamboo. In this chapter, you'll mainly use Jenkins to implement continuous integration for your To Do application because it has the biggest market share. Before you can emulate a typical CI workflow on your local machine, you'll have to set up your components.

13.2 *Setting up Git*

Continuous integration is best demonstrated by seeing it in action. All you need is a CI server installed on your local system, access to a central VCS repository, and a project you can build with Gradle. This section assumes that you've already installed a Java version on your machine.

Jenkins is the perfect candidate for getting started quickly. Its distribution can be downloaded and started in literally a minute. For your convenience, I uploaded the sample To Do application to GitHub, an online hosting service for projects. GitHub is backed by the free and open source VCS named Git. Don't be intimidated by this suite of tools if you haven't used them yet. You'll install and configure each of them step by step. You'll start by signing up on GitHub if you don't yet have an account.

13.2.1 *Creating a GitHub account*

Creating a free account on GitHub (https://github.com/) is as easy as entering your username, email address, and a password in the signup form on the homepage, as shown in figure 13.2.

That's it; you don't even need to confirm your account. A successful signup will bring you to your account's dashboard. Feel free to explore the functionality or update your profile settings. To establish a secure SSH connection between your computer and GitHub, you'll need to generate SSH keys and add the public key to your GitHub account. GitHub offers a comprehensive guide (https://help.github.com/articles/generating-ssh-keys) that explains the nitty-gritty details of achieving this.

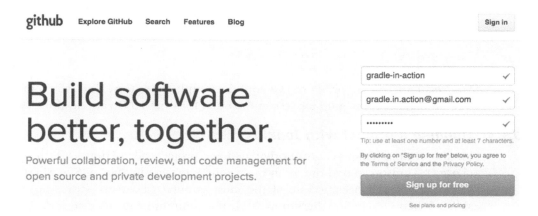

Figure 13.2 Signing up for a free GitHub account

13.2.2 Forking the GitHub repository

The sample To Do application is available as a public GitHub repository under https://github.com/bmuschko/todo. Because you're not the owner of this repository, you won't be able to commit changes to it. The easiest way to get push permission on a repository is to *fork* it from your own account. A fork is a local copy of the original repository that you can modify at will without harming the original repository. To fork a repository, navigate to the sample repository URL and click the Fork button in the navigation bar shown in figure 13.3.

    After a few seconds, the project will be ready for use. To interact with your remote GitHub repository you'll need to install and configure the Git client.

13.2.3 Installing and configuring Git

You can download the client distribution from the Git homepage (http://git-scm.com/). The page offers you installers for the most common operating systems. Follow the instructions to install Git onto your system. After a successful installation, you should be able to execute Git on the command line. You can verify the installed version with the following command:

```
$ git --version
git version 1.8.2
```

Commits to a remote repository can be directly mapped to your GitHub account. By setting your client's username and email address, GitHub will automatically link the

Figure 13.3 Forking the sample repository

change to your account. The following two commands show how to set both configuration values:

```
$ git config --global user.name "<username>"
$ git config --global user.email "<email>"
```

You're all set; you've configured Git and the sample repository. Next, you'll install Jenkins and configure a build job to run the build for your To Do application.

13.3 *Building a project with Jenkins*

Jenkins (http://jenkins-ci.org/) originated as a project called Hudson (http://hudson-ci.org/). Hudson started out as an open source project in 2004 at Sun Microsystems. Over the years, it became one of the most popular CI servers with a huge market share. When Oracle bought Sun in 2011, the community decided to fork the project on GitHub and call it Jenkins. While Hudson still exists today, most projects switched to using Jenkins because it provides the best support for bug fixes and extensions. Jenkins, which is entirely written in Java, is easy to install and upgrade and provides good scriptability and over 600 plugins. You're going to install Jenkins on your machine.

13.3.1 *Starting Jenkins*

On the Jenkins webpage, you can find native installation packages for Windows, Mac OS X, and various Linux distributions. Alternatively, you can download the Jenkins WAR file and either drop it into your favorite Servlet container or directly start it using the Java command. Download the WAR file and start up the embedded container with the Java command:

```
$ java -jar jenkins.war
```

After it starts up successfully, open the browser and enter the URL http://localhost:8080/. You should see the Jenkins dashboard. You're ready to install plugins and configure build jobs.

13.3.2 *Installing the Git and Gradle plugins*

Jenkins comes with a minimal set of features. For example, out of the box you can only configure a build job that pulls the source code from a project hosted on CVS or Subversion and invoke an Ant script. If you want to build a project with Gradle hosted on a Git repository, you'll need to install the relevant plugins. These plugins can be installed through the plugin manager. To access the plugin manager, click Manage Jenkins on the main dashboard page. Then, on the following page, click Manage Plugins. You'll end up on the Plugin Manager page, shown in figure 13.4.

The Plugin Manager page shows four tabs: Updates, Available, Installed, and Advanced. To install new plugins, navigate to the Available tab. In the upper-right corner, you'll find a search input box called Filter. Enter the search criteria "git plugin" and tick the checkbox next to the plugin named Git Plugin, as shown in figure 13.5.

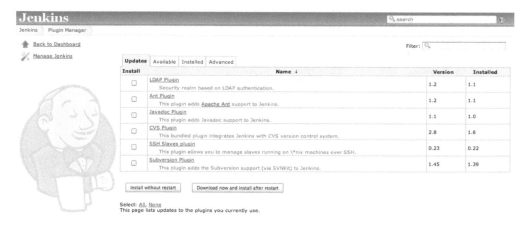

Figure 13.4   Jenkin's Plugin Manager page

Figure 13.5   Installing the Git plugin

After pressing the button Install Without Restart, the plugin is downloaded and installed. Using this technique, you'll also search for the Gradle plugin. Enter "gradle plugin" into the search box, as shown in figure 13.6.

After ticking the plugin's checkbox, press the button Download Now and Install After Restart. You'll see a screen similar to figure 13.7 that shows the downloaded and installed plugins. To use the plugins, Jenkins needs to be restarted. Ticking the checkbox Restart Jenkins When Installation Is Complete and No Jobs Are Running will take care of the restart.

Figure 13.6   Installing the Gradle plugin

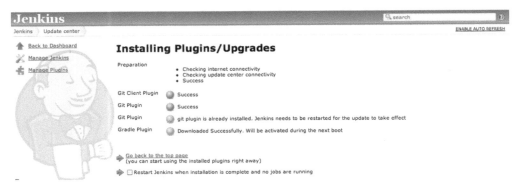

Figure 13.7   Restarting Jenkins through the browser

After a few moments, Jenkins is restarted and the plugins are fully functional. You're ready to define your first build job.

13.3.3   *Defining the build job*

Jenkins defines the actual work steps or tasks in a *build job*. A build job usually defines the origin of source code that you want to build, how it should be retrieved, and what action should be executed when the job is run. For example, a build job can be as simple as compiling the source code and running the unit tests. You'll create a build job that does exactly that for your To Do application.

On the Jenkins main dashboard, click the link New Job. This opens a screen that lets you enter the job name and select the type of project you want to build. For the job name, enter "todo" and press the radio button Build a Free-style Software Project. A free-style project allows you to control all aspects of a build job; for example, the VCS and build tool you want to use. Figure 13.8 shows the selected values.

When you're done, click OK. The build job is created and you'll be presented with the job configuration page.

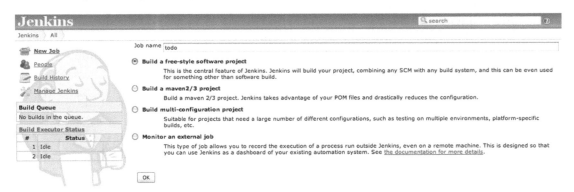

Figure 13.8   Creating the free-style build job

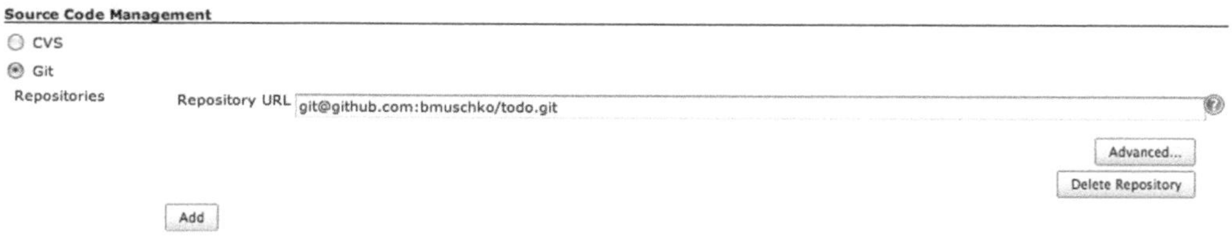

Figure 13.9 Configuring the Git repository

CONFIGURING THE REPOSITORY

First, you'll configure the GitHub repository for your build job. By configuring the repository, you ensure that Jenkins will know where to find the source code of your project when the job is executed. If you scroll down a little in the configuration screen, you'll find a section named Source Code Management.

You want to build your project stored in a Git repository. Click the Git radio button and enter the repository URL, which is the SSH URL you'll find in the forked repository of your GitHub account. It usually has the following form: git@github.com:<username>/todo.git. Figure 13.9 illustrates the filled-out Source Code Management section.

Now that you've told Jenkins where to retrieve the sources from, you'll also want to define when to pull them. In the next section, you'll set up a build trigger.

CONFIGURING THE BUILD TRIGGER

A build trigger is a standard feature of Jenkins. It determines when a build should be executed or *triggered*. Let's say you want to poll your repository on GitHub in certain time intervals, such as every minute. Scroll to the configuration section named Build Triggers, tick the checkbox Poll SCM, and enter the Unix cron expression "* * * * *" into the input box, as shown in figure 13.10.

The expression "* * * * *" means that the repository should be polled every single minute. Polling serves your purpose of periodically checking for changes. On the flip side, this method is fairly inefficient. Not only does it create unnecessary load for your VCS and Jenkins server, it also delays the build after a change is pushed to the repository by the timeframe you defined in your cron expression (in your case this is one minute).

A better way is to configure your Jenkins job to listen for push notifications from the repository. Every time a change is committed to the repository, the VCS will make a call to Jenkins to trigger a build. Therefore, a build is only executed if an actual

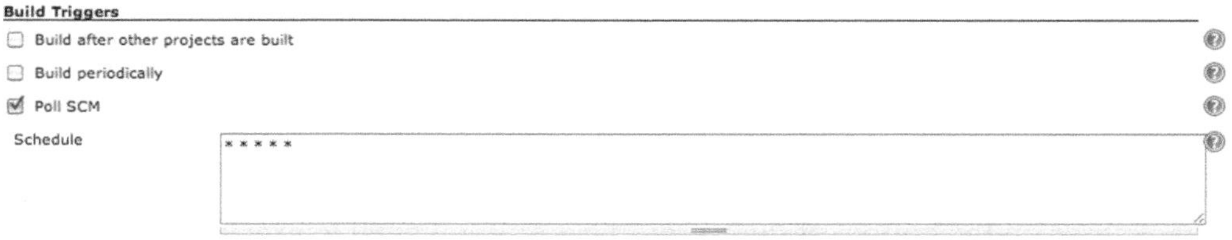

Figure 13.10 Polling the repository for changes minute by minute

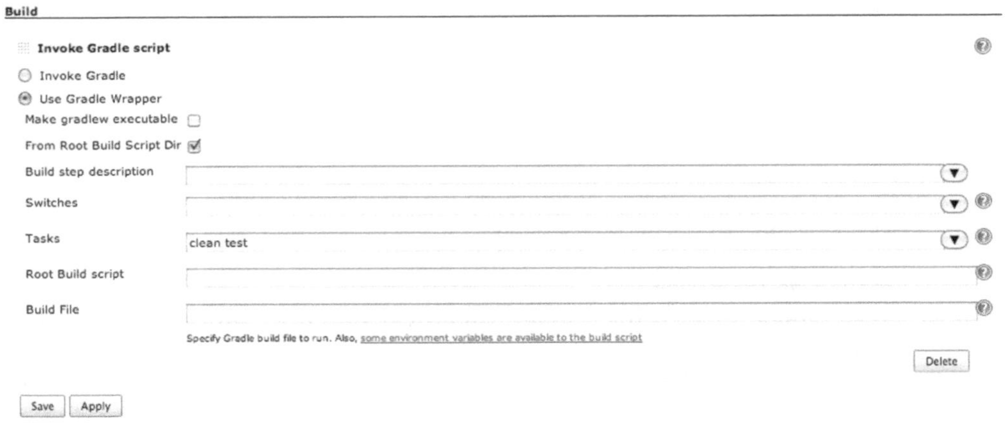

Build

Figure 13.11   Configuring the Gradle build invocation

change occurs. You'll find many examples online that describe the necessary setup for your VCS. Next, we'll define what a build means if it's triggered.

CONFIGURING THE BUILD STEP

Whenever a build is triggered, you want to execute your Gradle build script. Each task that should be executed is called a build step. Build steps can be added in the configuration section Build. Under Build, click the dropdown box Add Build Step and select Invoke Gradle Script. The options you see in figure 13.11 are provided by the Gradle plugin you installed earlier. Choose the radio button Use Gradle Wrapper and enter the tasks "clean test" into the Tasks input box.

This is one of the scenarios where the Gradle Wrapper really shines. You didn't have to install the Gradle runtime. Your build provides the runtime and clearly expresses which version of Gradle should be used.

If you're building the project on your developer machine, you'll want to make good use of Gradle's incremental build feature to save time and improve the performance of your build. In a CI setting, the build should be run from a clean slate to make sure all tests are rerun and recorded appropriately. That's why you added "clean test" to the list of tasks. Next, we'll touch on configuring build notifications.

CONFIGURING EMAIL NOTIFICATION

Email notifications are set up as a post-build action. Scroll down to the section Post-build Actions, click the dropdown box Add Post-build Action, and choose the option E-mail Notification. The only thing you need to do to receive emails on a failed build is to enter your email address into the Recipients input box, as shown in figure 13.12.

After adding this entire configuration, make sure you save the settings by pressing Save on the bottom of the screen. That's all you need to execute your build.

Figure 13.12 Setting up a post-build email notification action

13.3.4 *Executing the build job*

After saving the build job, you can find it listed on Jenkins' dashboard. The gray ball on the left side of the job indicates that it hasn't been built yet. A successful build will turn it blue, and a failed build is indicated by a red ball. You can either wait a minute until the job is triggered automatically or you can manually initiate the build by pressing the clock icon, which schedules the build. Figure 13.13 shows your first build in progress.

After a few minutes, the build is finished. You should see the ball turn blue and a sun icon will appear, which indicates the health status of your project. The job also reports on the last duration of the build and displays a timestamp that tells you the last time the build was successfully run. Figure 13.14 shows the successful build in the dashboard.

To get more information about the specifics of a build, you can click on the job name, which brings you to the project's homepage. The page lets you reconfigure the

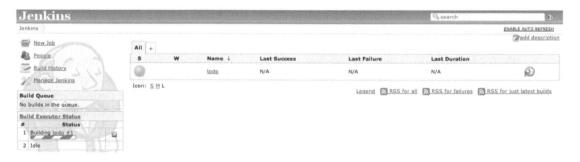

Figure 13.13 Build executing in progress

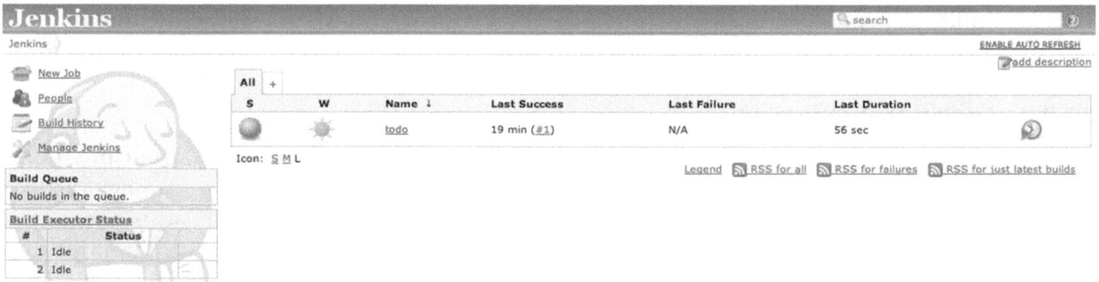

Figure 13.14 Build job executed successfully

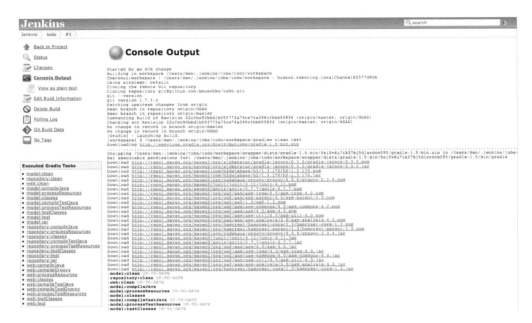

Figure 13.15   Job execution console output

job, trigger the build manually, and inspect the build history. You'll find your first build at #1 in the build history.

Click on it to examine what happened under the hood when the job was executed. One of the menu items on the left side is the console output. The console output recorded the steps that were executed during the build. First, the Git repository was checked out from the master branch. After pulling down the source code, the Gradle build was initiated for the tasks you defined. If you look closer, you can also see that the Gradle Wrapper and the dependencies were downloaded before the tasks were executed. Figure 13.15 shows an excerpt of the console output.

The console output is rendered in real time while a build is executing. This feature provides invaluable information if you want to track down the root cause of a failed build.

Congratulations, you set up a CI job for your project! To trigger a subsequent build, you can either push a code change to your repository or manually initiate it on the project's dashboard. Next, you'll improve on your project's reporting capabilities.

13.3.5   *Adding test reporting*

Jenkins provides extensive reporting capabilities. With minimal effort, you can configure your project to process the XML test results produced by testing frameworks like JUnit, TestNG, and Spock. In turn, Jenkins generates a graphical test result trend over time and lets you drill into the details of successfully executed and failed tests. Though limited in functionality, it can serve as an easy-to-set-up alternative to reporting provided by Sonar.

Post-build Actions

Publish JUnit test result report

Test report XMLs `**/build/test-results/unit/*.xml`

Fileset 'includes' setting that specifies the generated raw XML report files, such as 'myproject/target/test-reports/*.xml'. Basedir of the fileset is *the workspace root*.

☐ Retain long standard output/error

Figure 13.16   Configuring test reporting for all subprojects

PUBLISHING UNIT TEST RESULTS

You may remember that the XML test results produced by Gradle sit in the directory `build/test-results` for each of your subprojects. To create a clean separation between unit and integration test results, you reconfigured the project on GitHub to put the results for unit tests in the subdirectory `unit` and integration test results into the subdirectory `integration`.

After navigating back to the project configuration page, scroll down to the section Post-build Actions, click the dropdown box Add Post-build Action, and choose Publish JUnit Test Result Report. You can tell Jenkins to parse the test results of all subprojects by entering the expression "**/build/test-results/unit/*.xml" into the input field, as shown in figure 13.16.

For test results to be rendered on the project dashboard, you'll need to execute the build at least once. You're going to trigger a build manually. You'll find a new icon called Latest Test Results. If you click on it, you can view statistical information on your executed test suite. The test result trend determines the historical development over multiple data points. After executing the job at least twice, a graph is rendered. Successful tests are displayed in blue and failed tests in red. Figure 13.17 shows the test result trend in the project's dashboard.

Your unit test task is configured to produce code coverage metrics with JaCoCo. Next, you'll show the test coverage trend alongside the unit test results.

PUBLISHING CODE COVERAGE RESULTS

Rendering JaCoCo code coverage results is provided through a third-party plugin. You already know how to install a plugin for Jenkins. Go to the plugin manager page, search for jacoco plugin, and install the plugin. After restarting Jenkins, you can add a

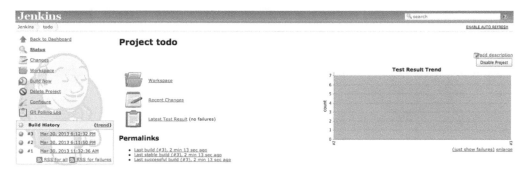

Figure 13.17   Test result trend graph

	Instruction	% Branch	% Complexity	% Line	% Method	% Class
☼	100	70	70	70	70	70
☁	0	0	0	0	0	0

Record JaCoCo coverage report

Path to exec files (e.g.: **/target/**.exec, **/jacoco.exec) — **/build/jacoco/test.exec

Path to class directories (e.g.: **/target/classDir, **/classes) — **/build/classes

Path to source directories (e.g.: **/mySourceFiles) — **/src/main/java

Inclusions (e.g.: **/*.class)

Exclusions (e.g.: **/*Test*)

Figure 13.18   Configuring code coverage reporting

new post-build action named Record JaCoCo Coverage Report. Figure 13.18 shows how to configure the plugin to point to the correct exec file, as well as directories that hold the class and source files.

Another useful feature of the plugin is the ability to act as a quality gate. Let's assume you want to make sure that your unit tests have to cover at least 70% of all classes and methods. In case your project's code coverage is below the expected quality threshold, Jenkins will appropriately reflect that as poor health status.

In figure 13.19 you can see the code coverage trend below the test result trend after creating at least two data points. You can directly drill into the coverage result by clicking on the graph or the menu item Coverage Trend on the left side of the project dashboard.

This concludes our discussion of setting up a basic build job with Jenkins. You'll now be able to use your knowledge to build your own projects. Later in this chapter, you'll expand your knowledge by chaining multiple build jobs to form a build pipeline. Before you do that, we'll discuss some cloud-based CI solutions.

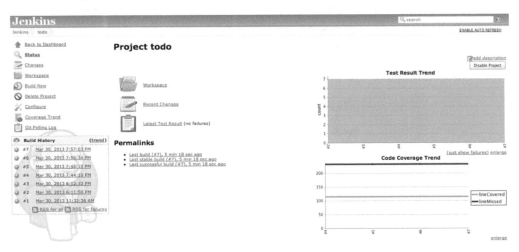

Figure 13.19   Code coverage trend graph

13.4 *Exploring cloud-based solutions*

Cloud-hosted CI servers deliver immediate benefits. First and foremost, you don't need to provision your infrastructure and maintain the software. Depending on the purpose of your build, the demand for hardware resources can be high. Continuous integration in the cloud promises to provide a scalability solution when you need it. Need more CPU power to satisfy the demand of multiple, concurrent compilation build jobs? Simply scale up by purchasing a plan that provides more hardware resources. Many cloud-based CI servers directly integrate with your online repository account like GitHub. Log into your account, select a project, and start building. The following list gives an overview of some of the popular CI server solutions in the cloud with Gradle support:

- *CloudBees DEV@cloud*: The DEV@cloud service (http://www.cloudbees.com/dev.cb) is a standard Jenkins server. The free version comes with limited server resources and plugin support. The paid plan gives you full access to all standard Jenkins plugins. DEV@cloud also allows you to limit the visibility of project reports and access to configuration options.
- *CloudBees BuildHive*: BuildHive (https://buildhive.cloudbees.com/) is a free service that lets you build projects hosted on GitHub. The service is backed by Jenkins with a limited feature set—for example, you can't add more Jenkins plugins or repositories hosted outside of GitHub. Build jobs are easy to set up and provide support for verifying pull requests before you merge them. Build-Hive is a good choice if you need basic compilation and testing support for open source projects.
- *Travis CI*: Travis CI (https://travis-ci.org/) is a CI service suitable for open source, small-business, and enterprise projects. The service provides its own homegrown CI product that lets you build projects hosted on GitHub. Projects need to provide a configuration file checked in with the source code to indicate the language and the command you want to execute.
- *drone.io*: Drone.io (https://drone.io/) lets you link your GitHub, Bitbucket, or Google Code accounts to CI build projects. In the free version, you can only build public repositories. Paid plans offer build support for private repositories as well. While reporting is limited, drone.io allows you to automatically deploy your application to environments like Heroku or AppEngine.

Choosing a hosted CI server might sound like a no-brainer. However, there are some drawbacks. Continuous integration can consume a lot of hardware resources, especially if you have to build a whole suite of applications and want quick feedback. The costs may easily spiral out of control. If you're playing with the idea of using a cloud-based CI solution, it's a good idea to try out the free tier first and diligently evaluate the pros and cons.

You already learned how to use Jenkins to build tasks for your To Do application. If you want to build a full pipeline that separates individual tasks into phases, you'll need

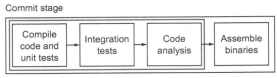

Figure 13.20   **Modeling the first phases of a build pipeline**

to create multiple build jobs and connect them. In the following section, you'll learn how to achieve that with Jenkins.

13.5   *Modeling a build pipeline with Jenkins*

While it may be convenient to run all possible tasks of your Gradle build in a single build job, it's hard to find the root cause of a failed build. It's much easier to break up the build process into smaller steps with their own technical responsibility. This leads to clear separation of concerns and faster, more specific feedback. For example, if you create a step for exclusively executing integration tests and that step fails, you know two things. On the one hand, you can be certain that the source code is compilable and the unit tests ran successfully. On the other hand, the root cause for a failed integration test is either an unsuccessful test assertion or a misbehaving integration with other components of the system. In this section, you'll model the first steps of your build pipeline, as shown in figure 13.20.

A build pipeline defines quality gates between each of the steps. Only if the result of a build step fulfills the requirements of its quality gate will the pipeline then proceed to the next step. What does this mean for your example? In case the suite of integration tests fails to run successfully, the pipeline won't trigger the next build step that performs code analysis.

13.5.1   *Challenges of building a pipeline*

When modeling a build pipeline, you face certain challenges that call for adequate solutions. The following list names a few very important points:

- Every build pipeline starts with a single initial build job. During the job's execution, the project's source code is checked out or updated from the VCS repository. Subsequent steps will work on the same revision of the code base to avoid pulling in additional, unwanted changes.
- A unique build number or identifier is used to clearly identify a build. This build number should be assigned by the first job of the pipeline and carried across all steps of the pipeline. Produced artifacts (for example, JAR files, reports, and documentation) incorporate the build number to clearly identify their version.
- A deliverable artifact should only be created once. If later steps require it (for example, for deployment), it should be reused and not rebuilt. The build number is used to retrieve the artifact from a shared binary repository.

- While many build steps are triggered automatically (for example, on a code change committed to VCS or when a previous step passed the quality gate), some of the steps need to be initiated manually. A typical example would be the deployment of an artifact to a target environment. Manual triggers are especially useful if you want to provide push-button release functionality to nontechnical stakeholders. In such a scenario, the product owner could decide when to release functionality to the end user.

At the time of writing, Jenkins doesn't provide a standardized and easy-to-use solution to implement those needs. The good news is that you can model a full-fledged build pipeline with the help of community plugins. The next section will give you a high-level overview of their features and use cases before you use them to configure your pipeline jobs.

13.5.2 Exploring essential Jenkins plugins

Wading through the feature lists of more than 600 Jenkins plugins is no fun if you need particular functionality. The following four plugins provide you with the most essential functionality to get started with a build pipeline. Please install every one of them while following along.

PARAMETERIZED TRIGGER PLUGIN

Jenkins provides out-of-the-box functionality for chaining individual build jobs. All you need to do is add a new post-build action called Build Other Projects. This action allows you to define the build job name that should automatically be triggered when the current build job completes. The problem with this approach is that you can't pass parameters from one job to another, a feature you need to clearly identify a build by an initial build number.

The Parameterized Trigger plugin extends the functionality of chaining build jobs with the ability to declare parameters for the triggered job. After installing the plugin, you can add a new post-build action named Trigger Parameterized Build on Other Projects. In the configuration section you can name the project to build, under what condition it should be triggered, and the parameters you want to pass along. Keep in mind that you can also trigger multiple jobs by declaring a comma-separated list of job names.

Let's say you want to define a parameter named SOURCE_BUILD_NUMBER in the first step of your pipeline that indicates the initial number of a build. As the value for this parameter, you can use the built-in Jenkins parameter BUILD_NUMBER. BUILD_NUMBER is a unique number assigned to every Jenkins build job at runtime. Figure 13.21 demonstrates how to define a build trigger on the build job running your integration tests from the job definition responsible for compilation/unit tests execution.

In the triggered build, you can now use the parameter SOURCE_BUILD_NUMBER as an environment variable in either the build job definition or the invoked Gradle build. For example, in your Gradle build script you can directly access the value of the parameter by using the expression System.env.SOURCE_BUILD_NUMBER.

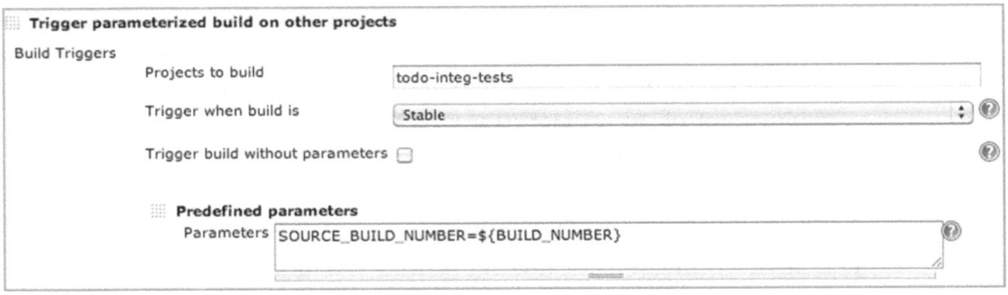

Figure 13.21   Passing a parameter from one build job to another when triggered

If you're unsure about what parameters have been passed to a build job, you can install the Jenkins plugin Show Build Parameters Plugin. It helps you verify parameters and their values by displaying them on the project page for a specific build.

BUILD NAME SETTER PLUGIN

By default, every Jenkins job uses the expression #${BUILD_NUMBER} to display the number for a particular build. On your project page, the expression looks similar to this: ,Build #8 (Apr 2, 2013 6:08:44 AM)., If you're dealing with multiple pipeline definitions, you may want a more expressive build name to clearly identify which pipeline a build belongs to. The Build Name Setter plugin allows you to adjust the build name expression. Figure 13.22 shows how you can add the prefix todo to the build name expression for the initial compilation/unit tests job.

After running a build, the name is displayed as follows: Build todo#8 (Apr 2, 2013 6:08:44 AM). We'll expand on using the plugin's functionality later when you model the full pipeline.

CLONE WORKSPACE SCM PLUGIN

As discussed earlier, you only want to check out the source code from the VCS repository once during the initial build job execution. Subsequent build jobs should work on the same change set. The Clone Workspace SCM plugin lets you reuse a project's workspace in other jobs. To achieve this, you'll need to configure the initial build job to archive the checked-out change set, as shown in figure 13.23.

In subsequent jobs, you can now select the new option Clone Workspace in the Source Code Management configuration section. Figure 13.24 demonstrates how to reuse the workspace of the parent project todo-initial in one of the subsequent build jobs.

Figure 13.22   Build name expression for initial job

Figure 13.23 Archiving the initial job workspace

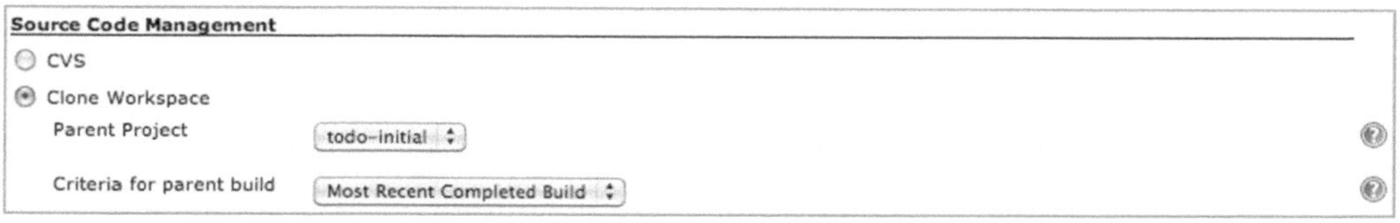

Figure 13.24 Cloning the archived workspace in subsequent jobs

Instead of checking out the source code again, you can now build on top of the already existing workspace. This gives you access to previously created artifacts like compiled class files and project reports.

BUILD PIPELINE PLUGIN

After chaining multiple build jobs, it's easy to lose track of their exact order if you don't name them appropriately. The Build Pipeline plugin provides two types of functionality. On the one hand, it offers a visualization of your whole pipeline in one single view. On the other hand, it allows you to configure a downstream build job to only execute if the user initiates it manually. This is especially useful for push-button deployment tasks. We'll explore this functionality in chapter 15 when discussing artifact deployments.

Creating a build pipeline view of the chained tasks is simple. After installing the plugin, click the + tab in the main Jenkins dashboard to add a new view. In the rendered page, select the radio button Build Pipeline View and enter an appropriate view name, as shown in figure 13.25.

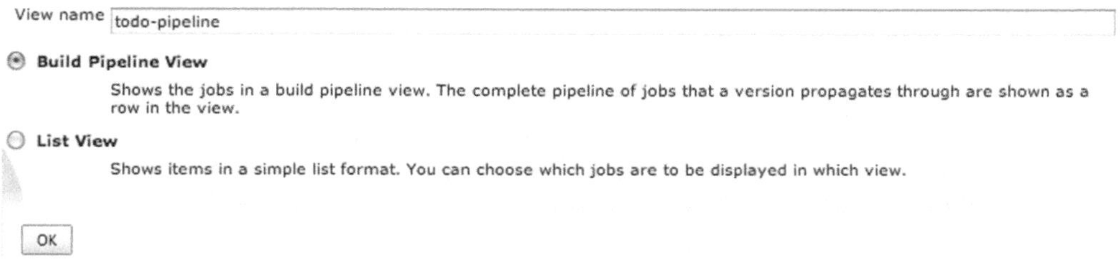

Figure 13.25 Creating a new build pipeline view

Figure 13.26   Build pipeline view

After pressing OK, you're presented with just one more page. Select the initial build job and you're ready to create the build pipeline view. Figure 13.26 shows an exemplary view produced by the plugin.

As shown in the figure, the pipeline consists of three build jobs. The arrows indicate the order of execution. The status of a build is indicated by the color.

Another option for creating a graphical representation of the pipeline is the Downstream Buildview plugin. Starting from the initial project, it renders a hierarchical view of downstream projects. The plugin you choose for your project is mostly a matter of taste. In this book, we'll stick to the Build Pipeline plugin. After getting to know these plugins, you're well equipped to build the first three steps of your pipeline.

13.5.3   *Configuring the pipeline jobs*

Modeling a build pipeline for your To Do application doesn't require any additional Gradle tasks. With the help of Jenkins, you'll orchestrate a sequence of build jobs that call off to your existing tasks. The full pipeline consists of three build jobs in the following order:

1   `todo-initial`: Compiles the source code and runs the unit tests
2   `todo-integ-tests`: Runs the integration tests
3   `todo-code-quality`: Performs static code analysis using Sonar

Earlier in this chapter, you set up a build job for compiling your source code and running the unit tests. With minor modifications, this job will serve as the initial step for your build pipeline. To indicate that the job is the entry point for your pipeline, you'll rename it `todo-initial`. Go ahead and create new free-style build jobs for steps 2 and 3 with the names mentioned above. Later, you'll fill them with life.

Declaring Jenkins build jobs can be a repetitive and tedious task. To keep it short, I'll stick to the most important points when explaining the configuration for each of the build steps.

Quick setup of Jenkins jobs

In its default configuration, Jenkins stores the definition of a build job in the directory `~/.jenkins/jobs` on your local disk. Don't worry if you feel lost at any point of time when configuring your pipeline. The source code of the book contains the job definition for each of the steps. All you need to do is copy the job definitions to the jobs directory and restart the server.

STEP 1: COMPILATION AND UNIT TESTS

You'll start by making some additional tweaks to the initial build job:

- To be able to use the same workspace in downstream projects, make sure to add the post-build action Archive for Clone Workspace SCM with the expression "`**/*`".
- Define the build name using the expression `todo#${BUILD_NUMBER}`.
- Add a parameterized build action that defines a build trigger on the job running your integration tests named `todo-integ-tests`. You'll also declare the downstream parameter `SOURCE_BUILD_NUMBER=${BUILD_NUMBER}`.

STEP 2: INTEGRATION TESTS

The integration test build step is only triggered if step 1 is completed successfully. This is only the case if there were no compilation errors and all unit tests passed. Make the following modifications to the default job configuration:

- In the Source Code Management configuration section, choose the option Clone Workspace and then the parent project `todo-initial`.
- As the build step, you want to trigger the execution of your integration tests. Add a build step for invoking your Gradle script using the wrapper and enter the task `integrationTest`.
- You separated the test results between unit and integration tests by writing them to different directories. For publishing the test reports, use the expression "`**/build/test-results/integration/*.xml`." You'll select the file "`**/build/jacoco/integrationTest.exec`" for code coverage reporting.
- Define the build name by incorporating the upstream build number parameter: `todo#${ENV,var="SOURCE_BUILD_NUMBER"}`.
- Add a parameterized build action that defines a build trigger on the job running your static code analysis named `todo-code-quality`. As far as parameters go, you'll reuse the existing ones by choosing the option Current Build Parameters.

STEP 3: CODE QUALITY

The code quality build step forms the last step in your pipeline for now. Therefore, you don't need to define a downstream project. You'll expand on your pipeline in the next two chapters by adding jobs for publishing the WAR file to a repository and deploying the artifact to different runtime environments. Most of the configuration for this job looks similar to the previous job definition:

- In the Source Code Management configuration section, choose the option Clone Workspace and then the parent project `todo-initial`.
- As the build step, you want to trigger the execution of Sonar Runner to produce code quality metrics. Add a build step for invoking your Gradle script using the wrapper and enter the task `sonarRunner`.
- Define the build name by incorporating the upstream build number parameter: `todo#${ENV,var="SOURCE_BUILD_NUMBER"}`.

Perfect, you built your first build pipeline with Jenkins by setting up a chain of Jenkins jobs. Make sure to configure at least one of the pipeline visualization plugins. It's exciting to see the job execution travel down the swim lane.

13.6   *Summary*

Continuous integration is a software development practice that delivers an instant payoff for your team and the project. By automatically integrating shared source code multiple times a day, you make sure that defects are discovered at the time they're introduced. As a result, the risk of delivering low-quality software is reduced.

In this chapter, you experienced firsthand how easy it is to set up continuous integration for a project. You installed the open source CI server Jenkins on your machine and created a build job for the To Do application. In a first step, you learned how to periodically retrieve the source code from a GitHub repository and trigger a Gradle build. One of Jenkins's strong suits is reporting. You configured your build job to display the unit test results and code coverage metrics. Hosting a Jenkins instance on a server requires hardware resources and qualified personnel to maintain it. We explored popular, cloud-hosted CI solutions and compared their advantages and disadvantages. While hosting a CI server in the cloud is convenient, it may become costly with an increasing number of build jobs and features.

A CI server is more than just a platform for compiling and testing your code. It can be used to orchestrate full-fledged build pipelines. You learned how to model such a build pipeline with Jenkins. Though Jenkins doesn't provide a standardized pipeline implementation out of the box, you can combine the features of various community plugins to implement a viable solution. We discussed how to set up build jobs for the first three stages of a continuous delivery commit phase and tied them together.

In the next chapter, you'll learn how to build the distribution for your project and how to publish it to private and public artifact repositories. In later chapters, you'll extend this pipeline by creating jobs for publishing the WAR file and deploying it to a target environment.

Artifact assembly and publishing

This chapter covers

- Building artifacts and distributions
- Publishing artifacts to local, remote, and public Maven repositories
- Artifact assembly and publishing as part of the build pipeline

As a developer, you mainly deal with two kinds of artifacts during the software development process: source code and binary artifacts as results of your build. We've already seen examples of binary artifacts in this book, including JAR, WAR, and ZIP files.

Source code repositories provided by version control systems like Git or Subversion are designed to manage source code. They provide features like storing the changes between two versions of a file, branching, tagging, and many more. A source code file is usually small and can be handled well by a source code repository. Larger files, typically binaries, can degrade the performance of your repository, slow down the developer's check-out process, and consume a lot of network bandwidth.

Binary repositories like JFrog Artifactory and Sonatype Nexus are well suited for storing binary artifacts. One of the most prominent binary repositives is Maven

Central. They're equipped to handle binary artifacts of large file sizes, provide a way to organize them, describe them with the help of metadata, and expose an interface (a user interface and/or API) to publish and download these artifacts.

In this chapter, we'll look at how to define the artifacts your build is supposed to produce. We'll also discuss how to generate metadata for these artifacts and publish them to local and remote repositories. The CloudBees plugin you wrote in chapter 8 is a perfect example to demonstrate this functionality. By publishing the artifact of the plugin, you can make its capabilities available to other Gradle users within your organization or to anyone on the web interested in using the plugin.

In the context of continuous delivery, publishing your artifact plays a crucial role. Once you package the delivery with a specific version, it's ready to be deployed to various target environments for acceptance testing or to be given into the hands of the end user. It's a good practice to build the artifact only once, deploy it to a binary repository, and reuse it whenever needed. We'll discuss how to apply this concept to your To Do application as part of your build pipeline introduced in the last chapter.

Let's start by bringing back your plugin code from chapter 8 and reviewing its assembly process.

14.1 *Building artifacts and distributions*

By default, every project that applies the Java plugin generates a single JAR file when the lifecycle task `assemble` is executed. In chapter 8, you made good use of this functionality when you created the plugin artifact for further distribution. The artifact filename consists of a name, which is derived from the base name (usually the project name), and a version number if it was set via the `version` property. The following directory tree shows the plugin artifact after generating it:

The file type of an archive might change based on the project type. For example, if you apply the War plugin, the generated archive is turned into a web archive (WAR file) with all its specific packaging characteristics.

While a single, project-type-specific artifact is sufficient for most applications, you may want to create additional artifacts as part of the assembly process. Gradle doesn't impose any limitations on how many artifacts a project can produce. If you're coming from Maven, which gives you a hard time for wanting to create more than one artifact per project, you may find this feature a welcome change.

So how do you add custom archives to your project? Gradle provides archive tasks like `Zip`, `Tar`, and `Jar`, available through the API package `org.gradle.api.tasks.bundling`.

Chapter 4 presented an example of adding an enhanced task that packages a Zip file. It may be helpful to have a quick peek at the example again to refresh your memory.

To produce the output of a custom archive task, you'll need to execute it on the command line or add it as a task dependency to another task. If you consider nonstandard artifacts part of your project's delivery consumed by other users or projects, you'll want to include them into the assembly process. Gradle offers a convenient and declarative way to add artifacts.

14.1.1 *Declaring additional artifacts*

Understanding how to declare additional project artifacts requires a bit of background information: every project that applies the Java plugin is equipped with the configuration archives. You can check its existence by invoking the dependencies task, as shown in the following command-line output:

```
$ gradle dependencies
:dependencies

------------------------------------------------------------
Root project
------------------------------------------------------------

archives - Configuration for archive artifacts.
No dependencies

...
```

Standard configuration used to declare outgoing artifacts

The archives configuration declares the outgoing artifacts of a project. For Java projects, the artifact assigned to this configuration is the standard JAR file. Whenever you execute the task assemble, all declared artifacts are built. You're going to enrich your plugin project by adding some more outgoing artifacts.

You'll learn how to achieve this by example. As the popularity of your plugin grows, you'll want to give your users deeper insights into the inner workings of your code. Plugin consumers are especially interested in learning about the exposed API. What could better serve this purpose than to provide them with the source code and the Groovydocs of your code?

It's common practice to deliver the source code and Groovydocs of a project in the form of JAR files. For your plugin project, this means that you'll have to create two new tasks of type Jar. The source code JAR task needs to include the source files of all SourceSets. You'll name the task sourcesJar. The task groovydocJar creates a JAR file containing the API documentation of your Groovy classes. To be able to include the project's Groovydocs into a JAR file, you'll need to generate them first. This can easily be achieved by letting the jar task depend on the groovydoc task provided by the Java plugin. Figure 14.1 shows the new archive tasks as part of the assemble task graph.

Let's discuss the implementation shown in listing 14.1. To clearly identify that the resulting JAR files belong to your plugin, it's helpful to align the naming. For that purpose, you'll add the suffix (also called classifier) sources to the JAR file containing source code and the suffix groovydoc to the JAR file containing the Groovydocs.

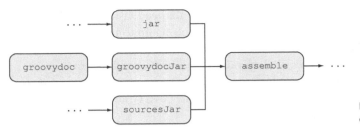

Figure 14.1   Tasks for creating additional artifacts

When looking at some of the libraries on Maven Central, you'll notice that this naming convention is a fairly common practice.

Listing 14.1   Declaring additional artifacts

```
ext.artifactBaseName = 'cloudbees-plugin'

task sourcesJar(type: Jar) {                    ⊲── Task for creating JAR file
   baseName artifactBaseName                        containing all source files
   classifier 'sources'
   from sourceSets.main.allSource
}

task groovydocJar(type: Jar, dependsOn: groovydoc) {   ⊲── Task for creating JAR file
   baseName artifactBaseName                               containing Groovydocs
   classifier 'groovydoc'                                  of project
   from groovydoc.destinationDir
}

artifacts {                    ⊲── Registers additional
   archives sourcesJar             artifacts by assigning them
   archives groovydocJar           to archives configuration
}
```

There are two ways to make the new archive tasks part of the `assemble` task graph. You can go down the imperative route by adding the `sourcesJar` and `groovydocJar` as task dependencies. This approach probably looks the most familiar and straightforward to battle-scarred Ant users:

```
assemble.dependsOn sourcesJar, groovydocJar
```

This works fine and is a valid way to hook up the creation of all artifacts for a project. However, Gradle offers a more declarative mechanism. You can express what outgoing artifacts a project produces without saying how they're created. Being declarative offers two benefits. On the one hand, it's more readable and expressive. On the other hand, projects participating in more complex builds can directly refer to the outgoing artifacts of another project with the help of Gradle's API.

   To declaratively make the new archive tasks part of the `assemble` task graph, you'll need to register them with the project's instance of `ArtifactHandler`. The interface `org.gradle.api.artifacts.dsl.ArtifactHandler` is responsible for defining and publishing artifacts. To register new artifacts with the project, the method

`Project#artifacts` is used. Within the closure, you can assign a task of type `org` `.gradle.api.tasks.bundling.AbstractArchiveTask` (for example, `Jar`, `Zip`, or `Tar`) to the archives configuration. Alternatively, you can also assign an instance of type `java.io.File` in case the artifact isn't generated by an archive task.

After assigning your archive tasks to the `archives` configuration, executing the assemble task will automatically invoke the creation of your custom JAR files:

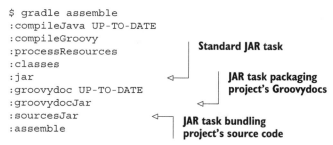

```
$ gradle assemble
:compileJava UP-TO-DATE
:compileGroovy
:processResources          Standard JAR task
:classes
:jar                       JAR task packaging
:groovydoc UP-TO-DATE      project's Groovydocs
:groovydocJar
:sourcesJar                JAR task bundling
:assemble                  project's source code
```

As expected, these files end up in the `build/libs` directory side by side with the standard JAR file of the project:

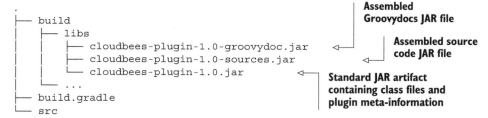

```
.
├── build
│   ├── libs
│   │   ├── cloudbees-plugin-1.0-groovydoc.jar    Assembled
│   │   ├── cloudbees-plugin-1.0-sources.jar      Groovydocs JAR file
│   │   └── cloudbees-plugin-1.0.jar
│   └── ...                                        Assembled source
├── build.gradle                                   code JAR file
└── src
                                                   Standard JAR artifact
                                                   containing class files and
                                                   plugin meta-information
```

You learned how easy it is to declare tasks that produce additional project artifacts and how to register them with the assembly lifecycle process. As part of your software delivery process, you may also want to create a single archive or even multiples archives containing a unique set of these artifacts. This requirement usually arises if you need to assemble distributions targeted toward different operating systems, specific groups of end users, or diverse product flavors of your software. Let's see how creating distributions is supported in Gradle.

14.1.2 Creating distributions

Creating custom distributions in Gradle is a no-brainer. For each archive you want to create, you can add an enhanced task of type `Zip` or `Tar`. While this approach works great for a project with a small set of distributions, you'll have to come up with a naming pattern for the tasks to clearly express their intent.

Gradle's distribution plugin offers a more streamlined and declarative approach to solving this problem. The plugin exposes an expressive language that lets you describe a number of distributions for a project without having to manually declare tasks. The task creation is handled by the plugin under the hood. The plugin lets you generate a distribution in the form of a ZIP or TAR file.

Let's say you want to create a distribution for your CloudBees plugin project that bundles the plugin JAR file, the sources JAR file, and the Groovydocs JAR file into a new archive. The following listing demonstrates how to apply the distribution plugin and specify the target directory content you want to bundle with the archive.

Listing 14.2   Building a distribution

```
apply plugin: 'distribution'

distributions {                    Standard distribution
    main {                         configuration closure named
                                   main by convention
        baseName = archivesBaseName        Base name of
                                           distribution file
        contents {
            from { libsDir }       Packages all files
        }                          in build/libs
    }
}
```

With this code in place, you can decide whether you want to create a ZIP or TAR file for the distribution. The ZIP file can be generated by the task distZip, and the TAR file is built by the task distTar. Usually, you'll just need one of these file formats. A TAR file is oftentimes a preferred format on UNIX operating systems. For a cross-platform distribution, a ZIP file is usually the preferred format. The following command-line output shows the creation of a ZIP distribution:

```
$ gradle assemble distZip
:compileJava UP-TO-DATE
:compileGroovy
:processResources
:classes
:jar
:groovydoc UP-TO-DATE
:groovydocJar
:sourcesJar
:assemble
:distZip
```

Distributions are placed into the directory build/distributions. The following directory tree shows the generated file:

```
.
├── build
│   ├── distributions
│   │   └── cloudbees-plugin-1.0.zip          ZIP distribution
│   ├── libs
│   │   ├── cloudbees-plugin-1.0-groovydoc.jar     Source files included
│   │   ├── cloudbees-plugin-1.0-sources.jar       in distribution
│   │   └── cloudbees-plugin-1.0.jar
│   └── ...
├── build.gradle
└── src
```

The distribution plugin is designed to support more than a single distribution. For each additional distribution, you'll need to add another named configuration block within the distributions closure. Listing 14.3 demonstrates an example. On top of the standard distribution that bundles all JAR files from the directory build/libs, you want to create a distribution that solely contains documentation files. As documentation files, you classify the source files JAR and the Groovydocs JAR.

Listing 14.3 Configuring a custom distribution

```
distributions {
    main {
        ...
    }
    docs {                                          ◁─── Custom distribution
                                                         configuration closure
        baseName = "$archivesBaseName-docs"         ◁─┐ Base name of
                                                        distribution file
        contents {
            from(libsDir) {
                include sourcesJar.archiveName      │ Only packages sources and
                include groovydocJar.archiveName    │ Groovydocs JARs in build/libs
            }
        }
    }
}
```

You may have noticed that the configuration block of the distribution is named docs. The plugin automatically derives the distribution task names for nonstandard distributions from the declared name. In addition to the already existing tasks, you can now generate the documentation distribution by using the tasks docsDistZip and docsDistTar. Generate the distribution—this time as a TAR file:

```
$ gradle assemble docsDistTar
:compileJava UP-TO-DATE
:compileGroovy UP-TO-DATE
:processResources UP-TO-DATE
:classes UP-TO-DATE
:jar UP-TO-DATE
:groovydoc UP-TO-DATE
:groovydocJar UP-TO-DATE
:sourcesJar UP-TO-DATE
:assemble UP-TO-DATE
:docsDistTar
```

The distribution output directory now also contains the expected TAR file:

```
.
├── build
│   ├── distributions
│   │   ├── cloudbees-plugin-1.0.zip          ◁─┐ Standard distribution
│   │   └── cloudbees-plugin-docs-1.0.tar     ◁   as ZIP file
│   ├── libs                                     │ Documentation
│   │   ├── cloudbees-plugin-1.0-groovydoc.jar  │ distribution as TAR file
│   │   ├── cloudbees-plugin-1.0-sources.jar
```

```
|    |    └── cloudbees-plugin-1.0.jar
|    └── ...
├── build.gradle
└── src
```

You saw how to declare and build distributions for your plugin project. Though descriptive and powerful, the requirements in your project may call for more complex or platform-specific functionality; for example, creating a desktop installer or generating an RPM package. If you feel like the distribution plugin doesn't cut the mustard, make sure to look at third-party Gradle plugins. Some of them may provide the functionality you're looking for.

Let's summarize what you've done so far: you enabled your project to produce the plugin JAR file and two documentation archives containing the project's source code and Groovydocs. Now you're ready to share the plugin with the world. Next, I'll show how to publish these artifacts to a binary repository.

14.2   *Publishing artifacts to a binary repository*

In chapter 5, we mainly talked about dependency management from a consumer's perspective. You learned how to declare dependencies and repositories within your build script. Gradle's dependency manager would in turn try to locate these dependencies, download and store them in a local cache, and make them available to your build.

In this chapter, you'll take on the role of the artifact producer. You'll learn how to publish build artifacts to a local or remote repository. An important step in the publishing process is to generate metadata for these artifacts. This metadata, usually stored in an XML-based text file, can give sufficient information about the corresponding artifacts. The following list should give you an idea of some common types of metadata:

- General information about the artifact, like name, description, involved developers, and links to source code or documentation
- The available version of the artifact
- Transitive dependencies the artifact relies on
- The software license of an artifact a consumer has to comply to

Gradle can help with producing customized metadata and uploading the artifacts of a build to different types of repositories. Figure 14.2 demonstrates the interaction among a Gradle build, its produced artifacts, and some targeted binary repositories.

The most common repository formats you'll find in the wild are based on either Maven or Ivy. At the time of writing, Gradle doesn't provide its own, specialized repository format. For our examples, you'll see how to publish to the most widely used repository format: Maven.

14.2.1   *Publishing to a Maven repository*

Remember earlier in this chapter when you modified your plugin build to produce three different artifacts? You ended up with these files in your `build/libs` directory:

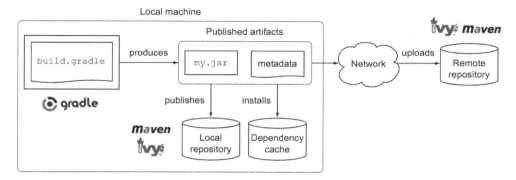

Figure 14.2   Publishing artifacts to local and remote repositories

- `cloudbees-plugin-1.0.jar`
- `cloudbees-plugin-1.0-groovydoc.jar`
- `cloudbees-plugin-1.0-sources.jar`

It's time to publish them to a Maven repository for later consumption. We'll look at how to publish them to three types of Maven repositories, as shown in figure 14.3:

- The local cache located in the directory `<USER_HOME>/.m2/repository`.
- A repository in an arbitrary directory on your local file system.
- A remote, binary repository accessible via HTTP(S). The following examples use the popular JFrog product Artifactory.

Projects in an enterprise setting shouldn't rely on Maven Central as their primary source of dependency management. To be able to produce reliable and reproducible builds, an internal repository should be set up for catering to your projects.

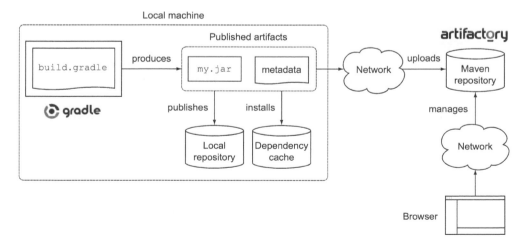

Figure 14.3   Publishing artifacts to a Maven repository

There are various products that can be used; for example, Sonatype Nexus (http://www.sonatype.org/nexus/) and JFrog Artifactory (http://www.jfrog.com/home/v_artifactory_opensource_overview). We won't discuss how to set up such a repository. Please refer to the product's installation manual for more information. For now, let's assume you already set up Artifactory as your manager for dependencies running on the URL http://localhost:8081/artifactory.

14.2.2   *Old versus new publishing mechanisms*

Publishing artifacts is an important step in the lifecycle of a software component. Gradle came with support for publishing artifacts to a repository early on with the Upload task included as part of the Maven plugin. While the Maven plugin is used by early Gradle adopters and works well in production environments, it became apparent that a more descriptive and elegant DSL is needed to describe publications of a project.

Starting with version 1.3 of Gradle, a new publishing mechanism was introduced by the plugins maven-publish and ivy-publish. Even though it's still an incubating feature, it coexists with the existing methods for publishing artifacts, but will supersede them in an upcoming version of Gradle. Given this outlook, most of our discussions will be based on the new publishing mechanism, because it'll make your build script future-proof. In the following sections, you'll use the maven-publish plugin for publishing the artifacts produced by your CloudBees plugin project to a Maven repository. A similar approach can be taken with the ivy-publish plugin if you prefer to use the Ivy repository format. The DSL exposed by both plugins looks fairly similar, so with minor modifications you can make it target Ivy as well. Let's jump right in and see how to publish the plugin JAR to a Maven repository.

14.2.3   *Declaring a software component as a Maven publication*

Gradle projects that apply a specific plugin are preconfigured to produce a primary, outgoing artifact whenever the assemble task is executed. You already got to know various examples of this behavior. A project that applies the Java or Groovy plugin creates a JAR file, and a project that applies the War plugin packages a WAR file. In the context of the publishing plugin, this artifact is called a software component.

The following listing applies the Maven publishing plugin to your CloudBees project and uses its DSL to declare a single publication: a Java software component. When I speak of a Java software component, I mean the generated JAR file.

Listing 14.4   Publishing JAR component to a Maven repository

```
apply plugin: 'maven-publish'

publishing {
    publications {
        plugin(MavenPublication) {
            from components.java
            artifactId 'cloudbees-plugin'
        }
    }
}
```

Declares publication name of type MavenPublication with the name plugin

Adds JAR component of your project to list of publications

Declares artifact ID for publishing

```
        }
}
```

This configuration is all you need to generate the metadata for your JAR file and publish the file to a Maven repository. Because you haven't yet defined a repository, you can only publish these files to the local Maven cache located in the directory .m2/repository. Check the list of publication tasks available to the project:

```
$ gradle tasks
:tasks

------------------------------------------------------------
All tasks runnable from root project
------------------------------------------------------------

...

Publishing tasks
----------------
publish - Publishes all publications produced by this project.
publishPluginPublicationToMavenLocal - Publishes Maven publication
   'plugin' to the local Maven repository.
publishToMavenLocal - Publishes all Maven publications produced by
   this project to the local Maven cache.

...
```

Only publishes software component to local Maven cache →

Publishes all artifacts of project

Publishes all declared artifacts to local Maven cache

The project exposes three different publication tasks. This may look confusing at first, but it makes a lot of sense if you need fine-grained control over the publication process. By picking the right task, you can selectively say which artifact(s) you want to publish to what repository. You may have noticed that the arbitrary name you used for your publication became part of a task name: the name plugin became part of the task name publishPluginPublicationToMavenLocal. This makes for a very declarative way to construct a publication task name. Next, we'll see these tasks in action.

14.2.4 Publishing a software component to the local Maven cache

The local Maven cache is of particular relevance for Gradle users for two reasons. In chapter 5, you learned that Gradle tries to reuse artifacts found in the local Maven cache. This is a major benefit to migrating Maven users, because the artifacts don't have to be downloaded again. The other reason why you'd want to publish to the local Maven cache is if you work with a variety of projects that use different build tools. One project may use Gradle to publish an artifact; another project may use Maven to consume it.

Let's assume you want to publish your plugin JAR file, including the generated POM file. The following console output shows the executed tasks:

```
$ gradle publishToMavenLocal
:generatePomFileForPluginPublication
:compileJava UP-TO-DATE
:compileGroovy UP-TO-DATE
:processResources UP-TO-DATE
:classes UP-TO-DATE
```

Generates POM file for publication

```
:jar UP-TO-DATE
:publishPluginPublicationToMavenLocal
Uploading: com/manning/gia/cloudbees-plugin/1.0/cloudbees-plugin-
➥ 1.0.jar to repository remote at file:/Users/Ben/.m2/repository/
Transferring 43K from remote
Uploaded 43K
:publishToMavenLocal
```

Uploads Java component to local Maven repository

In the process of publishing the JAR file, the POM file is generated by the task generate-PomFileForPluginPublication. Similar to the task publishPluginPublicationToMavenLocal, its name is derived from the declared name of the publication. You may wonder why the POM file isn't listed as an uploaded artifact in the console output. No worries—it's simply not logged. What you end up with are the following artifacts in the local Maven cache directory:

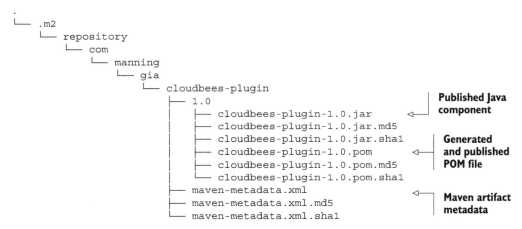

The uploaded artifacts follow the typical format for dependencies within a Maven repository. The directory com/manning/gia is derived from the project's group property, the artifact ID (in your case, cloudbees-plugin) follows the project name, and the version reflects the value of the version property in your project. Files with the extension .md5 and .sha1 are checksum files. They're used to check the integrity of the associated file.

How to change the artifact publication name

By default, the name of the published artifact is derived from the project name. You may remember from earlier chapters that the project name corresponds with the name of your project directory. It's important to understand that any change to properties like archivesBaseName won't have an effect on the publication name, even though the assembled archive may have the naming you desire.

Sometimes you may want to use a different publication name. Every MavenPublication allows for configuring custom publication attributes. One of these attributes is the

> **(continued)**
>
> artifact ID of the publication, as shown in listing 14.4. Alternatively, you can also set the project name in your `settings.gradle` file. The following example demonstrates how to change the project name to `my-plugin`:
>
> ```
> rootProject.name = 'my-plugin'
> ```
>
> As a result, the published artifact would have the name `my-plugin-1.0.jar`, and the name of the directory in the local Maven cache would be `com/manning/gia/my-plugin`.

The same naming pattern is reflected in the dependency attributes `groupId`, `artifactId`, and `version` of the generated POM file. The following listing shows the full content of the file named `cloudbees-plugin-1.0.pom`.

Listing 14.5   Generated POM for published software component

```
<?xml version="1.0" encoding="UTF-8"?>
<project xsi:schemaLocation="http://maven.apache.org/POM/4.0.0
        http://maven.apache.org/xsd/maven-4.0.0.xsd"
        xmlns="http://maven.apache.org/POM/4.0.0"
        xmlns:xsi="http://www.w3.org/2001/XMLSchema-instance">
    <modelVersion>4.0.0</modelVersion>
    <groupId>com.manning.gia</groupId>            Dependency attributes
    <artifactId>cloudbees-plugin</artifactId>     for published artifact
    <version>1.0</version>
    <dependencies>                                Transitive dependencies
        <dependency>                              required by published
            <groupId>com.cloudbees</groupId>      artifact to function
            <artifactId>cloudbees-api-client</artifactId>   correctly
            <version>1.4.0</version>
            <scope>runtime</scope>
        </dependency>
    </dependencies>
</project>
```

At the time of the POM generation, the publication plugin automatically determines the project's dependencies from the configuration `runtime` and declares them as transitive dependencies. Here, you can see that this is the case for the CloudBees API client library. Keep in mind that the publication API will only declare the dependencies that are relevant to the consumers of the JAR file. Dependencies that are used to build your project (for example, test libraries) aren't included. Though this is a minor shift from Maven's default philosophy of including both types of dependencies in the POM, build, and runtime information, it makes for much cleaner metadata without any drawbacks.

Great, you were able to publish the default outgoing project artifact. But what if you want to publish additional artifacts? Your plugin project has the specific need to provide the sources JAR and Groovydocs JAR for consumption as well. Let's look at how these files can be declared using the publishing DSL.

14.2.5 *Declaring custom artifacts for publication*

Additional artifacts can be registered for publication by using the method `artifact` provided by the API class `MavenPublication`. The method requires you to provide one parameter. This parameter can either be any task of type `AbstractArchiveTask`, which is the case for both of your documentation JAR file tasks, or any object that can be translated into a `java.io.File`. The Javadocs of the publication API will give you examples that demonstrate the use of both types of declarations. The next listing shows how to assign the archive tasks `sourcesJar` and `groovydocJar` as Maven publications.

Listing 14.6   Publishing additional artifacts to a Maven repository

```
apply plugin: 'maven-publish'

publishing {
    publications {
        plugin(MavenPublication) {          Declares publication name of type MavenPublication
            from components.java             Adds JAR component of project to list of publications
            artifactId 'cloudbees-plugin'    Declares artifact ID for publishing

            artifact sourcesJar              Adds custom artifacts to list of publications
            artifact groovydocJar
        }
    }
}
```

There's one important detail to keep in mind when declaring custom artifacts. The publication plugin only allows a single artifact to be published with an empty classifier attribute. Usually this is the software component, which has the name `cloudbees-plugin-1.0.jar`. All other artifacts need to provide a classifier. For your sources JAR file, the classifier is `sources`, and for the Groovydocs JAR file this is `groovydoc`. Initiate the previously used publication task again and see if you can deliver your custom artifacts to the Maven cache:

```
$ gradle publishToMavenLocal
:generatePomFileForPluginPublication
:compileJava UP-TO-DATE
:compileGroovy
:processResources
:classes
:groovydoc
:groovydocJar
:jar
:sourcesJar
:publishPluginPublicationToMavenLocal
Uploading: com/manning/gia/cloudbees-plugin/1.0/cloudbees-plugin-
➥ 1.0.jar to repository remote at file:/Users/Ben/.m2/repository/
Transferring 43K from remote
Uploaded 43K
Uploading: com/manning/gia/cloudbees-plugin/1.0/cloudbees-plugin-1.0-
➥ sources.jar to repository remote at file:/Users/Ben/.m2/repository/
Transferring 7K from remote
Uploaded 7K
```

```
Uploading: com/manning/gia/cloudbees-plugin/1.0/cloudbees-plugin-1.0-
    groovydoc.jar to repository remote at file:/Users/Ben/.m2/repository/
Transferring 33K from remote
Uploaded 33K
:publishToMavenLocal
```

The console output now shows that all declared publications were uploaded to the repository. A quick check of the directory tree reveals the desired end result:

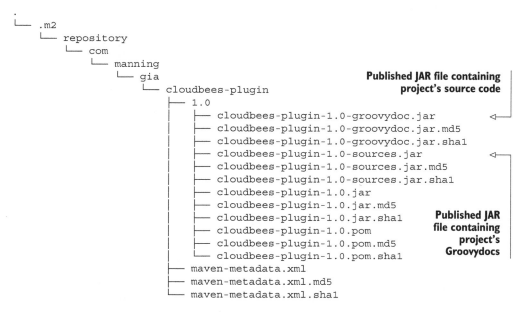

Perfect—all artifacts you wanted to make available to the Maven cache could be published. Consumers of the artifacts rely on the default POM metadata to resolve the plugin JAR file and its transitive dependencies. In section 14.2, we talked about the data a POM file can contain. The publishing API makes this data fully customizable. In the next section, we'll discuss how to modify the generated POM.

14.2.6 *Modifying the generated POM*

The POM file that describes an artifact within a repository should be as informative as possible. At the very least, you should provide details about the purpose of your artifact, the software license, and a pointer to the documentation so that end users can get a lead on *what* functionality is provided and *how* to use it within their project. The best way to find out what information can be configured is to the check the POM reference guide at http://maven.apache.org/pom.html. The guide describes the XML structure and available tags for configuring a POM.

The generated standard POM can be modified with the help of the hook `pom.withXml`. By calling the method `asNode()`, you can retrieve the root node of that POM. New nodes can be added or existing ones modified (except for the identifiers groupId, artifactId, and version). The following listing shows how to add more information to your plugin POM.

Listing 14.7 Publishing additional artifacts to a Maven repository

```
apply plugin: 'maven-publish'

publishing {
    publications {
        plugin(MavenPublication) {
            from components.java
            artifactId 'cloudbees-plugin'          ⟵ Method for configuring
                                                        POM XML elements
            pom.withXml {
                def root = asNode()
                root.appendNode('name', 'Gradle CloudBees plugin')
                root.appendNode('description', 'Gradle plugin for managing
                              ➥ applications and databases on CloudBees
                              ➥ RUN@cloud.')
                root.appendNode('inceptionYear', '2013')

                def license = root.appendNode('licenses').appendNode('license')
                license.appendNode('name', 'The Apache Software License,
                                    ➥ Version 2.0')
                license.appendNode('url', 'http://www.apache.org/licenses/LICENSE-
                                    ➥ 2.0.txt')
                license.appendNode('distribution', 'repo')

                def developer = root.appendNode('developers')
                              ➥ .appendNode('developer')
                developer.appendNode('id', 'bmuschko')
                developer.appendNode('name', 'Benjamin Muschko')
                developer.appendNode('email', 'benjamin.muschko@gmail.com')
            }

            artifact sourcesJar
            artifact groovydocJar
        }
    }
}
```

The next listing shows the regenerated POM file, which now reflects your changes to the metadata.

Listing 14.8 Modified plugin POM

```
<?xml version="1.0" encoding="UTF-8"?>
<project xsi:schemaLocation="http://maven.apache.org/POM/4.0.0
        ➥ http://maven.apache.org/xsd/maven-4.0.0.xsd"
        ➥ xmlns="http://maven.apache.org/POM/4.0.0"
        ➥ xmlns:xsi="http://www.w3.org/2001/XMLSchema-instance">
    <modelVersion>4.0.0</modelVersion>
    <groupId>com.manning.gia</groupId>
    <artifactId>cloudbees-plugin</artifactId>
    <version>1.0</version>
    <dependencies>
```

```
    <dependency>
        <groupId>com.cloudbees</groupId>
        <artifactId>cloudbees-api-client</artifactId>
        <version>1.4.0</version>
        <scope>runtime</scope>
    </dependency>
</dependencies>
<name>Gradle CloudBees plugin</name>
<description>Gradle plugin for managing applications and databases on
            ➡ CloudBees RUN@cloud.</description>
<inceptionYear>2013</inceptionYear>
<licenses>
    <license>
        <name>The Apache Software License, Version 2.0</name>
        <url>http://www.apache.org/licenses/LICENSE-2.0.txt</url>
        <distribution>repo</distribution>
    </license>
</licenses>
<developers>
    <developer>
        <id>bmuschko</id>
        <name>Benjamin Muschko</name>
        <email>benjamin.muschko@gmail.com</email>
    </developer>
</developers>
</project>
```

So far, you've installed the published artifacts to the local Maven cache. What if you wanted to publish them to a Maven repository on your local file system or the Artifactory repository you set up earlier? Nothing easier than that—the publishing API allows for declaring repositories as well.

14.2.7 *Publishing to a local Maven repository*

In chapter 8, you used the "old" Maven plugin to upload your project's artifact to a local Maven repository so it could be consumed by another Gradle project. You used this technique for testing your plugin functionality on your local machine without having to make it public. The same functionality is provided by the Maven publishing plugin.

Every repository you want to target needs to be declared in a `repositories` configuration block exposed by the publishing DSL. In the following listing, you'll declare a single Maven repository located in the directory named `repo` parallel to the project directory.

> **Listing 14.9 Publishing to a local Maven repository**

```
apply plugin: 'maven-publish'

publishing {
    publications {
        plugin(MavenPublication) {
            ...
        }
    }
}
```

```
    repositories {
       maven {
          name 'myLocal'                          ⟵┐  Optional name for
          url "file://$projectDir/../repo"         │  Maven repository
       }                                              ⟵┐  File URL to local
    }                                                  │  Maven repository
}
```

The name attribute of a repository is optional. If you assign a name, it becomes part of the corresponding publishing task. By assigning the name `myLocal`, your task is automatically named `publishPluginPublicationToMyLocalRepository`. This is especially useful when dealing with multiple repositories at the same time. Run the task:

```
$ gradle publishPluginPublicationToMyLocalRepository
:generatePomFileForPluginPublication
:compileJava UP-TO-DATE
:compileGroovy UP-TO-DATE
:processResources UP-TO-DATE
:classes UP-TO-DATE
:groovydoc UP-TO-DATE
:groovydocJar UP-TO-DATE
:jar UP-TO-DATE
:sourcesJar UP-TO-DATE
:publishPluginPublicationToMyLocalRepository
Uploading: com/manning/gia/cloudbees-plugin/1.0/cloudbees-plugin-
➡ 1.0.jar to repository remote at file:/Users/Ben/Dev/books/gradle-in-
➡ action/code/chapter14/publish-maven-local-repository/repo
Transferring 43K from remote
Uploaded 43K
Uploading: com/manning/gia/cloudbees-plugin/1.0/cloudbees-plugin-1.0-
➡ sources.jar to repository remote at file:/Users/Ben/Dev/books/gradle-
➡ in-action/code/chapter14/publish-maven-local-repository/repo
Transferring 7K from remote
Uploaded 7K
Uploading: com/manning/gia/cloudbees-plugin/1.0/cloudbees-plugin-1.0-
➡ groovydoc.jar to repository remote at
➡ file:/Users/Ben/Dev/books/gradle-in-action/code/chapter14/publish-maven-
➡ local-repository/repo
Transferring 33K from remote
Uploaded 33K
```

Gradle is smart enough to automatically create the local repository even though its root directory doesn't exist yet. As expected, you'll find the uploaded artifacts in the correct location:

```
.
├── cloudbees-plugin                    ⟵┐  CloudBees plugin project
│    └── ...                             │  that publishes artifacts
└── repo
     └── com                            ⟵┐  Local Maven
          └── manning                    │  repository parallel
               └── gia                   │  to plugin project
                    └── cloudbees-plugin
```

```
├── 1.0
│   ├── cloudbees-plugin-1.0-groovydoc.jar
│   ├── cloudbees-plugin-1.0-groovydoc.jar.md5
│   ├── cloudbees-plugin-1.0-groovydoc.jar.sha1
│   ├── cloudbees-plugin-1.0-sources.jar
│   ├── cloudbees-plugin-1.0-sources.jar.md5
│   ├── cloudbees-plugin-1.0-sources.jar.sha1
│   ├── cloudbees-plugin-1.0.jar
│   ├── cloudbees-plugin-1.0.jar.md5
│   ├── cloudbees-plugin-1.0.jar.sha1
│   ├── cloudbees-plugin-1.0.pom
│   ├── cloudbees-plugin-1.0.pom.md5
│   └── cloudbees-plugin-1.0.pom.sha1
├── maven-metadata.xml
├── maven-metadata.xml.md5
└── maven-metadata.xml.sha1
```

In the next section, we'll also look at how to publish the same artifacts to a remote repository via HTTP.

14.2.8 *Publishing to a remote Maven repository*

Remote repositories are extremely helpful for making artifacts available to other teams or stakeholders within your organization. For testing purposes, we set up an Artifactory instance on our local machine. Keep in mind that this repository could sit anywhere within your corporate network as long as it's accessible via HTTP(S). Artifactory preconfigures two Maven repositories with its default installation:

- `libs-snapshot-local`: Used for publishing artifacts that are considered under development with the version suffix `-SNAPSHOT`
- `libs-release-local`: Used for publishing production-ready artifacts without the `-SNAPSHOT` version suffix

Both of these repositories expose a dedicated HTTP URL and control how and who can upload artifacts. A secured repository requires you to supply the configured authentication credentials. If you don't provide these properties, your build will fail because it couldn't authenticate your upload. To prevent having to check in this sensible data into version control, you'll feed these properties through your `gradle.properties` file. Gradle will read the contents of this file automatically at runtime and make the properties available to your build script. For now, you're going to use the default Artifactory administration credentials:

```
artifactoryUsername = admin
artifactoryPassword = password
```

Next, you'll write some code to publish your artifacts to one of these repositories based on the `version` property of your project. The following listing doesn't look too different from previous examples. The biggest difference is that you also provide the credentials to the repository to authenticate the upload.

Listing 14.10   Publishing to a remote Maven repository

```
apply plugin: 'maven-publish'

ext {
    artifactoryBaseUrl = 'http://localhost:8081/artifactory'
    artifactorySnapshotRepoUrl = "$artifactoryBaseUrl/libs-snapshot-local"
    artifactoryReleaseRepoUrl = "$artifactoryBaseUrl/libs-release-local"
}

publishing {
    publications {
        plugin(MavenPublication) {
            ...
        }
    }

    repositories {
        maven {
            name 'remoteArtifactory'
            url project.version.endsWith('-SNAPSHOT') ?
                artifactorySnapshotRepoUrl : artifactoryReleaseRepoUrl

            credentials {
                username = artifactoryUsername
                password = artifactoryPassword
            }
        }
    }
}
```

Properties declaring Artifactory repository URLs

Optional name for Maven repository

Picks snapshot or release repository based on project version

Sets credentials needed to upload artifacts to secured Artifactory repository

You named the remote repository remoteArtifactory. The publishing plugin incorporates the repository name into the name of the task used to upload your project artifacts to Artifactory:

```
$ gradle publishPluginPublicationToRemoteArtifactoryRepository
:generatePomFileForPluginPublication
:compileJava UP-TO-DATE
:compileGroovy
:processResources
:classes
:groovydoc
:groovydocJar
:jar
:sourcesJar
:publishPluginPublicationToRemoteArtifactoryRepository
Uploading: com/manning/gia/cloudbees-plugin/1.0/cloudbees-plugin-
    1.0.jar to repository remote at
    http://localhost:8081/artifactory/libs-release-local
Transferring 43K from remote
Uploaded 43K
Uploading: com/manning/gia/cloudbees-plugin/1.0/cloudbees-plugin-1.0-
    sources.jar to repository remote at
    http://localhost:8081/artifactory/libs-release-local
Transferring 7K from remote
Uploaded 7K
```

```
Uploading: com/manning/gia/cloudbees-plugin/1.0/cloudbees-plugin-1.0-
➥ groovydoc.jar to repository remote at
➥ http://localhost:8081/artifactory/libs-release-local
Transferring 33K from remote
Uploaded 33K
```

After uploading the artifacts to Artifactory, you should be able to browse the repository by the provided group ID. There's a directory with the specified version containing the POM and JAR files of your CloudBees plugin (figure 14.4).

Simplifying the publishing code with product-specific plugins

Some binary repository products provide a Gradle plugin to simplify the process of publishing. Such a plugin provides a standardized, product-specific DSL and can't be used with other binary repositories. Think of it as a higher-level API sitting on top of the Gradle publishing API, while at the same time adding more features (for example, build information). Using a vendor plugin can reduce the code you need to write for publishing artifacts. These plugins should only be used if you know that your project is sticking with a particular product long term.

JFrog provides such a plugin for Artifactory. We won't discuss how to use it, but feel free to check out its documentation at the following Wiki page: http://wiki.jfrog.org/confluence/display/RTF/Gradle+Artifactory+Plugin.

14.3 *Publishing to a public binary repository*

Publishing artifacts to a repository within your corporate network is a practical solution for sharing binaries among teams. It also takes care of protecting intellectual property from the outside world.

Figure 14.4 Uploaded artifacts in Artifactory repository browser

Organizations with a stake in open source software like to contribute their hard work to the Gradle community or anyone interested in using their code. This can either be achieved by making their binary repository internet-accessible or by uploading the artifacts to a public repository. The most popular public repositories are JFrog Bintray's JCenter and Maven Central. In this chapter, you'll learn how to publish your CloudBees plugin to both repositories. Let's start by looking at Bintray.

14.3.1 *Publishing to JFrog Bintray*

JFrog Bintray (https://bintray.com/) is the new kid on the block among the public repositories. Bintray is more than just a provider for hosting binary repositories. It comes with a web dashboard, integrated search functionality, social features, artifact download statistics, and a RESTful API for managing your repositories and artifacts. Bintray was launched in early 2013 but quickly grew in popularity within its first months of existence. Currently, you see a lot of open source projects moving to Bintray. Before you can publish any artifacts to Bintray, you'll need to set up an account.

GETTING SET UP ON BINTRAY

Bintray requires you to create an account, a repository, and a package before you can get started. This involves the following simple steps:

1 Open a browser, navigate to the URL https://bintray.com/, and sign up for a new account if you don't have one yet.
2 After completing the signup process, log into the newly created account. Press the button New Repository to configure a repository. For your purposes, name this repository gradle-plugins and choose the Maven repository format.
3 Click the repository and create a new package with the name gradle-cloudbees-plugin. A package acts as a container for artifacts produced by a specific project. You can store any number of artifacts in a package.
4 Any artifact you publish to this package can only be downloaded as a Gradle project dependency if you provide your credentials in the repository configuration. To make this package public to any Gradle user, you can request it to be synced with Bintray's JCenter, a free-of-charge public Maven repository. Only after JFrog approves your request will you be able to make your artifacts public.

Don't worry if you get lost anywhere during the setup procedure or have additional questions. The Bintray user guide (https://bintray.com/docs/help/bintrayuserguide.html) can give you a more detailed insight into Bintray's terminology and serves as a good quick-start manual. You're going to bring your plugin artifacts into Bintray.

UPLOADING ARTIFACTS TO A BINTRAY PACKAGE

Architecturally, uploading artifacts to Bintray doesn't look any different from your regular upload to a remote Maven repository (figure 14.5). The main difference is that you can share an artifact located in a private repository with JCenter, a public repository.

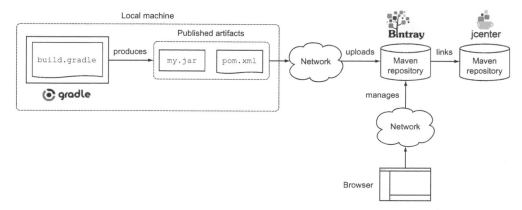

Figure 14.5 Publishing artifacts to Bintray

Bintray doesn't require you to sign your artifacts before you upload them, but gives you the option of signing them after the fact. Therefore, you'll only need some minor modifications to your original build script, as shown in the following listing. You'll need to define a new Maven repository, provide the repository URL of your package, and give the Bintray credentials of your account.

Listing 14.11 Publishing to Bintray repository

```
ext {
    bintrayBaseUrl = 'https://api.bintray.com/maven'
    bintrayUsername = 'bmuschko'                          Properties required for
    bintrayRepository = 'gradle-plugins'                  building Bintray API URL
    bintrayPackage = 'gradle-cloudbees-plugin'
}

apply plugin: 'maven-publish'

publishing {
    publications {
        ...
    }

    repositories {
        maven {
            name 'Bintray'
            url "$bintrayBaseUrl/$bintrayUsername/$bintrayRepository/
                ➥ $bintrayPackage"                        Puts together
                                                          Bintray API URL
            credentials {                                 and assigns it
                username = bintrayUsername   Bintray credentials    to Maven URL
                password = bintrayApiKey     needed for upload      property
            }
        }
    }
}
```

For security reasons, keep the credentials in the gradle.properties file under your home directory. The contents of this file should look similar to the following properties:

```
bintrayUsername = bmuschko
bintrayApiKey = 14a5g63385ad861d4c8210da795
```

You used an API key instead of a password in the credentials configuration block. You can find your API key in Bintray's dashboard under the link Your Account > Edit > API Key. You're all set; time to make the world a better place by publishing your plugin artifacts:

```
$ gradle publishPluginPublicationToBintrayRepository
:generatePomFileForPluginPublication
:compileJava UP-TO-DATE
:compileGroovy UP-TO-DATE
:processResources UP-TO-DATE
:classes UP-TO-DATE
:groovydoc UP-TO-DATE
:groovydocJar UP-TO-DATE
:jar
:sourcesJar UP-TO-DATE
:publishPluginPublicationToBintrayRepository
Uploading: org/gradle/api/plugins/gradle-cloudbees-plugin/0.1/gradle-
➥ cloudbees-plugin-0.1.jar to repository remote at
➥ https://api.bintray.com/maven/bmuschko/gradle-plugins/gradle-
➥ cloudbees-plugin
Transferring 179K from remote
Uploaded 179K
Uploading: org/gradle/api/plugins/gradle-cloudbees-plugin/0.1/gradle-
➥ cloudbees-plugin-0.1-sources.jar to repository remote at
➥ https://api.bintray.com/maven/bmuschko/gradle-plugins/gradle-
➥ cloudbees-plugin
Transferring 23K from remote
Uploaded 23K
Uploading: org/gradle/api/plugins/gradle-cloudbees-plugin/0.1/gradle-
➥ cloudbees-plugin-0.1-groovydoc.jar to repository remote at
➥ https://api.bintray.com/maven/bmuschko/gradle-plugins/gradle-
➥ cloudbees-plugin
Transferring 83K from remote
Uploaded 83K
```

Looks like the upload worked! You can also view the uploaded artifacts in the Bintray dashboard. The file browser under the package gradle-cloudbees-plugin > Versions > 0.1 > Files should look similar to figure 14.6.

Managing public artifacts

Never underestimate the power of open source. Once you put an artifact on a public repository, other developers may start to use it. Bintray doesn't prevent you from deleting already-published versions of an artifact. Try to stay away from deleting existing versions of your artifacts because it might break other developer's builds. If you need to fix a bug in your code, make sure to release a new version of your artifact and communicate the bug fix.

Figure 14.6   Uploaded artifacts in Bintray dashboard

CONSUMING DEPENDENCIES FROM BINTRAY'S JCENTER

You published the artifacts and made them available on JCenter. They're now ready for consumption. To configure a Gradle project to use your plugin from Bintray, declare a new reference to the JCenter repository available under the URL http:// jcenter.bintray.com, as shown in the next listing.

Listing 14.12   Consuming the published plugin from Bintray

```
buildscript {
    repositories {
        jcenter()                                       Defines Bintray
    }                                                   JCenter repository

    dependencies {                                                          Defines a
        classpath 'com.manning.gia:gradle-cloudbees-plugin:0.1'            dependency on
    }                                                                      your previously
}                                                                          uploaded
                                                                           plugin JAR file
apply plugin: 'cloudbees'
```

Looks pretty straightforward, right? Let's also discuss what steps are required to publish the same plugin to Maven Central.

14.3.2   Publishing to Maven Central

Maven Central (http://repo1.maven.org/maven2/) is probably the most popular public repository for binary artifacts, particularly open source projects. Sonatype Nexus,

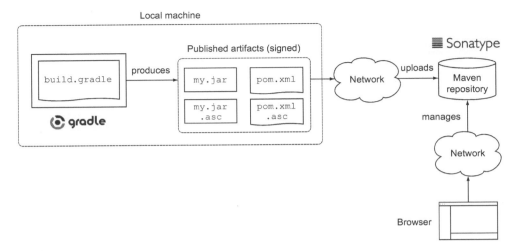

Figure 14.7   Publishing artifacts to Sonatype OSS

responsible for managing the artifacts, forms the backbone of the repository. Figure 14.7 shows the interaction with Sonatype OSS.

Sonatype OSS has more specific requirements for publishing artifacts than Bintray. The following checklist (described in more detail in the usage guide under https://docs.sonatype.org/display/Repository/Sonatype+OSS+Maven+Repository+ Usage+Guide) explains how to make binaries available to the world:

1 Sign up for a new Sonatype JIRA account at https://issues.sonatype.org/. You'll need to wait until your account has been approved.

2 Create a new JIRA ticket at https://issues.sonatype.org/browse/OSSRH/ that describes the meta-information of your artifact (for example, groupId, project URL, and so on). Once your request is approved, you can start publishing with the requested groupId. For publishing with a different groupId, you'll need to create another JIRA ticket.

3 Generate GNU Privacy Guard (GPG) signatures for all artifacts you wish to publish (shown in figure 14.7 with the file extension .asc). To generate these signatures, you can use the Gradle signing plugin. Check out the plugin documentation page for more information. One word of warning: at the time of writing, the new publishing API doesn't provide out-of-the-box signing support. You may have to fall back to the old publishing API to achieve this.

4 Publish the artifacts with Gradle.

5 Log in to the Sonatype OSS user interface at https://oss.sonatype.org/. Navigate to the Staging Repositories page, choose your artifact, and press the Close button. After staging the artifact, it's ready to be released. Press the Release button to initiate final release.

6 Before the promoted artifact can be accessed via Maven Central, Sonatype OSS needs to sync it with the central repository. This usually takes several hours.

7 Once an artifact is published, it can't be deleted or modified.

The publishing process to Sonatype OSS requires a lot of manual steps and even more patience to wait for approvals. If you're unsure which public repository to choose for your project, I recommend using Bintray over Sonatype OSS. Next, you'll learn how to apply the concepts we've discussed so far to your To Do application.

14.4 Artifact assembly and publishing as part of the build pipeline

In the last chapter, you learned how to set up and configure Jenkins jobs to model a build pipeline for your To Do application. After getting to know the core concepts of creating a distribution and publishing it to a binary repository, you can now apply your knowledge to your web application. First, you'll make some extensions to your existing Gradle build, and then you'll extend your build pipeline by configuring a Jenkins job. Figure 14.8 shows where you stand in the process.

In the context of continuous delivery, there are some important practices to discuss. They ultimately determine how you'll implement the artifact packaging and publishing.

14.4.1 Build binaries once

Before an application can be deployed to a target environment—for example, a UAT (user acceptance test)—for manual testing by the QA team, or to production to give it into the hands of the end users, the deliverable, also called the deployable artifact, has to be built. It's not uncommon for teams to rebuild this deliverable for each environment individually. This practice is often based on the fact that they need to include environment-specific configuration; for example, to point to a dedicated database set up for that environment. While this approach works, it creates the unnecessary risk of introducing a difference to the deliverable. For example, the dependency manager may pick a newer version of a third-party library that became available on a repository that you didn't intend to include. To avoid any side effects, you should only build your deliverable once and store it in a central location. As you learned earlier, a binary repository is the perfect fit for this use case.

14.4.2 Publish once, reuse later

Binary repositories require you to publish an artifact with unique attributes. In chapter 5, you learned that a Maven repository describes these attributes as `groupId`,

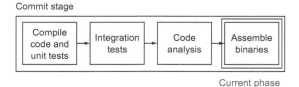

Commit stage

Current phase

Figure 14.8   Creating the distribution in the context of the build pipeline

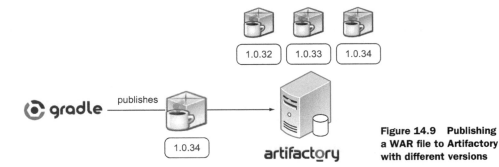

Figure 14.9   Publishing a WAR file to Artifactory with different versions

artifactId, and version, also called coordinates. The main distinguishing difference between each artifact built by your pipeline is the version. The two other attributes, groupId and artifactId, will likely never change once you've settled on a meaningful value. Over time, you'll notice that more and more versions of your artifact will be stored. Uploaded artifacts will stay in your repository until you delete them. Please refer to the product's documentation on how to best achieve this. Figure 14.9 illustrates the process of publishing to a repository with incremental versions.

Once the artifact is uploaded to a binary repository with a specific version, you can retrieve it by these attributes and reuse it for later steps in the pipeline. A typical use case would be the deployment to various environments. Many repository products expose a RESTful API for downloading artifacts via HTTP(S). The URL includes the dependency attributes to uniquely identify the artifact. Figure 14.10 shows the download of a published artifact with a particular version from Artifactory for successive deployment purposes.

With this background information in mind, you'll start by defining the versioning scheme for your project.

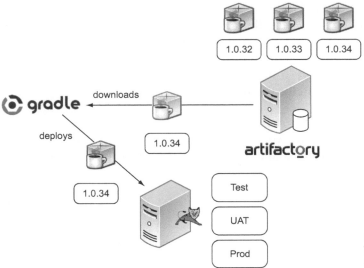

Figure 14.10   Retrieving a WAR file from Artifactory for deployment purposes

14.4.3 *Picking an appropriate versioning scheme*

Versioning your artifact becomes important at the time of assembly. In this section, we'll discuss which versioning scheme plays well with the core principles of continuous delivery and how to implement an appropriate strategy with Gradle. Some build tools propose a standard format for your versioning scheme. Let's see how Maven does it.

MAVEN'S VERSIONING SCHEME

Conceptually, Maven distinguishes between snapshot and release versions. A snapshot version of an artifact indicates that it's still under development and not ready to be released to production. This status is indicated by the filename suffix -SNAPSHOT (for example, todo-webapp-1.0-SNAPSHOT.war). Whenever the artifact is published to a binary repository, it's uploaded with the same version. Any consumer of this artifact will only be able to retrieve the latest version of that snapshot version. Because there's no concrete version attached to an artifact, you can't link it to a unique revision in the VCS. This can become a major drawback when trying to debug an issue. For that reason, snapshot versions of a deliverable should never be deployed to the production environment.

At some point in development, it's determined that the software is feature-complete. Once it passes the QA process, it's ready to be released to production. At that time, the -SNAPSHOT suffix is taken off the version and it's released to production. Now you're dealing with a release version of the artifact. Ultimately, this means having to modify the version attribute in the POM file and checking it into VCS. Figure 14.11 demonstrates this versioning scheme.

A new development cycle starts by bumping up the major and/or minor version of your project; the -SNAPSHOT suffix is added again. What's wrong with this way of assigning a project version? This is best explained by one of the core principles of continuous delivery.

EVERY COMMIT CAN BECOME A RELEASE

An important principle of continuous delivery is that every commit to your code base under version control can become a potential release to production. Of course, this will only happen if the software passes all phases defined by the build pipeline with the quality standards agreed on by the team.

Maven's versioning philosophy is diametrically opposed to this release strategy. It assumes that you work on a feature for a certain period of time until it's actually released. To be able to uniquely identify a version of an artifact during development, as well as in the live environment, you'll need to set an appropriate version at the initial

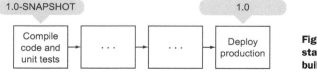

Figure 14.11 Applying Maven's standard versioning scheme in a build pipeline

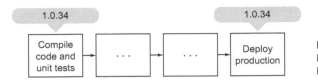

Figure 14.12   Setting a dynamic, incrementing version number at the initial phase of the build pipeline

stage of your build pipeline. This version will carry through all the way to the pipeline stage that deploys the deliverable to production (figure 14.12).

Next, we'll look at how such a versioning scheme can be implemented with Gradle.

VERSIONING SCHEME FITTED TO CONTINUOUS DELIVERY

In chapter 4, you learned how to assign an instance of a custom class to determine the project version. You can directly apply this knowledge to build the project version for your To Do application. The exemplary version format will look like figure 14.13. It consists of three attributes: major version, minor version, and a build number.

Figure 14.13   Versioning scheme for To Do application

The major and minor attributes of the versioning scheme are configured in Gradle. They'll change less often (for example, to indicate a new feature) and have to be incremented manually. The dynamic part of this versioning scheme is the build number. It's incremented every time a build is kicked off—that is, at the initial step of the build pipeline.

Let's look at the actual implementation of this versioning scheme in Gradle. The Groovy class named `ProjectVersion`, which resides in the package `com.manning.gia`, backs the version representation. Because you want to share this class among all projects of your build, you'll create the class in the `buildSrc` directory, as shown in the following directory tree:

```
.
├── buildSrc
│   └── src
│       └── main
│           └── groovy
│               └── com
│                   └── manning
│                       └── gia
│                           └── ProjectVersion.groovy   ◁─┐  Groovy class
│                                                          │  backing project
│                                                          │  versioning
│                                                          │  scheme
├── gradle
├── model
├── repository
├── web
├── build.gradle
└── settings.gradle
```

Let's look at the class. The following listing shows the contents of the file `Project-Version.groovy`.

Listing 14.13   Groovy class representing the project version

```
package com.manning.gia

class ProjectVersion {
    final Integer major
    final Integer minor            Fields representing major
    final String build             version, minor version,
                                   and build number

    ProjectVersion(Integer major, Integer minor, String build) {
        this.major = major
        this.minor = minor
        this.build = build
    }

    @Override
    String toString() {                              ◁┐  Builds String
        String fullVersion = "$major.$minor"            representation of
                                                        project version
        if(build) {
            fullVersion += ".$build"
        }

        fullVersion
    }
}
```

You know that Gradle automatically compiles every class under the directory `buildSrc` when the build is run. This compiled class can now be used in any of your build scripts to implement the versioning scheme. For a clean separation of concerns, you'll create a new script plugin in the directory `gradle` named `versioning.gradle`. As shown in the next listing, you import the class `ProjectVersion`, instantiate it with appropriate values, and assign it to the property version of `org.gradle.api.Project`.

Listing 14.14   Setting build information as script plugin

```
import com.manning.gia.ProjectVersion         Sets a build timestamp property to
                                              determine when build was initiated

ext.buildTimestamp = new Date().format('yyyy-MM-dd HH:mm:ss')     ◁┘
project.version = new ProjectVersion(1, 0, System.env.SOURCE_BUILD_NUMBER) ◁┐

                                              Assigns a new instance of ProjectVersion
                                              to project property version
```

The build number you set here is an environment variable named `SOURCE_BUILD _NUMBER`. This variable is automatically available to your build when you execute it as part of your Jenkins build pipeline. In the last chapter, you set it as part of your initial job configuration via the parameterized trigger plugin. For a quick refresher, you may want to quickly jump back to section 13.5.2. With your versioning script plugin in place, you can now apply it to all projects of your build with the help of the `allprojects` configuration block, as shown in the following listing.

Listing 14.15   Providing the version to all projects of the build

```
allprojects {
   ...
   apply from: "$rootDir/gradle/versioning.gradle"
}
```

You can easily emulate building your WAR artifact without having to execute the Jenkins build pipeline. All you need to do is set the environment variable SOURCE_BUILD_NUMBER on the command line. The following example demonstrates how to assign the build number 42:

- **nix:* export SOURCE_BUILD_NUMBER=42
- *Windows:* SET SOURCE_BUILD_NUMBER=42

If you assemble the WAR file now, you'll see that the correct version number is applied to your artifact. You'll find the correctly named file web-1.0.42.war under the directory web/build/libs.

Being able to identify a unique version of your artifact is essential for two reasons. It implies a releasable version and enables you to map the binary to the source code by tagging it in your VCS. The same versioning information can be included into the artifact to make it self-describing.

14.4.4   *Including build information in a deployable artifact*

Versioning information isn't only useful at build time. On occasion, you may also want to know what version of your application is deployed to a given environment. This can be achieved by including the build information as a property file generated by a new task named createBuildInfoFile. At runtime, this property file can be read and displayed anywhere in your web application. The following listing demonstrates the required task configuration in the build file of your web subproject.

Listing 14.16   Including build information in a WAR file

```
task createBuildInfoFile << {
    def buildInfoFile = new File("$buildDir/build-info.properties")
    Properties props = new Properties()
    props.setProperty('version', project.version.toString())
    props.setProperty('timestamp', project.buildTimestamp)
    props.store(buildInfoFile.newWriter(), null)
}

war {
    dependsOn createBuildInfoFile
    baseName = 'todo'

    from(buildDir) {
        include 'build-info.properties'
        into('WEB-INF/classes')
    }
}
```

Annotations:
- **Property file for storing build information** → points to `def buildInfoFile = new File("$buildDir/build-info.properties")`
- **Adds properties to represent project version and build timestamp** → points to the `props.setProperty` lines
- **Writes properties to file** → points to `props.store(buildInfoFile.newWriter(), null)`
- **Adds a task dependency on task that writes build information file** → points to `dependsOn createBuildInfoFile`
- **Bundles build information file in directory WEB-INF/classes of WAR file** → points to the `from(buildDir) { ... }` block

To give you an idea of how the generated file may look, see the following example:

```
#Tue Apr 23 06:44:34 EDT 2013
version=1.0.134
timestamp=2013-04-23 06:44:11
```

We won't discuss the custom code required to read and display these properties in your To Do application. Please refer to the book's code examples to see how to achieve this with Java. With your artifact well prepared, you're ready to push it to an internal binary repository for later deployments. Next, you'll adapt the publishing code you wrote at the beginning of this chapter to upload the WAR file.

14.4.5 *Publishing your To Do application WAR file*

Publishing the WAR file to an internal Artifactory repository isn't magic. You already have the essential knowledge on how to do this. The major difference here is that the software component you're about to publish is a WAR file instead of a JAR file, as shown in the following listing.

Listing 14.17   Publishing to a remote Maven repository

```
apply plugin: 'maven-publish'                                    Artifactory
                                                                 repository URL
ext {
    artifactoryBaseUrl = 'http://localhost:8081/artifactory'
    artifactoryReleaseRepoUrl = "$artifactoryBaseUrl/libs-release-local"
}

publishing {                                          Declares web
    publications {                                    software component
        toDoWebApp(MavenPublication) {                as publication
            from components.web
            artifactId 'todo-web'                         Declares published
                                                          artifact ID
            pom.withXml {
                def root = asNode()
                root.appendNode('name', 'To Do application')
                root.appendNode('description', 'A simple task management
                              application.')
            }
        }
    }

    repositories {
        maven {
            name 'remoteArtifactory'
            url artifactoryReleaseRepoUrl

            credentials {
                username = artifactoryUsername
                password = artifactoryPassword
            }
        }
    }
}
```

All it takes to upload the WAR file is to run the task with the name `publishToDoWeb-AppPublicationToRemoteArtifactoryRepository`. Remember that this task name is put together by the publishing API based on the assigned publication and repository name. If you check the generated POM file, you may notice that a WAR publication doesn't define any external dependencies. This is for a good reason: they're already bundled with the WAR file in the directory `WEB-INF/lib`. In the next section, you'll wire up this phase of your build pipeline to the existing jobs in Jenkins.

14.4.6 *Extending the build pipeline*

Creating the distribution and publishing it to a binary repository is an essential step for delivering your To Do application. You already implemented the Gradle side to support this functionality. Now it's time to extend your build pipeline by configuring the corresponding job on Jenkins. From the last chapter, you may remember that you set up three Jenkins jobs executed in the following order:

1 `todo-initial`: Compiles the source code and runs the unit tests.
2 `todo-integ-tests`: Runs the integration tests.
3 `todo-code-quality`: Performs static code analysis using Sonar.

Bring up the Jenkins dashboard and add a new job called `todo-distribution`. To simplify its creation, feel free to clone it from the existing job named `todo-code-quality`. After the job is created, you'll need to make some additional changes to step 3 of your build pipeline.

STEP 3: CODE QUALITY

Add a parameterized build action that defines a build trigger on the job named `todo-distribution`. As far as parameters go, you'll reuse the existing ones by choosing the option Current Build Parameters.

Perfect, you connected step 3 to step 4 by making it the downstream project. Next, you'll put in some finishing touches on your newly created job.

STEP 4: DISTRIBUTION AND PUBLICATION

The configuration for this job looks very similar to the previous one. Have a quick look at this checklist to see if it's set up correctly:

- In the Source Code Management configuration section, choose the option Clone Workspace and choose the parent project `todo-initial`.
- As the build step, you want to assemble the WAR file and publish it to Artifactory. Add a build step for invoking your Gradle script using the wrapper and enter the tasks `assemble publish`.
- Define the build name by incorporating the upstream build number parameter: `todo#${ENV,var="SOURCE_BUILD_NUMBER"}`.

With this configuration in place, your build pipeline view in Jenkins should look similar to figure 14.14. To verify its correct behavior, make sure to take the pipeline for a test drive.

Figure 14.14   Build pipeline view

Given the current status of your build pipeline, you're close to deploying your To Do application to various target environments. Keep on reading to learn how to approach this task.

14.5   Summary

Most software needs to be assembled before it can be deployed to a target environment or installed to a particular location. During the assembly process, individual software components need to be put together in a meaningful, consumable format. A software delivery doesn't have to be limited to a single artifact. Often it consists of multiple artifacts or distributions cut for a specific group of stakeholders or runtime environments.

Gradle supports creating artifacts for a wide range of archiving formats through core custom tasks like `Jar` or `Zip`, some of which are automatically preconfigured for your project if you apply a certain plugin. In addition to this functionality, the Gradle distribution plugin can be used to describe custom distributions through an expressive DSL, without actually having to define tasks in your build script. With these tools in your toolbox, it's simple to produce the artifacts you need and flexibly react to new requirements for your delivery process.

Once the deliverable artifacts are built, they can be shared with other projects, teams, or literally every developer on the planet. Binary repositories provide the infrastructure for uploading, managing, browsing, and consuming any number or type of artifacts. In this chapter, you learned how to use Gradle's publishing plugin to interact with a local or remote Maven repository. You took your plugin project from chapter 8, assembled the plugin JAR file, generated individualized metadata, and uploaded it to Artifactory, a popular binary repository. The most convenient option for sharing open source projects is to bring them into a public, internet-accessible repository. We discussed how to set up an account on Sonatype OSS (a.k.a. Maven Central) and JFrog Bintray and applied the publishing process to both repositories.

In the context of continuous delivery, assembling and publishing artifacts plays a crucial role. Whenever possible, you'll want to package the artifacts just once to avoid potential side effects. After uploading the artifacts to a repository, they can be reused in a later step of the process for deployment purposes. You learned how to implement a flexible versioning strategy to clearly identify a set of artifacts. Later, you extended your build pipeline with a new job for packaging and publishing the WAR file produced by your To Do application.

In the last chapter of this book, you'll finally roll out your To Do application to various target environments, write smoke tests to verify a successful deployment, and tag the release in version control.

Infrastructure provisioning and deployment

This chapter covers

- Driving infrastructure provisioning from Gradle
- Automated deployment to different target environments
- Verifying the outcome of a deployment with smoke and acceptance tests
- Deployment as part of the build pipeline

Software deployments need to be repeatable and reliable. Any server outage inflicted by a faulty deployment—with the biggest hit on production systems—results in money lost for your organization. Automation is the next logical and necessary step toward formulating and streamlining the deployment process. In this chapter, we'll talk about how to automate the deployment process with Gradle by the example of your To Do application.

Before any deployment can be conducted, the target environment needs to be preconfigured with the required software infrastructure. Historically, this has been the task of a system administrator, who would manually provision the physical server machine and install the software components before use. This setup can be defined as real code with tools like Puppet and Chef, checked into version control, and tested like an ordinary piece of software. Using this infrastructure-as-code approach helps prevent human error and minimizes the cycle time for spinning up a new environment based on the same software stack. While Gradle doesn't provide native tooling for this task, you can bootstrap other tools to do the job for you.

Deploying software to use as build masters means more than just copying a file to a server. In your build, you'll need to be able to configure and target different environments. Automating the full deployment lifecycle often requires cleaning out previously deployed artifacts, as well as restarting remote runtime environments like web containers. This chapter covers one viable approach to achieving this.

Once you deploy a new version of your software, you need to verify the outcome. Automated smoke and acceptance testing can help to detect the correct functioning of the software. You'll set up a sufficient suite of tests and execute them with Gradle.

All of these processes—deployment to different environments and the verification of a successful deployment—need to be part of your build pipeline. After setting up the supporting tasks in Gradle, you can invoke them from corresponding jobs in Jenkins. Deploying software for authorized stakeholders within an organization should be as easy as pushing a button. You'll extend your build pipeline by deploying jobs for different environments. Before we can dive into the details of deploying software, let's review the tools that are helpful for provisioning an infrastructure.

15.1 *Infrastructure provisioning*

Before any application can be deployed, the hosting infrastructure needs to be provisioned. When I talk about infrastructure provisioning in the traditional sense, I mean setting up the hardware as well as installing and configuring the required operating system and software components.

Nowadays, we see a paradigm shift toward cloud provisioning of infrastructure. Unlike the traditional approach, a cloud provider often allocates preconfigured hardware in the form of virtual servers. Server virtualization is the partitioning of a physical server into smaller virtual servers to help maximize the server resources. Depending on the service offer, the operating system and software components are managed by the cloud provider.

In this section, we'll talk about automating the creation of virtual servers and infrastructure software components with the help of third-party open source tools. These tools will help you set up and configure streamlined target environments for your To Do application. Later, you'll learn how Gradle can integrate with these tools.

15.1.1 *Infrastructure as code*

Developers usually work in a self-contained environment—their development machine. Software infrastructure that's needed to run an application has to be set up by hand. If you think back to your To Do application, this includes the Java runtime, a web container, and a database. What might sound unproblematic for a single developer can transform into a huge issue the moment the team grows in size. Now, each developer needs to make sure that they install the same version of the same software packages with the same configuration (optimally on the same operating system).

A similar process has to be followed for setting up the hardware and software infrastructure for other environments (for example, UAT and production) that are part of the deployment pipeline. In larger organizations, the responsibility for performing this task traditionally falls on the shoulders of the operations team. Without proper communication and documentation, getting these environments ready ends up becoming a lengthy and nerve-wracking procedure. Even worse, if any of the configuration settings need to be changed, they have to be propagated across all environments manually.

While shell scripting is a good first step to mitigate this pain, it doesn't fully automate the infrastructure provisioning end-to-end across environments. The paradigm of infrastructure as code aims to bridge the gap between software development and system administration. With sufficient tooling, it's possible to describe a machine's configuration as executable code, which is then checked into version control and shared among different stakeholders. Any time you need to create a new machine, you can build a new one based on the instructions of your infrastructure code. Ultimately, this allows you to treat infrastructure code like any other software development project that can be versioned, tested, and checked for potential syntactical issues.

In the past couple of years, several commercial and open source tools have emerged to automate infrastructure provisioning. We'll focus on two of the most popular open source infrastructure automation tools: Vagrant and Puppet. The next section will give you an architectural overview of how both tools can be used together to build a virtual machine from scratch. The end result will be a runtime environment equipped to serve your To Do application.

15.1.2 *Creating a virtual machine with Vagrant and Puppet*

Vagrant (http://www.vagrantup.com/) is an infrastructure tool for configuring and creating virtual environments. A machine can be managed with the help of the Vagrant executable. For example, you can start and stop a machine with a simple, one-line shell script. Even better, you can directly SSH into it and control it like every other remote *nix server.

The software configuration of a machine is described through shell scripts or provisioning tools such as Chef and Puppet. The provisioning provider you use often boils down to personal preference and knowledge of the tool. We'll concentrate on Puppet.

Puppet (https://puppetlabs.com/puppet/) provides a Ruby-based DSL for declaring the software components and their required state on a target machine. If you think back to the runtime environment required for your To Do application, you can identify the following software packages and their configuration:

- A Java runtime (JRE) installation. You'll use version 6.
- A Servlet container to host the web application. You'll use Apache Tomcat with version 7.

- An H2 database to manage your application data. To function properly, the database schema needs to be set up.

It's beyond the scope of this book to fully describe the configuration needed to set up such a scenario. However, you can find a working example in the source code of the book. Let's examine the basic structure of your Vagrant project to get a high-level understanding:

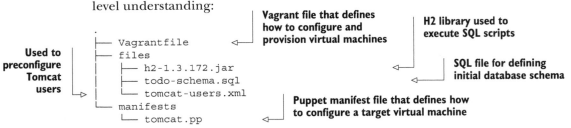

Figure 15.1 illustrates how the individual components of a Vagrant project play together. At a minimum, every Vagrant project needs to contain a `Vagrantfile`. Based on this file, virtual machines are configured and created. You're going to go with Puppet as the configuration provider. The configuration you want to apply to the virtual machine is set up in a Puppet manifest file, which is referenced in the `Vagrantfile`. In this case, the name of the manifest file is `tomcat.pp`. To be able to version and share the Vagrant project with other developers, you need to check it into version control like regular source code.

Before any virtual machine can be initiated from the infrastructure definition, you'll need to install the Vagrant executable and Virtual Box (https://www.virtualbox.org/). Please refer to the Vagrant documentation for more information. After a successful installation, you can invoke the Vagrant executable from the command line.

Let's explore some of the commonly used commands. To bring up your Vagrant machine, navigate to the Vagrant project in your shell and execute the command `vagrant up`. Vagrant is fairly wordy, so we won't show the command-line output here. After a few moments, you should see the notice that the virtual machine was brought up successfully.

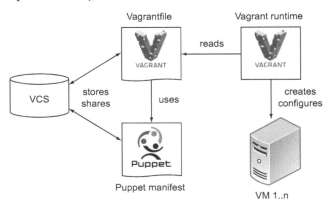

Figure 15.1 Creating test environments with Vagrant and Puppet

In the `Vagrantfile`, you configured the virtual machine to be accessible by the IP address 192.168.1.33. As part of your provisioning code, you defined Tomcat to run on port 8080. To verify a successful installation of the web container, open the browser of your choice and enter the URL http://192.168.1.33:8080/. You should see the Tomcat 7 dashboard. To shut down the virtual machine, use the command `vagrant destroy`. In the next section, you'll learn how to bootstrap Vagrant commands from Gradle.

15.1.3 *Executing Vagrant from Gradle*

At this point, you may be thinking, "Why would I want to execute Vagrant commands from Gradle?" The short answer is automation. Any workflow that incorporates interacting with a virtual machine provided by Vagrant needs to be able to call the corresponding command from Gradle. To show you a simple workflow, let's assume you want to execute functional tests on a virtual machine that mimics the infrastructure setup of a production server. The following steps are involved:

1 Start the virtual machine via the command `vagrant up`.
2 Deploy the web application to the Tomcat server.
3 Execute a suite of functional tests.
4 Shut down the virtual machine via the command `vagrant destroy`.

This use case is fairly advanced and requires some complex setup. For now, you'll start simple and enable your build to wrap Vagrant command calls with Gradle tasks. You're going to write a custom task. The task defines the Vagrant commands you want to execute as an input parameter. Additionally, you need to point the task to the Vagrant project you'd like to target. The following listing demonstrates a reusable task that allows executing Vagrant commands.

> **Listing 15.1 Custom task for executing Vagrant commands**

```
package com.manning.gia.vm

import org.gradle.api.DefaultTask
import org.gradle.api.GradleException
import org.gradle.api.tasks.Input
import org.gradle.api.tasks.TaskAction

class Vagrant extends DefaultTask {
    static final String VAGRANT_EXECUTABLE = 'vagrant'          List of provided Vagrant
                                                                 commands (doesn't include
    @Input                                                       Vagrant executable)
    List<String> commands

    @Input
    File dir                                     Directory where
                                                 Vagrant box is located
    @TaskAction
    void runCommand() {
        commands.add(0, VAGRANT_EXECUTABLE)
        logger.info "Executing Vagrant command: '${commands.join(' ')}'"
```

```
    def process = commands.execute(null, dir)          Executes Vagrant command
    process.consumeProcessOutput(System.out, System.err)   as external process
    process.waitFor()                                   (waits until finished)

    if(process.exitValue() != 0) {          If process didn't
        throw new GradleException()         finish successfully,
    }                                       throw an exception
  }
}
```

Depending on the complexity of your configuration, some Vagrant commands (especially vagrant up) may need a few minutes to finish. If you have a chain of tasks that build on each other, you need to make sure that task execution is delayed until Vagrant completes the actual work. Your task implementation takes care of this requirement by letting the current thread wait until the Vagrant command responds with an exit value. Next, you'll put your Vagrant task to the test. The following listing demonstrates the use of the custom task to expose important Vagrant commands to a Gradle build.

Listing 15.2 Enhanced tasks for important Vagrant commands

```
import com.manning.gia.vm.Vagrant                    Directory pointing
                                                     to targeted
ext.targetedVagrantProjectDir = file('../vagrant-tomcat-box')   Vagrant box

task vagrantUp(type: Vagrant) {          Creates and configures a machine
    commands = ['up']                    according to Vagrantfile
    dir = targetedVagrantProjectDir
}

task vagrantDestroy(type: Vagrant) {     Stops a running Vagrant machine
    commands = ['destroy', '--force']    and destroys all its resources
    dir = targetedVagrantProjectDir
}

task vagrantSshConfig(type: Vagrant) {   Outputs configuration of SSH configuration
    commands = ['ssh-config']            file (needed to SSH into a running machine)
    dir = targetedVagrantProjectDir
}

task vagrantStatus(type: Vagrant) {      Reports on state of a Vagrant machine
    commands = ['status']                (for example, running, suspended)
    dir = targetedVagrantProjectDir
}

task vagrantSuspend(type: Vagrant) {     Suspends a running Vagrant machine by
    commands = ['suspend']               creating a snapshot of its current state
    dir = targetedVagrantProjectDir
}

task vagrantResume(type: Vagrant) {      Resumes a previously
    commands = ['resume']                suspended Vagrant machine
    dir = targetedVagrantProjectDir
}
```

Congratulations, you just implemented a way to integrate Vagrant into your build! Running Vagrant on a local machine is great for simulating production-like environments. When it comes to interacting with existing environments other than your local machine, your build needs to have a way of configuring the connection information. In the next section, we'll explore a flexible way of storing and reading environment-specific configuration.

15.2 *Targeting a deployment environment*

The main maxim of continuous delivery is to get the software from the developer's machine into the hands of the end users as quickly and frequently as possible. However, that doesn't mean that you assemble your deliverable and deploy it in the production environment right away. In between these steps, a build pipeline usually verifies functional and nonfunctional requirements in other environments, as shown in figure 15.2.

At the beginning of this chapter, you created a virtual machine on your developer machine. Though the virtual machine has a production-like setup, you use this environment solely for testing purposes. The test environment brings together code changes from multiple developers of the team. Therefore, it can be seen as the first integration point of running code. On the deployed application in the test environment, you can run automated acceptance tests to verify functional and nonfunctional requirements. The user acceptance test (UAT) environment typically exists for the purpose of exploratory, manual testing. Once the QA team considers the current state of the software code to be satisfactory, it's ready to be shipped to production. The production environment directly serves to the end user and makes new features available to the world.

If you want to use the same code for deploying to all of these environments, you'll need to be able to dynamically target each one of them at build time. Naturally, the test, UAT, and production environments run on different servers with potentially different ports and credentials. You could store the configuration as extra properties in your build script, but that would quickly convolute the logic of the file. Alternatively, you could store this information in a `gradle.properties` file. In both cases, you'd end up with a fairly unstructured list of properties. At build time, you'd have to pick a set of properties based on a naming convention. Doesn't sound very flexible, does it? There's a better way of storing and reading this configuration with the help of a standard Groovy feature.

15.2.1 *Defining configuration in a Groovy script*

Configuration, especially if you have a lot of it, should be as readable and structured as possible. One of Groovy's language features allows for defining properties with the

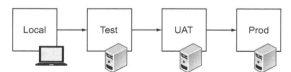

Figure 15.2 Software propagation through different environments

help of closures within a Groovy script. The following listing shows an example of composing an environment-specific configuration in the form of a mini DSL.

Listing 15.3 Groovy-based, environment-specific configuration

```
environments {                              Element for grouping
    local {                                 configuration by environment
        server {
            hostname = 'localhost'          Configuration for local
            sshPort = 2222                  development environment
            username = 'vagrant'
        }

        tomcat {
            hostname = '193.168.1.33'
            port = 8080
            context = 'todo'
        }
    }
    test {                                  Configuration for
        ...                                 test environment
    }
    uat {                                   Configuration for
        ...                                 UAT environment
    }
    prod {                                  Configuration for
        ...                                 production environment
    }
}
```

Each of the environments that you want to define properties for is enclosed in the environments configuration block. For each environment, you assigned a closure with a descriptive name. For example, you can define the server hostname, SSH port, and username to log into the server. Use this configuration data and save it to a Groovy script under the directory gradle/config/buildConfig.groovy, as shown in your project directory tree:

```
.
├── buildSrc
├── gradle                            Groovy-based,
│   └── config                        environment-specific
│       └── buildConfig.groovy        configuration file
├── model
├── repository
├── web
├── build.gradle
└── settings.gradle
```

You now have a Groovy-based configuration file in place, but how do you read its content from the Gradle build? Groovy provides a handy API class named groovy.util .ConfigSlurper that's designed to parse a treelike data structure. Let's take a closer look at its functionality.

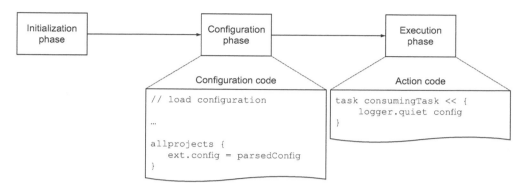

Figure 15.3　Reading Groovy script during Gradle's configuration phase

15.2.2　*Reading the configuration with Groovy's ConfigSlurper*

ConfigSlurper is a utility class for reading configuration in the form of Groovy scripts. Configuration can either be defined as properties on the root level of the script or as environment-specific properties wrapped by the environments closure. Once this configuration is parsed, the property graph can be navigated by dot notation. We'll see how this looks in practice.

Reading this configuration file from Gradle requires some thinking. You need to make sure that the configuration is read before any task action is executed. Remember when we discussed Gradle's build lifecycle phases in chapter 4? This is best done during the configuration phase, as shown in figure 15.3.

The task that reads the Groovy script doesn't need to contain a task action. Instead, you'll create an instance of the class ConfigSlurper in the configuration block of the task and provide the specific environment you want to read in its constructor. The method parse points to the location of the configuration file. The following listing demonstrates how to parse the Groovy script based on the provided property env.

Listing 15.4　Reading configuration during configuration phase

```
def env = project.hasProperty('env') ? project.getProperty('env') : 'local'
logger.quiet "Loading configuration for environment '$env'."

def configFile = file("$rootDir/gradle/config/buildConfig.groovy")
def parsedConfig = new ConfigSlurper(env).parse(configFile.toURL())

allprojects {
    ext.config = parsedConfig
}
```

- Groovy file containing configuration ⟵
- Reads configuration file for targeted environment ⟵
- Assigns read configuration to extra property config available to all projects of build

The parsed configuration is made available to all projects of your build through the extra property config. Next, you'll actually use the property in another task that requires the parsed configuration.

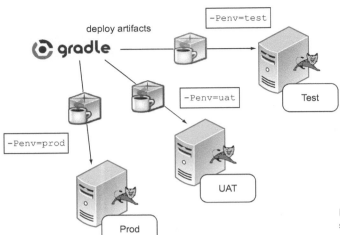

Figure 15.4 Targeting specific environments by providing a project property

15.2.3 *Using the configuration throughout the build*

A typical usage pattern for the configuration shown in listing 15.3 is the deployment of the To Do web application to a specific environment. Key to targeting a specific environment is to provide a value for the property env on the command line. For example, if you want to target the UAT environment, you'd provide the project property -Penv=uat. The value of this project property directly corresponds to the closure named uat in the Groovy configuration script. Using this simple mechanism, you enable your build to run the same task logic—for example, deployment of code via environment-specific configuration, as shown in figure 15.4.

You're going to emulate a deployment task to see if your mechanism works. In the web project, you'll create a new task named deployWar, as shown in listing 15.5. For now, you won't bother with actually implementing deployment logic. To verify that the settings appropriate to the targeted environment are parsed correctly, the task's doLast action will use Gradle's logger to print the read hostname and port.

Listing 15.5   Using the configuration extra property

Logs configured server hostname and port

```
task deployWar << {
    logger.quiet "Deploying WAR file to $config.server.hostname via SSH
                ➥ on port $config.server.sshPort."
}
```

When you run the task deployWar for the environment local, you can see that the proper settings are parsed and rendered on the command line:

```
$ gradle deployWar -Penv=local
Loading configuration for environment 'local'.
:todo-web:deployWar
Deploying WAR file to 'localhost' via SSH on port 2222.
```

Just printing out the configuration is pretty boring. In the next section, you'll actually use these settings to deploy the To Do application WAR file to a server.

15.3 Automated deployments

The end game of every build pipeline is to deploy the software to a production environment once it passes all automated and manual testing phases. The deployment process should be repeatable and reliable. Under all circumstances, you want to avoid human error when interacting with a production environment to install a new version. Failure to deploy the software properly will lead to unexpected side effects or downtime and actual money lost for your organization.

I think we can agree that the task of deploying software to production should be a nonevent. Deployment automation is an important and necessary step toward this goal. The code used to automate the deployment process shouldn't be developed and exercised against the production environment right away to reduce the risk of breakages. Instead, start testing it with a production-like environment on your local machine, or a test environment. You already set up such an environment with Vagrant. It uses infrastructure definitions that are fairly close to your production environment. Mimicking a production-like environment using a virtual machine for developing deployment code is cheap, easy to manage, and doesn't disturb any other environment participating in your build pipeline. Once you're happy with a working solution, the code should be used for deploying to the least-critical environment in your build pipeline. After gaining more confidence that the code is working as expected, you can deploy it to more mission-critical environments like UAT and production.

Writing deployment code is not a cookie-cutter job. It's dependent on the type of software you write and the target environment you're planning to deploy to. For example, a deployment of a web application to a Linux machine has different requirements than client-installed software running on Windows. At the time of writing, Gradle doesn't offer a unified approach for deploying software. The approach we'll discuss in this chapter is geared toward deploying your web application to a Tomcat container.

15.3.1 Retrieving the artifact from the binary repository

In the last chapter, you learned how to upload an artifact to a binary repository. You're going to retrieve it for deployment purposes. Now that you have the Groovy configuration file in place, you can also add the Artifactory repository URL. In this example, you only use a single repository that isn't specific to an environment. `ConfigSlurper` also reads any properties declared outside of the `environments` closure independent of the provided `env` property. The following listing demonstrates how to declare common configuration—in this case, the binary repository.

> **Listing 15.6 Adding binary repository settings to buildConfig.groovy**

```
binaryRepository {                                        Artifactory
    baseUrl = 'http://localhost:8081/artifactory'   ◁┘   base URL
```

```
        releaseUrl = "$baseUrl/libs-release-local"      ◁─┐  URL of Maven
    }                                                        release repository
    environments {
        ...
    }
```

In listing 15.7, you use the settings from the file `buildConfig.groovy` to download the WAR file with the current version of your project from Artifactory. In this example, Gradle's dependency management does the heavy lifting of downloading the file from the repository. Executing the task `fetchToDoWar` will put the artifact into the directory `build/download/artifacts`. Please note that it's not mandatory to use Gradle's dependency management for retrieving the file. You could also use the Ant task `Get` and write a lower-level implementation in Groovy.

Listing 15.7   Downloading the WAR file from a remote repository

```
repositories {
    maven {                                            Defines Artifactory
        url config.binaryRepository.releaseUrl    ◁─┘  URL as repository
    }
}
configurations {                          Introduces new configuration
    todo                              ◁── for application-specific
}                                         dependencies
                                                          Declares To Do
dependencies {                                            application WAR
    todo group: project.group, name: project.name,       files as dependency
    ➥   version: project.version.toString(), ext: 'war' ◁─┘
}
ext.downloadDir = file("$buildDir/download/artifacts")  ◁──  Extra property
                                                             that defines
task fetchToDoWar(type: Copy) {                              target download
    from configurations.todo    Task for downloading         directory
    into downloadDir            WAR file from
}                              Artifactory
```

Try out the task. Assume your project version is 1.0.42. After executing the task, you'll find the expected file in the download directory:

```
.
└── build
    └── download
        └── artifacts
            └── todo-web-1.0.42.war
```

Of course, it makes sense to download the artifact just once, even though you'll deploy it to different environments. The task `fetchToDoWar` automatically implements the incremental build functionality. Executing the task a second time will mark it UP-TO-DATE, as shown in the following command-line output:

```
$ gradle fetchToDoWar
:fetchToDoWar UP-TO-DATE
```

Now things are getting exciting. You downloaded the artifact with the correct version. Before you can take care of business by deploying the web application to Tomcat, you should plan out the necessary steps to implement the process.

15.3.2 *Identifying necessary deployment steps*

The deployment process for a web application to a remote server needs to follow a workflow to ensure a smooth transition from the current version to a new one. What kind of aspects should be considered?

First, you need to make sure that all artifacts of the old version, like the exploded WAR file, are properly removed. Under all circumstances, you need to avoid mixing up old artifacts with the new ones.

Some deployment solutions like Cargo (http://cargo.codehaus.org/) allow for deploying a web application while the container is running, a technique also known as hot deployment. While it might sound attractive at first, because you don't have to restart the server, hot deployment isn't a viable solution for production systems. Over time, long-running JVM processes will run into an OutOfMemoryError for their Perm-Gen space, which will cause it to freeze up. The reason is that the JVM will not garbage-collect class instances from previous deploys even if they're now unused. Therefore, it's highly recommended to fully stop the web container JVM process before a new version is deployed.

An efficient deployment process can look like the following steps:

1 Push new artifact to server.
2 Stop the web container process.
3 Delete the old artifact and its extracted files.
4 Deploy the new artifact.
5 Start the web container process.

In the following section, you'll implement this process with the help of Gradle. The previously created Vagrant instance will act as a test bed for your deployment script.

15.3.3 *Deployment through SSH commands*

We didn't go into any specifics about the operating system of the virtual machine you set up before. Assume that the box is based on the Linux distribution Ubuntu. You may know that transferring a file to a remote machine running a SSH daemon can be achieved with Secure Copy (SCP). SCP uses the same security measures as SSH. For authentication purposes, SCP will ask for a password or a pass phrase. Alternatively, the private key file can be provided to authenticate the user. Vagrant automatically puts this identity file into the directory <USER_HOME>/.vagrant.d.

You could model the whole deployment process in a shell script and call it from Gradle by creating an enhanced task of type Exec. That's certainly a valid way of implementing the necessary steps. However, in this section we'll discuss how to model each step with a corresponding Gradle task.

FILE TRANSFERS WITH SCP

You'll start by implementing the file transfer via SCP. If you're familiar with Ant, you may have used the SCP task before. The Ant task provides a nice abstraction on top of a pure Java SSH implementation named JSch (http://www.jcraft.com/jsch/). The next listing shows how to wrap the Ant SCP task with a custom Gradle task declared in the buildSrc project.

> **Listing 15.8   Custom task wrapping the optional Ant SCP task**

```
package com.manning.gia.ssh

import org.gradle.api.DefaultTask
import org.gradle.api.GradleException
import org.gradle.api.file.FileCollection
import org.gradle.api.tasks.*

class Scp extends DefaultTask {
    @InputFiles
    FileCollection classpath

    @InputFile
    File sourceFile

    @Input
    String destination

    @Input
    File keyFile

    @Input
    Integer port

    @TaskAction
    void transferFile() {
        logger.quiet "Copying file '$sourceFile' to server."
        ant.taskdef(name: 'jschScp', classname:
                'org.apache.tools.ant.taskdefs.optional.ssh.Scp',    ◁─── Declares Ant SCP task
                classpath: classpath.asPath)
        ant.jschScp(file: sourceFile, todir: destination, keyfile:
                keyFile.canonicalPath, port: port, trust: 'true')
    }
}
```

Uses Ant SCP task to copy a file to server ▷

You'll use this SCP abstraction in the build script of your web project to copy the WAR file to the remote location. In listing 15.9, you declare the JSch Ant task dependency with the help of a custom configuration named jsch. This dependency is passed on to the classpath property of the enhanced task responsible for transferring the WAR file to the remote server. You also incorporate the server settings read during the configuration phase of your build.

> **Listing 15.9   Transferring the WAR file to the server via SCP**

```
configurations {
    jsch
}
```

```
dependencies {
    jsch 'org.apache.ant:ant-jsch:1.9.1'
}

ext {
    warFile = configurations.todo.singleFile
    tomcatRemoteDir = '/opt/apache-tomcat-7.0.42'

    userHome = System.properties['user.home']
    vagrantKeyFile = file("$userHome/.vagrant.d/insecure_private_key")
    remoteTmpDir = "$config.server.username@$config.server.hostname:/tmp"
}

import com.manning.gia.ssh.Scp

task copyWarToServer(type: Scp, dependsOn: fetchToDoWar) {
    classpath = configurations.jsch
    sourceFile = warFile
    destination = remoteTmpDir
    keyFile = vagrantKeyFile
    port = config.server.sshPort
}
```

Before SCPing the WAR file to server, make sure it's downloaded from Artifactory

Assigns optional Ant tasks to task classpath

Defines downloaded WAR as source transfer file

Declares remote target directory WAR file is transferred to

This listing only implements step one of the deployment process. You have four more to go. All of the other steps need to execute shell commands on the remote server itself.

EXECUTING REMOTE COMMANDS WITH SSH

The SSH command makes it very simple to achieve such an operation. Instead of running an interactive shell, SSH can run a command on the remote machine and render the output. The following listing shows the custom task SshExec that internally wraps the SSH Ant task.

Listing 15.10   Custom task wrapping the optional Ant SSH task

```
package com.manning.gia.ssh

import org.gradle.api.DefaultTask
import org.gradle.api.GradleException
import org.gradle.api.file.FileCollection
import org.gradle.api.tasks.*

class SshExec extends DefaultTask {
    @InputFiles
    FileCollection classpath

    @Input
    String host

    @Input
    String username

    @Input
    String command

    @InputFile
    File keyFile
```

```
                                    @Input
                                    Integer port

                                    @TaskAction
                                    void runSshCommand() {
                                        logger.quiet "Executing SSH command '$command'."
                                        ant.taskdef(name: 'jschSshExec', classname:
                                                ➡ 'org.apache.tools.ant.taskdefs.optional.ssh.SSHExec',
                                                ➡ classpath: classpath.asPath)
                                        ant.jschSshExec(host: host, username: username, command: command,
                                                ➡ port: port, keyfile: keyFile.canonicalPath,
                                                ➡ trust: 'true')

                                    }
                                }
```

Uses Ant SSH task to copy a file to server

Declares Ant SSH task

In the next listing, you use this custom SSH task to run various shell commands on the Vagrant virtual box. As a whole, this script implements the full deployment workflow we discussed earlier.

Listing 15.11   SSH commands for managing Tomcat and deploying WAR file

```
import com.manning.gia.ssh.SshExec

tasks.withType(SshExec) {
    classpath = configurations.jsch
    host = config.server.hostname
    username = config.server.username
    keyFile = vagrantKeyFile
    port = config.server.sshPort
}

task shutdownTomcat(type: SshExec, dependsOn: copyWarToServer) {
    command = "sudo -u tomcat $tomcatRemoteDir/bin/shutdown.sh"

    doFirst {
        logger.quiet "Shutting down remote Tomcat."
    }
}

task deleteTomcatWebappsDir(type: SshExec, dependsOn: shutdownTomcat) {
    command = "sudo -u tomcat rm -rf $tomcatRemoteDir/webapps/todo"
}

task deleteTomcatWorkDir(type: SshExec, dependsOn: shutdownTomcat) {
    command = "sudo -u tomcat rm -rf $tomcatRemoteDir/work"
}

task deleteOldArtifacts(dependsOn: [deleteTomcatWebappsDir,
                                    deleteTomcatWorkDir]) {

    doFirst {
        logger.quiet "Deleting old WAR artifacts."
    }
}

task copyWarToWebappsDir(type: SshExec, dependsOn: deleteOldArtifacts) {
    command = "sudo -u tomcat cp /tmp/$warFile.name
            ➡ $tomcatRemoteDir/webapps/todo.war"
```

Configures all tasks of type SshExec

Shuts down the Tomcat JVM process

Deletes existing exploded To Do web application directory

Deletes Tomcat temporary work directory

Copies WAR file to Tomcat's webapps directory

```
    doFirst {
        logger.quiet "Deploying WAR file to Tomcat."
    }
}

task startupTomcat(type: SshExec, dependsOn: copyWarToWebappsDir) {  ⟵  Starts
    command = "sudo -u tomcat $tomcatRemoteDir/bin/startup.sh"           Tomcat JVM
                                                                         process
    doFirst {
        logger.quiet "Starting up remote Tomcat."
    }
}
                                                             Deployment
                                                             lifecycle task
task deployWar(dependsOn: startupTomcat)  ⟵
```

That's all you need to implement a full deployment process. Bring up the Vagrant box and give it a try. The following command-line output shows the execution steps in action:

```
$ gradle deployWar -Penv=local
...
Loading configuration for environment 'local'.
:todo-web:fetchToDoWar
:todo-web:copyWarToServer
Copying file 'todo-web-1.0.42.war' to server.
:todo-web:shutdownTomcat
Shutting down remote Tomcat.
Executing SSH command 'sudo -u tomcat /opt/apache-tomcat-7.0.42/
➥ bin/shutdown.sh'.
:todo-web:deleteTomcatWebappsDir
Executing SSH command 'sudo -u tomcat rm -rf /opt/apache-tomcat-
➥ 7.0.42/webapps/todo'.
:todo-web:deleteTomcatWorkDir
Executing SSH command 'sudo -u tomcat rm -rf /opt/apache-tomcat-
➥ 7.0.42/work'.
:todo-web:deleteOldArtifacts
Deleting old WAR artifacts.
:todo-web:copyWarToWebappsDir
Deploying WAR file to Tomcat.
Executing SSH command 'sudo -u tomcat cp /tmp/todo-web-1.0.42.war
➥ /opt/apache-tomcat-7.0.42/webapps/todo.war'.
:todo-web:startupTomcat
Starting up remote Tomcat.
Executing SSH command 'sudo -u tomcat /opt/apache-tomcat-7.0.42/
➥ bin/startup.sh'.
:todo-web:deployWar
```

After restarting Tomcat again, it may take some seconds until your web application is up and running. After giving Tomcat enough time to explode the WAR file and start its services, navigating to the URL http://192.168.1.33:8080/todo in a browser will present you with a To Do list ready to be filled with new tasks.

Running SSH commands isn't the only approach for tackling deployment automation. There are many other ways to achieve this goal. Due to the diversity of this topic, we won't present them in this chapter. Don't feel discouraged from trying out new, automated ways of getting your software deployed in the target environment. As long as the process you choose is repeatable, reliable, and matches your organization's needs, you're on the right path.

15.4 Deployment tests

Every deployment of an application should be followed by rudimentary tests that verify that the operation was successful and the system is in an expected, working state. These types of tests are often referred to as *deployment tests.*

If for whatever reason a deployment failed, you want to know about it—fast. In the worst-case scenario, a failed deployment to the production environment, the customer shouldn't be the first to tell you that the application is down. You absolutely need to avoid this situation because it destroys credibility and equates to money lost for your organization.

The harsh reality is that deployments can fail even with the best preparation. Knowing about it as soon as possible is worth a mint. As a result, you can take measures to bring back the system into an operational state; for example, by rolling back the application to the last "good" version.

In addition to these fail-fast tests, automated acceptance tests verify that important features or use cases of the deployed application are correctly implemented. For this purpose, you can use the functional tests you wrote in chapter 7. Instead of running them on your developer machine against an embedded Jetty container, you'll configure them to target other environments. Let's first look at how to implement the most basic types of deployment tests: smoke tests.

15.4.1 Verifying a successful deployment with smoke tests

Your deployment automation code should incorporate tests that check that your system is in a basic, functional state after the deployment is completed. These tests are called *smoke tests.* Why this name, you ask? Smoke tests make an analogy to hardware installation like electronic circuits. If you turn on the power and see smoke coming out of the electrical parts, you know that the installation went wrong. The same conclusion can be drawn for software.

After a deployment, the target environment may need time to reach its fully functional state. For example, if the deployment process restarts a web container, it's obvious that it won't be able to serve incoming requests right away. If that's the case for your environment setup, make sure to give some leeway before executing your suite of smoke tests.

How do smoke tests look for a web application like your To Do application? Simple—you can fire basic HTTP requests to see if the Tomcat server is up and running. You also want to find out if the application's homepage URL responds with the HTTP status code 200.

Making HTTP requests from Gradle tasks is easily achieved with Java's standard API classes (`java.net.HttpUrlConnection`) or third-party libraries like Apache Http-Components (http://hc.apache.org/). You'll make your life even easier by using a Groovy

library named HTTPBuilder (http://groovy.codehaus.org/modules/http-builder/).
HTTPBuilder wraps the functionality provided by HttpComponents with a DSL-style
configuration mechanism, which boils down the code you need to write significantly.
You'll use HTTPBuilder from a custom task named `HttpSmokeTest` that acts as an
abstraction layer for making HTTP calls. To make this task available to all projects of
your build, the implementing class becomes part of the `buildSrc` project, as shown in
the following directory tree:

```
.
├── buildSrc                                    Build script for buildSrc project
│   ├── build.gradle                            declaring a dependency on the
│   └── src                             ◄────    HTTPBuilder library
│       └── main
│           └── groovy
│               └── com
│                   └── manning
│                       └── gia                      Custom tasks
│                           └── test                 for defining
│                               └── smoke            HTTP smoke
│                                   └── HttpSmokeTest.groovy  ◄──  tests
├── gradle
├── model
├── repository
├── web
├── build.gradle
└── settings.gradle
```

Before any class under `buildSrc` can use the HTTPBuilder library, you need to declare
it in a build script for that project. The following listing references the version 0.5.2.

Listing 15.12 Build script for `buildSrc` project

```
repositories {
    mavenCentral()                                          Declares a
}                                                        dependency on
                                                       library HTTPBuilder
dependencies {
    compile 'org.codehaus.groovy.modules.http-builder:http-builder:0.5.2'   ◄──┘
}
```

As you can imagine, you may implement other types of smoke tests later; for example,
for testing the functionality of the database. For this reason, you'll group smoke tests
in the package com.manning.gia.test.smoke. Let's have a closer look at the implementation in the next listing for smoke tests that fire an HTTP request.

Listing 15.13 Custom task for executing HTTP smoke tests

```
package com.manning.gia.test.smoke

import org.gradle.api.DefaultTask
import org.gradle.api.GradleException
import org.gradle.api.tasks.Input
import org.gradle.api.tasks.TaskAction
```

```
import groovyx.net.http.HTTPBuilder
import static groovyx.net.http.ContentType.TEXT

class HttpSmokeTest extends DefaultTask {
    @Input
    String url

    @Input
    String errorMessage

    @TaskAction
    void letThereBeSmoke() {
        boolean success = isUp(url)

        if(!success) {
            throw new GradleException(errorMessage)
        }
    }

    private boolean isUp(String url) {
        def http = new HTTPBuilder(url)
        def responseStatus = http.get(contentType: TEXT) { resp, reader ->
                                    resp.status
                                        }

        responseStatus != HttpURLConnection.HTTP_OK
    }
}
```

Makes HTTP Get request for provided URL and checks if response code comes back OK

Fail smoke test task if HTTP response code is anything other than OK

Makes HTTP Get request for provided URL and parses response status code

In your build script, you can set up as many smoke tests as you need. As with the URL, provide the HTTP endpoint of your web application that was read from the Groovy configuration file earlier. Figure 15.5 shows how to use the env project property to target a particular environment.

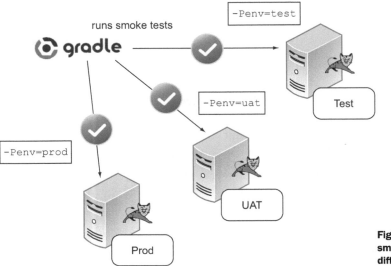

Figure 15.5 Running smoke tests against different environments

Let's look at some exemplary smoke test implementations. The following listing shows two different smoke tests: one for verifying that Tomcat is up and running and another for checking if your web application was deployed successfully.

Listing 15.14 Smoke tests for verifying HTTP URLs

```
import com.manning.gia.smoke.HttpSmokeTest

ext {
    tomcatUrl = "http://$config.tomcat.hostname:$config.tomcat.port"
    toDoAppUrl = "$tomcatUrl/$config.tomcat.context"
}

task checkTomcatUrl(type: HttpSmokeTest) {
    url = tomcatUrl
    errorMessage = "Tomcat doesn't seem to be up."
}

task checkApplicationUrl(type: HttpSmokeTest,
                         dependsOn: checkTomcatUrl) {
    url = toDoAppUrl
    errorMessage = "Application doesn't seem to be up."
}

task smokeTests(dependsOn: checkApplicationUrl)
```

Constructs environment-specific Tomcat URL from configuration file

Verifies if main Tomcat container homepage URL is reachable

Verifies if deployed To Do application URL is reachable

I'm sure you can imagine a whole range of smoke tests for your real-world applications. It's certainly worth experimenting with options, as long as they're cheap to write and fast to execute.

If all smoke tests pass, you can rightfully assume that your application was deployed successfully. But does it work functionally? As a next step, you should determine whether the provided application functionality works as expected.

15.4.2 *Verifying application functionality with acceptance tests*

Functional tests, also called acceptance tests, focus on verifying whether the end user requirements are met. In chapter 7, you learned how to implement a suite of functional tests for your web application with the help of the browser automation tool Geb.

Of course, you want to be able to run these tests against a deployed application in other environments. Acceptance tests are usually run during the automated acceptance test phase of the continuous delivery build pipeline. This is the first time in the pipeline that you bring together the work of the development team, deploy it to a test server, and verify whether the functionality meets the needs of the business in an automated fashion. In later phases of the build pipeline, acceptance tests can be run to get quick feedback about the success of a deployment on a functional level. The better the quality of your tests, the more confident you can be about the determined result.

In listing 15.13, you added a new task of type Test for running functional tests against remote servers. Geb allows for pointing to an HTTP endpoint by setting the system property `geb.build.baseUrl`. The value you assign to this system property is derived from the read environment configuration, as shown in the following listing.

Listing 15.15   Task for exercising functional tests against remote servers

```
ext {
    functionalTestReportDir = file("$test.reports.html.destination/functional")
    functionalTestResultsDir = file("$test.reports.junitXml.
                             ⇒ destination/functional")
    functionalCommonSystemProperties = ['geb.env': 'firefox',
                                    ⇒ 'geb.build.reportsDir':
                                    ⇒ reporting.file("$name/geb")]
}

task remoteFunctionalTest(type: Test) {
    testClassesDir = sourceSets.functionalTest.output.classesDir
    classpath = sourceSets.functionalTest.runtimeClasspath
    reports.html.destination = functionalTestReportDir
    reports.junitXml.destination = functionalTestResultsDir
    systemProperties functionalCommonSystemProperties
    systemProperty 'geb.build.baseUrl', toDoAppUrl
}
```

Task of type Test for running functional tests against different environments

Defines HTTP endpoint of deployed web application

15.5   *Deployment as part of the build pipeline*

In the previous chapters, we discussed the purpose and practical application of phases during the commit stage. We compiled the code, ran automated unit and integration tests, produced code quality metrics, assembled the binary artifact, and pushed it to a repository for later consumption. For a quick refresher on previously configured Jenkins jobs, please refer to earlier chapters.

While the commit stage asserts that the software works at the technical level, the acceptance stage verifies that it fulfills functional and nonfunctional requirements. To make this determination, you'll need to retrieve the artifact from the binary repository and deploy it to a production-like test environment. You use smoke tests to make sure that the deployment was successful before a suite of automated acceptance tests is run to verify the application's end user functionality. In later stages, you reuse the already downloaded artifact and deploy it to other environments: UAT for manual testing, and production environment to get the software into the hands of the end users.

Let's look at these stages with Jenkins. As a template for these stages, you'll duplicate an existing Jenkins job. Don't worry about their configuration at the moment. You'll modify their settings in a bit. The end result will be the following list of Jenkins jobs:

- `todo-acceptance-deploy`
- `todo-acceptance-test`
- `todo-uat-deploy`
- `todo-uat-smoke-test`
- `todo-production-deploy`
- `todo-production-smoke-test`

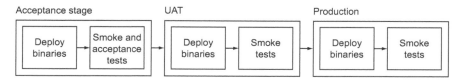

Figure 15.6   Acceptance, UAT, and production stages as part of the build pipeline

Together these jobs model the outstanding stages of your build pipeline, as shown in figure 15.6.

In the next sections, we'll examine each of these stages one by one. Let's start with the acceptance stage.

15.5.1 *Automatic deployment to test environment*

You'll start by configuring the Jenkins job `todo-acceptance-deploy` for automatically deploying the WAR file to a test server. Figure 15.7 illustrates this stage in the context of later deployment stages of the build pipeline.

Have a quick look at this checklist to see if it's set up correctly:

- In the Source Code Management configuration section, choose the option Clone Workspace and the parent project `todo-distribution`.
- As with the build step, you want to download the WAR file from Artifactory and deploy it to the test environment. Add a build step for invoking your Gradle script using the wrapper and enter the task `deployWar`. In the field Switches, you'll provide the appropriate environment property: `-Penv=test`.
- Define the build name by incorporating the upstream build number parameter: `todo#${ENV,var="SOURCE_BUILD_NUMBER"}`.
- Add a parameterized build action that defines a build trigger on the job running your deployment tests named `todo-acceptance-test`. As far as parameters go, you'll reuse the existing ones by selecting the option Current Build Parameters.

15.5.2 *Deployment tests*

Deployment testing should follow directly after deploying the application to the test environment (figure 15.8).

There are two important points you need to consider when configuring the corresponding Jenkins job. The execution of the job has to be slightly delayed to allow the

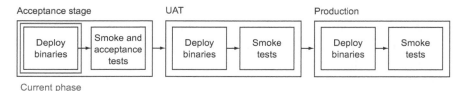

Current phase

Figure 15.7   Deploying the WAR file to a test server for acceptance testing

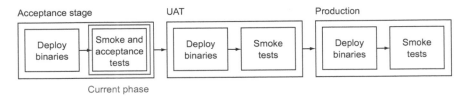

Current phase

Figure 15.8   Deployment tests against deployed WAR file

test environment to come up properly. Also, the downstream project (the deployment to UAT) may not be executed automatically. The following list explains the necessary configuration steps:

- In the Source Code Management configuration section, choose the option Clone Workspace and the parent project `todo-acceptance-test`.
- In the Advanced Project Options configuration section, tick the checkbox Quiet Period and enter the value `60` into the input field. This option will delay the execution of the job for one minute to ensure that the Tomcat server has been properly started. Because this method can be kind of brittle, you may want to implement a more sophisticated mechanism to check whether the server is up and running.
- As with the build step, you want to run smoke and acceptance tests against the test environment. Add a build step for invoking your Gradle script using the wrapper and enter the tasks `smokeTests remoteFunctionalTest`. In the field Switches, you'll provide the appropriate environment property: `-Penv=test`.
- Define the build name by incorporating the upstream build number parameter: `todo#${ENV,var="SOURCE_BUILD_NUMBER"}`.
- Add a parameterized build action that defines a manual build trigger on the job deploying the WAR file to the UAT environment named `todo-uat-deploy`. To define the manual trigger, choose the option Build Pipeline Trigger → Manually Execute Downstream Project from the Add Post-build Action drop-down menu. The build pipeline view will indicate the manual trigger by displaying a Play button for this job.

When executing the full pipeline in Jenkins, you'll notice that the job for deploying to UAT requires manual intervention. Only if you actively initiate the deployment will the pipeline execution resume—that is, until it hits another push-button, downstream job.

15.5.3   *On-demand deployment to UAT and production environment*

You already configured a push-button deployment in step 6. The same configuration needs to apply to the job that deploys the artifact to the production environment, as shown in figure 15.9.

We won't go into too much detail about the configuration of these jobs. In fact, they look very similar to the jobs that you set up to implement the acceptance stage.

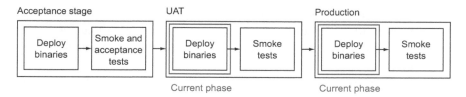

Figure 15.9 Performing push-button releases to UAT and production environments

The big differentiator is the environment they target. In the Gradle build step, the UAT deployment job needs to set the `-Penv=uat` switch. The deployment job to the production environment applies the setting `-Penv=prod`.

The build pipeline view in Jenkins can be configured to keep a history of previously executed builds. This is a handy option if you want to get a quick overview of failed and successful builds. This view also enables the stakeholders of your build to deploy artifacts with a specific version. Typical scenarios for this use case could be one of the following:

- The product team decides to launch a new feature included in a specific version of your application.
- Rolling back the application version in production to a known "good" state due to a failed deployment or broken feature.
- Deploying a given feature set for manual testing by the QA team into the UAT environment.

Jenkins needs to know which version should be deployed when you hit the release button. Thankfully, the parameterized build plugin helps you to provide the appropriate version to the job. For each of the deployment jobs, make the following configuration. Tick the checkbox This Build Is Parameterized. From the drop-down menu Add Parameter choose String Parameter. In the Name input box, enter the value `SOURCE_BUILD_NUMBER`.

15.6 *Summary*

Software deployments need to be repeatable and reliable. Any server outage inflicted by a faulty deployment—with the biggest hit on production systems—results in money lost for your organization. Automation is the next logical and necessary step toward formulating and streamlining the deployment process.

Deployable artifacts often look different by nature, follow custom project requirements, and demand distinct runtime environments. While there's no overarching recipe for deploying software, Gradle proves to be a flexible tool for implementing your desired deployment strategy.

A configured target environment is a prerequisite for any software deployment. At the beginning of this chapter, we discussed the importance of infrastructure as code for setting up and configuring an environment and its services in an automated fashion. Vagrant can play an instrumental role in creating and testing infrastructure templates. You learned how to bootstrap a virtual machine by wrapping Vagrant management commands with Gradle tasks. Later, you implemented an exemplary deployment process using SSH commands and exercised the functionality on a running Vagrant box.

To ensure repeatability for your deployments, the same code should be used across all environments. This means that the automation logic needs to use dynamic property values to target a particular environment. Environment-specific configuration becomes very readable when structured with closures and stored in a Groovy script. Groovy's API class `ConfigSlurper` provides an easy-to-use mechanism for parsing these settings. To have the property values available for consumption across all projects of your build, you coded a task that reads the Groovy script during Gradle's configuration lifecycle phase.

The outcome of every deployment needs to be verified. Automated deployment tests, invoked after a deployment, can provide fast feedback. Smoke tests are easy to implement and quickly reveal breakages. Functional tests, also called acceptance tests, are the natural extension of smoke tests. This type of test assesses whether functional and nonfunctional requirements are met.

By the end of this chapter, you extended your build pipeline by manual and push-button deployment capabilities. In Jenkins, you set up three deployment jobs for targeting a test, UAT, and production environment, including their corresponding deployment tests. With these last steps completed, you built a fully functional, end-to-end build pipeline. Together, we explored the necessary tooling and methods that will enable you to implement your own build pipeline using Gradle and Jenkins.

appendix A
Driving
the command line

Gradle's command-line interface (CLI) is a user's primary tool of choice for discovering available options, inspecting the project, and controlling execution behavior by providing configuration information. It consists of three parts: discovery or help tasks, build setup tasks, and configuration input. The gradle command has the following usage:

```
gradle [option...] [tasks...]
```

A.1 Discovery tasks

Many discovery tasks provide information about the build. If you're new to a project, they're a good place to start discovering the configuration. They're implemented as Gradle tasks. Every Gradle build provides the discovery tasks shown in table A.1 from the get-go.

Table A.1 Discovery tasks available to all Gradle projects

Name	Description	Where To Go for More Information
dependencies	Emits a list of your project's dependencies, including transitive dependencies. For an in-depth discussion of declaring and consuming dependencies in your project, jump to chapter 5.	Section 5.4.2

Table A.1 Discovery tasks available to all Gradle projects *(continued)*

Name	Description	Where To Go for More Information
dependencyInsight	Explains how and why a dependency is selected in the dependency graph. The task requires you to provide the mandatory parameters `--dependency` to inspect a particular dependency. To inspect a dependency assigned to a configuration other than `compile`, use the parameter `--configuration`. Example: `gradle dependencyInsight --dependency apache-commons`.	Section 5.7.2
help	Displays a help message on the basic usage of the Gradle command line; for example, listing all existing tasks and running a specific task. If you run the `gradle` command without specifying a task, the `help` task is executed.	Gradle online manual
projects	Displays all subprojects in a multiproject build. A single-project build has no subprojects.	Section 6.2
properties	Emits a list of all available properties in your project. Some of these properties are provided by Gradle's `Project` object, the build's internal representation. Other properties are user-defined properties originating from a property file, property command-line option, or directly declared in your build script.	Section 4.1.3
tasks	Displays all runnable tasks of your project, including their descriptions. Plugins applied to your project may provide additional tasks. To print additional information about the available tasks, this task can be run with the option `--all`.	Section 2.6.1

A.2 *Build setup tasks*

At a minimum, every Gradle project requires a `build.gradle` file to define your build logic. This file can be created manually or conveniently generated by tasks of the build setup plugin. Table A.2 shows the build setup tasks for initializing a new Gradle build.

Table A.2 Build setup tasks for initializing a new Gradle build

Name	Description	Where To Go for More Information
setupBuild	Initializes a Gradle project by creating `build.gradle`, `settings.gradle`, and the wrapper files. If a `pom.xml` is found, Gradle tries to derive a Gradle project from the Maven metadata (see task `maven2Gradle`).	Gradle online manual

Table A.2 Build setup tasks for initializing a new Gradle build (*continued*)

Name	Description	Where To Go for More Information
generateBuildFile	Creates a `build.gradle` file with the standard setup for building a Java project. This task is only available if no `pom.xml` file can be found in the project directory.	Section 3.2.1
generateSettingsFile	Creates a `settings.gradle` file, usually used for configuring a multiproject build. This task is only available if no `pom.xml` file can be found in the project directory.	Gradle online manual
maven2Gradle	Translates a Maven project into a Gradle project (usually as part of a build migration) by inspecting the POM file in the project directory. After running this task, `build.gradle` and `settings.gradle` files are created. This task is only available if a `pom.xml` can be found.	Section 9.2.2
wrapper	Generates the Gradle wrapper files in the project directory with the same version as the Gradle runtime.	Section 3.4.1

A.3 Configuration input

Build configuration information can be provided through the CLI. Options that don't require a value can be combined; for example, `-is` for running the build on the INFO log level and printing out the stack trace if an error occurs.

A.3.1 Common options

Table A.3 describes common command-line options that don't belong to a particular functional grouping. These options may come in handy in your day-to-day use of Gradle, so feel free to explore them.

Table A.3 Commonly used command-line options

Name	Description	Where To Go for More Information
-?, -h, --help	Prints out all available command-line options, including a descriptive message.	Gradle online manual
-a, --no-rebuild	Avoids rebuilding all subprojects participating in a multiproject build other than the project that the command issues for (also called a partial build). By using partial builds, you can avoid the cost of checking the subproject model and bring down your build execution time.	Section 6.3.3

Table A.3 Commonly used command-line options *(continued)*

Name	Description	Where To Go for More Information
`-b, --build-file`	The default naming convention for a Gradle build script is `build.gradle`. Use this option to execute a build script with a different name (for example, `gradle -b test.gradle build`).	Section 8.3
`-c, --settings-file`	The default naming convention for a Gradle settings file is `settings.gradle`. Use this option to execute a build with a nonstandard settings filename (for example, `gradle -c mySettings.gradle build`).	Gradle online manual
`--continue`	Gradle will continue execution when a task fails to execute. This option is particularly useful in a multiproject build with many subprojects. It'll discover all possible issues with a build, and allows you to fix them at once without having to fix problems one by one.	Gradle online manual
`--configure-on-demand`	This option aims for optimizing the configuration time required to initialize a multiproject build. The configuration on-demand mode attempts to configure only projects that are relevant for requested tasks. This option can be activated for all Gradle builds by setting the property `org.gradle.configure-ondemand` in a `gradle.properties` file.	Gradle online manual
`-g, --gradle-user-home`	Gradle's default home directory is located in the directory `.gradle` under the user's home directory. Use this option if you want to point to a different directory.	Gradle online manual
`--gui`	Launches a Swing-based user interface as an alternative to executing Gradle tasks from the command line.	Gradle online manual
`-I, --init-script`	Specifies an initialization script used for the build. This script is executed before any of your project tasks are executed.	Gradle online manual
`-p, --project-dir`	By default, a build is executed based on the current directory. With this option, you can specify a different directory to execute the build.	Gradle online manual
`--parallel`	Builds participating subprojects of a multiproject build in parallel. Gradle automatically determines the optimal number of executor threads. This option can be activated for all Gradle builds by setting the property `org.gradle.parallel` in a `gradle.properties` file.	Gradle online manual

Table A.3 Commonly used command-line options *(continued)*

Name	Description	Where To Go for More Information
`--parallel-threads`	When building a multiproject build in parallel, this option can be used to override the number of executor threads (for example, `--parallel-threads=5`).	Gradle online manual
`-m, --dry-run`	Prints the order of tasks without executing their actions. This option comes in handy if you want to quickly determine the task execution order of your build.	Gradle online manual
`--profile`	Apart from the total build time output on each build run, you can break down the execution time even more. The profile option generates a detailed HTML report under `build/reports/profile` listing task execution times and time spent during configuration phases.	Gradle online manual
`--rerun-tasks`	Reruns all tasks in the determined task execution graph. This option ignores any `UP-TO-DATE` status of previous task executions.	Gradle online manual
`-u, --no-search-upwards`	Tells Gradle to not search for a settings file in parent directories. This option is useful if you want to avoid the performance hit of searching all parent directories in a deeply nested project structure.	Section 6.2.4
`-v, --version`	Prints the version of the Gradle runtime that executes the command.	Section 2.4
`-x, --exclude-task`	Specifies a task that's excluded from task execution. A practical example for this option is if you want to execute a full build of a Java project without running the unit tests (for example, `gradle -x test build`).	Section 2.6.2

A.3.2 *Property options*

Properties provide a way to configure your build from the command line. Besides the standard Java system properties, Gradle defines project properties. Table A.4 describes their specific use cases.

Table A.4 Providing properties to Gradle JVM process or the Gradle project

Name	Description	Where To Go for More Information
`-D, --system-prop`	Gradle runs as a JVM process. As with all Java processes, you can provide a system property like this: `-Dmyprop=myvalue`.	Section 4.1.3

Table A.4   Providing properties to Gradle JVM process or the Gradle project *(continued)*

Name	Description	Where To Go for More Information
`-P, --project-prop`	Project properties are variables available in your build script. You can use this option to pass a property to the build script directly from the command line (for example, `-Pmyprop=myvalue`).	Section 4.1.3

A.3.3   Logging options

Gradle allows access to all log messages produced by your build. Depending on your use case, you can provide logging options to filter the relevant messages important to you, as shown in table A.5.

Table A.5   Controlling the runtime logging level

Name	Description	Where To Go for More Information
`-i, --info`	A Gradle build does not output a lot of information in the default settings. Use this option to get more informative messages by changing Gradle's logger to the INFO log level. This is helpful if you want to get more information on what's happening under the hood.	Section 7.3.1
`-d, --debug`	Running Gradle on the DEBUG log level will give you a vast amount of low-level logging messages, including stack traces. Use this option if you want to troubleshoot a build problem.	Gradle online manual
`-q, --quiet`	Reduces the log messages of a build run to error messages only.	Section 2.6.1
`-s, --stacktrace`	If you run into errors in your build, you'll want to know where they stem from. The option `-s` prints out an abbreviated stack trace if an exception is thrown, making it perfect for debugging broken builds.	Gradle online manual
`-S, --full-stacktrace`	Prints out the full stack trace for all exceptions.	Gradle online manual

A.3.4   Caching options

Gradle uses caching on various levels to improve the performance of the build. With the options presented in table A.6, you can change the default caching behavior.

Table A.6 Managing Gradle's caching functionality

Name	Description	Where To Go for More Information
`--offline`	Often your build only declares dependencies on libraries available in repositories outside of your network. If these dependencies weren't stored in your local cache, running a build without a network connection to these repositories would result in a failed build. Use this option to run your build in offline mode and only check the local dependency cache for dependencies.	Section 5.6.2
`--project-cache-dir`	The default dependency cache directory sits under `.gradle` in the user home directory. This option can be used to point to a different directory.	Gradle online manual
`--recompile-scripts`	Gradle compiles every script by default and stores them in a local cache to improve the performance of the build. To flush the cache of compiled scripts, execute the build with this option.	Gradle online manual
`--refresh-dependencies`	Manually refreshes the dependencies in your cache. This flag forces a check for changed artifact versions with the configured repositories.	Section 5.7.4

A.3.5 Daemon options

The daemon runs Gradle as a background process. Once started, the `gradle` command will reuse the forked daemon process for subsequent builds, avoiding the startup costs altogether. Table A.7 gives an overview of the available options for controlling the daemon process.

Table A.7 Managing the daemon

Name	Description	Where To Go for More Information
`--daemon`	Executes the build with the Gradle daemon for better performance. If a daemon process exists, it's reused. If it doesn't exist, a new daemon process is started. The daemon can be activated for all Gradle builds by setting the property `org.gradle.daemon` in a `gradle.properties` file.	Section 2.6.4
`--foreground`	Starts the Gradle daemon in the foreground of your console for debugging and monitoring purposes.	Section 2.6.4

Table A.7   Managing the daemon *(continued)*

Name	Description	Where To Go for More Information
`--no-daemon`	Executes the build without using an existing Gradle daemon process.	Section 2.6.4
`--stop`	Stops an existing Gradle daemon process.	Section 2.6.4

appendix B
Groovy for Gradle users

Gradle's core functionality is built with Java. On top of this functionality sits a domain-specific language (DSL) written in the dynamic programming language Groovy. When writing a Gradle build script, you automatically use the language constructs exposed by this DSL to express the desired build instructions. Gradle build scripts are executable Groovy scripts, but they can't be run by the Groovy runtime. When the need to implement custom logic arises, you can use Groovy's language features to build out the desired functionality directly in the Gradle build script. This appendix is a primer to Groovy and explains why it's important for users of Gradle to learn the language. Later, I'll also demonstrate how some of Gradle's configuration elements are implemented with Groovy.

B.1   *What is Groovy?*

Groovy is a dynamic programming language for the Java Virtual Machine (JVM). Its syntax is close to the one provided by Java. The language integrates with existing Java classes and libraries, which makes it easy for Java developers to learn it. Not only does Groovy build upon the strengths of Java, it also provides powerful programming features inspired by those of Ruby, Python, and others. Groovy can be used as a scripting language without having to compile the code. Alternatively, Groovy code can be compiled to Java bytecode. In this book, you use both approaches.

While this appendix will give you a head start on Groovy's most important language features, it's highly recommended that you explore it further on your own. There are great resources out there in the form of books and dedicated Groovy web pages. The definitive guide to Groovy is the book *Groovy in Action, Second Edition* by Dierk Konig, et al (Manning, 2009). It explains all language features in great detail. The DZone reference guide on Groovy provides a cheat sheet that's handy to every beginner of the language. You can download it for free at http://refcardz.dzone.com/refcardz/groovy. A useful resource for people experimenting with Groovy is the blog *Groovy Goodness* by Hubert A. Klein Ikkink, at http://mrhaki.blogspot.com/search/label/Groovy% 3AGoodness. Each posting demonstrates a unique Groovy language feature by example. The author recently condensed his blog posts into a book titled *Groovy Goodness Notebook* (Leanpub, 2013).

B.2   *How much Groovy do I need to know?*

If you're new to Gradle you may wonder how much Groovy you actually need to know to write your first build scripts. The simple answer is very little. However, it's highly recommended that you know some Java. Groovy is almost 100% compatible with Java. When implementing trivial task actions within your build script, you can choose to write plain Java code or use Groovy's expressive language constructs.

Let's look at an example. Assume you want to determine all files within a directory and write their names to a new file named allfiles.txt. Sounds pretty simple, right? The following listing demonstrates the Java version of the task action doLast.

Listing B.1   Gradle task written with Java syntax

```
task appendFilenames << {                                          Gradle task
    File inputDirectory = new File("src");                         definition
    File outputFile = new File(getBuildDir(), "allfiles.txt");
    File outputDirectory = outputFile.getParentFile();

    if(!outputDirectory.exists()) {
        outputDirectory.mkdirs();
    }

    outputFile.createNewFile();                                    Task action
    FileWriter fileWriter = new FileWriter(outputFile, true);      implemented
                                                                   in Java
    try {
        for(File file : inputDirectory.listFiles()) {
            fileWriter.write(file.getName() + "\n");
        }
    }
    finally {
        fileWriter.close();
    }
}
```

Apart from the task definition itself, which is defined with Gradle's DSL, no Groovy code was required to implement the scenario. Next, we'll compare this task implementation with the Groovy version. In the following listing, the task action code is much shorter and more concise than the Java version.

Listing B.2 Gradle task written with Groovy syntax

```
task appendFilenames << {
    def inputDirectory = new File('src')
    def outputFile = new File(buildDir, 'allfiles.txt')
    def outputDirectory = outputFile.parentFile

    if(!outputDirectory.exists()) {
        outputDirectory.mkdirs()
    }

    outputFile.createNewFile()
    inputDirectory.eachFile { outputFile << "$it.name\n" }
}
```

◁─┤ Gradle task
     definition

Task action
implemented
in Groovy

A mixture of Java and Groovy works just fine for trivial builds, especially if you're in the process of learning Groovy. For more complex builds that include custom tasks and plugins, you'll need to know more about the language. And for a deep understanding of how Gradle works internally, knowing about advanced Groovy features is key.

B.3 Comparing Java and Groovy syntax

In the last section, we compared a task implementation written in Java and Groovy. In Groovy you can become extremely productive while at the same time writing less code. To get a good understanding of how this plays out in practice, let's talk about the main differentiators between both languages. As an example, we'll look at the class ProjectVersion.java from chapter 4 of this book. The class describes the major and minor version of a Gradle project. The next listing shows a simplified version of the class.

Listing B.3 A typical Java POJO class

```
package com.manning.gia;

public class ProjectVersion {
    private Integer major;
    private Integer minor;

    public ProjectVersion(Integer major, Integer minor) {
        this.major = major;
        this.minor = minor;
    }

    public Integer getMajor() {
        return major;
    }

    public void setMajor(Integer major) {
        this.major = major;
    }

    public Integer getMinor() {
        return minor;
    }
}
```

```
      public void setMinor(Integer minor) {
         this.minor = minor;
      }
}
```

As a Java developer, you probably see this kind of boilerplate code every day. Plain old Java objects (POJOs), classes that don't implement or extend third-party library classes, are often used to represent data. The class exposes two private fields via getter and setter methods. The following listing demonstrates how to express the same logic in Groovy.

Listing B.4   Project version class written in Groovy

```
package com.manning.gia

class ProjectVersion {
   Integer major
   Integer minor

   ProjectVersion(Integer major, Integer minor) {
      this.major = major
      this.minor = minor
   }
}
```

I think we can agree that the Groovy version of the class looks far less noisy. Groovy assumes sensible defaults for any class you write, particularly the following optimizations:

- The use of semicolons at the end of an expression is optional.
- Every class, constructor, and method is `public` by default.
- In Groovy, the last expression in the body of a method is returned. This means that the use of the `return` statement is optional.
- The Groovy compiler adds getter/setter methods automatically so you don't have to write them yourself.
- Fields of a class (also called properties in Groovy) can be accessed by dot notation, which looks exactly as if they were public in Java. However, under the hood Groovy calls the auto-generated corresponding getter/setter method.
- If you compare two instances of a class with `==`, Groovy automatically calls the method `equals()` under the hood. This operation also avoids potential `NullPointerExceptions`.

B.4   *Essential Groovy features*

So far, we've only scratched the surface of the feature set Groovy provides. In this section, we'll explore language aspects used on a regular basis when programming in Groovy. The features we'll discuss in the following sections aren't listed in a particular order. Feel free to follow along and try out the examples one by one on your computer. There are two tools that are extremely helpful in running code snippets.

The Groovy console is automatically available after installing the Groovy runtime. It provides an interactive user interface for entering and executing Groovy scripts. The console can be launched by running the command `groovyConsole` or `groovy-Console.bat`, located in the directory `<GROOVY_HOME>/bin`.

The Groovy web console (http://groovyconsole.appspot.com/) provides an even easier way to try out Groovy code snippets. You can run Groovy scripts on the web without installing the Groovy runtime. Keep in mind that the language features used in your script are bound to the bundled Groovy version of the web console indicated on the page.

B.4.1 Assert statement

If you're coming from Java, you may know the keyword `assert`. It's used to verify pre- and post-conditions in your code. Unlike Java's pendant, which only works if you enable assertion checking by setting a runtime flag (`-ea` or `-enableassertion`), Groovy's assert statement is always evaluated. The following listing shows a usage example.

Listing B.5   Groovy's power assert

```
def version = 12
assert version == 12
version++                      Provokes
assert version == 12           a failed
                               assertion
```

Careful readers will note that the second assertion should fail, because you incremented the `version` variable by 1. Groovy's assert statement, also called *power assert*, provides helpful output to identify the root cause of an issue. The following output demonstrates a sample output for the listing:

```
Exception thrown
Jul 29, 2013 8:06:04 AM org.codehaus.groovy.runtime.StackTraceUtils
sanitize
WARNING: Sanitizing stacktrace:
Assertion failed:
assert version == 12
       |         |
       13        false
```

You'll use the `assert` statement in the upcoming code examples as a tool to verify and document the desired behavior.

B.4.2 Optional data type declaration

Groovy doesn't force you to explicitly declare a type of variable, method parameter, or return type. Instead, you can simply mark it with the keyword `def`, a placeholder for `java.lang.Object`. At runtime, Groovy figures out the type based on the assigned value. The next listing demonstrates some examples of optional typing.

Listing B.6   Optional typing for variables and methods

```
def buildTool = 'Gradle'
assert buildTool.class == java.lang.String

def initProjectVersion(major, minor) {
   new ProjectVersion(major, minor)
}

assert initProjectVersion(1, 2).class == com.manning.gia.ProjectVersion
```

This feature is helpful for certain use cases, but you may still prefer explicit, strong typing. Particularly in projects that expose a public API, strong typing automatically improves documentation, makes it more obvious what parameter types need to be provided, and enables IDE code completion. For the same reasons, declaring void instead of def as a return type should be used if a method doesn't return a value.

B.4.3   *Optional parentheses*

Method calls in Groovy can omit the parentheses if the method signature requires at least one parameter. Without going into too much detail, this feature is often used to create more natural-looking DSLs, a human-readable language understandable by domain experts. The following listing compares two method calls with and without the parentheses.

Listing B.7   Omitting parentheses for top-level expressions

```
initProjectVersion(1, 2)
initProjectVersion 1, 2

println('Groovy is awesome!')
println 'Groovy is awesome!'
```

B.4.4   *Strings*

There are three different ways to declare Strings in Groovy. A single-quoted String always creates the Java equivalent of a String. The second form follows the Java way of creating a String. It wraps the text with double quotes. Multiline Strings, wrapped by triple double quotes, are helpful if you want to assign wordy text or impose formatting (for example, multiline SQL statements). The next listing shows the full range of creating Strings in Groovy.

Listing B.8   String notations in Groovy

```
def myString1 = 'This is a single-quoted String'
def myString2 = "This is a double-quoted String"
def myString3 = """
   This
   is a
   multiline
   String
"""
```

B.4.5   *Groovy Strings (GStrings)*

Double-quoted Strings in Groovy are more powerful than traditional Java Strings. They can interpolate embedded variables or expressions denoted by a dollar sign and curly braces. At runtime, the expression is evaluated and forms a String. In Groovy, these types of Strings are also known as GStrings. The following listing gives an example of their practical use.

Listing B.9   String interpolation with GStrings

```
def language = 'groovy'
def sentence = "$language is awesome!"
assert sentence == 'groovy is awesome!'

def improvedSentence = "${language.capitalize()} is awesome!"
assert improvedSentence == 'Groovy is awesome!'
```

B.4.6   *Collections API*

Groovy offers a concise syntax for implementations of the Collections API, which makes them easier to use than their Java equivalent. Next, we'll discuss Lists and Maps.

Lists

By putting a comma-separated list of values in square brackets, you can initialize new Lists. Under the hood, Groovy creates an instance of java.util.ArrayList. Groovy also adds syntactic sugar to simplify the use of a List. A perfect example is the left shift operator (<<) that allows for adding a new element to the List. Under the hood, Groovy calls the method add. The following listing shows some of this functionality.

Listing B.10   Managing Lists in Groovy

```
def buildTools = ['Ant', 'Maven']
assert buildTools.getClass() == java.util.ArrayList
assert buildTools.size() == 2
assert buildTools[1] == 'Maven'

buildTools << 'Gradle'
assert buildTools.size() == 3
assert buildTools[2] == 'Gradle'          Iterate over
                                          the values
                                          in List
buildTools.each { buildTool ->     <──┘
   println buildTool
}
```

Maps

Maps are easier to handle than Lists. To initialize a new Map with a new value, create a comma-separated list of key-value pairs in square brackets. The default implementation of a Map is java.lang.LinkedHashMap. The next listing shows usage examples of a Groovy Map.

Listing B.11   Managing Maps in Groovy

```
def inceptionYears = ['Ant': 2000, 'Maven': 2004]
assert inceptionYears.getClass() == java.lang.LinkedHashMap
assert inceptionYears.size() == 2
assert inceptionYears.Ant == 2000
assert inceptionYears['Ant'] == 2000

inceptionYears['Gradle'] = 2009
assert inceptionYears.size() == 3
assert inceptionYears['Gradle'] == 2009

inceptionYears.each { buildTool, year ->
    println "$buildTool was first released in $year"
}
```

Iterate
over values
in Map

B.4.7   Named parameters

Earlier we talked about the simple bean class ProjectVersion. The class exposes a constructor to initialize its fields with values. Assume you didn't define a constructor. Groovy provides another handy way of setting property values, called *named parameters*. This mechanism first calls the default constructor of the class and then calls the setter methods for each of the provided parameters. The following listing shows how to set the values for the fields major and minor through named parameters.

Listing B.12   Setting field values with named parameters

```
class ProjectVersion {
    Integer major
    Integer minor
}

ProjectVersion projectVersion = new ProjectVersion(major: 1, minor: 10)
assert projectVersion.minor == 10
projectVersion.minor = 30
assert projectVersion.minor == 30
```

B.4.8   Closures

A closure is a block of code of type groovy.lang.Closure, similar to lambdas in other programming languages. Closures can be assigned to variables, passed to methods as parameters, and called like regular methods.

IMPLICIT CLOSURE PARAMETER

Every closure that doesn't explicitly define any parameters has access to an implicit parameter named it. The parameter it refers to the first parameter passed to a closure when calling it. If no parameter is provided, the value of the parameter is null. Let's look at an example to make this concept less abstract. The following listing shows the definition and invocation of a closure, including the implicit parameter it.

Listing B.13   Closure with single, implicit parameter

```
def incrementMajorProjectVersion = {          Explicit closure
    it.major++                                 parameter it
}

ProjectVersion projectVersion = new ProjectVersion(major: 1, minor: 10)
incrementMajorProjectVersion(projectVersion)
assert projectVersion.major == 2               Calls closure and provides
                                               required parameter
```

EXPLICIT CLOSURE PARAMETERS

Instead of using the implicit closure parameter, you can be more descriptive by assigning your own parameter name. In the next listing, you define a parameter named version of type ProjectVersion.

Listing B.14   Closure with single, explicit parameter

```
def incrementMajorProjectVersion = { ProjectVersion version ->    Implicit,
    version.major++                                               named closure
}                                                                 parameter

ProjectVersion projectVersion = new ProjectVersion(major: 1, minor: 10)
incrementMajorProjectVersion(projectVersion)
assert projectVersion.major == 2               Calls closure and provides
                                               required parameter
```

Keep in mind that typing is optional in Groovy. You could have used the identifier version without the type. Groovy doesn't limit the number of parameters a closure can define. The following listing shows how to declare multiple, untyped parameters for a closure.

Listing B.15   Closure with multiple, untyped parameters

```
def setFullProjectVersion = { projectVersion, major, minor ->    Declares three
    projectVersion.major = major                                 untyped closure
    projectVersion.minor = minor                                 parameters
}

ProjectVersion projectVersion = new ProjectVersion(major: 1, minor: 10)
setFullProjectVersion(projectVersion, 2, 1)
assert projectVersion.major == 2               Calls closure and provides
assert projectVersion.minor == 1               required parameters
```

CLOSURE RETURN VALUE

A closure always returns a value. This is either the last statement of the closure if no explicit return statement is declared, or the value of the executed return statement. If the last statement of a closure doesn't have a value, null is returned. The closure shown in the following listing returns the value of the last statement, the project's minor version.

Listing B.16   Closure return value

```
ProjectVersion projectVersion = new ProjectVersion(major: 1, minor: 10)
def minorVersion = { projectVersion.minor }
assert minorVersion() == 10
```
Closure returns with value of last statement

CLOSURE AS METHOD PARAMETER

As mentioned earlier, you can also use a closure as a method parameter. The following listing shows an example.

Listing B.17   Closure as method parameter

Invokes closure and uses its return value to add a count →

```
Integer incrementVersion(Closure closure, Integer count) {
    closure() + count
}

ProjectVersion projectVersion = new ProjectVersion(major: 1, minor: 10)
assert incrementVersion({ projectVersion.minor }, 2) == 12
```
Method that defines a closure as first parameter

Invokes method and provides closure as first parameter

CLOSURE DELEGATION

The code of a closure is executed against the delegate of a closure. By default, the delegate is the owner of the closure. For example, if you define a closure within a Groovy script, the owner is an instance of groovy.lang.Script. The implicit variable delegate of a closure allows for redefining the default owner. Consider the scenario in the next listing. You set the delegate to the instance of ProjectVersion. This means that every closure is executed against it.

Listing B.18   Setting the delegate for a closure

```
class ProjectVersion {
    Integer major
    Integer minor

    void increment(Closure closure) {
        closure.resolveStrategy = Closure.DELEGATE_ONLY
        closure.delegate = this
        closure()
    }
}

ProjectVersion projectVersion = new ProjectVersion(major: 1, minor: 10)
projectVersion.increment { major += 1 }
assert projectVersion.major == 2
projectVersion.increment { minor += 5 }
assert projectVersion.minor == 15
```
Internal method of class ProjectVersion that takes a closure as parameter

Only resolve property references of delegate

Sets delegate of closure →

Calls provided closure

Invokes method that internally executes closure on instance of ProjectVersion

B.4.9   *Groovy Development Toolkit*

The Groovy Development Kit (GDK) extends the Java Development Kit (JDK) by providing convenience methods to the standard JDK classes. You can find a Javadoc-style HTML catalog at http://groovy.codehaus.org/groovy-jdk/. You'll find many useful methods in classes like `String`, `Collection`, `File`, and `Stream`. Many of these methods use a closure as a parameter to add a functional flavor to the language. You already saw one of these methods in action in listings B.10 and B.11: `each`. You used the method to iterate over the elements of a `Collection`. Let's look at some other examples in the following listing.

Listing B.19 Examples of methods added by the GDK

```
def buildTools = ['Ant', 'Maven', 'Gradle']
assert buildTools.find { it == 'Gradle' } == 'Gradle'      Methods added
assert buildTools.every { it.size() >= 4 } == false        for Collections

assert 'gradle'.capitalize() == 'Gradle'                   String convenience
                                                           method
new File('build.gradle').eachLine { line ->     Simplifies
    println line                                 iterating through
}                                                each line of a file
```

B.5 *Applied Groovy in Gradle build scripts*

Gradle build scripts are valid Groovy scripts. Within the build script, you can use every Groovy feature the language provides. This means that the code has to strictly adhere to Groovy's syntax. Invalid code will automatically result in a runtime error when executing the build.

Gradle comes with a DSL written in Groovy for modeling typical build concerns. You learned in chapter 4 that every build script corresponds to at least one instance of `org.gradle.api.Project`. In most cases, properties and methods you invoke in the build script automatically delegate to the `Project` instance.

Let's examine the sample build script shown in listing B.20. After getting to know some of Groovy's language features by example, you may have a hunch how they work internally. I hope this example can demystify some of the "magic" beginners to Gradle and Groovy encounter.

Listing B.20 Applied Groovy syntax in a sample Gradle build script

```
apply plugin: 'java'          Calls method apply on Project. As parameter, provides
                              a Map with a single key–value pair (see section B.4.6).
                              Method call omits parenthesis (see section B.4.3).

version = '0.1'               Sets a new value for property version by calling setter
                              method of Project under the hood (see section B.3).

repositories {                Calls method repositories on Project with a
    mavenCentral()            single closure parameter (see section B.4.8).
}

dependencies {                              Calls method dependencies
    compile 'commons-codec:commons-codec:1.6'    on Project with a single
}                                                closure parameter
                                                 (see section B.4.8).
```

Calls method mavenCentral() on object that closure delegates to (see section B.4.8).

Calls method compile with a String as parameter on object that closure delegates to (see section B.4.8). Method call omits parentheses (see section B.4.3).

index